The Innovating Organization

The Innovating Organization

edited by

Andrew M. Pettigrew and Evelyn M. Fenton

SAGE Publications
London • Thousand Oaks • New Delhi

Editorial arrangement and Chapters 1, 2, 3, 10 © Evelyn
M. Fenton and Andrew M. Pettigrew 2000
Chapters 4 and 6 © Winfried Ruigrok, Leona
Achtenhagen, Mathias Wagner and Johannes Rüegg-
Stürm 2000
Chapter 5 © Raymond A. van Wijk, and Frans A.J. van
den Bosch 2000
Chapters 7 and 9 © Javier Quintanilla and Carlos J.
Sánchez-Runde 2000
Chapter 8 © Tomas Müllern 2000

First published 2000

 SAGE Publications Ltd
6 Bonhill Street
London EC2A 4PU

SAGE Publications Inc.
2455 Teller Road
Thousand Oaks, California 91320

SAGE Publications India Pvt Ltd
32, M-Block Market
Greater Kailash – I
New Delhi 110 048

British Library Cataloguing in Publication data

A catalogue record for this book is
available from the British Library

ISBN 0-7619-6433-9
ISBN 0-7619-6434-7 (pbk)

Library of Congress catalog card number
00–132716

Typeset by M Rules
Printed and bound in Great Britain by Athenaeum Press,
Gateshead

Contents

Notes on Contributors

Leona Achtenhagen is currently a Visiting Fellow at the Centre for Creativity, Strategy and Change at the Warwick Business School, UK. She was formerly a Research Fellow at the Research Institute for International Management at the University of St Gallen, Switzerland, and is currently finishing her doctorate on 'coordinating new forms of organizing'. Previously, she studied business administration in Germany, Italy and Switzerland.

Evelyn M. Fenton is a Senior Research Fellow at the Centre for Creativity, Strategy and Change at the Warwick Business School, where she gained a PhD on strategic agenda building and change in the water industry. She is currently engaged in research in the public and private sector. Her current research interests are in professional services, the management of organizational networks and strategies for leveraging their intellectual and social capital.

Tomas Müllern is Associate Professor in Business Administration at Jönköping International Business School. His research is focused on leadership, culture and new forms of organizing. He has published several books in the field of leadership and organizational culture. Among his recent research interests is managerial rhetoric in strategic change projects.

Andrew M. Pettigrew is Professor of Strategy and Organization at Warwick Business School where between 1985 and 1995 he founded and directed the Centre for Corporate Strategy and Change. He is the author, co-author and editor of 15 books and has published over 100 papers and chapters in scholarly journals and monographs. He is also a

Fellow and distinguished scholar of the Academy of Management and a founding Academician of the Academy of Social Sciences.

Javier Quintanilla has a PhD from the University of Warwick and is Assistant Professor at IESE, University of Navarra, Madrid. His current main research interests are international human resource management and the personnel implications of new forms of organizing.

Johannes Rüegg-Stürm is currently an Assistant Professor at the Institute of Management at the University of St Gallen. His research and teaching interests are in the management of (strategic) change processes, new forms of organizing and leadership, organizational communication, systemic-constructionist epistemology in organization and leadership theory. He is currently working on a project looking at 'Learning Dynamics' – an investigation of organizational change and innovation capabilities with six companies, which have leading worldwide market positions.

Winfried Ruigrok is Professor of International Management at the University of St Gallen, Switzerland. A Dutch national, he has previously worked in the Netherlands, Belgium and the UK. His research focuses on organizational innovation in international firms, the integration of foreign nationals in top management teams and boards, and comparative corporate governance issues.

Carlos J. Sánchez-Runde has a PhD from the University of Oregon and is Assistant Professor at IESE, University of Navarra, Barcelona. His interests are in international and cross-cultural management. He has taught in the United States, Chile and Argentina. He has published a book and several papers on strategic human resource management and organizational behaviour.

Frans A. J. van den Bosch is Professor of Management and Chairman of the Department of Strategic Management and Business Environment of the Rotterdam School of Management, Erasmus University, Rotterdam. His research interests are innovative intra- and interorganizational forms, knowledge creation and sharing strategies, strategic renewal and co-evolutionary theory building, strategic decision-making processes and corporate governance. He has published in, amongst others *Organization Science, Journal of Management Studies, Long Range Planning* and *Corporate Governance*.

Raymond A. van Wijk is a Research Associate at the Rotterdam School of Management, Erasmus University Rotterdam. He is examining how innovative forms of organizing contribute to managing knowledge.

Several papers reporting his research have been awarded Best Paper prizes at the Academy of Management and Strategic Management Society conferences.

Mathias Wagner has worked as a project assistant at the Research Institute of International Management, University of St Gallen. He was involved in several consulting and research projects in the areas of knowledge management and new forms of organizing. He is currently in the final stage of his doctoral thesis which deals with the topic 'Knowledge Transfer within Multinational Corporations'.

Preface

This book is very much a collective effort. It is a product of the INN-FORM programme of research which is being carried out by an international network of scholars based in seven European universities and one each in Japan and the USA. The aims of the programme are to map the contours of contemporary organizational innovation, to examine the management practices involved in the processes of innovation, and to test for the performance benefits of these changes. The programme was initiated at Warwick Business School in a successful research submission to the Economic and Social Research Council's (ESRC) Innovation Programme which was jointly funded by Coopers & Lybrand Europe (now part of the merged entity, PricewaterhouseCoopers) (Pettigrew et al., 1995). The research is being carried out in cooperation with colleagues from Erasmus University (The Netherlands), ESSEC (France), Hitotsubashi University (Japan), IESE (Spain), Jönköping (Sweden), Oxford University (UK) and St Gallen (Switzerland). Duke University joined the network in 1997 to carry out the US survey component of the programme. Our special and primary thanks are to the lead researchers from each of these institutions: Frans van den Bosch, Hamid Bouchikhi, Tsuyoshi Numagami, Carlos Sánchez-Runde, Leif Melin, Richard Whittington, Winfried Ruigrok and Arie Lewin. Other team members who have contributed to the programme include Leona Achtenhagen, Tomas Ericsson, Silvia Massini, Tomas Müllern, Javier Quintanilla, Simon Peck, Raymond van Wijk, Johannes Rüegg-Stürm and Mathias Wagner. Some of their analytical and written work is represented in this volume and we thank them all.

The initial funding of the research idea was made possible by generous grants from the ESRC and Coopers & Lybrand. These three-year awards were then supplemented by one year extensions from the ESRC (to carry out the US survey) and by PricewaterhouseCoopers (PWC) to enable crucial analytical and dissemination activities to occur. We are most grateful for this financial support. We would also like to recognize the practical advice and support of Adrian Alsop of the ESRC and Dr Fiona Steele the coordinator of the ESRC Innovation Programme. Fiona has supported our work in every conceivable way from its inception and certainly way beyond the call of duty. Fiona, we applaud you.

Paul Batchelor, then partner in charge of Coopers & Lybrand Europe, helped us to prepare the initial submission to the ESRC and offered co-funding. Vic Luck (Managing Partner for PWC in Europe, Middle East and Africa), has also supported the fourth year of PWC funding and has joined the UK team in a high profile dissemination event. We would also like to acknowledge the support of Andy Embury, Head of Organisation and Change Strategy, PWC Europe, Middle East and Africa. Crucial to the success of the programme has been PWC's willingness to act not just as co-funders but also co-producers and co-disseminators of knowledge. Our initial project link into PWC was Chris David, Director in the Global Pharmaceuticals Consultancy Group. This role has now been taken up by David Shaw, Director in the Organisation and Change Strategy Practice. Chris and David have been great collaborators and in different ways have enriched the INNFORM programme. David Shaw is now playing a crucial role in the co-dissemination of knowledge from the programme, not just in PWC but also more widely.

Case study research can be demanding and intensive for researcher and host company and we never take research access for granted. All of our case study companies have been experimenting with organizational innovations and are already under pressure without the additional encumbrance of business school researchers. We would like to recognize and thank everyone in the eight case studies who have in some way assisted our research efforts. In Ove Arup we are grateful in particular for the help of the current Chairman Duncan Michael and also Stella Littlewood, the Human Resource Director. Colleagues at Erasmus wanted to acknowledge the support of all the managers at Rabobank who helped them. In Sociedad General de Aguas de Barcelona, S.A. – AGBAR we would like to thank Mr Fernando Porta, Assistant Manager to the Executive Management and in FREMAP the Human Resource Manager, Mr Juan Gabriel Fernandez. IESE colleagues also thank Professor Rafael Andreu, the Director of Research Division, IESE – University of Navarra.

Our St Gallen University network members have had great support from ABB and Hilti and would like especially to acknowledge Dr Andreas Steiner and Mr Rene Lichtsteiner, both Executive Vice-Presidents of Asea Brown Boveri AG, Baden, Switzerland. At Hilti AG the St Gallen team were grateful for the guidance and practical help of

Mr Egbert Appel, member of the Executive Committee and Mr Mathias Oertle, Head of Technical Projects. From Saab we were thankful for the help of Mr Börje Persson, Personnel Manager.

The Warwick team would like to thank Gill Drakeley and Caroline Conneely who have provided sterling administrative and secretarial support to the INNFORM network.

We often characterize the INNFORM programme as a network studying networks. Building and making networks work can be a precarious exercise and no more so than when it involves an international team studying complex processes over international boundaries. We are a team who have benefited from intellectual diversity and personal compatibility. We have been innovating in the social production of knowledge whilst studying others exploring and exploiting innovative forms of organizing. Such are the risks and blessings of knowledge generation at the beginning of the twenty-first century.

Andrew Pettigrew and Evelyn Fenton
Warwick Business School
January 2000

1

Theoretical Perspectives on New Forms of Organizing

Evelyn M. Fenton and Andrew M. Pettigrew

This book is the collective endeavour of an international research network engaged in the study of *Innovative Forms of Organizing* (INNFORM). The INNFORM programme was a multidisciplinary, multitimethods and multiresearch-site study which aimed to empirically examine the claims made in the theoretical and practitioner literature on new and innovative forms of organizing. In addition, and most crucially, this research sought to link the adoption of new forms of organizing with performance. The programme adopted two main methods of capturing empirical data: survey questionnaire and 18 case studies. The case studies were conducted by the UK and European teams, of companies who had adopted innovative forms of organizing. This book presents eight of these case studies, designed to illustrate innovative organizational transformations.

Here it seems most pertinent to address the question: what do we mean by innovative forms of organizing? Innovation suggests radical change in Schumpeter's terms (1934) which we have adopted alongside criteria from theories of knowledge creation (Cohen and Levinthal, 1990; Kogut and Zander, 1992; Boisot, 1995) concerning the combination of ideas. Together, these perspectives suggest that innovation concerns radical new combinations of elements. We propose four instances of innovation as guidelines for our case studies. In the first instance, innovation may refer to a genuine widespread organizational innovation, such as the development of the Multidivisional form in the 1930s or the

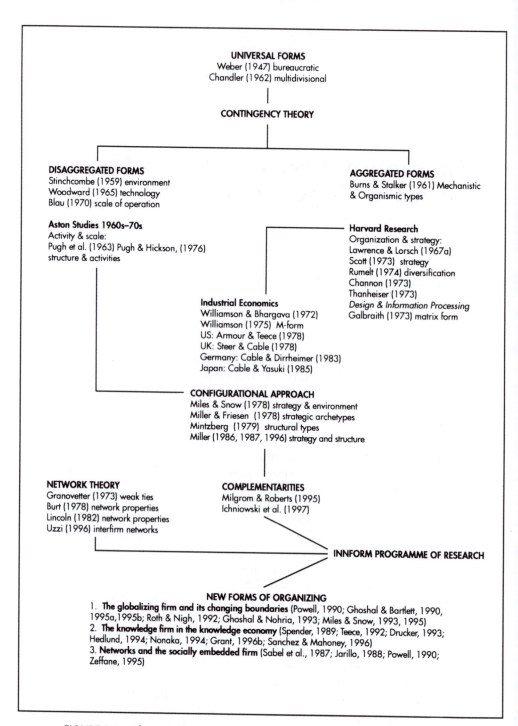

FIGURE 1.1   *Theoretical perspectives on organizational design 1950–2000*

possibility of its equivalent in the 1990s. Secondly, innovation may be some novel combination of organizational processes and/or structures not previously associated. Thirdly, innovation could refer to some novel recombination of previously associated structures and/or processes. Finally, innovation could refer to some organizational initiative which is new for the industry sector in that particular economy, but more generally may not be new. The important criterion was that the changes which the organizations adopted were perceived as new by their members (Knight, 1967; Zaltman et al, 1973; Kanter, 1983; Damanpour and Evan, 1984; Van de Ven, 1986). All of our innovative forms of organizing were expected to provide novel theoretical insights or to add new perspectives to the field of organizational design and/or strategy.

In this first chapter our aim is to set innovative forms of organizing in their theoretical context by attempting to characterize the field of organizational design between the early 1950s and 2000. We begin by giving an overview of the more recent 'New Forms of Organizing' literature and set out the key themes as we see them. This is an area in which few comprehensive reviews of the literature exist and in which the road marks for signalling the discrete intellectual areas are few and far between. We then turn to a review of the antecedent writings on organizational design. Space does not permit a comprehensive review of the literature; instead we have attempted to capture thematically the history of the field. This thematic representation is one both of continuity and of disjunctures in intellectual thought. To assist the reader we have drawn a thematic road map (see Figure 1.1) which indicates the intellectual lineage and cross-fertilization of the chief schools of thought. Following our review is a more detailed thematic account of the new forms of organizing literature, after which we turn to the INNFORM programme, its aims, mode of research and key findings. In the final section we give a brief review of the eight case study chapters, highlighting their findings and significance for innovative forms of organizing.

New Forms of Organizing

Over the last decade or so there has been a proliferation of writings heralding the advent of new organizational forms. This literature has yet to be united under an overarching theory or perspective and therefore may only be weakly classified as a research focus. What is significant about the last decade's writing is its very eclecticism, drawing on a diverse range of theories and perspectives such as the resource-based view of the firm (Wernerfelt, 1984), interorganizational theory (Powell, 1990; Perrone, 1997), cognitive and decision-making perspectives (Rumelt and Stopford, 1996), network theory (Granovetter, 1982, 1992; Uzzi, 1997), knowledge-based views (Hedlund, 1994; Nonaka, 1994;

Blackler, 1995; Grant, 1996b) complementarities (Milgrom and Roberts, 1995; Ichniowski et al., 1997) and relational perspectives (Ghoshal and Bartlett, 1990; Roth and Nigh, 1992; Ghoshal and Nohria, 1993; Easton and Araujo, 1994). What these diverse perspectives agree upon is that the form, process and role of organizations on the brink of the twenty-first century have fundamentally changed and continue to do so.

The new organizational form literature has also provided ample opportunity for prescription. For instance, Bartlett and Ghoshal (1995a) see the problems which companies have in coping with the new competitive challenges as inherent in the strategy-structure-systems doctrine which produced the tools of planning and control systems. They suggest managers must create an 'individualized corporation' in which executives are the coach, and middle- and front-line managers monitor themselves. Numerous writers have urged organizations to change their structure (Peters, 1992) and management style (Davis, 1993); strategy (Knorr, 1990b) and processes (Knorr, 1990a); to implement internal markets inside corporations (Rothschild, 1993) and adopt the manufacturing of knowledge as the first principle (Peters, 1992). Moreover US firms may only remain competitive if a transformation of organizational and managerial practices comparable to the managerial revolution of the early part of the twentieth century takes place (Gummer, 1995).

The evidence for organizational change in face of the new competition is a bewildering cocktail of responses, some single initiatives focused on structure, such as delayering to reduce costs (Nienstedt, 1989; Galagan, 1992; Zeffane, 1992; Shaw and Schneier, 1993), work redesign and redesigning operations into autonomous operating units (Donovan, 1989b), or process-oriented initiatives, such as team-based continuous improvement (Peters, 1992; Tompkins, 1993) and empowering employees (Donovan, 1989a; Clutterbuck, 1993). Other single initiatives have focused on the customer, such as developing total customer service strategies (Rummler and Brache, 1991; Peters 1992; Davis, 1993) or responsive operational measures such as service response logistics (Ripley and Ripley, 1992; Davis, 1993). There is also evidence of multiple initiatives such as automating information and strategic restructuring (Knorr, 1990b), business process re-engineering (Leth, 1994; Meckstroth, 1994; Alavi and Yoo, 1995) which is often linked to TQM (total quality management) programmes (Donovan, 1989a). Other commentators have raised the possibility of behavioural and attitudinal effects, for instance altering organizational psychology (Bartlett and Ghoshal, 1990), and creating learning organizations (Taylor, 1992; Bennett and O'Brien, 1994). It is clear that much of this conjecture is about process, which has implications for structure. As Stewart (1992) notes, organizing around processes permits greater self-management and allows companies to dismantle unneeded supervisory structures.

Few authors have attempted to construct theoretical perspectives to unify the field. One exception to this is Denison (1997) who has argued for a process-based theory of organizational design which draws on the concepts of the value chain and networks. Employing a range of organizational innovations or 'process perspectives', such as quality, re-engineering and virtual organization, Denison develops a process perspective divided into managing, organizing and designing the value chain. In this way Denison claims to describe the emerging form of the process organization. Essentially an ideal type, this form is constructed around the value chain. Its primary control system is more market driven than hierarchy driven, with increasing emphasis being placed on its external relations. This type of firm will then face a market dynamic of competing sources for supply of resources between the internal and external firms. In this model while the hierarchy remains intact it is configured to match the management, organization and design of the value chain. Denison's process view of organizing remains to be empirically tested.

A recurrent expression of the new organizational forms literature has been the proliferation of ideal types, particularly with regard to the multinational firm. For instance Ghoshal and Bartlett (1998) make a case for the individualized corporation as one where people and their management are central to the achievement of organizational success in the twenty-first century. Similarly, Ashkenas et al. (1995) argue for the boundaryless organization where goods and services move freely across borders within and between firms to achieve competitive advantage. A particularly evocative type to emerge has been the virtual organization, as a result of the growth and importance of information technology. The virtual organization marks a sharp break with the tangible and very visible organizations of the past. Monolithic global organizations are being replaced with flatter, more responsive, real-time information-rich configurations. This is said to be particularly true of knowledge-based organizations where human resources are the company's chief asset. This, in combination with the outsourcing of non-core competencies and contractual arrangements with networks up and down the value chain, enables firms to be flexible and cost effective. However, the empirical evidence for such large scale changes in global organizing is weak, being based either on high profile case studies or more rarely on a small population of firms (see Nohria and Ghoshal, 1997).

The most extreme form of virtual organization is described by Handy (1996: 188) as a 'box of contracts' and he makes the salient point that although one can describe what it does, it cannot be seen. This elimination of physicality has profound consequences for our conceptualization of organizational form. For now organization becomes more of a verb than a noun, that is, a means of organizing rather than a physical presence with tangible structures. Handy (1996) adopts a relational view when he suggests organizations are more properly viewed as patterns of relationships. In this way it is the quality of internal and external relationships that is important, not the role positions occupied by people. Thus our understanding of organizing comes from an analysis of relationships, coordination mechanisms, intangible assets and legal contractual arrangements.

The virtual organization is of necessity a rather extreme and futuristic view. It is a perspective which may be associated with certain industries, particularly knowledge-intensive ones such as professional services without tangible assets. However, there are many features of this view which pervade the literature on new organizational forms, not least of which is a relational perspective and the notion that the object of empirical study should be organizational processes and patterns of relationships. For instance, the global structuring perspective contributes key insights into the larger pattern of changes within multinational companies. It is apparent that size and complexity (both internal and external) are important drivers for new ways of organizing and hierarchy is not adequate to handle the resultant information uncertainty (Galbraith, 1973). Firms have responded by adding new coordination mechanisms alongside the established principles of hierarchy and multidivisional structures. In this way, the focus on what is new moves hierarchical reporting relationships backstage while lateral and informal relationships move frontstage. This new structuring of activities nevertheless preserves the hierarchy principle as the constitutional backcloth of the firm.

However, closer inspection of the literature reveals that many of the new forms are not entirely new but reminiscent of earlier typologies, such as Burns and Stalker's (1961) organic and mechanistic forms and Galbraith's (1973) preoccupation with lateral relations. Further, many of the recent new forms of organizing literature are either anecdotal, requiring greater generalizability in the field, or theoretical, remaining to be empirically tested. Ideal types make prescription easier and more attractive to managers, for one substantial theme may be played out in endless permutations of advice to firms. But the natural partiality of specialist fields and interests means that no one has attempted to characterize the new organization writing in all its diversity. We will attempt to do this here in terms of the recurring themes in the literature which we see as marking out the fundamental changes within and between organizations over the last decade.

Themes in the new organizational forms literature

Our enquiries into the nature of the new organizational forms has been at the heart of the INNFORM programme and has led us to identify three major interrelated themes which permeate the different writings in this area. When these are drawn together, one sees that a new managerial logic underlies the new forms of organizing. We have labelled these three themes as follows:

The globalizing firm and its changing boundaries   Powerful forces for globalization, rapidly changing technologies, including information technology, and intense competition have shifted the emphasis of organizational goals from economizing to adding value. Increasingly, large global firms are discovering that customers are demanding added value in products and services and not just cheaper products. Thus the economies of scale derived from the vertically integrated firm are giving way to a focus on core competencies while all other activities are being outsourced. This has led large firms to experiment with new forms of organizing around, for instance, technology, processes and or resources. The emphasis on processes has highlighted the importance of organizational relations in the global structuring literature, especially in the work of Ghoshal and Bartlett, (1990), Roth and Nigh (1992) and Ghoshal and Nohria (1993). This work has led to a reconceptualization of the global firm as an entity for capturing and utilizing strategic internal competencies.

The knowledge firm in the knowledge economy   This phenomenon is particularly evident in the influential literature on the knowledge-based view of the firm where the requirement to leverage intellectual capital (Nahapiet and Ghoshal, 1998) involves new forms of organizing around social and relational dimensions. There is a concern with managing intangible assets, their acquisition and integration, within and between firms. An emphasis on intangible rather than tangible assets has profound consequences for organization. This brings a new perspective on organizational design based on new principles such as multiplication and combination, integration and interdependence.

Networks and the socially embedded firm   Inter- and intra-organizational networks represent a shift away from transactions as the primary unit of analysis to relationships in the exchange (Easton and Araujo, 1994). The theme of organizational relations appears predominantly in the interorganizational network literature as a key social control and cohesion mechanism. This literature regards interdependence, including interdependency with other social and political institutions, as vital for the survival of firms.

A preoccupation with developing a firm's strategic capability or adding value to firm activities underlies a large tranche of the literature on, for instance, global organizing, strategic alliances, inter-firm networks and outsourcing. Strategic capability here is as much about developing tangible as intangible assets and competencies. The influence of the resource-based view of the firm is evident in all of these themes where developing capability in the management and sharing of knowledge is a strategic imperative.

The new forms literature has also blurred the boundaries of the firm in terms of scope and depth. By scope we mean the inclusion of a much larger constituency of interests, from owned and affiliated subunits, to joint ventures, strategic partnerships and networks, including political and social institutions shared by similar firms. By depth we mean the flattening of hierarchies and the breaking down of barriers between functions in order to create the horizontal and vertical integration of knowledge. At the same time, the vertical integration of the value chain is being dismantled to allow the firm to concentrate on its core competencies. To this end, integration or interdependence becomes the principal activity of organizations for competitive advantage. This necessitates flexible organizational boundaries and requires greater cooperation and therefore relational forms of organizing.

As firms add value via relationships and require ever greater internal and external interdependence to create, share and transfer knowledge, so the basis for organizational activity and configuration is centred on relationships and the wider social context within which firms are embedded.

One may demonstrate the interconnectedness of these themes by considering the rationale for interorganizational networks. Here non-market, non-hierarchical modes of exchange represent a particular form of collective action which may be sustained in the long term, is conducive to knowledge transference and subsequent firm action, suited to demand conditions of resource and environmental uncertainty and provides a feasible means of utilizing intangible assets such as tacit knowledge and technological innovation. The driver for these organizational arrangements is less a concern with minimizing transaction costs than strategic considerations, in terms of gaining access to critical resources or redefining competitive strategy. This perspective problematizes other approaches to economic organization (Powell, 1990). For instance the exclusive focus on the transaction – rather than the relationship – as the primary unit of analysis is misplaced. In this sense, Powell (1990) argues for historically contingent and context dependent explanations in understanding the diversity of organizational forms, for no single explanation ties all the cases together.

The new forms literature portrays organizing as fundamentally concerned with both structure and process. The evidence appears to be that formal hierarchical organization is still present as an institutional backdrop but not so crucial in determining organizational activities or capabilities. Instead, 'new' subtle coordination mechanisms stress the informal and social processes of organization. There is also a move away from defining organizations purely in distributional terms toward more relational notions. The new forms literature has uncovered a myriad of processual issues which have hitherto been separate from theories of design. For instance the concept of trust within organizations may be seen as integral to the design of group and team dynamics. Meyerson et al.'s (1996) work on 'swift trust' which develops within temporary teams under intense task situations, illustrates that trust can both create organizational forms and be created by them. Relational concerns are also evident in the repetition of the network theme and use of network concepts to describe multinational firms and interorganizational arrangements. Here the work of Easton and Araujo (1994) is important for their very considered approach to exchange theory which contains an appreciation of relationships in the exchange process, the temporal context of exchange and the performance consequences of their inter- action.

A recognition of the dual nature of organizational design as encom- passing both formal structure and processes is not new in organizational theory (see for example Ranson et al., 1980; Skivington and Daft, 1991). These dualities have been theorized by Sryker and Statham (1985) who take a social psychological perspective on design while Galunic and Eisenhardt (1994) refer to both formal organizational form and sociostructure. A configurational approach is adopted by many authors in explaining the two sides of design. For instance, Hinings et al. (1996) have looked at structure and organizational values; Pennings (1992) conceives of formal designs and spontaneous 'grassroots' configura- tions while Rapert and Wren (1998) look at structural frameworks and communication networks. These writings all give equal weight to the duality of organizing. This appreciation of a variety of social mecha- nisms, control mechanisms, incentives and authority structures all coexisting within organizational arrangements, signals a deeper appre- ciation of organizational complexity. Viewed in this light, organizing becomes a strategic act, one which must orchestrate holistic change and carefully manage contradictory organizational imperatives. Before dis- cussing the three themes of organizing in more detail, we turn to an overview of antecedent theories of organizational design.

Organizational Design: 1950–2000

The history of the field of organizational design may be characterized more generally as that of a recurrent interest in aggregated and disag- gregated conceptualizations of form. Each approach has its own methodology, focus and language. In Figure 1.1 this was demonstrated by the progression of the field from universalistic models to the split between the disaggregated and aggregated approaches of contingency theorists. In parallel with contingency theory, the industrial economic literature was exploring the relationship between firm structure and performance. This led to a proliferation of organizational categories or ideal types (see Hill, 1988a) which found a resonance with the work of the aggregated contingency theorists at Harvard. At the same time as the ideal types of the configurationists sought to find a middle ground between these conceptual approaches, one finds a dwindling of interest in design in general and the disaggregated approach in particular. This left design in the hands of industrial economists who dominated the pages of management and strategy journals.

This disjuncture in the profile of organizational design theorists was brought about in the first instance by a dissatisfaction with contingency theory and secondly by a deflection of academic interest towards other theoretical perspectives and foci, such as process, politics and networks in organizations. The current resurgence of interest in organizational form differs from its predecessors in the blurring of the boundaries between structure and process. In this sense, the new organizational forms literature, while still seeking a coherent theory and paradigm to explain the phenomenon, does mark a distinctive conceptual break from previous design schools of thought.

Universal organizational forms

A preoccupation with universal organizational forms marks the earliest influential theories of organizational design. The bureaucratic form was the earliest documented and most influential for the emerging contingency theorists. The multidivisional form may be seen as a later expression of a desire to capture developments in Western capitalism, initially in the United States and later in other Western countries.

Bureaucracy　The field of organizational design consolidated during the 1950s with Merton's focus on dysfunctional organizational learning derived from Weber's (1947) earlier writings at the turn of the century on the bureaucratic organization. Much of the literature in the 1950s emphasized on the bureaucratic organization, its dynamics (Blau, 1956), and dysfunctional consequences (Merton, 1940; Selznick, 1949; Gouldner, 1955; Bendix, 1956; March and Simon, 1958). This literature is based on the 'machine' model of organizational behaviour, where the independent variable is some form of organizational procedure designed to control the activities of organizational members. Criticism of this school has taken the form of the empirical demonstration of the paradox that although people are necessary for an organization to function at all, their presence gets in the way of its rationally efficient functioning (Pugh and Hickson, 1976).

Essentially, the bureaucratic organization is a highly rational and highly efficient organization with universal applicability. Its superiority in terms of efficiency enabled this model to be applied to all kinds of administrative tasks. Weber saw the development of the modern form of organization as identical with the development and spread of bureaucratic administration, which he saw as the most crucial phenomenon of the Western state. Bureaucracy was the central element in large scale administration and therefore aided the development of Western capitalism. In this way the bureaucratic organization was a product of its time and became the dominant form of organization discussed in the academic literature.

Critics of the normative implications of Weber's work emphasized the dysfunctional consequences of bureaucracies. Other critiques were of a more profound nature, such as that by Bennis (1959) who criticized Weber for only considering the formal aspects of organizational structure and function, which was like being concerned with organizations without people. Friedrich (1952) criticized the logical status of the 'ideal type' and pointed out the value judgements implicit in Weber's formulation. All critiques regarded bureaucracy as a unitary concept although many questioned the elements of bureaucracy laid down by Weber as requiring reformulation (Friedrich, 1950; Blau, 1956; Stinchcombe, 1959). It was not until the Aston studies in the 1960s that any attempt was made to deconstruct bureaucracy into the constituent 26 characteristics postulated by Weber (Pugh et al., 1963) and develop the concept further. Until the Aston studies, the general view appeared to be that the bureaucratic form was of a particular type rather than a variable.

The multidivisional   The drivers for the bureaucratic organization must be seen in the context of the development of Western capitalism, with its requirement for technical knowledge and the increasing complexity of society. A very similar conclusion was adopted by Chandler (1962) in his seminal work on the evolution of large scale corporations in the United States. He charted the development of the multidivisional in terms of historical determinism, seeing it as representing a solution to the increasing scale and complexity of industrial enterprise. The diversification of resources led to the creation of multiple divisions within large organizations in order to manage these resources effectively. This adoption of the multidivisional structure in its turn 'institutionalized' the strategy of diversification. In this way the multidivisional was also a highly rational and adaptive model of organizational form which was seen to hold universal applicability. Chandler's premise was that large industrial firms in advanced economies all over the world would follow the logic of corporate development and over time would converge on increasingly similar strategies and structures.

Whittington et al. (1999a) illustrate the importance of the historical context of theorizing when they note that Chandler (1962) proposed the notion of diversification at a time when strategies of unrelated conglomerate diversification were largely unknown. Therefore Chandler had no need to distinguish between types. From an institutionalist perspective the empirical evidence for the diffusion of the M-form out of the US into Europe during the 1960s occurred at a time of American political and economic pre-eminence in the world (Fligstein, 1990; Whitley, 1994). This diffusion was aided by the pre-eminent consultancy firm McKinsey, who propagated the M-form design. The intellectual climate in which Chandler constructed his work was one in which the common social project of modernization by society was pre-eminent. Thus like Weber's bureaucratic organization, Chandler's framework was both universalistic and borderless (Kogut, 1992), as it was deemed essential for economic growth and the political stability of all advanced economies (Servan-Schreiber, 1967; McArthur and Scott, 1968; Guillen, 1994; Djelic, 1998).

The M-form, as it came to be known, held sway in academic accounts and empirical analysis, particularly in the US. Both the bureaucratic and the multidivisional were normative models, driven to their continuing function by powerful internal interests. In particular, the separation of ownership from control in large firms was dependent upon discipline and technical training. Here we have the genesis of the rise of the managerial elite who would manage the large corporations which fuelled Western capitalism. Both models are based on hierarchy, and formalization, the division of labour, specialization and utilitarianism are the guiding organizational principles.

Contingency theorists

The work of Weber and Chandler spawned influential streams of work under the rubric of contingency theory. In particular, two large scale quantitative research programmes will be highlighted here. These programmes both challenged and developed the notion of ideal types by recognizing the greater diversity of organizational forms. These were principally the Aston studies in the UK and the work of a number of Harvard doctoral students in the 1970s. Although each of these research streams was in the mould of its intellectual forebear and built upon that earlier work, they were widely different in their approach to organizational design. The Aston studies took a disaggregated approach in developing quite fine-grained design variables while the Harvard School's more aggregated approach focused on the study of three or four organizational designs. Meanwhile, numerous influential contingency studies were being conducted by single and small groups of researchers and these captivated academic thought from the 1950s to the late 1970s.

The contingency theorists of the late 1950s and 1960s created theoretical models derived from statistically established patterns of association between contextual and organizational variables. The main interpretation from these studies was that there was no one best way of organizing a business. Instead, the criteria of appropriateness of any organizational structure must be the extent to which it furthers the objectives of the firm. There occurred both in the United States and in Britain systematic comparative investigations of the relationships between organizational structure and situational variables. Researchers attempted to discover the degree of empirical variation in organizational structures and to establish the conditions of such variation. Such structurally determined models posit associations between dimensions of organizational structure and contextual factors such as environment (Stinchcombe, 1959; Burns and Stalker, 1961; Emery and Trist, 1965; Haige and Aiken, 1967; Lawrence and Lorsch, 1967b), technology (Woodward, 1965, 1970; Perrow, 1967, 1970) or scale of operation (Pugh et al., 1969; Blau, 1970). All of these authors accounted for variations in structure between organizations by analysing task predictability and diversity.

While such studies give accounts of the diversity of organizational form they usually leave the underlying processes to be inferred (Child, 1972) and thereby fail to pay due attention to the agency of choice by organizational decision makers. This was one of the key criticisms of the Aston studies, which nevertheless placed a marker in the ground for their particular conceptualization of structure and their methodological approach.

The Aston studies   One of the most intensive and longstanding research programmes to examine bureaucracy was carried out under the directorship of Derek Pugh at the University of Aston in the UK between 1961 and 1968. The Aston researchers saw critics of bureaucratic theory as failing to distinguish between structural, behavioural characteristics and achievement of purpose. There had been no rigorous analysis or formal definition of bureaucracy. Its characterization had remained limited and partial, with writers adding still further characteristics (Blau, 1956; Presthus, 1958). Pugh and Hickson (1976) argued for an explicit synthesis of conceptual theory and empirical field research. They attempted to develop empirically based multi-dimensional analyses of structural variables within organizations, what Donaldson (1996) has described as a Cartesian framework. To do this they had to first isolate the conceptually distinct elements that went into Weber's formulation of bureaucracy. Then the relationships between these elements became the subject of empirical investigation; they were not postulated a priori. The insights of Weber were then translated into a set of empirically testable hypotheses (Pugh et al., 1963). This finely grained way of modelling organizations is seen to be more accurate and useful than analysis in terms of ideal types (Donaldson, 1996).

The Aston programme sought to address the lack of empirical studies of bureaucracy as a structural variable and to empirically validate the notion that organizational structure was made up of a number of dimensions. Based on a sample of local organizations around Birmingham they defined scales along key dimensions so that clear comparisons could be made between organizations. The result was a typology based on empirical generalizations (Pugh et al., 1963, 1968, 1969). Conceptually, the Aston School stood in the Weberian tradition as the basic dimensions were derived from Weber's bureaucratic model (Pugh and Hickson, 1976). But the radical idea for the time was in trying to move away from unitary conceptualizations to the idea of dimensions as variables. In this way unitary concepts could be seen to have a number of meanings conceptualized as dimensions. What the Aston studies attempted was revolutionary in organizational theory at the time: to conceptualize Weber's bureaucracy as a variable within organizations rather than an undifferentiated ideal type.

Emphasis with the Aston taxonomy of organizational types was on the ability to measure and state precise relationships between structure, context and behaviour. The Aston studies' empirical taxonomy of organizations was elaborated from four main types: workflow bureaucracy in manufacturing firms, personnel bureaucracy in public sector organizations, full bureaucracy as a mixture of the last two types and non-bureaucracy characteristic of small firms. Pugh and Hickson write of their findings: 'Of such, then, are the organizations of today in Britain and probably elsewhere too. In terms of structural characteristics, it can be suggested that these are the principal forms of organization of which late twentieth century organizational society is composed' (1976: 16). Here Pugh and Hickson make strong claims for their taxonomy. The world of organizations has now shifted from one model to four, of which the basic building blocks are derived from the former model. This taxonomy is as much bound by time and place as Weber's bureaucracy and Chandler's multidivisional. The empirical data represent the character of 1960s Midlands organizations in the United Kingdom: small, medium and large scale manufacturing, mixed with public sector organizations. Nevertheless, the legacy of the Aston studies has been enormous, as seen in the proliferation of research in many countries which essentially replicated their methodology (Clark, 1997). However, this did not prevent this work from being eclipsed in the Anglo-Saxon academic world by the increasing dominance of American managerial thought, one of the most influential institutions being the Harvard Business School.

The Harvard research on organization and strategy

The two most influential writers on contingency theory were Lawrence and Lorsch (1967b) who came from the organizational behaviour field in

Harvard. Their work on the design principles of differentiation and integration had a profound impact on organization theory and managerial practice. Noticeably, unlike the Aston studies, their work included a performance variable and was crucial in propagating contingency theory more widely amongst academics.

Later, Chandler's work on the multidivisional inspired a whole programme of research throughout the 1970s looking at strategy and structure in the United States and Western Europe. The lead researcher here was Scott (1973), who devised a three-stage model of corporate development: undiversified, undiversified with functional organization and diversified and divisionalized on product-market lines. This evolutionary model retained Chandler's basic premise that structure followed strategy. In general the Harvard studies were supportive of the Chandlerian framework and a stream of research by doctoral students examined the relationship between strategy and structure and the effects of structure on performance (Channon, 1973; Thanheiser, 1973; Rumelt, 1974).

Industrial economics

The theoretical justification for the multidivisional was based on the transaction cost economics argument (Williamson, 1975) that the M-form separated strategy and capital allocation from operations in the divisions, and reduced transaction costs by creating an internal capital market. Industrial economists were theoretically separate from contingency theorists in developing the M-form argument that certain organizational attributes are more likely to yield superior corporate performance. Thus organizational categories such as the H-form (Holding Company), M-form, CM-form (Centralized Multidivisional) or U-form (Functional) were tested for performance effects. The reasoning here is that one type of organizational structure is more suited to resolve agency costs and alleged capital market failure than other organizational types. This work began with Williamson and Bhargava (1972) and was replicated in the US (Armour and Teece, 1978; Teece, 1981; Markides and Williamson, 1996), the UK (Steer and Cable, 1978; Grinyer et al., 1980; Hill and Pickering, 1986; Hill 1988b; Ezzamel and Watson, 1993), Germany (Cable and Dirrheimer, 1983) and Japan (Cable and Yasuki, 1985)

However, from an institutionalist perspective the success of the multidivisional does not rest just on economic universals but is linked to the importance of the US as a country (Djelic, 1998). This system of industrial production is seen to rely on strong institutional supports: the predominance of the American way of management (Locke, 1996) and the politically motivated programme of 'Americanization' of European management dating from the Marshall Plan (Guillen, 1994; Djelic, 1998).

Additionally, the multidivisional was promoted by McKinsey, the leading American consultancy of the day (McKenna, 1997). The evidence from Europe supports the institutional determinism of organizational form where the indigenous traditions of organizations have resulted in enduring national differences (Zysman, 1994; Whitley, 1994; Calori et al., 1997).

Moreover, the work of micro-economists in the strategy field led to a proliferation of organizational types to accommodate the empirical diversity of organizational forms. These types were all constructed from the relationship between the two variables of strategy and structure. These were then tested for performance, with largely inconclusive results. For a time, industrial economists gained in popularity as academics lost interest in contingency theory. But more recently, academic interest has faded here too, with the sterility of organizational types and inconsistent findings. Additionally, this literature has ignored the processual and contextual dimension of organizations, which make this approach outmoded in the context of new organizational forms.

The matrix form   During the 1970s large organizations began to display increasingly complex structural arrangements, the most widely reported being the matrix form with its dual lines of accountability up the hierarchy. An analytical framework for the design of such organizations which applied lateral decision processes was put forward by Galbraith (1973) at MIT. This work was firmly in the contingency school and took as its underlying premise the Lawrence and Lorsch (1967b) conceptualization of the organizational design problem as differentiation and integration. Galbraith added the importance of information requirements to the dictum that the best way to organize was contingent upon uncertainty and diversity. The greater the task uncertainty, the greater the amount of information that must be processed by decision makers during the task execution in order to achieve given levels of performance. In this way, alternative organizational designs were contingent upon the degree of task uncertainty as this represented alternative capacities for processing information.

Galbraith's (1973) framework provided a justification for the multidivisional in that the creation of self-contained tasks would reduce the interdependence of subunits and therefore reduce information requirements. Another information reduction strategy, the creation of lateral relations, would find support in the new forms of organizing literature some 20 years later. Here the creation of task forces and teams would enable managers to solve problems at their own level instead of referring problems up the hierarchy. Galbraith's framework was based on limited empirical study and had little room for alternative organizational forms. He regarded the matrix as essentially an overlay on what was still a bureaucratic structure with hierarchically distributed power.

In this respect, the basic organizing principles of the Weberian inheritance prevailed, and contingency theory underwent a further refinement to accommodate the increasing complexity of organizational form.

The waning of interest by academic researchers in contingency theory has been attributed to the antimanagerial nature of newer organizational theories (Donaldson, 1997) and the difficulties in operationalizing its concepts in terms of decision making (Argyris, 1972; Child, 1972). Starbuck's (1981) withering critique of the Aston studies singled out their methodology as using too highly aggregated agglomerations of variables and constructs which lacked meaning at an operational level. Essentially, contingency theory suffered from overcomplicated and abstract constructs, a disconnection from decision variables and did not deal in robust, parsimonious ideas (Pfeffer, 1997). But Pfeffer (1997) also argues for the importance of the institutional context of the field of organization studies in understanding the declining interest in the contingency approach. This context is one in which there is a preoccupation with what is new and unique, making cumulative research unattractive. Additionally Pfeffer (1997) cites a preoccupation with ideas that have practical outcomes and the influence of economic theories which are invariably non-contingent.

The dwindling of interest in the contingency approach was supplemented from the mid-1970s onwards by new theories, such as population ecology (Hannan and Freeman, 1977), institutional theory (Powell and DiMaggio, 1991), resource dependency theory (Pfeffer and Salancik, 1978), agency theory (Jensen and Meckling, 1976) and transaction cost economics (Williamson, 1985). Each explicitly or implicitly rejected structural contingency theory and led to its own programme of research. However, one approach, that of the configurationists, attempted to bridge the divide between the aggregated and disaggregated contingency approaches.

The configurational approach

In parallel with the Harvard School there developed another stream of work focusing on ideal types but which attempted to look at strategy and structure from a more multidimensional point of view. For instance, Miles and Snow (1978) showed how unique configurations of strategy adapted to their environments and indicated how this might influence the organization's technology and structure. Miller and Friesen's (1977, 1978) types or archetypes were derived from an empirical taxonomy of organizations. Similarly they looked at common adaptive strategies and their structural and environmental correlates. Mintzberg (1979) identified five structural types and Miller (1986) reduced this to four strategy-structure gestalts.

The configurational approach to structure takes its departure from the strategy and structure studies of the Harvard School. The chief proponent of this approach is Danny Miller (1986) who critiques the simplistic approach of the Harvard School in equating strategy and structure with diversification and divisionalization respectively. Rather than linking a myriad of individual variables in the two respective categories, Miller suggests identifying and interrelating common configurations of strategy and structure. He identifies a central gap in the literature in that the rich content of strategies has never been related to structure. He sought to include the work on micro-economics by Porter (1980) and the empirical studies of the PIMS (Profit Impact of Marketing Strategy) data by Hambrick (1983) and Hambrick and Schecter (1983).

The central theme of Miller's approach is that there are ties which unite strategy and structure and therefore organizational form is determined by strategy. Not a controversial proposition but one which sought to unite contingency theory with theories of strategy. Miller argues for the pervasiveness of ideal or common types in the strategy and structure literature and that these now remain to be united. The innovation in this line of thinking is the premise that organizational elements form common gestalts such that '. . . *each can best be understood in relation to the other elements in the configuration*' (Miller, 1986: 235, our italics). These tight constellations of mutually supportive elements occur in a large proportion of high-performing firms. It is the presence of certain elements in these firms which can lead one to reliably predict the remaining elements (Miller and Mintzberg, 1984). Further, configurations can be a source of competitive advantage (Miller, 1996) in that the complexity and ambiguity of their components may give some organizations non-imitable capacities.

The argument for the prevalence of common configurations is based on the population ecology (Hannan and Freeman, 1977; Aldrich, 1979; McKelvey, 1981) premise that firms will converge upon viable configurations thereby limiting the available repertoire of strategic and structural configurations. Secondly, organizations are driven towards common configurations in order to achieve internal harmony among strategy, structure and context. In this way the number of possible permutations of elements will be limited. Finally, organizations will remain with successful configurations for fairly long periods because of the disruption and expense of change. Because piecemeal changes destroy complementarities among elements of the configuration these will be avoided, and change programmes will act either to extend existing configurations or move to a totally new one which is retained for a long time. Miller (1987) argues for four imperatives which restrict organizational variety and help give rise to organizational configurations: environment, organization structure, leadership and strategy. He argues for a single dominant imperative for most configurations where imperatives are the cause and the configurations the effects.

The debate on aggregated versus disaggregated approaches continues with the configurationists. Their central claim is that organizations can be reduced to a few types that are internally coherent (Mintzberg, 1979; Miller, 1986). However, Donaldson's (1997) analysis shows this idea of internal coherence to be theoretically flawed, the researchers having recourse to hybrid forms when their data fail to fit their configurations. He advocates a return to the Cartesian approach of the Aston programme if one is to account for empirically observed structures and organizational change. What has been lacking in the configurational perspective is any dedicated empirical work to support its arguments. Ten years after Miller's (1986) seminal article on configurations of strategy and structure he wrote in the *Strategic Management Journal*: 'For all its promise, the literature on configuration remains underdeveloped . . . there remains a great deal of work to be done' (Miller, 1996: 506). Organizational form as a serious research endeavour has remained diverted throughout the 1980s by alternative research themes and practitioner interests, such as culture, change and internationalization. There was, however, significant interest in organizational form from another direction, that of networks within and between organizations.

Network analysis

The influence of sociology, and in particular economic sociology, has been prevalent with the introduction of network concepts into the organizational design field. Deriving their ideas from early anthropological studies of kinship and sociological studies of class and job mobility, network theorists brought a more social and relational perspective to the study of organizations. Network analysis in general and social network theory in particular offer alternative conceptualizations of design and techniques of analysis. The distinctiveness of the network approach is encapsulated by Tolbert et al. (1995) as a focus on the organization of actions rather than the actions of individual organizations.

A network focus involves the identification of patterns of direct and indirect linkage among persons and positions based on diverse ties. This processual orientation of the network approach may be illustrated by a quote from Lincoln (1982: 12): 'Organizations divide administrative and functional responsibilities among positions, then recombine them through a collective meshing of roles to generate an organizational action.' Thus networks of work and authority roles arise from an interdependence of individual lines of action. The important point here is that the fact of transmission is secondary to the relation itself.

Lincoln (1982) describes the relationship between distributional form and the internal network structures of organizations as complex and reciprocal. Given that classical management theorists were in part seeking solutions to the problem of managing relational complexity, the prescribed principles of formal structuring were based upon early management writers' conception of network form. In this historical sense, Lincoln argues, the network form has shaped the modern organizations' distributional forms. He is, however, more interested in addressing the reverse question: how does the configuration of organizational positions, and distribution of members in them, condition the internal network? Where distributional form is a relatively fixed, exogenous organizational property, network properties are contingent emergent outcomes. He gives as examples the relational consequences, such as cohesion, interdependence and connectivity, of the key distributional dimensions of vertical and horizontal differentiation.

As a conceptual tool for organizational analysis the network perspective is particularly constructive. Lincoln (1982) lists the network properties at three levels of analysis: the dyad, network and node. The concept of nodes is useful either at the firm or the actor level to characterize positions in a network. Dyadic properties such as symmetry, multiplexity and strength give insights into the microprocesses of organizations while global network properties such as density, connectivity and hierarchy explain system-wide processes. It has been argued that global properties are not reducible to the sum of their parts (Burt, 1978; Aldrich, 1979; Wellman, 1980) but this distinction is still meaningful and theoretical propositions can usefully be cast at both levels. A useful bridge between the dyadic and global properties is provided by the concept of embeddedness (Granovetter, 1992) and the distinction between relational and structural embeddedness. Relational embeddedness (Uzzi, 1997) captures the quality of dyadic exchanges (for example trust, confiding, information exchange) while structural embeddedness refers to the entire network system: 'the extent to which a dyad's mutual contacts are connected to one another' (Granovetter, 1992). When there is too much relational embeddedness in a system, that is, overreliance on strong ties, the formation of cliques can act to isolate parts of the system and prevent integration such that overembeddedness results.

Network techniques are also particularly useful in empirical analysis for investigations into differences in internal roles, relations and tasks of different affiliated units (Ghoshal and Bartlett, 1990), where techniques such as block modelling (Boorman and White, 1976; White et al., 1976) and analysis of functional equivalence are especially suited. Alternatively, assessing how internal coordination mechanisms might be differentiated to match the variety of subunit contexts may be approached using Burt et al.'s (1983) analysis on 'distinguishing relational contents'. Additionally, network theory can contribute to an understanding of the flows of resources and people and to the development of theories of decision making, strategic control, knowledge flows (Van Wijk and Van den Bosch, 1998a) and innovation within companies (Burt, 1987).

New Forms of Organizing

As the academic interest in the structure of organizations has been replaced by an examination of process and networks, the question remains whether organizations have significantly changed over the last 50 years. A more recent study by Whittington et al. (1999a) replicates the Harvard studies using longitudinal data from 1950 to 1993. Their findings show that Europe has continued in the direction of increased diversification as predicted by Dyas and Thanheiser (1976) but with a steady rise in conglomerate diversification. Amongst the top 500 firms in three major economies, the multidivisional form was found in 70 per cent of firms in France, 79 per cent in Germany and 89 per cent in Britain. The general pattern of their findings, then, is consistent with the model of corporate development advocated by Chandler (1962) and Scott (1973). These show institutionalism to be less important than critics of Chandler would claim. It appears that the divisional organization has been steadily absorbed into the European mainstream, even after what may be a decline of American influence in business. Thus amongst the largest European firms the multidivisional is robust with enduring and generalizable qualities over other forms.

It would seem that large organizations at the end of the twentieth century have the same structural characteristics as they did 50 years ago. But would it be the same for the individuals who work in these organizations? We think not. One of the conceptual issues arising from the Harvard studies was the limitations of their measures (Pfeffer, 1997). Divisionalization does not capture much of a range of design variables (Pfeffer, 1997) and is a gross oversimplification (Starbuck, 1981). Whittington et al. (1999a) note that their structural categories refer mainly to formal organizational characteristics and say little about the ways in which managers actually behave within them. These authors make the point that the character of the divisional organization of the 1960s is not the same as that in the 1990s given new technology, management fads and internal processes. So while there is no formal break with the essential character of the multidivisional, that is, its distributed form, there is less evidence for the continuity of its internal processes. These internal processes and their links with a range of other organizational variables became the dominant subject of analysis and discussion in the debates on new forms of organizing.

The new organizational forms phenomena is however still emerging

and therefore remains underspecified and nebulous in its conceptualization within the literature. Given the lack of empirical research and
theoretical development we have had to capture the phenomenon thematically and attempt to provide specificity amidst the linguistic
plurality and confusion. It seems right, given the emergent nature of the
phenomenon, to set it within its equally emergent and ever changing
context.

The new context and the new competition

One of the key drivers for the new forms of organizing literature has
been the rapidly changing organizational context. The writing on this
new competitive environment is at times apocryphal and dramatic.
Here the new context of organizations has been described variously as
a 'silent industrial revolution' (Prahalad and Hamel, 1994), or as hypercompetitive (D'Aveni, 1994; Volberda, 1996), brought about by
globalization and the recessions of the late 1980s and early 1990s. The
new competition is shown to have quickened trends in corporate refocusing (Geroski and Gregg, 1994); to herald a change in world
economies brought about by globalization (Bartlett and Ghoshal, 1986)
and be influenced by new technologies, particularly IT (information
technology) (Miles and Snow, 1986; Halal, 1993; Malone et al., 1996). The
new features of organizations which these literatures highlight include
the breakdown of vertically integrated structures and the disintegration
of industries (Prahalad and Hamel, 1994).

The 1980s and 1990s, with their environmental and business trends,
has been described variously as a period of rapid structural change
(Meckstroth, 1994), a time of discontinuous change in the Age of
Unreason (Handy, 1990), the Age of Re-engineering (Hammer and
Champy, 1993), or as an age of increased competition (Donovan, 1989b;
Ross, 1993), economic and technological change (Drucker, 1988) or globalization (Knorr, 1990a). Goldhar and Lei (1991) list the most common
events contributing to the upheaval of the competitive environment:
increasing fragmentation and volatility of consumer buying patterns,
faster diffusion of the latest advances in science and technology, the
spawning of new learning organizations and the enormous propagation
of different technologies and skills needed for companies to compete.
Prahalad and Hamel (1994) give a comprehensive overview of the forces
impacting on the nature of the competitive environment within industries in Europe, the US and Japan. They cite deregulation, structural
changes due to technological and customer expectations, excess capacity, increasing merger and acquisition activity, environmental concerns,
less protectionism, technological discontinuities, the emergence of trading blocks and global competition. These or a subset of these, have
impacted upon almost all industries during the 1990s.

Change itself is said to be a permanent condition of companies if they are to survive in today's competitive environment (Horton, 1992). In the UK the pace of organizational change since the mid-1980s has been very high (Geroski and Gregg, 1994). The recession of the early 1990s is shown to have quickened trends in corporate refocusing, and both holding and divisionalized companies are prone to change. The organization of the future is seen to comprise a high-involvement workplace (for example, self-managing teams), an emphasis on managing business processes rather than functional departments and the evolution of information technology (Stewart, 1992). Drucker (1988) predicted that in 20 years the typical large firm will have fewer than half the management levels of today and be overridingly knowledge-based as a result of economic and technological changes.

The importance of technology as a driver for organizational change is a dominant theme within this literature: for instance, the value of a strong technology infrastructure in holding the global corporation together (Williamson, 1994). IT is having a widespread impact on information flows within and between firms, on the structural configuration of the firm (Konstadt, 1990) and on management's ability to integrate change (Shani and Sena, 1994). This has led to a proliferation of technical writings on systems design, for instance, to link branch networks (Bransky et al., 1995) and popularist speculations on coming organizational forms such as the cybercorp (Betts, 1995) with cross-functional teams (Dow, 1995).

Perrone (1997) starts from a contingent view when he makes the case for a particular set of interorganizational arrangements which arise due to the influence of changes in the environmental context of organizations. In particular he focuses on the evolution of competition towards hypercompetitive environments (D'Aveni, 1994) and the evolution of technology towards an 'information age'. These two facets of modern environments are responsible for a set of organizational relationships in which a focal firm shares a common strategic goal with a network of organizations. The flexibility of the focal firm combined with the differentiated resources of the network enable the N-form (Network-form) to perform well in the context of a hypercompetitive environment.

The collective impact of these writings is suggestive of widespread and rapid changes within organizational populations. However, the empirical evidence is fragmented and piecemeal, coming from different organizational perspectives and different sampling methods, mainly from single industries or small populations across industries. The extent of organizational transformation within or across Western economies has yet to be systematically mapped (see Geroski and Gregg, 1994; Ezzamel et al., 1994 and Fenton et al., 1997 for extensive surveys of the UK). Also, the degree of change undertaken within organizations is unclear. Very few studies have examined the extent to which organizations have moved from traditional bureaucratic and hierarchical modes to radically new forms of organizing. Furthermore, we lack a clear understanding of the sequencing of the change initiatives, the configuration of changes which are complementary to performance (see Whittington et al., 1999b) and the long term impact of the above considerations upon the organization.

The new competitive environment literature emphasizes the importance of organizational context, such as history and institutional change, as a driver for organizational form. For instance, Miles and Snow (1993) posit the network form as part of a continuous evolution of capitalist enterprise from the functional organization in the late nineteenth century, to the divisionalized corporation and later the matrix form. Similarly, Whittington and Mayer (1997) emphasize the continuities between the M-form and newer forms which are seen as an adaptation in structure during the evolution of the M-form. Therefore the temporal dimension and the location of organizations in their social and economic circumstances cannot be ignored if we are to understand the development and transformation of these firms.

The new competition literature also stresses the interactive role of firms with their environment, acknowledging the importance of economic and social change, and firms' roles in creating this wider context of change. The global firm literature has taken some significant steps towards isolating some of the key social and institutional variables while the interorganizational literature is perhaps most advanced in this area. The view taken here is that all change is both continual and disjunctive in that new structures contain remnants from the past. These remnants may remain *in situ* alongside or behind newer features, where their role will most likely change, or be reconfigured into new ways of organizing. The important question then becomes: what is different about organizing to accommodate the new environmental imperatives?

We now discuss these emerging differences in innovative forms of organizing in relation to the three themes of the globalizing firm and its changing boundaries, the knowledge firm in the knowledge economy, and networks and the socially embedded firm.

The globalizing firm and its changing boundaries

The decline of rigid compartmentalism within organizations in terms of hierarchies and functions is evident in much of the new forms literature. In particular, IT is seen to integrate the firm by making knowledge and information transparent (Konstadt, 1990). Thus even global firms are no longer constrained by geographical boundaries in the sharing of real time information. Global networks are emerging in a variety of guises (Williamson, 1994) due to their technology infrastructure: private, public carriers, virtual private and software-defined networks. New manufacturing systems have implications for work design, organizational structure and systems that are likely to necessitate a realignment of the entire organization (Shani et al., 1992). For instance, the use in Japan of continuous improvement systems has improved current performance and radically reshaped organizational structure and processes (Melcher et al., 1992). The new technology context of Korean firms is associated with less centralized structures and a higher degree of group dynamics (Lee, 1993).

There is also an emphasis on managing business processes rather than functional departments (Stewart, 1992) which has led to a variety of new organizational configurations such as cross-functional and self-managed teams, task forces and diagonal slice teams. This type of horizontal integration around processes allows the organization to dismantle the hierarchy as well as functional compartmentalization. Kogut and Bowman (1995) advocate the twin design principles of permeability, where information and action flow across boundaries, and modularity, or flexible design. When barriers are dismantled in this way, they emphasize cooperation as a basis for coordination, thereby highlighting the relational basis of organizing. The principle of integration becomes a further basis of organizing, as discussed in the knowledge-based view of the firm. For it is through the firm activities of combination and recombination that the tacit knowledge of organizational members is accessed and new knowledge is both created and transferred (Grant, 1996a).

A resource-based view of the firm underlies much of the analysis of new global firm modes of organizing, particularly in the concern with developing organizational capability and core competencies. For instance, Miles and Snow (1993) adopt a resource perspective when they describe the network structures of internal markets inside large firms as having three main variants: the stable, the dynamic, and the internal network which has a focus on internal resources, particularly the development and exchange of knowledge. They have subsequently developed their ideas to focus on the ability to distribute resources as contingencies arise (Miles and Snow, 1995). This necessitates a HR management philosophy that stresses employees as partners. In this way Miles and Snow are alluding to a cultural perspective as a social control mechanism governing relations within the organization.

There have also been some important theoretical developments in reconceptualizing the firm from the global firm literature. The theoretical treatment of the multinational company (MNC) as an interorganizational network by Ghoshal and Bartlett (1990) is interesting in its adaptation of interorganizational theory, from which they employ the concepts of organizational sets and networks. By combining exchange theory (Cook, 1977) and network methodologies they are able to explain variation in interactions between different units of an MNC. Such concepts as density and centrality measures, although crude, capture internal structural characteristics while the distribution of resources explains process characteristics. In this way they overcome the limitations of traditional intra-organizational theory, which is explained in distributional and categorical terms. Ghoshal and Bartlett depart from purely technical or economic rationality in explaining MNC structure and focus instead on the social and institutional structure of their environments. This is in line with their use of interorganizational theory and is particularly pertinent to the situation of internationally dispersed subunits.

Support for a relational approach has appeared in empirical work by Roth and Nigh (1992) whose survey responses from 105 subsidiaries indicated that more effective HQ–subsidiary relationships were associated with greater levels of coordination between HQ and subsidiaries, greater use of personal integrating mechanisms and lower levels of conflict. Additionally, and of particular interest, was the finding that the use of bureaucratic mechanisms had no impact on the effectiveness of these relationships. When they disaggregated their measure of bureaucratization it became clear that it was the specification by HQ of the subsidiaries' ends that was critical to effective relationships, rather than the specification of means. Roth and Nigh highlight the need to study informal aspects of the organization and identify a new, but no less important, role for bureaucratic mechanisms – backstage.

Ghoshal and Nohria (1993) extend this work when they look at the relationship between HQ–subsidiary relations and environmental fit. Here too the emphasis is on the pattern or nexus of relationships between different national subsidiaries and HQ but this is elaborated to include the variable of a matching environment for certain types of relationships. The theme of building processes was continued by Ghoshal and Bartlett (1995a, 1995b) who see the emphasis in the new MNC to be on developing organizational relationships and management behaviours. They explain this in terms of overcoming the insularity of the divisional structure which prevented integration of subunits, so vital for resource exchanges. This alternative of regarding organizations as portfolios of processes emphasizes the informal, behavioural and relational aspects of organizing.

At a broad theoretical level this literature reflects a disappointment with the 1970s strategy and structure literature and the inconclusive results on the link between performance and the M-form (Farley and Kobrin, 1995). The evocative nature of the network metaphor has heralded a return to a consideration of organizing principles away from the sterility of organizational types. This literature, then, is a radical departure from models that define MNC structure in terms of function, geography, product division or matrix, so characteristic of the formal organization. What this literature reveals is that the organizational chart is a poor representation of how an organization really functions

(Lincoln, 1982). Instead, these authors have demonstrated the need for a relational perspective, in that large organizations exist within a network of exchange relationships which may be highly variable throughout the system.

This acknowledgement of internal complexity implies that comparisons between organizations should focus on the way in which organizations manage their relationships, including a concern with informal behaviour and socialization. This throws into relief the roles of the formal organization, such as HQ and authority relations, which are no less important, but it includes their interrelationship with informal behaviour and processes.

Similarly, we have seen how the global firm literature challenges the hegemony of the divisional structure with its emphasis on subunit integration and the sharing of resources (Ghoshal and Bartlett, 1995a, 1995b). Here the boundaries of the MNC are drawn around constellations of shared resources and interests, thereby creating a concern with developing organizational relationships and the socialization of individuals. In this way the activities of the firm may now be seen in terms of their interdependences, resource analysis, and the relations between the different 'boundaries' of resources, activities and actors (Penrose, 1959).

The knowledge firm in the knowledge economy

The firm as a knowledge-creating entity has been given a historical interpretation by Drucker (1993), who documents the shift in the relationship between knowledge and wealth creation brought on by the demands of contemporary capitalism. Hence new approaches are necessary for defining the nature of organization and management (Reich, 1991; Blackler, 1995). The knowledge-based view of the firm evolves out of the requirement to add value in highly competitive and technologically challenging environments. The nature of the knowledge traded is a key motivator for new modes of organizing. Much sophisticated technological knowledge is tacit in character (Nelson and Winter, 1982) and cannot easily be transferred by licensing. Much firm-specific knowledge is also unwritten and intangible, while technological innovation requires cumulative knowledge of the linkages among design, production and sales. The firm thus becomes an entity for both knowledge access and creation.

Hedlund's (1994) model of knowledge management relies to a large extent on the assumption that a significant role for multinational companies is one of knowledge creation and transfer. His concept of heterarchy is based on the principles of multiplication and combination rather than the principle of division so characteristic of hierarchies. This type of structure has implications for role assignments at all levels, particularly highlighting lateral communication, and integrating mechanisms become more important than differentiating ones. Additionally, his catalytic and architectural role for top management involves a more substantial knowledge of the organization by HQ, necessitated by strategies aimed at focusing and economies of depth. Here Hedlund is referring to the degree of experience and involvement in a field, company or industry that is necessary for the generation of new and the transfer of related knowledge. In the heterarchic organization several strategic apexes shift over time and several ordering principles are at work. Where knowledge management is the primary role, we are witnessing a complex organization, without one clear structure but requiring a high degree of integration both horizontally and vertically.

In a similar vein, Grant's (1996b) knowledge-based view of the firm makes interdependence the focus of organizational design. The general issue is devising mechanisms for integrating individuals' specialized knowledge to perform discrete productive tasks. This is the essence of organizational capability, requiring a hierarchy of knowledge integration – from the base level where specialized knowledge is held by individuals, to the middle levels where the span of specialized knowledge broadens into functional capabilities such as marketing and R&D, through to the highest levels of integration, requiring wide-ranging cross-functional integration, such as is required for new product development (Clark and Fujimoto, 1991). The key point which Grant (1996b: 118) makes about structure is that: 'Once firms are viewed as institutions for integrating knowledge, a major part of which is tacit and can be exercised only by those who possess it, then hierarchical coordination fails.'

The idea of the organization as a knowledge institution is supported by the work of Sanchez and Mahoney (1996) who focus on the internal structural characteristic of modularity. This is an organizational design which enables autonomous organizational structures to carry out concurrent and coordinated processes. They explore the relationships between the structure of the knowledge built into the firm's products and the structure of the firm as it manages that knowledge and transforms it into products. In this way, the firm's knowledge is measured as both product and organizational structure. This also fits in with the presupposition of organization theory that the firm is an administrative structure which must in some way fit with the knowledge manifest in the firm's products. This work provides support for Daft and Lewin's (1993) concept of the 'modular organization' as a new organization form that uses 'interconnected, coordinated self-organizing processes' to support continuous learning and flexible responses to problems posed by a changing environment.

Other reconceptualizations using the knowledge theme have been attempted by Spender (1996) to capture knowledge as a dynamic theory of the firm, Nonaka (1994) who proposes a paradigm for managing dynamic aspects of organizational knowledge-creating processes and Tsoukas (1996) who views the firm as a distributed knowledge system. Further, Liebeskind (1996) argues for a view of the firm as an institution that protects knowledge from expropriation and imitation and does so more effectively than market contracting. These writings conceptualize the firm as an institution for capturing, creating, protecting and integrating knowledge. The key question for this literature, given that knowledge is the new form of capital giving competitive advantage, is how to achieve coordinated action by connecting and integrating individuals' knowledge within the firm.

This view of the role of the firm as a knowledge-integrating institution relates to Demsetz's (1991: 171–175) rationale for the existence of the firm as a response to a fundamental asymmetry in the economics of knowledge. As knowledge acquisition requires greater specialization than is needed for utilization, production requires the coordinated efforts of individual specialists possessing many different types of knowledge. However, markets are unable to undertake this coordination role because of failure in the face of (a) immobility of tacit knowledge and (b) the risk of expropriation of explicit knowledge by a potential buyer.

This new role of the firm is somewhat differently emphasized in the literature. As Grant notes, most research into organizational learning (Levitt and March, 1988; Huber, 1991) and the knowledge-based view of the firm (Spender, 1989; Nonaka, 1991, 1994) focuses upon the acquisition and creation of organizational knowledge. This is in the sense of the organization as an institution for knowledge and in Collins' (1993) terminology the knowledge would be described as encultured (shared understanding), embedded (systemic routines) and encoded (conveyed by signs and symbols). Grant, on the other hand, assumes that knowledge creation is an individual activity and that the primary role of firms is in the application of existing knowledge to the production of goods and services. This would fall into Collins' other two categories of knowledge as embrained (dependent upon conceptual skills and cognitive abilities) and embodied (action oriented). The focus of organizational theory then becomes how to facilitate individual creativity and learning while knowing how to transfer this knowledge effectively into value added outputs.

Thus Grant (1996b) interprets many organizational form initiatives as attempts to access and integrate the tacit knowledge of organizational members while recognizing the barriers to the transfer of such knowledge. A knowledge-based view favours integration mechanisms which bring the varied knowledge of small numbers of individuals together to deliver organizational solutions. The question of the boundary of the firm is then analysed in terms of the relative efficiency of knowledge utilization. Thus both the horizontal and vertical boundaries of the firm are drawn at the gaps occurring between constellations of products and knowledge. For instance, the stages of production need only be vertically integrated where knowledge at one stage is crucial to production at the next stage.

Networks and the socially embedded firm

At an abstract level the interorganizational forms literature concerns the notion of the boundaries of the firm (Adams, 1980) in which both the market (Arndt, 1979; Easton and Araujo, 1994; Boxer and Wensley, 1997) and the nature of the firm itself are problematized (Powell, 1990; Mingers, 1995). Strategic networks of interfirm relations have been conceptualized as a mode of organization (Jarillo, 1988). Further, Powell (1990) suggests that international joint ventures, often both long term and stable, represent a different form of interorganizational exchange, one in which continuity rests on continual mutual dependence.

The increasing rate of joint venture formations and outsourcing during the past decade has led to claims that strategic alliances and networks are becoming an integral part of contemporary strategic organizational thinking (Zeffane, 1995). Contracting out and strategic alliances are said to enable small industrial firms to accomplish the work of much larger diversified companies (O'Leary, 1992). At a general economic level, strategic alliances and supplier networks are said to be crucial if US manufacturing is to compete in fast response global manufacturing (Goldhar and Lei, 1991). These trends in large manufacturing are echoed by Hagedoorn (1991), who notes increasing strategic partnerships, outsourcing and co-makership. Further, he sees this development as a new form of quasi-integration.

The literature on strategic alliances and partnerships has provided widespread evidence of experimentation with various new kinds of interfirm agreements and collaborations (Friar and Horwitch, 1985; Teece, 1986; Hergert and Morris, 1988; Mowery, 1988). These novel cooperative relationships are usually designed to create value through synergy as partners achieve mutually beneficial gains that neither would have been able to achieve individually (Teece, 1992). Alliances increase firms' capability by creating economic advantages such as leveraging their market presence (Ohmae, 1989; Lewis, 1990; Lorange and Roos, 1992), providing vertical integration and scale economies at a greatly reduced cost (Anderson and Weitz, 1992), and mitigating the effects of transaction-specific assets, channel uncertainty, performance variability and production costs (John and Weitz, 1988).

Alongside economic value, alliances are found to provide intellectual and social capital. This is evidenced by reciprocity, interdependence and learning (Borys and Jemison, 1989), the fact that the perceived effectiveness of the relationships themselves creates strategic advantage (Hamel et al., 1989) and that relational norms are found to safeguard against opportunism and help prevent the abuse of control (Heide and John, 1992) and the capture of new knowledge (Parkhe, 1991). Thus there has been a proliferation of such developments in technology-intensive industries (Mariti and Smiley, 1983; Contractor and Lorange, 1988). This is necessary where technological developments are fast moving. Porter and Fuller (1986) suggest that coalitions such as international joint ventures seem well suited to the process of industry and firm globalization.

Similarly, industrial district networks are seen as a viable alternative to vertical integration (Dore, 1983) and work done on the Japanese textile industry supports this view. The industrial districts literature is rich with examples of networking to add value between (usually small) firms. For instance Sabel et al. (1987) described the German textile industry as associated experts and flexible specialists in different phases or types of production. Although a traditional craft industry, it employs a highly refined system of production that links small and medium-sized firms with a wide range of institutional arrangements that further the well-being of the industry as a whole. The interdependences within this system are apparent when Sabel et al. (1987) argue that the more distinctive each firm is, the more it depends on the success of the other firms' products to complement its own. The performance consequences suggested by Dore (1983) include investment by suppliers encouraged by the security of close relationships and the accelerated flow of information from trust and mutual dependence.

From the interorganizational literature, the basis of Perrone's (1997) configuration is deemed to be a multidimensional and multilevel organizational concept, whereby the nature of interfirm contracts, structures and coordination processes is matched at the level of both the focal firm and the wider network. This configuration is not only highly adapted to a rapidly changing environment but its main innovation is the ability to transform social capital into competitive advantage. So organizational design becomes concerned with behavioural processes between and within firms, such as managing relationships, trust and cooperation.

Further, the extensive subcontracting system identified in Sabel et al.'s (1987) work, in which key technologies are developed in a collaborative manner and the overlapping inter-industry supplier networks, serves to strengthen the social structure in which textile firms are embedded and to encourage cooperative relations that attenuate the destructive aspects of competition. Similarly, the North Italian industrial district model is comprised of small firms grouped in specific zones according to their product, in which all firms have a very low degree of vertical integration (Brusco, 1982). Production is conducted through extensive, collaborative subcontracting agreements, which is preferred

to expansion or integration. The socially embedded nature of this industrial district is illustrated through the significant role played by political
and social institutions, including the dominance of the Communist
Party and the extended family (Powell, 1990).

These writings have in common a strong sense of the historical and
cultural context of these firms. From industry institutional arrangements, to political, ideological and economic factors, the development of
these organizational arrangements cannot be explained solely in terms
of traditional theories of the firm. The implications for a theory of the
firm are first, to blur the boundaries of the firm and to extend them to
include a much larger constituency of interests. Secondly, economic success is not only dependent upon economic relationships but on
cooperation with and proximity to government and social agencies.
Thirdly, the growth in the number of technologically advanced, smaller
units of enterprise is not dependent upon notable direct investment or
significant employment increase but is a result of expansion through
various cooperative interorganizational relationships (Lorenzoni and
Ornati, 1988).

New forms in organization studies

The current preoccupation with organizational forms is indicative of a
significant shift in the focus of theoretical enquiry away from the study
of purely formal structures (Pugh et al., 1968; Blau and Schoenherr,
1971), and purely economic motivations, so characteristic of organizational researchers during the 1960s and 1970s. The network dimension
of formal structures was neglected and only referred to in terms of
imagery in organizational charts. Instead, researchers operationally
defined organizational properties almost exclusively in distributional
terms, that is, the configuration of positions and distribution of persons
among them. How these positions combined to form an organizational
unit appeared not to be worthy of research scrutiny (Lincoln, 1982).

The general tenor of the new forms of organizing literature places
structure and design backstage with strategy and process front stage.
For instance, structure is now seen as just one aspect of design by Farley
and Kobrin (1995), who stress that what matters are the hidden operating systems of measurement, process and coordination. The whole
language and focus of theorizing point to a greater concern with human
interaction, social context, organizational processes and intangible
assets. The most important characteristic of the field is its dynamic quality – 'organizing': Handy (1996) uses the verb status to define modern
organizations. The phenomenon appears to be less about the stable
physicality of organizational divisions, roles and rules and more about
the processual quality of organizational systems and participants.
Perhaps that is why theory is problematic here, for existing frameworks

cannot adequately account for the intangible and fluid nature of the phenomenon.

But it would be wrong to think that the study of organizations had never been concerned with these types of phenomenon. There is, for instance, a well established literature in the areas of culture, human relations and power and politics within organizations. It is just that these have always been advanced under the rubric of organizational behaviour, whereas for the last 30 years the organizational design literature in the US has been closely affiliated to strategy and micro-economics. It would seem that the new context of organizations has highlighted organizational behaviour issues, some of which are now being incorporated into new economic thinking (Milgrom and Roberts, 1995).

The implications for research

The sheer numbers and diversity of organizational forms which have arisen out of the new forms of organizing is not unlike the complexity of variables spawned by contingency theory. The real difference in the field at this time appears to be the variety and questionable robustness of many theoretical frameworks which are working in isolation from each other. As Donaldson (1996: 39) remarks: 'In essence the problem in the USA is the rapid proliferation of fads and fashions.' This state of affairs may be traced to the conditions under which the production of knowledge takes place. These include the influence of practitioner academics and the location of management studies within business schools where teaching MBAs and executive programmes is primarily an applied, normative and weakly critical distillation of management and organization studies (Denison, 1997; Pfeffer, 1997).

Moreover, the fads and fashions approach places little emphasis on rigorous empirical research (Denison, 1997). Donaldson (1996) calls for a return to replication studies, long term programmes of work and the accumulation of knowledge in organization studies. The other major problem in this field is the startling lack of robust empirical evidence and theory testing. Many of the most high profile studies rely upon descriptive case studies, where there is a dual problem. Often the nature and quality of the data collected is unclear and the resulting monographs move uneasily from description to prescription. So the reader is often uncertain when findings are being reported or when prescriptions are being made. The evidence is piecemeal: for all the publicity of new forms of organizing, both academic and practitioner, there have been no large scale mapping studies to corroborate this assumed tide of organizational change.

This institutional context of the creation of knowledge about organizations must make us critical of anecdotal and normative texts which seem to abound at a time when organizations are looking for new answers – or at least are being told they should be looking for them. Pfeffer (1997) echoes the criticism of the profusion of theories and notes a diminished consensus on the important research questions, directions and methodology. He singles out the proximity of business schools to economics as influencing the topics chosen for study and the research paradigm. Pfeffer (1997) further bemoans this lack of theoretical and methodological consensus as resulting in increased differentiation in the field and subsequent lack of integration in organization studies. Moreover, given the significant changes in the context of organizations, this poses challenges for organizational theories that were developed to explain a prior organizational context. As Pfeffer rightly remarks: 'One way of evaluating organizational models and theories is to ask to what extent they provide a productive way of understanding and predicting the evolving nature of organizations' (1997: 24).

While we are not convinced by the argument that economics represents the intellectual bogeyman, there is a case for arguing for greater reflection and integrity in the research endeavour. What seems to be lacking in the field of organizational studies generally, and organizational design in particular, is a theoretical research agenda which can accommodate novelty without being distracted into new intellectual cul-de-sacs. Pfeffer (1997) and Donaldson (1996) both argue for more emphasis on data collection and engagement with the phenomena which are the object of theorizing. This implies programmatic research, using multiple methods and international comparisons and a commitment to theory building which will enhance our knowledge of organizations.

The INNFORM Programme of Research

The INNFORM programme is a research network of scholars from Europe, Japan and the US with the focal group at Warwick Business School, led by Andrew Pettigrew. Our research has sought to engage with the claims about new forms of organizing in the literature. The programme was essentially phenomenon driven and sceptical as to the existence of a new form or ideal type such as the 'network form'. Therefore, the aim of the research was in the first instance to address the problem of the lack of empirical evidence for these claims. Related to this, we aimed to provide data from different methodologies to supplement and enhance our knowledge of what was happening within organizations. In the second instance, the programme was concerned with analysing the performance consequences of organizational form. Thirdly, we were concerned to expose and understand the transition processes of firms as they moved from more traditional to innovative forms of organizing. Before we turn to the findings of our first survey, it seems pertinent to outline our theoretical assumptions, which derive from the notion of complementarities. It is this approach which leads to the key theme of our research: that holistic change, in the form of complementarities, drives organizational performance.

An important theoretical development has come from the economics field with the concept of complementarities. This notion develops the thinking from contingency through to configuration theory. In terms of the contingency perspective it sees performance as dependent on the 'fit' between key organizational variables such as size and structure (Donaldson, 1996). However, it develops contingency by seeking to address the multilateral kinds of fit required for organizational effectiveness (Drazin and Van de Ven, 1985; Meyer et al., 1993b). In this way it resembles configurational theory (Miller, 1986, 1996) with its emphasis on the more holistic and systemic nature of organizations.

In their study of modern manufacturing, Milgrom and Roberts (1995) define the basic notion of complementarity as follows: doing more of one thing increases the returns of doing more of another. Performance is therefore dependent upon a set of complementary changes within organizations. They use the example of the introduction of CAD (computer aided design) technology to show that it paid best when associated with complementary inventory, production, marketing and management policies. Thus Milgrom and Roberts go beyond the simple one-to-one associations governing performance relationships in contingency theory. These complex interaction effects develop the configurational notion that changing any variables must be in association with change in others that are complementary to it, otherwise the returns may well be negative.

The complementarities approach goes beyond configurational analysis by suggesting that a disaggregated approach to performance testing is needed. In this way, complementarities suggests a simultaneously aggregated and disaggregated approach that compares the contributions of individual organizational practices, with the performance pay-off being an expression of their combined effort. Thus the reverse effect is expected, where piecemeal change, that is, without the full complement of practices, results in negative performance. Moreover, as Ichniowski et al. (1997) argue from their study of HR practices, complementarity amongst practices implies that the magnitude of the performance effects of the full system is larger than the sum of the marginal effects from adopting each practice individually. When analysed together, the individual effects on performance should be exhausted by the full system effects.

Similar conclusions on complementary effects have been posited from qualitative case study work. For instance, Starbuck's (1993) case study of a high performing New York law firm (Wachtell) uncovered ambiguity and contradiction in the organization, brought about by complexity, internal inconsistencies and incoherence. Starbuck discovered that to explain this firm's success he needed to resort to the metaphor of a house of cards: ' Wachtell contains many elements that fit together and reinforce each other. Each element is individually a flimsy component with which to build an institution, and some elements are individually farfetched. Yet, they fit together so well that removing one element might undermine the whole structure' (1993: 916).

From the INNFORM programme, Pettigrew (1999b) has attempted to capture complementarities in action by his case study account of BP Amoco over a ten-year period of change. Simultaneous alterations in BP Amoco's structure, processes and boundaries were explored over the period 1988–1998. This account seeks to go beneath the generalities of statistical analysis to expose the micro-level processes of continuity and change which can explain the long term history and consequences of complementary change. Another recent application of complementarities has been to the survey data of the INNFORM programme (Whittington et al., 1999b), to be discussed in the next section. The work on complementarities therefore shows fruitful signs of activity in both qualitative and quantitative methodologies.

The INNFORM survey

Our first survey in Europe (Whittington et al., 1999b) was the template for subsequent surveys in Japan and the US. We surveyed three regions because we were mindful that organizational change takes place in the context of socio-economic, institutional and historical factors. It is the idiosyncratic interplay of organizations with the competitive environment, institutional systems and other natural phenomena which will give rise to particular regional developments (Lewin et al., 1999). In particular, we wanted to survey firms in Japan as we felt there were significant socio-economic and institutional factors which would have a bearing upon organizational form. This is evident from the literature, with the Japanese reputation for adopting project and horizontal forms of organizing.

The questionnaire used was a standardized instrument which drew on the new organizational forms literature to ask questions about innovative organizational practices. The survey had three main objectives: to map contemporary organizational change, to understand the content of this change and to test for the performance consequences. The main thrust of the questionnaire concerns change and its complements, so that most questions compared 1992 with 1996. Our measure of performance was a financial one in the UK while in Continental Europe self-reported scales of financial performance were used: this was due to the difficulties in obtaining reliable and comparable published performance data.

After adjustments following a pilot test, the questionnaire was mailed during 1997 to the chief executives of large and medium-sized (that is, with more than 500 employees), independent, domestically owned firms throughout Western Europe. For the United Kingdom, these were the largest 1,500 independent businesses by employment. For the remainder of Western Europe, these were 2,000 large and medium-sized firms sampled in proportion to home country GDP. Except for the Dutch and Scandinavian samples, the Continental European questionnaires were translated into German, Italian, Spanish or French as per country, using native translators, and checked for accuracy by local team members. We mailed to initial non-respondents and subsequently used telephone follow-ups. The overall response rate was 13.1 per cent, comparable to other recent European surveys of organizational change (Coulson-Thomas and Coe, 1991; Ezzamel et al., 1996). Corresponding to their original sampling proportions, the largest groups of respondents were British (40.7 per cent) and German (15.8 per cent): no other country accounted for more than 10 per cent of responses. Tests for the UK sample indicated no response biases for size, industry or profitability.

The more complete presentation of our European results are in Whittington et al. (1999b) and Ruigrok et al. (1999). These results have now been extended by the preliminary comparative analysis of our European and Japanese survey findings (Pettigrew et al., 2000). During 2000 we expect to publish the survey results comparing all three regions: Europe, Japan and the USA.

The survey instrument measured three sets of aggregated variables (see Figure 1.2): changing structures, changing processes and changing boundaries. Changing structures measured delayering, the existence of project-based structures and operational and strategic decentralization. Changing processes measured horizontal interactions, IT infrastructure and strategies, and new human resource practices. Changing boundaries measured outsourcing, alliances and diversification trends.

A trends analysis of this data (Ruigrok et al., 1999; Pettigrew, 1999a) showed an overall movement in European organizations toward the new organizational practices, although tendencies are not always simple and one way. In terms of structure, 30 per cent of organizations took out organizational layers between 1992 and 1996 while at the same time 20 per cent of firms actually increased their layers – presumably because of growing size or managerial complexity. Project-based structures became more pervasive, with 51 per cent of firms placing a greater emphasis on them in 1996 compared to 1992. Operational decentralization increased in 47 per cent of firms (see Figure 1.3).

However, it was the dimensions of process and boundaries that showed the greatest activity. In particular, there were significant

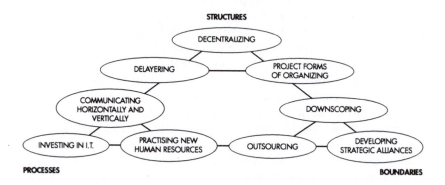

FIGURE 1.2   *New forms of organizing: the multiple indicators*

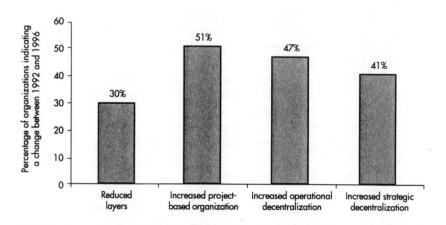

FIGURE 1.3   *Structural change in Europe, 1992–1996*

increases in horizontal interactions. We asked the companies to compare the importance of various horizontal linkages such as sharing of R&D knowledge across units, joint purchasing, common distribution channels and shared marketing information in 1992 and 1996. Overall, 74 per cent of companies claimed to increase the importance of these kinds of horizontal linkages. At the same time, 82 per cent of firms were increasing their investments in the various information technology infrastructures capable of sustaining these kinds of horizontal exchanges. Decentralized and more intensely interacting organizations need new kinds of human resource practices. In all, 65 per cent of companies claimed greater use of new human resource practices such as team building, internal labour markets and corporate mission building. Thus there seemed to be considerable increases in the emphasis put on HRM to provide the skills and the glue to make the flatter and more horizontal organizational structures work (see Figure 1.4).

The new types of competition, and the new forms of organization designed to cope with it, are reshaping the scope of the firm as well (see Figure 1.5). Outsourcing increased markedly between 1992 and 1996, with 65 per cent of firms claiming increases. At the same time, firms were resorting extensively to alliances, with 65 per cent claiming the formation of long term strategic alliances over this period. Diversification trends were complex, and the net de-diversification was small. However, again consistent with the simultaneous focus on resource advantages and the leveraging of those into related business areas, 11 per cent of firms reduced their diversification over the period.

We then analysed the impact of these changes by approaching performance pay-offs in a more holistic fashion, using the notion of complementarities (Milgrom and Roberts, 1990, 1995). In common with much configurational research (Ketchen et al., 1993), we approached the performance questions both inductively and deductively. The inductive approach derived configurations directly from the data and lent

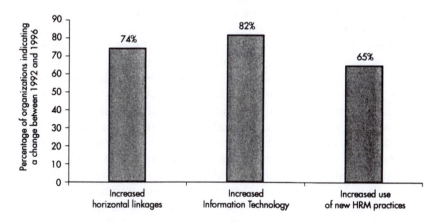

FIGURE 1.4   *Process change in Europe, 1992–1996*

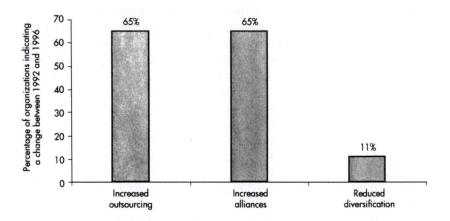

FIGURE 1.5   *Boundary change in Europe, 1992–1996*

itself to the first of the two performance questions: what are the organizational innovations that high performing firms seem to bring together? The deductive approach was aimed at the second question, examining the extent to which a theoretically derived full system of new organizational practices does yield performance benefits superior to those of its constituent parts taken separately.

The results of the inductive analysis showed, as expected, a denser set of related changes amongst the high performers than the low performers. The high performers are characterized by a denser set of connections between structure, process and boundaries variables. For instance, there are strong links between outsourcing and five variables: use of IT, new human resource practices, operational and strategic decentralization and project-based structures. Delayering also has strong links with downscoping, use of IT and new human resource practices. Moreover, amongst the high performers all variables have at least one significant correlation, suggesting that all link back with others in some sort of system of relationships. Amongst low performers, high commitment to IT is noticeably left outside the web of relationships while no one organizational variable is connected to more than two others. In short, high performers are doing more things together than low performers, and not leaving anything out. The inductive approach therefore provided some support for complementarities, but did not tell us whether the system effects were greater than the individual effects. This was the task of the deductive approach, which tested the system effects against the components separately.

We classified firms in our sample according to whether they were:

changing structures (A), changing processes (B) and changing boundaries (C). Our results showed that 50 per cent of the firms were making sets of boundary changes, 28 per cent sets of process changes and 20 per cent sets of structural changes. We then examined the four systems of changes with the resulting percentages of firms from our sample having adopted each of them:

System 1 (A + B + C)	4.5%
System 2 (A + B)	9.3%
System 3 (B + C)	14.3%
System 4 (A + C)	11.2%

While only a few companies carried out the full multidimensional raft of innovative practices, the results of this analysis confirmed the importance of system-wide change, with System 1 firms enjoying an average performance premium of more than 60 per cent. Also consistent with the notion of complementarities were the dangers of partial change, as evidenced by the negative performance associated with those companies implementing the most minimal change.

However, population ecology (Hannan and Freeman, 1989) and co-evolutionary (McKelvey, 1997) perspectives led to our proposition that the kind of comprehensive change represented by System 1 would, at this stage at least, be only thinly represented. Again, this expectation was broadly met, with less than one in 20 firms adopting System 1 type change. From the population ecology perspective, the firms of our sample, all with over 500 employees by 1996, might be expected to be too mature to be leaders of this kind of change (Baum, 1996). However, inertia was not complete, as just over half the firms emerged as highly committed to structural changes. What appears more difficult for these firms is the 'systemic' kinds of transformation required of the new organizational forms (Miles and Snow, 1992; Nohria, 1996). There is little evidence yet of the kind of widespread and radical organizational revolution implied by claims for the replacement of the M-form by the N-form (Hedlund, 1994).

Country and business contingencies proved important influences on the propensity to change. Following the co-evolutionary emphasis on institutional context of Lewin et al. (1999), German-based companies, associated with more 'patient' capital, proved to be disproportionately capable of the exploration types of initiative represented by widespread organizational change. They emphasize strategic decentralizing and human resource innovations. British firms are more likely to emphasize operational decentralizing and downscoping. Knowledge-intensive firms, meanwhile, resort most to project structures, strategic decentralizing and downscoping. Although R&D intensity was positively associated with some kinds of new organizational practices, internationalization most consistently promoted wider kinds of change, including comprehensive System 1 type change.

In terms of our first two initial objectives, therefore, our findings suggest that change was pervasive amongst medium-sized and large European firms during this period, while being conditioned by important country and business contingencies. It is notable that change was evolutionary and not radical, as some of the literature has suggested. Effective change was found to be associated with definite patterns, in particular comprehensive rather than piecemeal initiatives; and the performance benefits of the new organizational practices depended on the context of the other changes in which they were set. These benefits were particularly strong when combined with comprehensive organizational change. Our findings also provide strong support for the use of complementarities in continuing research into organizational form.

However, while survey findings can illuminate the central tendencies of organizational populations, they cannot give us deeper insights into how firms manage such initiatives as complementary change. It is clear that this type of whole system change requires distinct management skills and abilities. In particular, we wanted to know what configurations of structure, process and boundary changes were being made in our case study firms, what was the sequencing of initiatives and the pace of change through time, in adopting new configurations and processes. This process agenda is the third objective of our research and is developed in the eight case studies within this volume.

The Innovating Organization

The eight case studies in this book are the first set of the 18 cases undertaken to complement the findings of our survey. The prime purpose of the cases was to both illuminate and develop the context, content and processes of innovating forms of organizing (Pettigrew, 1985b, 1990, 1997). In this way the idiographic case study is crucial in aiding our understanding of organizational development and change (Tsoukas, 1989). All the cases were accounts of organizations experimenting with new configurations and processes and in this sense, the changes documented were innovative, given the history of these organizations. Thus the phenomena under investigation were both significant for the organization under study and represented what was innovative in terms of the four criteria given in the first part of this chapter. The innovation criteria had also to be supported by real evidence to testify what was novel. The element of change is a strong theme which runs through all the case studies and each author has attempted to demonstrate the character of the organization before and after the organizational innovation.

We wanted to provide accounts of the transition process from old to new arrangements. This could only be accomplished by adopting a longitudinal case study method. These cases are therefore distinguished from previous work on new and innovating organizational forms by their longitudinal accounts of change. The timescales analysed here vary from 5 to 50 years, so they fill an important empirical gap in our understanding of the sequencing and pace of change in innovating organizations.

The following chapters are then our first set of organizational accounts to provide flesh to the bones of our survey. The theoretical perspectives are diverse because these cases deal with both different levels of analysis and different phenomena of organizing. But each builds upon existing theory to provoke and inspire debate in the field of organizational design.

The first two cases deal with professional service organizations and their transformation to network forms of organizing as part of a drive to be globally integrated organizations. In Chapter 2 we use a network theory of governance (Jones et al., 1997) to explain, the drivers for adopting a network form and, the use of social mechanisms of control to guide behaviour. The first case is Ove Arup, an engineering design consultancy with a global presence. Here the authors examine organizational transformations at the level of the whole firm. There are two key transformations: one concerns the reorganization of the owned subunits while the other concerns the integration of affiliated but independent firms in a wider Arup network. The drivers for these changes are shown to reside in strong customer and competitive pressures, as well as in the project-based nature of Arups with its emphasis on knowledge creation and transfer. We develop the case to look at the problems and advantages of using social controls to condition firm behaviour.

Chapter 3 provides a focused look at the pharmaceutical network within Coopers & Lybrand Europe. This case develops the theory of network governance by focusing on the social controls which guide behaviour in this network. These social controls include developing small but coherent groups within the network; establishing strong cultural ties to coordinate behaviour; the use of collective sanctions; and the use of reputation to control behaviour. These four social controls are analysed at four levels of analysis: member firms, partners, consultants and project teams. We look at the interaction of social controls within and between these groups to determine the effectiveness of the current configuration of the pharmaceutical network. We conclude on the importance of these controls in integrating and guiding behaviour but caution against their sole use as the network increases in size.

In Chapter 4 Ruigrok, Achtenhagen, Wagner and Rüegg-Stürm present the oft-cited exemplar of a new organizational form in ABB. Based on intensive fieldwork in Switzerland, they trace the development of the firm over a ten-year period from 1988, through three major reorganizations of this global company. The authors conclude that ABB still retains many of the elements of the global matrix while transforming them in several important ways, namely strengthening product focus and maintaining the country dimension. ABB has adopted a network multidivisional form with shared strategic decision making between business areas and segments. In this way it is attempting to cross divisional boundaries to create synergies and reduce costs. Additionally, it has supplemented a strong internal capital market with an internal labour market. The authors conclude that ABB's last reorganization in 1998 involved both continuity and change. This case is less about radical change than the successive reconfiguring of the parameters of the matrix form in ABB.

Networks are again the focus of organizational transition in Van Wijk and Van den Bosch's account of the Dutch-based multinational Rabobank in Chapter 5. What is distinctive and additive about this case is that the authors look at this financial services company at three levels of analysis: the whole organization, the member banks and an internal service unit set up specifically as a network. Their analysis at all levels is guided by three themes: structure, management and knowledge processes. The unique character of this embedded case study provides evidence of differential pace of change in all three levels in the move toward a network organization. The focus here is on the importance of knowledge processes and a relationship is established between horizontal knowledge flows and the degree of internal networking within an organization. The enabling factors in the transition toward a network organization are complementarities between structure and management processes while size of firm or subunit is shown to restrict the pace of change.

A strong process orientation is adopted by Ruigrok, Achtenhagen, Rüegg-Stürm and Wagner in their minutely observed and carefully analysed Hilti case in Chapter 6. This is a firm which in the construction industry is globally known by its product but remains firmly based in Liechtenstein. The case traces the development of Hilti since its establishment in 1941 through eight phases of development. This case asks questions about process sequencing when moving beyond what the authors term the post-Chandlerian organization. Here they focus on the role of communication and leadership within Hilti. Their findings suggest that leadership style and the nature of the hierarchy were important components of the change process. Leadership was actively distributed throughout the firm with the decentralization of operational decisions, leaving top management to set strategic parameters but increasing the transparency of decision making. The divisional structure was nevertheless difficult to disengage, leading to a faltering of the transformation process. Here tensions centred on finding a balance between direct sales and product innovation within the company.

Ultimately, communication proved a singularly effective tool, in the transformation process, for changing the culture and attitudes within the company.

In Chapter 7, the Fremap case takes a configurational approach to human resource management in new forms of organizing. This Spanish firm is a particularly interesting example of how an organization managed to overcome the constraints of its business context to fashion its own destiny. The authors Quintanilla and Sánchez-Runde demonstrate that this is an innovative organization, both for its sector of mutual insurance and in the conservative Spanish business environment more generally. Fremap charted an ambitious organizational transformation in which human resource management was pivotal in formulating, facilitating and implementing a new work organization. This case stresses the role of corporate culture in driving the transformation internally. It is also about managing dualities within new organizational forms such as simultaneous centralization and decentralization. The configurational approach adopted by Fremap shows how an organization may effectively transform itself through a programme of simultaneous initiatives, including HRM practices, IT and management accountability systems. These initiatives interacted to provide a catalyst for change, illustrating the need to adopt a systemic approach when conducting radical change programmes.

The transition from a functional to a team-based structure is the focus of our only small firm case, SAAB Training Systems (Chapter 8). This is a high-tech company within the defence industry which has adopted a team-based structure to support business processes within the organization. Müllern provides us with an account of how an organization which has adopted teams as the basic building block for design may manage to combine horizontal and vertical coordination and communication. Müllern asks how a team-based structure, labelled a cross-functional heterarchy, can be organized to reflect the basic business processes in the company and the advantages and disadvantages of such a form within a highly competitive environment. The clear contribution of this chapter is its description of the microprocesses of organizing with a strong focus on operations. In evaluating the effectiveness of the team-based approach, Müllern strikes a cautious note. For while teams were found to be highly effective in production processes, allowing the re-engineering of operations and close customer contact, they were weak on development issues. For instance, knowledge sharing and coordination between teams was poor, which reduced innovation. The challenge for organizations is to create cooperation between teams in order to counteract their tendency to departmentalize and form boundaries. This means linking cooperation with the formal planning systems of the company and balancing the team approach with a strong focus on the whole business process. This way echoes the other chapters' findings of the necessity for a holistic approach to change.

Two transformational initiatives within an international water services provider are the focal point for the case of Aguas de Barcelona (AGBAR) in Chapter 9. AGBAR is a major player in the Spanish economy and is highly diversified into related and unrelated sectors. A cautious approach in experimenting with new forms of organizing marks this case, whereby the organization uses two subunits as a test-bed before committing the whole organization to such change. These initiatives concern the creation of two new subunits: the AGBAR foundation to coordinate the firm's environmental R&D and a firm-wide corporate purchasing unit. The first initiative provides the reader with insights into processes of knowledge management and virtual teamwork through informal, non-hierarchical coordination mechanisms. The second initiative demonstrates how an internal organizing function may find a balance between centralizing and decentralizing through debate and negotiation within the organization. Sánchez-Runde and Quintanilla demonstrate in this study that innovative forms of organizing require the balancing of seemingly opposing organizational dualities. They illustrate the value of a holistic understanding of this type of change: how, for instance, all the organizational factors interact to produce a configurational whole which is greater than the sum of its parts. The AGBAR case reminds us that innovative forms of organizing tend to supplement rather than supplant more traditional forms of organizing and that organizational development involves balancing the old with the new.

2

Integrating a Global Professional Services Organization: The Case of Ove Arup Partnership

Evelyn M. Fenton and Andrew M. Pettigrew

This case applies a network theory of governance (Jones et al., 1997) to a professional service organization from the construction industry. Ove Arup comprises a global network of subunits with differing ownership structures which are in the process of moving from a loose federation to an integrated network form. Our findings support Jones et al.'s view that the drivers for this form of organization are demand uncertainty in the competitive environment, customized exchanges between highly skilled personnel, high task complexity within project groups and frequent exchanges between groups and individuals. We also found strong evidence for the use of social mechanisms of control to safeguard and coordinate exchanges between and within groups. However, there were limitations to the use of purely social mechanisms of control where the network is global and complex such as the one under study. In considering what other organizational and network variables were implicated in the effective management of this form, we saw the need for sound leadership, a balance between strong and weak ties in the network, a heterogeneous organizational design and incentive systems.

This and the following chapter are concerned with professional service organizations, which are of particular interest in the context of new forms of organizing. Professional services are different from other firms, in particular from manufacturing, as being at the extreme end of a number of dimensions (Lowendahl, 1997). These firms have been characterized by Lowendahl (1997) as being knowledge intensive, having a high degree of customization, relying almost exclusively on discretionary effort and subjective interaction with clients and guided by the norms of professional conduct.

All these characteristics signal the extreme reliance of these firms upon human resources. There is a particular reliance upon named individuals, rather than the tangible entity of the firm to drive the business in value creation. Moreover, these reputations are built up over time and are not replaceable or imitable in the marketplace.

The other extreme characteristic of these firms is the nature of their business activity, which does not easily lend itself to analysis by traditional management concepts (Lowendahl, 1997). For instance the predominance of project team structures means work activity does not follow a linear model from idea to transformation to output, but is often a chaotic and emergent process. Similarly, the nature of income generation means markets cannot be measured in the same way as they are for other firms because the only meaningful measure is the current number and size of projects. These characteristics present professional service organizations with unique challenges around managing human resources and intangible assets. Not least, for the current study, are the efficient and effective capture and dissemination of knowledge in the context of a growing global business.

This chapter will outline the development of Ove Arup since the beginning of the firm in 1946 and detail the more recent change initiatives, Reformation and Seamless Arup, which are part of an overall vision to become a global network. The Reformation initiative marks a significant break on two counts, in what has been a continual evolution of growth and development of capabilities within the firm. In the first instance, Reformation challenges the hitherto loose structure of the firm by creating divisions and an explicit hierarchy. In the second instance, Reformation has sought to break with isolationist tendencies of the previous group structure by creating linkages within and between divisions. There have thus been simultaneous vertical and horizontal moves: to separate policy from operational decision making and create market and skill networks to integrate the groups. The Seamless Arup initiative is an attempt to bring the independent affiliate firms into a shared vision of service delivery and create a more integrated global network. This case therefore takes a macro perspective on the applicability of network governance to a global network.

This case builds upon the theoretical work of Jones et al. (1997) on network governance in two important ways. First we empirically test the theory in the field. Secondly, we have added analytically to the theory by including conditions of exchange relationships which may confound cooperation based on social controls. These confounding factors are shown to reduce trust and motivation, create goal incongruence and reduce the efficient spread of information through the wider network. In this way we demonstrate the importance of behavioural, relational and contextual features in any theory of exchange. In extending and refining this theory of network governance, the notion of optimizing embeddedness (Granovetter, 1985), or maximizing network interconnectedness, is shown to be a useful construct which takes account of the evolutionary nature of organizational change.

The chapter is organized as follows: A literature review on network forms of organizing and governance is followed by an explanation of the methods used. The case study is presented in terms of its context and history, then a general theory of network governance (Jones et al., 1997) is applied to the current organization of the firm in order to illustrate both the validity of the exchange conditions and the social mechanisms, proposed by the theory, for optimal functioning of this form. This is followed by an analysis of integration issues in Ove Arup, in terms of a network theory of governance. A discussion then explores organizational and network variables which are important for optimal functioning of a global network form. We conclude with an evaluation of a network theory of governance and implications for future research.

Network Forms of Organizing

In recent years much has been written about network forms of organization. In the strategy field this has concentrated on global organizations, described by Malnight (1995) as integrated network models. An emerging theme in this literature was the treatment of multinational companies (MNCs) within integrated network models, viewing worldwide operations as specialized and interdependent (Bartlett, 1986; Bartlett and Ghoshal, 1986). A key proposition behind this view was that operating a network created additional value directly from being multinational in nature, associated with cross-border exchanges among operating units. The MNC literature review undertaken by Martinez and Jarillo (1989) suggests that during the 1980s there was an important development of coordination mechanisms within MNCs. As MNCs moved towards network forms of organization, new cross-departmental, informal and more subtle mechanisms were added to – not substituted for – the existing structural and formal managerial devices (Ferlie and Pettigrew, 1996).

Kogut (1983) and Porter (1986) developed important dimensions of the emerging approach. Their work emphasized the structuring of activities globally, based on flows among dispersed operating units, indicating the need both to strategically allocate tasks globally (impacting where resources are located), and to develop the organizational mechanisms to manage and maximize the benefits of resulting exchanges (impacting how activities are linked). In this way the organization can leverage its core competencies and disperse these economically throughout the organization. This view introduced a significant step away from reliance on the unity of command approach. As the interaction among worldwide operating units expanded, the need arose to extend coordination mechanisms beyond the hierarchical reporting relationships found in dyadic models.

Building on this integrated network approach and the seminal work of Perlmutter (1969), a number of organizational models were developed, including the heterarchy (Hedlund, 1986), the multifocal organization (Prahalad and Doz, 1987), the transnational organization (Bartlett and Ghoshal, 1989), and the horizontal organization (White and Poynter, 1990). Given rapid changes in the competitive environment of many industries, some writers have stressed the need to move toward these integrated network structures, claiming that the critical challenge facing MNC management is developing the 'organizational capability' (Bartlett and Ghoshal, 1989) necessary to acquire network characteristics. This last was reflected in Bartlett and Ghoshal's (1993) managerial theory of the firm, based on the principles of proliferation and subsequent aggregation of subunits from the bottom up. This radically different distribution of resources alongside a simplification of administrative systems creates a horizontal information processing capacity of equal weight to the vertical mechanisms.

In the new multinational company, functionality is separated from the concept of hierarchy. Although there may still be 'official' reporting responsibility to local subsidiary management, the concept of horizontal networks makes these 'official' reporting procedures and control mechanisms more 'dotted line' than direct chain of command. Network interactions are flexible and created according to need. Adjustments can be made without altering the formal vertical structure. As White and Poynter (1990: 106) note: 'Vertical structures are not allowed to get in the way of the pursuit of advantage. This internal flexibility is extremely valuable when confronted with high external variety – a changing, difficult to predict international environment.' The multinational firm thus represents a mode of economic governance that is well removed from the traditional conceptualizations of hierarchy. The virtue of the discrete nature of divisions with distinct horizontal separation, so characteristic of the multidivisional form (Williamson, 1975), has given way to a less rigid, more fluid organizational structure. The relationships between subsidiaries and between headquarters and subsidiaries is governed by a mix of incentives and control mechanisms combining price, authority and socialization (Hennart, 1993). The common theme running through these integrated network models is the significance of horizontal linkages alongside vertical ones (Bahrami, 1992).

Network governance

The growing body of work on network forms of organizing has so far provided insightful descriptions of the coordination mechanisms and structural and economic dimensions of these forms. To this end a convincing case has been made for a clear departure from traditional hierarchical forms of organizing. New organizing principles have been defined in terms of linkages, ties, integration and relationships, giving descriptive insights into these organizations, but without a comprehensive or theoretically consistent framework of understanding (Jones et al., 1997). Grandori (1997) has outlined the limitations of the network coordination mode, not least its ubiquitous presence in all governance structures, as well as its hybrid nature in employing a wide range of coordination mechanisms.

A more precise definition of an internal network organization is provided by Baker (1992) as one characterized by a high degree of integration across formal boundaries of multiple types of socially important relations, that covers vertical, spatial and horizontal differentiation. The critical distinguishing feature of a network organization is this high degree of integration. In the ideal-typical network organization, all members are well integrated: formal categories or groups such as formal position, geographic location and market focus are not significant barriers to interaction. Interpersonal ties of all types (for example, task-related communication, advice, socializing) are as easily established between as within formal groups or categories.

Baker (1992) uses the structural properties of differentiation and integration to advance a theoretical scheme which resolves the classic Lawrence and Lorsch (1967a) compromise between horizontal differentiation and integration. Baker makes a case for stating the precise relationship of formal differentiation and integration in an ideal type network organization. This is that intergroup relations in a network organization are associated with heterogeneity (opportunities for contact) rather than ingroup biases. Thus formal boundaries are a spur to rather than inhibitor of relational ties. Baker's argument derives much from Granovetter's (1973) theory of weak ties whereby organizational heterogeneity, in promoting a more extensive network of weak ties, acts to prevent the formation of cliques. In this way the opportunities for contact allow information and knowledge to move freely across the organization.

Few empirical studies on intra- and interfirm networks have set out the general conditions for the emergence of this governance form, or the way in which this form is sustained. A recent theoretical approach to understanding this phenomenon is outlined by Jones et al. (1997), who attempt to explain under what conditions network governance has competitive advantage and is therefore more likely to emerge and thrive. They deal with an important dimension for comparative analyses of coordination mechanisms: the process by which they are established and change (Grandori, 1997). Jones et al. achieve this by integrating transaction cost economics and social network theories. Their proposed definition of network governance is one which 'involves a select, persistent, and structured set of autonomous firms ... engaged in creating products or services based on implicit and open-ended contracts to adapt to environmental contingencies and to coordinate and safeguard exchanges. These contracts are socially – not legally – binding' (Jones et al., 1997: 914). While largely referring to legally independent firms, they 'do not exclude business units that may share common ownership or that may directly invest in each other' (1997: 916).

This latter definition reflects the status of the present study, of an engineering consultancy with 6,000 employees which is comprised of a federation of small owned and autonomous subsidiaries or partnerships. This study attempts to determine the nature of the network form in Ove Arup in terms of the firm's strategic aim to become a more integrated global network. Specifically, the aim was to test Jones et al.'s framework for the emergence of this governance form and to establish whether other organizational or external factors were relevant. We also sought to analyse the nature of the social controls which Jones et al. propose as maintaining this form, and to consider whether other social and/or institutional factors might support or undermine the network. To this end we conducted a contextualized case study in which the structure and processes of the firm were examined over time. Participants in the study were drawn from the centre and the periphery of the organization; with them a wide-ranging proforma was covered which explored the detail of organizational life. The application of Jones et al.'s theory in this way, to the present research, indicates strong support for their theory and provides insights into some of the design problems experienced by this firm.

Methods

The method adopted here derives from the recent tradition of process research in strategy (Chakravarthy and Doz, 1992; Pettigrew, 1992, 1997). Here is included the longitudinal field research on organizational change, with its contextualist theory of method, advocated by Pettigrew (1990) and the innovation studies of Van de Ven et al. (1989). In the best tradition of qualitative research, the strategy employed has been both iterative and developmental. Rather than imposing a theoretical framework from the start, being open to what the site had to say was deemed essential (Glaser and Strauss, 1967). This did not mean operating in a vacuum; rather, a tentative framework around network governance was created with propositions which informed the initial research strategy. Being open to what the data had to say also meant being flexible (Silverman, 1985) and therefore prepared to change direction as the emerging data dictated. Thus the sequence of the research was not a linear progression from fact-finding to analysis. A forwards and backwards motion from data to analysis, and back to the data again, more adequately describes the process.

Data collection

A processual study, aiming for pluralist accounts of historical and contextual organizational reality, means producing case studies and not just case histories (Pettigrew, 1990). This involves going beyond chronology to develop analytic themes. It also means collecting data at different levels of analysis and demonstrating how actors mobilize features of economic, sectoral and organizational contexts to legitimize or delegitimize ideas for change and continuity at organizational levels. This implies a triangulated methodology (Denzin, 1978; Jick, 1979) to gather different types of data which can be used as cross-checking for reliability. The aim is to draw on different strengths of various data collection methods. Crucially data collection is concerned with observation and verification, and in comparative process research these are iterative processes. One observes, follows themes and trails, identifies patterns, has those patterns disconfirmed or verified by further data, and then moves on.

The time period for data collection was between 1996 and 1997. This research involved two main types of data: in-depth interviews and documentary data. Initially a chronology needed to be established from documents and in-depth interviews, in order to extend the first proforma, which then had to be tested in further interviews. The company were very helpful in providing a number of documents including their monthly publication, books on the history of the company and its founder, and a number of internal memos.

Access to interviewees at board level, assisted by the gatekeeper to the organization, yielded a further four, including the Chairman of Ove Arup. The list for a second round of interviewees was drawn up by a senior partner on the board. All potential interviewees were then sent a letter outlining the project and requesting their participation. A further 12 agreed to participate, making a sample of 17. These interviewees comprised four functional heads of department: Finance, Human Resources, Legal, and Research and Development, and eight senior members who had a mixture of management, network and/or strategic responsibilities.

Ove Arup Partnership: Profile and Historical Development

From a small engineering consultancy founded by one man in London in 1946, Ove Arup Partnership had grown by the beginning of the 1990s to more than 50 offices in over 40 countries across the world. Approximately 6,000 staff members, a third of whom are in London, provide services across the full range of engineering disciplines. Arups is regarded as one of the top three firms in the industry and has a reputation for professionalism, skill and innovation.

There is a fundamental distinction between the structure of ownership and the legal organizational structure. Although having the word partnership in its name, Ove Arup is a holding company for an international network of firms which return profits to the centre. There is, in addition, a group of eight independently owned companies operating under the same name which work closely (and to the clients indistinguishably) with the subsidiaries. Since 1992 Arups has been a private company; since 1999 with limited liability and protected by professional indemnity insurance. All staff, including directors, are employees of the firm. Thus there is no individual ownership of the company, and the legal structure makes the company entirely independent. Ownership lies with two asset trusts: an employee trust and a company trust. The profits are shared among employees according to the length of service and level of responsibility, after a proportion is paid into reserves. There has never been an operational loss to be shared.

Fields of business activity

At the formation of the Ove Arup Consultancy the main field of work was structural engineering, chiefly in reinforced concrete, with particular emphasis on the architectural use of concrete in framed structures, folded plates and concrete shells. This type of expertise was to find its expression in high profile projects such as the Sydney Opera House. Building services design was established later, and in the decades that followed, Arups' activities have expanded to include all aspects of engineering related to the built environment.

The practice has always maintained a focus on fields of activity rather than on various sections or subsidiaries. Arups defines fields of activity as work sectors which constantly develop and change according to the needs of technologies and markets. The current fields of activity are listed in Figure 2.1.

Organizational structure

The formal structure of Arups shows complex divisions into a large number of different disciplines and groups. The smallest unit is the project team, headed up by a project manager and varies between six and 200 personnel. Every four months all groups and departments which operate as independent cost centres have to present a report on their financial status. Project directors, some 150 in total, are responsible for professional quality, time-cost planning and monthly cost control. Arups has maintained the sort of informal links typical of a smaller firm, so for any unusual technical problem, a manager has available in-house specialists, no matter which part of the practice they belong to. Small project teams are easy to manage and have their own identities and personalities, while small size guarantees rapid flow of information. For instance the Acoustics Principal described their formula for developing a successful group:

Building Engineering: structural engineering analysis and design along with building services engineering with a full range of HVAC, electrical and public health services design.

Civil Engineering: infrastructure projects usually with Arups in the role of prime agent.

Industrial Engineering: a range of commissions, including comprehensive planning of individual factories and entire industrial parks.

SPECIALIZED GROUPS
Facade Engineering: all aspects of building enclosure.
Arup Communications: IT requirements of projects.
Controls and Commissioning Group: building services commissioning, automation, management and control systems.
Project Management Services Group: projects on which Arups is the prime agent, acting directly for the client in planning, designing and monitoring work process. The brief sometimes extends beyond the design phase into construction management, where Arup coordinates the various contractors working on site.
Arup Economics and Planning: provides advice and technical skills across a broad range of development issues such as economics, town planning and business strategy.
Urban Design: planning, design and construction of urban centres, industrial parks and residential developments.
Arup Transportation: consultancy providing transportation planning and traffic engineering.
Arup Environmental: fastest growing of specialist groups involved in environmental assessment and audits, land use planning, pollution assessment and control, contaminated land reclamation and waste management.
Geotechnics, Fire Safety Engineering, Advanced Technology and **R&D**

FIGURE 2.1   *Fields of activity in Ove Arup (Sommer et al., 1994: 79–81)*

We say 'we want you to come in and enjoy your acoustics', and we generate what I would call something of a garden environment where you place a seed. If somebody wants to go and do vibration . . . we just feed them in training, and resources and so on. As long as they are pulling in the clients and developing the business, and we help them with all of that, that is how we build people up.

A flexible structure offers the advantages of a large company, with resources that allow project teams to be rapidly enlarged when the need arises and with specialist support in financial, legal and technical matters. This ideal situation does not, however, eliminate the various problems which can arise from complex relationships between knowledge, power and communications. This issue of suboptimal behaviour within the firm will be discussed in more detail in later sections.

Organizational growth and development

Ove Arup has shown continuous growth in size and expansion into new specialist fields since the early 1950s. New offices were opened early on in the UK and Commonwealth countries. The first office outside London opened in Dublin in 1946. This was followed by others in Africa, Australia and Malaysia. Only later were the United States and Europe included in this expansion and today there are offices in more than 40 countries with projects in a further 16. There are nine companies which make up the Arup Partnership: one company called Ove Arup and eight overseas offices, whose mixed ownership structures added a further complexity to the Arup network. Significantly, all of the specialisms have established their own groups in London over the years.

The company structure has adjusted to the special requirements of each overseas office: limited, fully independent (owned by directors), or owned by the UK firm. Building up and sustaining a strong Arup identity is one of the major challenges for all partners of the international network. In the past the network has expended considerable time and effort in ensuring that corporate principles are maintained by all the offices. Arups carefully guards its reputation and the right to use its name is controlled by the Council of the Arup Partnerships, which works to ensure that all the partnerships throughout the world subscribe to the same essentials and maintain the same high technical standards.

The new competitive environment

Until the late 1960s the company acted as a traditional consultancy and the industry was very much like a gentlemen's club. In this respect money was not an issue, there was little negotiation with clients over fees and no disputes. The clients accepted that they were getting a high level of expertise and paid accordingly.

This situation in the industry began to change during the 1970s and 1980s. Economic considerations led to a splitting up of projects and they were repackaged into areas such as project management, value management, quantity surveying, costing of work and so on. All these roles had formerly been undertaken by a professional advisor as a whole package. The result was that individual parts of the system did not achieve their full potential.

Arups is now revising this strategy to try to reintegrate all the parts because they have found that the drive for efficiency made them lose sight of the holistic aspects of their work. For instance, as the projects became more discipline oriented, particular types of engineering lost out on the advantages of cross-fertilization. Also the building boom of the 1980s allowed mismanagement to proceed and Arups got caught up in the boom like the rest of the industry. As one director reflected: 'Probably when we started we had a niche, there was a unique selling proposition of one kind or another – no one else worked in that particular way, we now have very able imitators many of whom are start-ups from us. We are very much more conscious of the competition.'

Despite the recession in the UK at the end of the 1980s there was a much stronger international orientation of the partnership. So although the building side of the company shrank by about 40 per cent, the firm overall shrank very little because of its international expansion: 'There was major growth in the Far East, we opened offices in mainland Europe, our American offices grew and the civil engineering side grew' (Director). Those made redundant were largely retrained in other skills. Thus due to their unique ownership structure Arups survived while many of their competitors have been taken over by other companies:

> a lot of the old names have gone and there are few left. But one of the key issues . . . We want to be independent we have always financed our own expansions, we have always been prudent in keeping a certain amount of cash in reserve, so we can finance R&D. Because we won't otherwise be innovative or be different. We have spent a lot on R&D and training. An awful lot by turnover. (Director)

A number of initiatives have followed in response to the changing economic environment. They all attempted to recognize the greater need for unifying the international firm, the need to facilitate project groups working together and maintaining quality in a constrained economic environment. Arups found it needed to become more decisive, businesslike and more financially aware and efficient. This did not come easy:

That was actually quite hard to do for the first few years, because those who were running the firm came from a previous age when that was not important. Engineers came in at a time when fee scales were sufficiently generous . . . there was always a profit to be made at the end of the day and we could actually afford to indulge ourselves. We cannot afford to do that today because the money is not there. (Director)

The top management responded with two initiatives. The first, called QED, was a highly focused one concerning the quality and efficiency of their work. The second, Dependence and Interdependence, was more wide ranging and concentrated on the structure of the organization. In 1990 the then Chairman, John Martin, implemented this initiative in response to a tendency toward hierarchy within the firm, and to bring the regions and the overseas offices together as a united organization. A tension had developed between London and the regions, especially over the setting up of London-based divisions, such as Industrial Engineering, which the regions felt were their own. John Martin did away with the intermediate divisional level and the company went back to 50 independent units, each reporting separately to the main board (See Figure 2.2). As one director put it: 'It was a question of authority, strength and power.' Similar tensions had also occurred with strong overseas locations because things seemed to be London-centric. As one director explained the thinking behind unifying the company:

If your client product and the way in which you serve your client matters, then it is important that there should not be an immensely variable standard in different parts of the firm. And therefore the different Arup companies round the world need to make a bit more effort to have a common aim, common vision, shared objectives.

Dependence and Interdependence was about giving people the independence to carry out their work without having always to refer up the hierarchy, while at the same time ensuring the interdependence of subunits in a common vision of the company. As one director elaborated: 'So you have got to give them independence and somehow or other make them aware of how they fit into the whole.' By creating a totally flat structure of 50 groups underneath the main board, the aim was to empower the groups and give them a direct link into the decision making. Unfortunately this structure confused decision making without integrating the groups.

The mid-1990s

By the mid-1990s Arups still faced many of the problems and issues which had come out of the recession. It was a radically changed firm

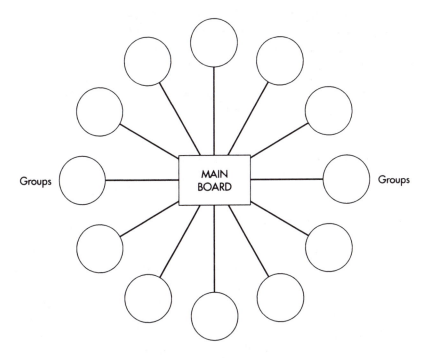

Groups   Groups

FIGURE 2.2 *Dependence and interdependence in Ove Arup:*
organizational structure

since earlier days, even though much of the culture of the organization
was the same. As one director said:

> Business is very much bigger and much more widely skill based. The skill
> base has moved off into civil engineering, into transportation, planning, into
> economic planning, into specialist skills of acousticians and vibration spe-
> cialists – so the range of product is dramatically different. Geographically it
> is very different – the biggest mass is still London, but it is now obviously
> much more geographically spread.

A different perspective has also been brought to the firm by a third generation of leaders since the founding partners. Now, more than ever
before, good organization is essential in order to fulfil the demands of
clients and perform well. As one director highlighted: 'There is now a
realization that the size of projects is so big, complex, the interactions are
more complex. To do well you need greater teamwork than ever before
inside and outside the firm. And therefore the interfaces are much more
complex.'

It was during 1994 that the global partnership attempted to read-
dress the issue of organizational unity. They launched Seamless Arup in

response to perceptions that the global network was drifting away from a common endeavour. As a first step it was decided to adopt six relatively straightforward things such as computer systems and training programmes throughout the partnership. These were deliberately chosen as self-evidently good ideas which would not challenge the control of individual offices. This was described by one director as a rehearsal for the Reformation initiative which followed:

> What is nice about it is you cannot make the reverse proposition, that we should not do it together . . . We won their hearts but not necessarily their actions . . . You then turn the screw. You then say 'Two years, is that all we have done? What is it all about?' Implying come in or get out.

There is still a lot to do in the Seamless programme, particularly countering the notion that the organization is London-centric, which is not helped by the fact that the central finance group and the human resource function are London based. The company now has to revise its written material so that it appeals to staff all over the world.

In 1995 Arups debated the general question, 'Where should we be in five years, time?' It was decided to develop a five-year plan for the owned subsidiaries and offices that would take the organization to the year 2000. The plan became known as Reformation, and in consultation with leaders of the firm, the board, headed by their Chairman Duncan Michael, set out the goals, philosophy and operational framework for their achievement.

Reformation initiative

In August 1995, Duncan Michael circulated a broad statement of what the board intended to achieve by the year 2000, which was a vision of the Ove Arup Partnership and 12 target objectives for the five years ahead. This 'statement of intent' formed the basis for the second stage 'implementation plan'. Implementation started on 1 January 1996 with the fully reformed firm up and running by 1 April 1996. Reformation, while being an organization-wide debate, is very much owned by the current Chairman: 'When you are faced with decaying business, dissatisfied people, a great reputation, and me being party to it for the last forty years – in other words I cannot say it is not my problem.'

Arups sees continuity as important, with its future built on and shaped by the past. It looked carefully at the principles and policies which had guided Arup in the past and in particular reaffirmed those set out by their founder Ove Arup in his 1970 'Key Speech'. Arups' shared vision is of a partnership serving the societies in which it operates by:

- Providing clients with an excellent service worldwide.
- Being widely known and respected for the quality of our work, for our multidisciplinary approach, for our concern about the environment, for our good design and our ability to deliver.
- Operating as a highly successful international firm where all the parts and all the people work together through shared values and knowledge and with mutual ambitions.

('Vision Statement', internal document, 1996)

The Chairman described the type of vision required by Arups as like that which underpinned the success of the Catholic Church:

Their ability to create continuity and to depersonalize it. Well I want Arups to see us as tenants personally, I love saying this to people, 'Look don't get too excited because if both of us fell out of the window tomorrow, actually it would make no difference. Arups is bigger than any of you.'

This institutional example had a resonance with a top executive at AGBAR (see Sánchez-Runde and Quintanilla Chapter 9 in this volume) who attributed the enduring nature of the Catholic Church to its shared organizational goals and culture.

Such a vision has implications for future decision making which will have a preference for the long term, and investment in expertise and skills for the future. To achieve these aims, realize its vision and become the kind of firm it wants to be, Arups has chosen 12 specific, identifiable and measurable targets (see Figure 2.3).

Essentially, Reformation is still tackling the issues of empowerment and coordination: 'We do need coordination and it's a balance between coordination, which can sometimes be seen as direction and independent authority or decision making, and it is a very delicate balance' (Director).

Reformation structure Several organizational models were considered, to make the vision, aims and targets possible. Although the existing culture was retained it was decided to reorganize the structure. The existing structure of individual units reporting directly to the board was seen to work potentially better if there were closer groupings and if a framework existed within which new initiatives could be developed and further changes incorporated. A firm with the management structure of 'One Firm' was needed.

A new structure was proposed which would reform the 'Partnership' Board into a Policy Board (see Figure 2.4). This in turn would devolve operating responsibility to five new operational boards, covering: operations, civil engineering and planning, industrial engineering, building engineering and East Asia.

The business operations of Arups are carried out by groups which

Target 1:   Highly motivated people working together to achieve the aims and visions
Target 2:   Good leaders in all parts of the firm
Target 3:   Recruit excellent people from diverse sources to join the firm and stay
Target 4:   Deliver the financial performance we seek and be confident that it will continue
Target 5:   Develop ongoing relationships with clients
Target 6:   Achieve significant and continuing improvements in the quality of our work over all areas of activity
Target 7:   Operate on the basis of developed and agreed strategic plans for our businesses
Target 8:   Have Central Services which are appropriate for the firm's plans and cost effective
Target 9:   Operate worldwide in a few businesses on a market basis
Target 10: Create a seamless international Arups satisfactory to the people in the firm and delivering on projects
Target 11: Have a world IT network that is well developed and contributing to our success
Target 12: Be well known to clients, government and communities for our good work, advice and quality of design

FIGURE 2.3   *12 targets for the future of Ove Arup (Bulletin 145, November 1995)*

report to an operational board. Arups refocused and aligned these groups into networks to bring the various parts of the partnership into alignment. It has operating groups according to technical, business or geographical interests rather than one principle alone, and in the main has avoided contract staff. The resourcing of staff for a particular project is done centrally by networking through the group leaders.

This arrangement allows the policy board to concentrate on policy matters and delegate operations to the body of the firm. This is designed to establish real operational power and responsibility on a much broader basis. The existing skills networks, strategy committees and committees for staff policy, financial planning and computing, continue to function within the existing framework. The strategy and functional committees provide horizontal links at board level while the skill and market networks link horizontally at the level of the group. In this way the policy board can unite the firm, steer it through a period of change and plan new phases. Thus the task of managing the operations of the firm is delegated to new people and this provides new managerial responsibilities.

There are two kinds of network which run horizontally across groups: skill networks and market networks (see Figure 2.4). Skill networks have been a part of the company structure for a long time and historically have evolved out of members' interest in their fields of activity. One of the earliest skill networks was that of geotechnics, which began informally in the late 1970s. The geotechnics network was particularly useful in linking specialists throughout the firm as every

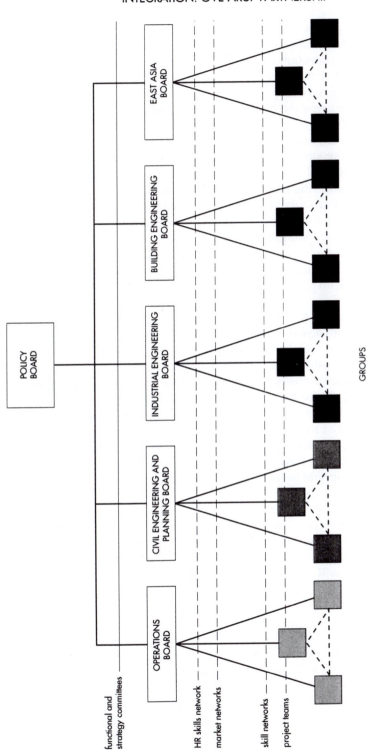

FIGURE 2.4 *Reformation structure in Ove Arup*

design group will usually have at least one geotechnics expert. The success of geotechnics inspired the formation of other groups and Arup now has a rich collection of specialist skill networks in every field of activity. Market networks are a recent innovation, arising out of the Reformation initiative, and they have a global reach. At the time of this study two were being established: transport and energy.

During the first quarter of 1996 a wide ranging consultation exercise was carried throughout the firm which took the form of conferences with all the major skill groups and in all the major geographical areas. At each conference, draft terms of reference for the policy board and the operational boards, the interaction of these boards, and the unit membership of the particular board were considered, including related matters, such as the role of the strategy committees and the skills networks. Views were sought on the size of the new boards, the unit membership, and how units which practise in more than one business should report. Throughout this time the partnership board met frequently to work on the detail of the Reformation proposals.

Operational boards Members of the operational boards are appointed for a period of three years but may offer themselves for reappointment. It is intended that membership shall be rotated, not least because it is important that most members retain a strong commitment to working on projects and with clients. Because of this rotation, some members will only serve initially for two years. It is accepted that some groups will move from the responsibility of one operational board to another as the need arises in the future. Some groups are small and in their formative period. During this stage it is likely that they will flourish most in the care of the operations board (see Figure 2.4). At some stage in the future it may be appropriate to move them to the board to which they most closely relate.

It will be necessary for each board to plan its business for the longer term. In the immediate future, it is expected that the strategy committees and skills networks will continue to provide leadership in business planning and professional activity. In the longer term, operational boards will be able to propose new arrangements for these matters.

Summary

Ove Arup has followed a steady path of organizational growth and expansion overseas with parallel diversification into wide ranging skill areas concerning all facets of the built environment. This progression was interrupted during the 1990s by the requirement to effectively utilize the core competence of the firm on a global scale. By the early 1990s Arups had reached a size both in the UK and abroad which made strategic and operational management difficult. The first initiative, Dependence and Interdependence, was an attempt to break the formation of dominant centres within the firm but failed, because it was not appropriate for the size of the firm. The second initiative, Reformation, tackled the problem by recreating a divisional structure to facilitate policy making, but with the innovation of horizontal networks to unite the divisions. In parallel with this last initiative is the ongoing Seamless Arup initiative which is also an attempt to integrate the firm on a global basis and includes the independent firms. More recently (1999), Ove Arup has started due diligence with Arup Australia, looking at a merger and joint operating from April 2000. This marks the beginning of the formation of the Global Arup Partnership, which will ensure global integration.

These last two initiatives, then, are significant both for their reaffirmation of the past growth and development of Arups and for their attempt to innovate in organizational systems and processes to integrate an increasingly large and complex global network.

Network Governance in Ove Arup Partnership

This section aims to apply Jones et al.'s (1997) theory of network governance to the Reformation structure and Seamless programme implemented by Arups' board in 1996 and 1994 respectively. It is divided into three sections: the first deals with the conditions under which a network governance emerges, the second discusses the social mechanisms which are used to coordinate this form of governance and the third analyses the problems with global integration in terms of this theory of governance.

Conditions for the emergence of network governance

Jones et al. (1997) lay out four conditions under which network governance emerges, defined as: demand uncertainty, customized exchanges, frequent exchanges among parties and task complexity. Their arguments are based on the transaction cost economics (TCE) logic that for a governance form to emerge and thrive it must address problems of adapting, coordination and safeguarding exchanges more efficiently than other governance forms (Williamson, 1991). They extend TCE by incorporating task complexity, thereby including group interactions and moving beyond purely dyadic exchanges. Also, they develop Williamson's notion of frequency in TCE by providing a link with social network constructs of relational and structural embeddedness (Granovetter, 1985, 1992; Uzzi, 1996, 1997). This section aims to apply these four conditions to the current Arup initiatives in order to demonstrate the applicability of Jones et al.'s theory.

Demand uncertainty   Two aspects of demand uncertainty identified by Jones et al. are particularly pertinent to this case: environmental uncertainty and rapid changes in knowledge or technology. The first is reflected in the tendency of the construction industry to track the economy quite closely, making firms like Arups sensitive to economic fluctuations. Hence the very buoyant period in the mid- to late 1980s followed by a downturn in profits with the recession of the early 1990s. One outcome of environmental uncertainty has been the tendency toward organic growth, as the spread of the partnerships and subsidiaries internationally has been largely due to opportunism rather than any planned strategy. In Arups directors have a great freedom to be entrepreneurial, take risks and open new offices. One director spoke of his experience of going into Europe: 'It works on this very free-form grapevine of acceptance, and it is a very good way because it is live. If we had sat and planned to be in Europe I don't think we would have been there.' Rapid changes in knowledge and technology in their sector have made the rapid dissemination of information critical; hence the requirement for an integrated network of subunits.

In the last five years demand uncertainty has led Arups to make the strategic decision to become globally integrated. It has perceived the necessity to leverage its competencies on a global basis in order to serve what are felt to be more sophisticated and demanding clients in an increasingly competitive environment. As a director explained: 'You cannot have a different level of service and culture under the same name in a shrinking world.'

Customized exchanges   The project-based nature of this organization means that there is a high level of customization, involving human asset specificity such as specialized skills, meetings and teamwork, derived from participants' knowledge and professionalism. Customization occurs, for instance, in exchanges between project groups or specialized individuals and groups, on specific project briefs. If these exchanges terminate, or enter into dispute, they are not outputs which can readily be transferred to another project.

The increasing emphasis on project management skills and the establishment of a skills network for this purpose serves to strengthen the basis for the coordination of project teams. As Jones et al. point out, this requires an organizational form 'that enhances cooperation, proximity, and repeated exchanges to transfer effectively tacit knowledge among parties' (1997: 920). The integrated network form to which Arups has moved is designed to achieve just such aims. For instance, cooperation and interdependence are achieved in the Arup global network by personnel transfers between overseas offices, e-mail, specialized skills networks, conferences, strategy committees and joint working on projects over time. All these are mechanisms for people getting to know others as individuals, which remains a significant factor in reducing uncertainty between consultants. As a senior director explained of his experiences:

> Since I have been here 30 years on and off, I just know the people . . . I used to boast and I think it is probably true, that I know personally the leader of every Arup office . . . I used to play cricket with the guy who leads the Johannesburg office in South Africa.

All the parties on a construction project must work together to effectively transfer tacit knowledge. Having a network of relationships can also be an asset in leveraging intellectual capital for strategic initiatives such as market development. The Chairman of Arups US firm attributed the success of setting up the New York office to the wide network of relationships which his engineers had acquired over the years from internal company transfers: 'So with our contacts and with our relationships it really makes you very powerful actually. Disproportionate to the fact that you have only got an office of six people.'

Task complexity The third exchange condition of task complexity under intense time pressure accurately reflects the working environment of this project-based firm. As project teams benefit from a number of specialized inputs by experts, there is of necessity a behavioural interdependence (Pfeffer and Salancik, 1978: 41) requiring coordination. In addition, staff are usually under enormous time pressures to complete, requiring parallel working patterns, coordination through meetings and group work. As a director explained: 'There is now a realization that the size of projects is so big, complex, the interactions are more complex. To do well you need greater teamwork than ever before, inside and outside the firm. And therefore the interfaces are much more complex.' There is also a need to speed information flows, as well as provide a focal point for advice giving. For instance the R&D department accepts an average of 200 telephone queries a day, from staff who often just want to bounce ideas off an expert. As the R&D director explained: 'They don't actually say will you go away and check it. They just want to talk it through.' Thus for Arups the need to integrate multiple autonomous, diversely skilled parties under intense time pressure requires network governance with a global reach.

Frequent exchanges Finally, frequent exchanges among parties exactly captures the interaction between specialized individuals on specific projects over time. As Jones et al. argue, these frequent interactions both justify and enable using intrafirm networks as an alternative governance form (cf. Jones et al., 1997: 281–282).

Thus, there is a significant amount of informal control exacted through embeddedness, or close contacts, due to the frequency of dyadic exchanges (Granovetter, 1992). Frequency of course becomes the basis for relational exchanges and determines the choice of project teams. A director explained the basis upon which he put together a large project in Germany: 'There are probably 25 key leaders on the project, maybe 30, and I personally targeted all of them and brokered into the introduction of all of them to the project . . . putting it together relied almost entirely on personal relationships.' In this one discerns the basis for continual reselection of individuals to projects, which results in the formation of cliques.

Two aspects of embeddedness, relational and structural, are identified as important to this theory (see Fenton and Pettigrew, Chapter 1 in this volume). Relational captures the quality of dyadic exchanges, and a significant amount of informal control through dyadic exchanges occurs in the context of project groups. This control is assisted by the learning-by-doing example set by engineer project leaders. Structural embeddedness (or the extent to which *a dyad's mutual contacts are connected to one another*) refers to the entire network system. Mutual contacts are connected by weak ties, or third party contacts to the rest of the network. At the systemic level structural embeddedness ensures a more efficient information spread about what members of a pair are doing and thus better ability to shape that behaviour (Granovetter, 1992: 35). The importance of frequent exchanges in informal control is the link Jones et al. make between TCE and social network theorists and which explains: 'the origins and persistence of structural embeddedness and social mechanisms that allow network governance to emerge and thrive' (1997: 923).

Linking exchange conditions to social control mechanisms   Jones et al. see the interaction effects of exchange conditions as promoting structural embeddedness which creates the foundation for social mechanisms of control. This explains the decision by Arups to integrate their global network during the last six years. For while they have always operated under conditions of customized and frequent exchanges, it is only in recent years that demand uncertainty and task complexity have become significant exchange factors. The increased competitive pressures brought by more sophisticated global clients and the increased pace of change in information and technology, have forced them to rethink the way they conduct their business. In addition, the size of these previously loose networks has grown to a point where they were losing coherence and control over information within the system. This was why the Dependence and Interdependence initiative ultimately failed. Thus size becomes an important empirical question in the emergence of this governance form (Jones et al., 1997).

Social control mechanisms arise because the more structural embeddedness there is in a network, the more transparency there is in the entire system for all individuals, leading to greater constraints on behaviour. A structurally embedded network therefore is one where, as with Arups, there are many weak ties, such that all the groups have relationships with each other and the same third parties (for example, contractors, clients, fellow professionals in other networks, and internal focal hubs such as the R&D Department).

Social mechanisms of control

Social mechanisms are used to overcome the problems of adapting, coordinating and safeguarding exchanges between autonomous groups operating under conditions of demand uncertainty and high interdependence, owing to customized complex tasks. Thus network governance overcomes these problems by using social mechanisms rather than authority, bureaucratic rules, standardization, or legal recourse (Jones et al., 1997: 925). Jones et al. isolate four social mechanisms: restricting access to exchanges, establishing a macroculture, imposing collective sanctions and instilling a reputation within the organization. It is the effectiveness of these four governance mechanisms within Arups which we shall now examine.

Restricting access to exchanges   Restricting access to exchanges is a strategic reduction in the number of exchange partners and therefore mitigates the problems of coordination and safeguarding. This control mechanism serves to reduce coordination costs, with fewer partners increasing interaction frequency. In this way relationships become more predictable, which facilitates mutual adjustment, and continued interaction may substitute for internal socialization processes. This further increases the safeguarding of exchanges, reduces monitoring and transaction costs (Jones et al., 1997: 928). It strengthens identification among parties and provides conditions for developing strong ties among those involved (Granovetter, 1973) which also has the effect of reducing opportunism. In a similar way, project teams and relationships built up over the years are an important social control. As the R&D Director described it: 'It is a firm that runs enormously on personal contacts and that is part of the business of this flexibility of deployment and fast team working.'

Reformation has reduced the size of the 'owned' network system into manageable subnetworks, defined by common markets, sectors, specialization or geography. Restricting access in this way has reduced vertical links and coordination costs, and given increased coherence and accountability to the subnetworks. The five boards have integrated the organization vertically by clarifying the links between the groups and the policy board. Additionally, horizontal links such as strategy and functional committees, skills networks and business networks have encouraged cross-fertilization of ideas and information. As a principal consultant explained: 'The structure we have been creating is a weave, there is a vertical operational system, and there is a horizontal skills sharing system, and a business intelligence system.' Ultimately, Reformation may be viewed as an attempt to serve client demands more satisfactorily and to leverage the competence of organizational members by integrating subnetworks to capture innovation and learning.

Jones et al. speculate that the relationship between the degree of access restriction and the contribution to adaptive fit of the network follows an inverted U shape: 'where too little restriction reduces performance because it impedes coordination of complex tasks, whereas too much restriction reduces performance because it provides inadequate incentives for quality and innovation' (1997: 928). The former scenario was well illustrated by the previous reorganization, Dependence and Interdependence, with its network of 50 groups: 'The idea was to really empower the groups and have direct links there to decision making. The problem with that is the horizontal network had so many interfaces, coordination was not working. There were too many nodes to interface with' (Director). This structure empowered the groups but detracted from system-wide embeddedness and the goal of being one international firm.

Macroculture   A macroculture is a system of widely shared assumptions and values, comprising industry-specific, occupational or professional knowledge, that guides actions and creates typical behaviour patterns among independent entities (Jones et al., 1997: 929). A director described the culture of Ove Arup as 'seeking to do well. The culture of wanting to look at the whole and not just do bits of something. It's still very much a design-based culture . . . but there is also a much, much bigger realization that good organization also matters.' A shared macroculture specifies roles and role relationships, and conventions to be employed by participants and in so doing, coordinates interdependent activities among independent entities so that complex tasks may be completed.

Jones et al. suggest three institutional means by which macrocultures are diffused and sustained. The first of these, socialization in professions, is easily applied to Arups. The profession of engineering has its own vocabulary, professional standards, formal schooling and conduct of behaviour. Senior engineers are regularly asked to organize seminars for junior staff members. There is a wide array of partnership publications: *Arup Journal* (a respected engineering journal now in its 29th year), *Arup Focus, Arup Bulletin* (monthly), *Arup News* (weekly), *Feedback Notes* (internally circulated to inform staff on technical topics such as specific methods of calculation and give advice on materials, thus ensuring that offices across the world are on the same technical level).

Trade journals and industry newsletters are an important feature of this socialization, supplemented by Arups' own internal newsletters and information. Industry events such as trade shows and conferences are reasoned to diffuse norms by providing role models, setting standards and exchanging information among participants. The equivalent of this is also achieved internally in Arups, which sets up its own conference venues, such as the yearly firm-wide conference or skills network conferences which serve to impart both organizational glue and current knowledge about specialist areas.

The culture which has historically pervaded Arups has been touched on in the previous section as underpinning the Reformation initiative. It is also a culture of great enthusiasm and dedication to the work, as the R&D Director explained: 'Arup acoustics started because one person had a bee in his bonnet about Haydn. And the firm now believes very strongly nothing runs unless there is a person who is – not just championing it – but who has got a real bee in his bonnet about it.' Additionally this director felt that psychologically the firm was against central policies. Arups has few central policies which must be rigidly adhered to and many strategic initiatives have been the result of individual interest and entrepreneurialism. This is reflected in a great ethos of democracy, as echoed by another director: 'We have no concepts of hierarchy and maestros for anything. We have submerged our individual egos into a firm and we have said everyone is equal here.'

Thus macroculture enhances coordination amongst autonomous partners by creating a convergence of expectations, allowing for idiosyncratic language to summarize complex routines (Williamson, 1975) and by specifying tacitly understood rules for appropriate actions under unspecified circumstances (Camerer and Vepsalainen, 1988). In general, Jones et al. point out that macrocultures are enhanced by close geographic proximity, because of the increased likelihood and ease of interaction. In Arups the detrimental effects of distance on culture brought about by globalization have been somewhat mitigated by the utilization of a common IT architecture, personnel transfers, internet technology, frequent flying and indeed the organizational glue provided by the macroculture itself. But the issue of culture remains a thorny one, as will be discussed in the section on integration issues.

Collective sanctions The third social control mechanism is that of collective sanctions, which involve group members punishing other members who violate group norms, values or goals and range from gossip and rumours to ostracism and sabotage. Collective sanctions within Arups is evidenced by a lot of informal communication about the performance of people which feeds into their promotion prospects and employment on assignments.

However, sanctions were a highly problematic issue as they counter-manded the democratic culture of the organization, and there were few mechanisms in place to encourage accepted network behaviour outside of informal sanctions. For instance, there were no mechanisms other than persuasion and moral obligation: 'We have a friendly relationship that says you will talk to us if you are going to talk to Tarmac . . . because we might not want to do it that way, but we have not got the authority to say you are not bloody doing that in Manchester' (Unit Leader).

Jones at al. (1997) have largely assumed the power of collective sanc-tions where the subunits of a network are interdependent. In partner-owned firms such as the independents of Arups this is not at forefront an issue, for each has control of its own profits and is inde-pendently managed. In practice, the Ove Arup name has never been withdrawn from an independent and there is no precedent for such a move, nor are there any alternative procedures in place to administer sanctions other than exclusion from projects.

As Jones et al. note, collective sanctions are limited in how accurately they may be applied: 'human asset specificity makes it difficult to dis-cern minimal versus best effort' (1997: 932). This may explain the absence of what Jones et al. describe as metanorms, or the norm for punishing those who do not punish rule breakers (Axelrod, 1985). It was clear from our empirical research that a lack of enforceable sanctions contributed in part to problems in achieving an integrated network. It was apparent that opportunism and uncertainty still prevailed in many quarters. The counterside of these arguments was the lack of incentives for good network behaviour within Arups.

Reputation The social mechanism of reputation is important under exchange conditions of uncertainty and customization. It is an estima-tion of one's character, skills, reliability, and other attributes central to exchanges. As uncertainty increases, exchange parties become more concerned with information about their own and others' reputation. It enhances cooperation by deterring and detecting deceptive behaviour (Jones et al., 1997: 932). Arups' reputation for excellence was outlined by one senior partner: 'What we are good at is our design capabilities, our conceptual design, our flair, in different ways of looking at things, inspi-ration, we are good at all the fluffy things up front of the job . . . and that is where we get most of our enjoyment.' In terms of industry percep-tions the following was a typical remark: 'We are still regarded as being one of the best training grounds and therefore we have some extremely good people; the industry tells us that' (Director). It is therefore vital for Arups to protect its international reputation by ensuring that the global network adheres to common standards of professionalism.

This background, of a sound reputation and a desire by individuals to be the best, naturally conditions the selection of individuals and groups for project teams. As a senior director reflected on his decision making in forming a team: 'There is a certain amount of reputation based on it. When you meet someone that you have not met a lot in the past, you have, however, got quite a lot of information about who the guy is and what he has done.' Reputation is key in reducing behavioural uncertainty and provides the basis for the development of trust. It promotes repeat exchanges and in this way the use of reputation risks the creation of cliques and hence overembeddedness in a network system.

Implementation of social controls

The key strategic driver for Reformation and Seamless Arup was integration of the global network, in order to leverage competencies and respond to market demands. It was felt this would be achieved by encouraging and enabling subunits to interact, exchange ideas and work more closely together. The sequencing in the implementation of social controls was as follows: initially, Seamless Arup introduced a shared vision and systems to the global network. This was followed by Reformation, which set about restricting access to exchanges through a divisional structure which improved coherence between groups while horizontal mechanisms leveraged competencies. In parallel to this move, the established macroculture was promoted around professionalism and quality of work, and in many ways the new structure was used to reinforce these values. Reputation is not easily disentangled in this case from an organizational culture which assumes it is the best in the industry, and as such, may be viewed as an important subset of the macroculture. Collective sanctions were found to be underdeveloped and operated more at the level of the individual than the group. It is this social control which has proved to be the most problematic for Arups.

Issues of integration within Arups

There was a discernible system-wide imbalance in the degree of integration within Arups' global network because of a variety of confounding factors. This has led to a situation where some members are actively involved in the network while others are less able or are resistant and hence do not feel well integrated. These problems are apparent with both the owned Arup subsidiaries and the independents. This lack of integration may be seen as a result of a variety of factors operating singly or together. Six factors of either a contextual or historical nature were identified as contributing to behavioural outcomes which undermined integration. The contextual factors concern the different market conditions and internal capabilities of individual practices. Historical factors which have developed over the years include perceptions of inequality, cultural fragmentation, lack of incentives and structural imbalances at the group level.

Market conditions   Individual country partnerships of Arups experience variations in their external markets, either because of market maturity or market structure. So for example, country practices with few multinational clients, or who are positioned in a national market, will exhibit parochial behaviour. The task here is to make sure that the essential ingredients of the Arup formula are subscribed to while at the same time respecting the cultural nuances of the independents. As one senior partner explained: 'It is different when you talk to an owner, you are talking a different language. These people are entrenched 20 or 30 years in the business and their culture.'

Differences in success could also be due to different growth rates or critical mass in one's market. For instance the US market generates much lower profit margins and therefore the US operations argue that they cannot expect to perform according to the same criteria as the UK. As the Chairman of the USA board explained: 'what is 10 per cent in the UK is different – you can't say you need 10 per cent in the United States, you just cannot achieve that outlook . . . we have not really adjusted how we do our work, how we approach it, to fit the environment that we are working in'. These differentials are in many cases a matter of time, until a country region develops its full potential. Such cultural and market differences in work orientation create goal incongruence between individual practices and the network. There is an ongoing debate on this issue within the company and it remains a barrier to optimal integration unless Arups can cope with the duality of standardization and customization of rules.

Internal capabilities   Goal incongruence is also evident where network members do not share the same level of experience of networking. For instance, some regional offices have better links than others, as a unit leader remarked: 'Some other places are much more separate and want to be much more separate.' Skill differences are also an issue when working with different national partners and some country practices with a lower skills profile are dropped from the network.

Perceptions of inequality   Over the years tensions have developed around the perceptions held by independent offices of the parent company. As the Chairman explained: 'Because things seem London-centric, the main board is here and most of the members . . . all the main central services are here. It looks as if London rules the world, even though we don't really.' These tensions undermine trust in cooperative behaviour while encouraging opportunism.

Lack of incentives In the way that Arups has not developed effective collective sanctions, similarly there was little in the way of reward and recognition systems to encourage positive behaviour under the new governance system. The firm has a history of modest rewards, as a senior manager explained: 'That is a big problem. It has been there for 20 years. Why the firm doesn't do it I just don't know . . . we would spend that on some stupid thing about the entrance to a building . . . [We] have never found a good way to reward our people.' In Arups reward and recognition are traditionally manifest in peer acceptance and honorary status and these informal recognition systems have not been updated to account for the new governance structure. For instance, no one could give examples of rewards for cooperative behaviour in the network. A lack of incentives will reduce the motivation of network members to cooperate, particularly where goal incongruence is already present.

Cultural fragmentation Arups shows evidence of a strong macroculture in the UK, but within some overseas firms subcultures have developed which now detract from an integrated global network. For instance, the independents and some subsidiaries have developed quite different cultures from the founding firm and so commitment to integration is weakened (see Ruigrok et al., Chapter 4 in this volume). In addition, the priorities of the independents are often different from the goals of the wider network. They are motivated by profits and need to be convinced about spending a lot of money on long term governance arrangements.

> It is no surprise that in Asia they have a very strong work ethic and profit related ethic, it's making sure that it's not to the detriment of what they are doing. We could argue in England there is a very high quality ethic and not very high profit ethic. Arups to a degree is going to reflect the culture of where you operate. But it is making sure that that does not dictate. That we maintain our difference . . . it is the way you innovate. (Director)

Convincing the independents to join an integrated network with the same goals, vision and standards is the most challenging part of the integration exercise for this firm. There was also evidence of different motivations due to specialization rather than geography. As the HR director explained: 'If you look at industrial engineering . . . their driver is to be profitable, commercially cute, do interesting work and be innovative, probably in that order. The other way round is building engineering.'

Structural imbalances Arups shows evidence of overembeddedness in a relational sense (Uzzi, 1997) where many strong and persistent ties lead to tight-knit cliques. Individuals are selected for project teams on the basis of who they know and reputation, so it is the same set of individuals over time. The HR director described it as a double network: 'where you have got one group of people who all talk to each other and the same names keep coming up again and again'. This overembeddedness extends to the power and influence in the company whereby:

> There is a very strong network for the people who are part of the network but for the ones who weren't, nobody knew about them. So you actually have two networks of communication and power. One network that actually says we know everybody and this is how we communicate, this is where the power is. And another sort of subliminal network where people are not spoken to from top to bottom. (HR Director)

The same result is found in very successful skill networks such as geotechnics, where strong ties between individuals confine their knowledge to within the group. As a director explained: 'One of the problems is actually broadening their outlook and taking more of a stronger role within civil engineering as a whole. They tended first to look after their own and were a bit inward looking.'

The opposite situation of incoherent social connections occurs where a group becomes underembedded in the network. This happens when specialists are located in larger groups and there is a tendency for them not to develop in a sufficiently sharply focused way, as the Head of Acoustics explained: 'They go native with the larger groups and don't push their disciplines. So feeding the strength of the discipline is the challenge if you start operating that way.' One solution to optimize the degree of embeddedness (or integration), was to create a total engineering skills network comprised of all the specialist subnetworks. This process of widening access for specialists would provide a cross-fertilization of skills and knowledge which could then diffuse to other groups. As the Head of Geotechnics explained: 'The big challenge now is to thread that strength in laterally, without losing the strength . . . I think the thing that the specialists can do is to infect those skills with specialism to give them the added value.' In this way over- or under-embedded groups require innovative design solutions for integration, in order to facilitate the potential spread of information and knowledge throughout the organization.

Summary As Jones et al. point out, congruent mechanisms reinforce one another to promote cooperation. However, the content of some social mechanisms may undermine others and create incoherence in the system (Jones et al., 1997: 923–924). For example, Arups experiences uncooperative behaviour by individual offices or partnerships as a result of the lack of sanctions, as well as the lack of incentives to coordinate fully with the wider network. Additionally, some elements of the macroculture undermine coordination. Like the importance of independence: 'people say "my business, my client, my field, my area, cross at your peril"' (Unit Leader). However, the evidence suggests that there are additional problems of a contextual and historical nature in integrating the global network, giving rise to a legacy of mistrust and opportunistic behaviour. Long-established relationship patterns may be incongruous with more recent initiatives and require adjustment, elimination or compensatory measures. Indeed, the passage of time and new contingencies will demand ongoing adjustments if Arups is to remain adaptable.

Discussion

A lack of integration in Arups' global network has been shown to be linked to differences in market conditions and internal capabilities combined with an accumulation of historical exchange patterns. This has resulted in an imbalance in the network, with some offices becoming more high profile, which in turn contributes to perceptions of inequality and reinforces cultural fragmentation abroad. The lack of integration resulting from these factors is to some extent a matter of time. For some subunits, new external contingencies will change behaviours, as will the support of the wider system in improving their internal capabilities. This section considers organizational and network variables which may be important in the strategic deployment of social control mechanisms within the network. We consider the role of leaders, the role of strong and weak ties and organizational heterogeneity. Finally, we turn to a consideration of formal rules and incentive systems to motivate integrative behaviour.

The focus on structural integration in Arups' global network should not be confined to purely structural considerations. As Granovetter (1982: 118) cautions: 'The active role of individuals in a culture cannot be neglected, lest the explanation become too mechanistic.' Thus the importance of key individuals within the network should not be neglected, and the way in which they can be cultivated and employed. For instance, leadership was crucial in the diffusion of the geotechnics specialism throughout Arups, as the former leader of their skills network explained:

> We were one of the first geotechnical groups of its kind to be established within a consultancy. And we developed a strong base in London, and various people then went out from London and established themselves in the regional offices . . . And the same thing was happening overseas too . . . So in short, we had a band of leaders if you like who were distributed around the world, who by and large knew each other, kept in touch with each other, and acted as a bit of a Mafia in a way.

In this sense, individuals are key in the dissemination of a macroculture, where 'chemistry' on the job and informally is a vital means of establishing trust and goodwill. Complex customized exchanges on multiple projects require particular personality profiles which must be fed into selection procedures. Leadership is also important in gaining identification with the organization and winning hearts and minds. Leaders must not only articulate the vision of the governance structure but provide example and inspiration. An example of such a leader was given by one engineering consultant, who described a former chairman as having 'black magic' which captured people's imagination.

Weak ties have been shown to be necessary for the diffusion of knowledge through the system, whereas strong ties lead to cliques which are not well integrated. However, the emphasis placed on weak ties in optimizing integration should not lead us to ignore the role of strong ties in the network system. Weimann (1980) finds that strong ties are not irrelevant in information flows, as credibility and especially influence are all greater when there are strong ties, and that in fact 'most of the influence is carried through strong ties' (1980: 12). This is borne out in determining the locus of power within Arups. Weimann suggests a division of labour between strong and weak ties: 'Weak ties provide "the bridges" over which innovations cross the boundaries of social groups . . . whereas the influence on the decision making is done mainly by the strong ties network within each group' (1980: 21).

This suggests that each subnetwork within the system needs a cluster of strong ties for the purposes of decision making and leadership, although the content of this decision making should be transparent to others within the subnetwork. There need to be effective and genuine mechanisms for all members of the network to voice their opinions and in so doing feel ownership of the governance arrangements. The strong ties in Arups are provided by the vertical links between the subunits and the operational boards to the policy board. But these arrangements were not always clear cut, given the orientation of the structure to a business area model. While this model worked well in the large London office employing around 500 people in one field, it is more problematic for smaller offices such as Manchester, which has one fifth of the staff and may be involved in up to three business areas. As one director candidly related:

> So those polycells still exist. And they now report to a board that is specially set up to deal with these special things. My judgement is it is a muddle, it has its strengths, I back it because change is necessary. Personal view is that I do not think it will last.

Thus Arups has had to create an operations board to deal with anomalies of multi-specialist and overseas offices in order to ensure they have adequate representative leadership.

Equally a balance needs to be struck with an adequate number of weak ties to provide the connections between subunits. It could be expected that those at the hub of strong ties would also perform a bridging role in diffusing information about the subnetwork through the system. Linked to this role would be that of facilitating bridging weak ties between subnetworks. Thus leadership in the context of an integrated network requires skills in the building of both strong and weak ties.

The problem of underembeddedness (or lack of integration) was shown to lead to incoherence within a subnetwork and between groups and the wider system. Where a group lost its identity, the wider network also lost the benefits of what it had to offer. It seems necessary, then, for a highly differentiated system of specialized staff relations to form subnetworks in order to retain their identity. This was the finding of Blau's (1980) case study of successful integration in a children's psychiatric hospital. She discovered that the subnetworks had many different foci of organization, reflected in a complex division of the hospital into departments, committee programmes, residential units and specialist clinical teams. Additionally, there was an intolerance of close dyadic ties and an overwhelming predominance of weak ties, which allowed each subnetwork to overlap extensively with many others. A large number of these weak ties were found to serve bridging functions.

It would seem that for optimal integration to occur between groups, a complex organization is an advantage in promoting a heterogeneity which creates the opportunity for contact (Baker, 1992). This, coupled with an intolerance of close ties other than for leadership purposes, and an emphasis on weak ties for the wide diffusion of information, would compel group members to sustain bridging intergroup connections. These would in turn serve to weaken the bonds of cliques (Blau, 1980: 20–21). To this end, the evidence from the case study suggests a need for an even greater variation in organizational design to encourage the cross-fertilization of ideas.

Finally, social controls such as collective sanctions are not adequate for the types of ownership structures found in Ove Arup, as they do not overcome problems of safeguarding and coordinating exchanges. Where there is separate ownership of member firms, market mechanisms may need to be introduced to encourage cooperation. In owned subsidiaries where negotiation is the usual coordination mechanism, controls may have to take the form of the establishment of rules and procedures of fair division (Grandori, 1997). Additionally, the lack of incentive systems was notable and creating an economic interest from cooperative behaviour may be the key to promoting cooperation in the network.

Conclusion

The application of Jones et al.'s (1997) theory of network governance to this case study has illustrated both the utility of the framework and the coherence of a theoretical approach linking TCE with social network theories. This theory of governance, in identifying the factors implicated in the emergence and sustainability of this form, is both broad enough to encompass a variety of network forms, and specific enough to enable comparison with other forms of economic organization. In this way, the network form of governance represents a meta-form which can accommodate a variety of coordination mechanisms and therefore is representative of complexity in economic life (Grandori, 1997). This form nevertheless distinguishes itself from traditional hierarchical governance forms in its utilization of the concept of embeddedness (Granovetter, 1985).

The comparability of Jones et al.'s theory could be further extended to include the degree of formalism of social control mechanisms (Grandori, 1997), and the role of leaders in coordinating and motivating. Further analytical force could be provided by including authority frameworks and incentive systems as additional control mechanisms to coordinate exchanges between groups. Additionally, the social mechanism restricting access to exchanges could be developed into a more inclusive category which recognizes the requirements of firms to both restrict and extend access to exchanges as contingencies arise. Thus the notion of optimizing embeddedness (or integration) would seem to capture the necessity of network governance forms to change and remain flexible.

It would seem that for Arups to leverage their core competencies and retain competitive advantage, they need to optimize embeddedness as contingencies dictate. These contingencies include both external competition factors and internal factors, such as history, capabilities and the size of the network. The process of optimizing embeddedness is not a one-off task. It involves both the strategic deployment of individuals and subnetwork boundaries, coupled with the creation of positive hub and periphery effects. These positive network patterns should comprise hubs of knowledge and decision making (strong ties) which are made transparent to the wider system by an extensive network of bridging weak ties.

Arups recognizes the need for flexibility in its design arrangements and the degree and pattern of embeddedness it employs will be largely dictated by the goals of the organization at any one time. In this way, optimizing embeddedness is not a permanent design feature but a flexible strategic tool which lends this social control mechanism an added desirability. For as organizations battle for competitive advantage, the impermanence and flexibility of any particular combination of social mechanisms make them especially difficult to imitate. However, the issue of delivering change is still at question here, for moving to this kind of responsive organization entails commitment from organizational members. People must feel that the new arrangements will enhance service delivery and that their cooperation will be recognized and rewarded. Orchestrating change at multiple levels and designing for complexity are a matter of resources and of time, both for the new form to bed down, and for organizational mindsets to come to terms with a future of ongoing change and uncertainty. These are not easy messages to sell, particularly when your staff are your key asset.

Further research could usefully focus on weak ties; for instance, Granovetter (1982) calls for more systematic investigation of the origin and development of those ties that bridge, as compared to those that do not. Conversely, the role of strong ties in leadership, decision making and power needs further development in the context of network governance. Granovetter (1982) also sees a need to move away from static analyses that observe a system at one point in time, toward a more systematic account of how such systems develop and change. This is particularly relevant for understanding the deployment of embeddedness as a strategic tool over time. Related to this is the question of network size in altering subnetwork boundaries.

A very important research stream identified by Jones et al. (1997) is the examination of the interaction of social mechanisms: for instance how social mechanisms reinforce, replace and undermine each other and the way in which they can be employed to strategic advantage. This is the focus of the next chapter, in which the interplay of social mechanisms employed by a management consultancy are analysed. Finally, Jones et al. (1997) note the importance of determining the emergence of networks as a result of efficiency or other institutional processes. They make the worthwhile point that the adoption of network governance may not necessarily be based on efficiency considerations but on processes of institutionalization. The time is now right for large scale organizational population studies to explore this key question.

Note

We acknowledge the support of the UK Economic and Social Research Council, PricewaterhouseCoopers and the consortium members of the Centre for Creativity Strategy and Change. Our thanks go to Stella Littlewood and Bente Lowendahl for helpful comments made on an earlier version of this work and all the participants in this study who gave so generously of their time.

3

The Role of Social Mechanisms in an Emerging Network: The Case of the Pharmaceutical Network in Coopers & Lybrand Europe

Evelyn M. Fenton and Andrew M. Pettigrew

A micro perspective on network governance is taken in this case of a professional service organization from the management consultancy sector. This is an account of the highly successful European pharmaceutical network within Coopers & Lybrand (C&L). Here we have sought to establish the significance of social mechanisms of control in network governance as distinct from authority and economic mechanisms. This study develops the network theory of governance (Jones et al., 1997) discussed in the previous chapter on Ove Arup. It does this by analysing the interaction effects of social mechanisms of control which coordinate and safeguard exchanges within the network.

This case supports the view that relational forms of organizing matter as much as formal structures and economic attributes to the performance consequences of organizations. We aimed to understand how these social mechanisms interrelated, that is, how they reinforced, substituted and undermined one another. Our findings support Jones et al.'s (1997) proposition that where there is congruence between social mechanisms, then the network will perform effectively. Additionally, it was clear that provided the network is not too large and complex, then some social mechanisms may substitute for each other in their role in safeguarding and coordinating exchanges. The success of the pharmaceutical network demonstrates how social mechanisms contribute to the social capital of organizations by adding value through the development of and the investment in relationships. In this way relational organizing provides firms with competitive advantage by being non-imitable and non-transferable, unable to be bought on the open market and requiring time to develop (Dyer and Singh, 1998).

This study traces the development of part of the C&L consulting practice in Europe from the late 1980s until prior to its merger with Price Waterhouse in 1998. It takes as its main theoretical focus the emergence and development of the European pharmaceutical (pharma) network from the early 1990s until early 1998. The study was conducted throughout the merger negotiations in late 1997 and early 1998, and therefore concerns the firm as the Coopers & Lybrand entity.

The adoption of a network mode of organizing by Coopers & Lybrand Europe (CLE) was a strategic response to market conditions with the objective of leveraging core competencies across the firm (Kogut, 1983; Porter, 1986). This form of organizing by CLE was essentially a set of coordination mechanisms overlaid upon a federal structure of dispersed and independent partner firms. The pharmaceutical network was one of four industry programmes and the most advanced network in terms of integration and coordination. This was a significant innovation for C&L because it marked an important first step in organizing globally. The interest for new forms of organizing is that this is an example of the normalization of a previously informal network. This process of formalization involves employing social control mechanisms which are a crucial success factor in this form of organizing (Dyer and Singh, 1998).

The structure of the chapter is as follows: a literature review on relational forms of organizing is followed by a brief explanation of the methods used. The case study is presented, first from the perspective of Coopers & Lybrand Europe in terms of its context and recent history. A detailed account of the European pharmaceutical network is given. This is followed by an analysis of the effectiveness with which the network was integrated across Europe, explained in terms of the interplay of social mechanisms that act to govern the network at different levels. A discussion follows on the interaction effects of social mechanisms of control and how they provide resources and competitive advantage for firms. We conclude with suggestions for future research and organizational practice.

Relational Forms of Organizing

The current interest in relational forms of organizing is indicative of a significant shift in the focus of theoretical enquiry away from the study of purely formal structures and purely economic motivations which have dominated organization studies (see Fenton and Pettigrew, Chapter 1 in this volume). The emphasis on economic motivations is represented by the transaction cost approach to organizing which is rooted in micro-economic preoccupations with efficiency (Williamson, 1981: 549). This approach has been challenged by Granovetter (1985) as providing an undersocialized account of organizations. Transaction cost economics (TCE) evolved from explaining why organizations exist to addressing the question of what organizational designs are appropriate under various circumstances (Williamson, 1985). The thrust of this argument is that governance structures are tailored to the specific needs of each type of transaction.

As Roberts and Greenwood (1997) note, the rationale for the existence of any given organizational design is its efficiency compared to the set of available alternatives, including markets (Winter, 1991). In this sense the transaction cost explanation is a comparative efficiency one. Further, they argue that given the lack of clarity with transaction cost's understanding of design adaptation and change, an intermediate position should be adopted. This position, spelt out, is that organizations seek efficiency subject to cognitive constraints and institutional influences. We add to this debate by arguing that organizations are efficiency seeking subject to relational influences as well (Uzzi, 1997).

Several authors have demonstrated, with regard to relational contracting, the relevance of the TCE framework for a relational view of organizations (Eccles, 1981; Mariotti and Cainarca, 1986; Jarillo, 1988). Jones et al. (1997) have taken this approach a stage further with their synthesis of TCE and social network theory. These authors' contribution to organizing has advanced our understanding of transaction costs and governance, and in so doing has clarified the basis for network relations which had hitherto been both partial and non-specific.

The view taken here is that exchange processes are embedded in a dense fabric of social relations. According to Easton and Araujo (1994: 75): 'economic exchange is rarely able to rid itself of non-economic exchange baggage such as social exchange, kinship and friendship networks, altruism and gift giving and a host of other psychological and sociological elements not liable to be reduced to the standardized metric of money'. The relational view of organizations has gained increasing prominence over a range of literature which highlights a number of important commonalities. There has been a move away from transactions as the primary unit of analysis to a focus on relationships in the exchange. This theme has appeared strongly in the global structuring literature (see Fenton and Pettigrew, Chapter 1 this volume), especially in the work of Ghoshal and Bartlett (1990), Roth and Nigh (1992) and Ghoshal and Nohria (1993). Defining organizations in relational terms has been particularly evident in the focus on networking and the use of networks in multinational companies and interorganizational arrangements.

A principal ordering activity of relational organizing appears to be integration or interdependency. In the multinational company (MNC) literature and knowledge-based views (Hedlund, 1994; Nonaka, 1994; Grant, 1996b; Tsoukas, 1996) this becomes the principal role of organizations that want to gain competitive advantage. Similarly, the interorganizational literature regards interdependency as vital for the survival of firms but takes a broader view, including interdependency with other social and political institutions (Brusco, 1982; Sabel et al., 1987; Powell, 1990).

The purpose of organizations has moved from a focus on economizing to adding value. Here the influence of the resource-based view of the firm is evident in the MNC literature and knowledge-based views, where developing capability in knowledge management is a strategic imperative. Easton and Araujo (1994) note that a greater variety of assets is generated by relationship-specific investments, with different degrees of specificity, compared to transaction-specific investments. Relationship-specific investments are a complex web of investments in tangible and intangible assets committed to a specific party.

Another related form of investment is a relationship development investment, allowing both parties to invest in the development of tangible and intangible assets, as opposed to the utilization of new and existing resources. The important distinction here is that the relationship has become a resource in itself and is being used to create other resources, product adaptations, new ways of doing things, access to third parties, etc. Thus the returns have now more to do with extending the scope, content and process of the relationship. While more difficult to measure, these relationships are likely to generate greater value.

One way of conceptualizing the returns from an investment in relationships is in the development of social capital as an organizational resource. Like physical and human capital, social capital is a productive resource which may facilitate a firm's business activities (Baker, 1990; Coleman, 1990; Burt, 1992). This concept was first developed by Nahapiet and Ghoshal (1998), building on Moran and Ghoshal's (1996) idea of value creation as arising from the combination and exchange of resources. Nahapiet and Ghoshal (1998) identify three dimensions of social capital: structural, relational and cognitive. They then provide a theoretical justification of how the attributes of each of these dimensions facilitate the combination and exchange of resources within firms. The structural dimension is where the location of an actor's contacts in the social structure of interactions provides certain advantages for the actor, such as information and access to resources. The relational refers to assets such as trust which are rooted in relationships and act as a governance mechanism for embedded relationships (Uzzi, 1996), while the cognitive dimension is embodied in attributes such as shared codes of behaviour which reduce coordination costs and facilitate cooperation.

The argument in favour of relationship-specific investments is that they are crucial in helping organizations to develop general purpose capabilities and to learn new skills. This is a direct result of interaction with others and is in sharp contrast to the static view of the transaction cost approach with its focus on economizing rather than adding value. Additionally, the stability and future oriented nature of the relationship reduces uncertainty and lowers the threshold of risk for new investments. Finally, there are returns from the totality of investments that firms make in the relationships they enter into. In the long term, the cumulative nature of the commitment of resources in the building up of dyadic and network relationships (Johansson and Mattsson, 1985), and the resultant intangible resources, generate a strategic identity for the individual firm in this total context. Thus there is a picture of interdependent consequences from investment decisions for which the timing is crucial. A firm's network position is one of opportunities and constraints: the opportunities to access resources and the constraints from the lock-in effect of the relationships which cause switching costs if broken. This is a complex and dynamic picture in which firms occupy positions in a network of relationships within a social, historical and temporal context.

Network governance

In recent years network governance has become increasingly important to new forms of organizing but as yet is poorly understood (Jarillo, 1988; Grandori, 1997; Jones et al., 1997, see Fenton and Pettigrew, Chapter 2 this volume). The increase in inter-firm networks of all kinds (alliances, franchises, joint ventures, supplier networks) makes this a critical area for research as the working patterns and business activities of these companies mean that traditional structural forms of control and coordination between subunits do not apply. Similarly, intra-organizational modes of activity may be seen to mirror these networking characteristics, of which professional services organizations represent a case in type. Also, as Jones et al. (1997: 937–938) state, network governance will become more prevalent because the exchange conditions of demand uncertainty, human asset specificity and complex tasks are increasing. This is true not only in the professional services but of many other sectors where the competitive environment demands more rapid response times, greater flexibility and lower managerial costs as well as higher entrepreneurialism and intellectual capital. In relation to this last, work has shifted increasingly to knowledge-based modes (Reich, 1991; Drucker, 1993; Blackler, 1995), where human asset specificity and transfer of tacit knowledge across and within firm boundaries are important.

In the previous chapter we outlined Jones et al.'s (1997) theory of network governance which identified the exchange conditions giving rise to social mechanisms of control. Jones et al. identified four social mechanisms: restricting access to exchanges, macroculture, collective sanctions and reputation which act to coordinate and safeguard exchanges. In applying this theoretical framework to Ove Arup we demonstrated that the failure to operate as an integrated network could be traced to inadequate development of collective sanctions, over- or under-restriction of exchanges, fragmented organizational culture and contextual features relating to subunits' capability and experience of networking. As Jones et al. (1997) point out, social mechanisms are critical to network performance as they involve implicit and open-ended contracts. Therefore it is important to have a better understanding of how social mechanisms reinforce, substitute or undermine one another and how this combination influences performance. Equally we do not understand whether some social mechanisms are more significant in predicting when networks emerge and others for predicting when networks will thrive.

The interaction effects of social mechanisms in network governance may promote cooperative behaviour while at the same time preventing opportunistic behaviour by providing greater incentives for cooperation. This economic rationale for behaviour of course ignores other fundamental psychological and sociological motivations for non-cooperation or cooperation. Such factors as friendship, politics and power, trust and temporal outlook all can (and often do) supersede profit-maximizing motives. Thus as Jones at al. point out: 'Restricted access, reputation and collective sanctions align well with Putnam's (1993) review of conditions that favour cooperation in the face of collective or social dilemmas' (1997: 934).

The social mechanisms of network governance enhance the cooperative behaviour needed for customization of complex tasks under conditions of uncertainty. Restricted access limits the number of players, macroculture enhances coordination through aligning expectations, behaviours and cognition, thereby reducing transaction costs. Reputation provides information about participants' actions and collective sanctions discourage participants from yielding to incentives for short-term opportunistic behaviour. Jones et al. theorize that all these mechanisms decrease the coordination costs and enhance the safeguarding of customized exchanges. Further, as more social controls are used, the likelihood of network governance emerging and thriving is enhanced.

In terms of assessing the effectiveness of these social mechanisms for adapting, coordinating and safeguarding exchanges, the key characteristic identified by Jones et al. is congruence of social mechanisms. Congruent mechanisms reinforce one another to promote cooperation in a network, so that for instance restricting access and macroculture coordinate specialized exchanges by clarifying behavioural routines and expectations while at the same time safeguarding exchanges by confining information access and providing rules for its dispersal.

However, the context of some social mechanisms may undermine others and create incoherence in the system. So for example, macroculture content may inhibit and collective sanctions may penalize information sharing and undermine coordination, even where there are appropriate social structures for dispersing information about reputations. Therefore Jones et al. hypothesize that the congruent content of social mechanisms influences coordination costs and safeguards complex customized exchanges. To this end they note the practical implications of their theoretical framework which highlights the dangers for those who might seek to use network governance without appropriate supporting social mechanisms. Without these mechanisms both coordination and safeguarding are likely to suffer.

The purpose of this study was to analyse the range of social control mechanisms used within an evolving network, to capture the interaction effects of these social controls and to consider what other contextual features are implicated in organizational behaviour. Further, we have considered to what extent relational organizing can provide an organization with resources and contribute to its competitive advantage.

Method

The methodology adopted here mirrors that described in the previous chapter (see Fenton and Pettigrew, Chapter 2, this volume), a processual and contextual case study approach involving data gathered from semi-structured interviews and supporting documentary material.

The evidence for this case was gathered from in-depth interviews conducted in the first instance with eight senior executives having a strategic brief within the firm. These interviews focused on the overall transformation within C&L including the establishment of Coopers & Lybrand Europe (CLE) from the mid-1980s until 1998. In the second instance the focus for interviews was on the pharmaceutical network, and ten consultants of varying seniority but with extensive experience were interviewed from around Europe. Seven of these interviews were conducted by telephone (to which a tape recorder was attached). This was due to their European location or because of unavailability for a face-to-face interview: for example if the consultant was located within a client firm. A total of 18 interviews was conducted and this evidence was supported by internal documents. The second round of interviews dealt with issues specific to the pharma network, such as its management agenda, cross-border working, team building and membership of specialist groups. The purpose of the interviews was to elicit processual detail concerning the social nature of the coordination mechanisms which govern exchanges and the way in which they facilitate and/or inhibit network effectiveness.

Coopers & Lybrand: Recent History and Business Development

Coopers & Lybrand was a professional services organization with over 70,000 employees worldwide in around 140 countries and more than 30,000 in Europe. The firm comprised a federation of small autonomous partnerships.

C&L international structure mid-1990s

From 1996 to 1998 the business environment was characterized by two interrelated factors: significant growth in consulting activity coupled with more sophisticated and demanding clients. This prompted a fundamental strategic review which established that C&L needed to restructure in a way that appealed to their main buyers. As a senior partner explained: 'Coopers needed to position itself as deep specialists.' C&L structured itself along the following main lines of business with the related percentage of income:

1	Business assurance (audit)	>40%
2	Tax and legal	20%
3	Management consulting services	20%
4	Corporate finance	<10%
5	Human resource advisory services	5%

Within these five business lines C&L had been developing specialisms, of which the pharmaceutical industry business within the management consultancy line is the focus of the analysis section. The model towards which the firm gravitated was a coordinated international network of businesses from that of a loose federal structure. This means that a greater degree of centralized control was required for both the standardization of business practice and services, and the integration of disparate partnerships for the purposes of shared skills and knowledge. In order to hasten and develop these strategic aims Coopers & Lybrand announced plans to merge with Price Waterhouse in November 1997.

Coopers & Lybrand Europe

In order to foster the integration of C&L firms in all service lines, the first regional unit: Coopers & Lybrand Europe was established in 1989. CLE was a more integrated network of national partner firms in 16 countries, sharing common business practices and costs. There was no head office but London and Brussels were hubs for the European operation where dedicated resources resided. It was the only substantial regional unit within C&L and was established: 'in frustration that we did not have a global mechanism' (Senior Partner). It developed as a bottom-up exercise by national firms deciding that they wanted to do it and fund it. But it was always without a shared economic interest and so avoided the issue of an authority framework. The firms did not share profits but shared some costs.

CLE organization   The European office in Brussels acted as a hub for each of the service lines with mechanisms to increase members' awareness, support the roll out of product and invest in various territories such as Eastern Europe. There were also centres of excellence which resided where the expertise happened to be most concentrated. However, the real power lay with the partner networks and sector heads who were partners in charge of consulting in a particular country, or responsible for a particular line of business. This wider group of some 400 people interfaced with the national firms.

Over the last 15 years the performance of CLE has tended to track the economy quite closely, so there was a very buoyant period in the mid- to late 1980s, followed by a downturn in profits with the recession in the early 1990s, and since 1993–1994 a period of quite extraordinary growth with European revenues growing at around 15 per cent. In terms of personnel CLE grew from 10,000 people in Europe in 1989 to about 33,000 in 1998, about half of which was organic growth and half merger related. Profitability as a percentage of turnover remained constant with the consultancy business growing more quickly in profit terms than the other lines in recent years.

Management Consultancy Services

Management Consultancy Services (MCS) was developed as an offshoot of CLE because it was felt that management consultancy needed to develop to respond to market forces and therefore needed additional resourcing from the CLE budget. Strategic decisions were taken globally by a peripatetic consulting board on which the main components such as geographic and service are represented. The sector heads then came together to form a European consulting board and took decisions about strategies, business plans, investments, products, sector priorities and who would direct them. From this it was expected that each country would conform to that strategic thrust. The European Consulting Board had a common investment budget of $10 million for 1998.

MCS organization   CLE was a virtual network in which the MCS executive team of around four to eight people formed the hub. The brief for MCS Europe was to coordinate the team plans in Europe of four industry programmes (retail and consumer, pharmaceuticals, telecoms, and financial services) and develop industry-tailored service initiatives. The reorganization of management consultancy into programmes created subnetworks, thereby creating greater focus and connectedness between national firms. These subnetworks were designed to service target clients with specialized industry knowledge and largely network within themselves, although cross-fertilization between groups occurred and was encouraged.

The degree of interaction of offices varied by the nature of the business sector. At the time of this study, approximately 15–20 per cent of the consulting business was transnational, either working across borders or in a cross-border team. This translated into at least 10 per cent of staff working regularly outside their domestic environment. The most integrated sector was pharmaceuticals which is the focus of this chapter. In this sector there is a relatively small number of company clients and virtually all of them operate in multiple countries, specialization is quite high and the pharmaceutical community is very interconnected, so there is a high degree of mobility.

MCS project teams   While there was no consistent organization, there was a hierarchy on each project. This consisted of a partner or director who was the person with contractual responsibility to commit the firm. Then the project manager with day to day responsibility for managing the delivery process, and on very big projects there was an additional layer of team leaders under the project manager. The service delivery was then carried out by two levels of consultants: experienced senior consultants and less experienced junior consultants.

One of the tensions within management consultancy had been in the way it used the term 'network'. As a senior consultant explained: 'We have tended to say, this decision-making body is a network because it has got a lot of representatives, but we have never had the authority framework which decision-making bodies actually need.' He regarded the decision to integrate not as a failure of the network model: 'It is a failure of the type of networking that we were doing as an international organization.' For instance, it was well known that the largest partner firms in Europe had a dominant position in terms of decision making on the executive, and there had been charges that lead firm requirements were taking precedence over opportunities in the marketplace.

The Pharmaceutical Network

MCS identified pharmaceuticals as a strategic area for development in the early 1990s, when it had existed substantially as an informal network for around five years. In 1996 the pharma network was formally established as a business development group. It was required to develop an integrated business plan across Europe, so that although its leaders were located in different regional offices they operated as a management team for business strategy. One member of this team described it as a 'virtual management team'. The network prioritized its potential clients and service delivery to them and invested in the development of service lines. The management team were accountable for top line growth, in which revenue was measured by service. There was some sharing of investment where there was a degree of risk. The network comprised around 200 consultants from across Europe. Between 1996 and 1998 they had grown by 30–40 per cent per year, from £20 million to around £45 million.

The pharmaceutical industry

There are three facets to understanding the client in pharmaceuticals. In the first place pharmaceuticals is a global industry because of the reach of the client firms. Secondly, the markets for pharmaceuticals are national and thirdly, it is a very fast growing knowledge sector and therefore the network had to create external alliances with competitors in order to compete. As a senior consultant explained: 'The way we develop a product today will be totally different from the way we develop it in the future.' There was thus a requirement for consultants in this sector to balance the competing requirements of globalization and national markets. Market changes are driven by two key factors: rising expectations of health care and fundamental changes in science and technology. The latter is a particular source of demand uncertainty which has influenced the adoption of a network governance form (Jones et al., 1997). In general, the size of the work had been getting bigger and the network had focused on larger accounts with subsequent fee scales to match.

Organization and management of the pharma network

The organization of the pharma network must be seen in the context of the MCS organization (see previous section). Structural and relational elements made up the MCS network of which pharmaceuticals were a part. First, the industry programmes were subnetworks which acted to restrict access to exchanges in the network, so that specialization along sector lines occurred, facilitating coordination. Leading the European industry programmes was a network of partners whose primary role was still at a country level. This second element was the locus of power in MCS: the networks of partners with industry and/or geographic responsibilities. All firms in MCS had separate financial and ownership arrangements. The pharma network, illustrated in Figure 3.1, may therefore be classified as complex (Biemans, 1992), being a network within a network.

National firms supplied the human resources for temporary project teams. The firms varied from one to 31 in the number of pharma specialists they employed. The seven largest firms (with number of pharma consultants) were London and Uxbridge (31), Basel (14), Utrecht (11), Brussels (11), Milan (8) and Frankfurt (7). All other firms had four or fewer pharma consultants. The pharma consultants owed an allegiance both to their firm and the pharma network. The Chairman of the pharma network explained: 'I have explicitly tried to build up loyalty to pharma over the individual country offices to generate a team spirit.' In this endeavour he noted that shared history counted for a lot, especially between the network leaders. There was an overall feeling that during the five or so years of pharma's history there had been a general convergence in values.

The management of the pharma network was led by a team comprising partners who were the national pharma leaders in the ten major countries in Western Europe:

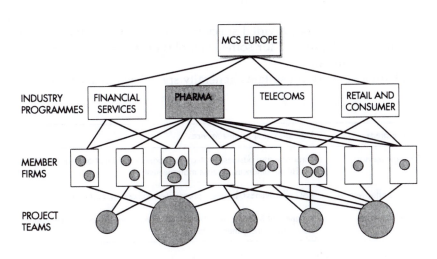

FIGURE 3.1   *The pharma network within the European management consulting business of Coopers & Lybrand*

Belgium	France	Italy	Norway	Switzerland
Denmark	Germany	Netherlands	Spain	United Kingdom

This team operated under the overall leadership of the Chairman who was a partner (from the UK) dedicated to the task and therefore no longer attached to a national firm. The European pharmaceutical management group had an explicit management agenda which was expressed as follows:

1 Coordinate the European management of our key client accounts
2 Optimize use of resources on a European basis
3 Build critical mass of resources in our major country practices
4 Undertake European product/service development
5 Create a knowledge sharing infrastructure
6 Develop the capabilities of our people
7 Achieve European revenue growth targets

(Internal document April 1997)

The reputation of partners was an important aspect of leadership within the pharma network and crucial in both client and colleague relationships. As a consultant remarked of the pharma leadership team:

> If you replace those personalities with others, it would probably disintegrate totally in my opinion. It works on the basis that they have a lot of knowledge, they have a good standing in the industry. People listen to them and they can knock on the right doors as well, and get some response.

The pharma network provided specialist services to industry in three key areas (see Figure 3.2 for some examples of the specialist services within these areas).

Pharma network consultants generally specialized in a service area

Service areas	Examples of specialist services
Strategic services	corporate and business strategy, corporate transformation, mergers and aquisition, alliances, disease management
Business effectiveness	R&D effectiveness, business process re-engineering, cost reduction
Systems delivery	commercial & financial systems (SAP), clinical data management systems, document management systems

FIGURE 3.2 *Specialist services provided by the pharmaceuticals network*

(and occasionally worked across more) but within that may have worked in more then one specialist field. Traditionally consultants had been labelled first by their specialism and second by their industry group, so being a member of the pharma network enabled consultants to have more opportunities for contacts with colleagues from different specialist areas.

The management team was felt to have been successful in providing references, methodologies and ideas but had now reached the limits of its success on a virtual network basis. One country leader gave the reason as a mismatch between business performance measures and business requirements. In other words, consultants were measured for performance on the basis of their national firm, not on the efforts they put into networking with the pharma group. He felt that goodwill and personal relationships were not adequate at this stage in the development of the network and that it should now move to a more formal mode of operation.

Pharmaceutical network resources

Most pharma network consultants had industry-specific skills such as R&D, disease management and clinical data management from their industry experience. They therefore shared both industry-specific knowledge and expertise which informed their working routines and common understandings. Pharma consultants were engaged in exchanges involving the customization of products and services, such as new methodologies and knowledge management systems, tailored to meet client needs. There was thus a requirement for cooperation, proximity and coordination, to effectively transfer tacit knowledge between parties (Jones et al., 1997) in the pharma network.

The optimal use of resources involved proactively managing potential staffing but the reality, as one consultant explained, was different: 'On a European basis there is no real coordination of resources, it tends to be on a project by project basis: he who shouts loudest.' There was a general feeling amongst participants in the study that resource management could not be optimized while the mentality of the national firm still predominated in the network.

The goal of achieving a critical mass of resources has also been somewhat variable across Europe, with core hubs of people in Switzerland and the UK while other countries were more sparsely resourced. This also varied by specialism, so that for instance the UK had a critical mass of resources in R&D. Given the target to develop a critical mass of resources in major country practices, the key issue became establishing what that critical mass for any one location would be. This reflected the need for strategic management and where firms were too small, critical resources could be achieved by a group of countries investing collectively in specialists. This approach was adopted in Scandinavia.

The development of human resource capabilities was generally considered to be very good, with many opportunities to develop skills and share information. For instance the pharma university, which was a three-day learning event open to the whole network, was often cited as an excellent forum for development and interaction. Primarily the development of capabilities was an individual responsibility and each consultant had a career development manager. There was however a frequent problem noted in the mismatch of skills between staff in different firms.

Reward and recognition

There was little in the way of reward and recognition systems in place to encourage positive behaviour in the network, such as sharing knowledge, resources and clients. The reward and recognition system was linked to the reward system of the individual country practices, and this did not explicitly encourage integrative behaviour. Indeed, at times it served to discourage integration, where for instance, the fees charged by one office were considerably higher than those charged by the bidding firm, making the use of those consultants too expensive for the client. Also, there were profit implications for national firms, as one consultant explained: 'Quite often the performance matrix works against multi-disciplinary working and involving people from other groups . . . you effectively lose the revenue for your group.' In this way the performance structure restricted exchanges in a manner which was counterproductive for the wider firm.

One consultant described the lack of measures to assess networking: 'still today, evaluation is made country by country. So it is a relationship between me and my country partner and office.' There was informal communication about the performance of people which could potentially feed into their promotion prospects and future employment on assignments. However, evaluation at the team level was rarely conducted, except within country practices.

A consultant reflected that they had gone as far as they could with the current structure in terms of rewards. The promotional structure had problems when there was a clash between the country firm and the network. This occurred when an assignment did more for the network than the country firm and therefore interfered with promotion prospects. One senior consultant felt that the performance matrix had to be aligned with the network structure. In other words, rewards would have to be factored into achievements for the greater good of the network.

However, dissenting opinions were expressed by some consultants on the issue of incentives. For instance, one felt that it was very useful for their work to avoid incentives: 'It is very necessary for our work that we don't have recognition but that we are doing it because it is mandatory to share.' This consultant favoured a recognition system for cooperative behaviour (see Figure 3.3, p. 99, showing accepted 'green card' behaviour). Another did not even favour rewarding cooperative behaviour, as he explained: 'To me it's a given. I believe that's the way you should operate rather than be rewarded for doing it. I would say if you don't do this then we need to understand why and fix it.' This consultant favoured better rewards for excellence in consulting practice.

Cultural influences

The pharma network may be seen to have had cultural influences which were nested at three levels: C&L firmwide, the pharma network and the pharmaceutical industry.

Firmwide culture   At the firmwide level, cultural influences were embedded in the C&L culture of professionalism. This included a cognitive mindset shared by individuals, so that even people not known to each other had a common understanding, manifested in behaviours and language. This was defined by a senior partner in the following way: 'Being technically excellent, setting oneself very high standards, being ethically concerned to do the right job for the client. And in addition to have a deep business understanding and business rapport.' The key here was to have complementary business and technical skills with quality and ethical standards: 'If you can't deal with that combination and the dilemmas that it creates, then you should not be in this business' (Senior Partner). This kind of thinking pervaded the general approach to working, as many of the partners and leaders of the network had grown up within C&L prior to the formation of CLE and still had strong links into the London hub.

Pharma network culture   At a level more specific to the coordination and integration of customized, human asset-specific exchanges, the pharma network employed a common set of methodologies and understandings. These enabled personalities to interact in a productive way, and for an organization whose prime asset was people, this was vital to their business. As a consultant put it: 'What makes us successful at the end of the day is the chemistry between our consultants and between the consultants and the client.' One consultant noted that having the same spirit, working style and relationships led people to be very willing to share ideas with others from different countries.

Increasingly the challenge was to bring together people from different countries and different service lines who might not know each other.

This made it all the more important that there was a common frame of reference and familiarity with common methods. To this end they had a corporate language and a common view of understanding clients, called a client understanding framework which was instilled into people: 'So it is a way of looking at and developing a shared under-standing of a client's business and their needs' (Senior Partner). This aim was supported by a common IT architecture and Lotus Notes throughout the organization. They also set up their own conference venues, such as the pharmaceutical university which imparted organi-zational glue and current knowledge about specialist areas. On a more informal level, pharma consultants spoke about the value of having fun together which was reinforced through events such as the university: 'Part of the university next week will be not just the formal presenta-tions but actively encouraging people to enjoy each others' company' (Consultant).

One significant and overt tool employed to safeguard exchanges was that of the guidance notes on cross-border working. These notes were lists of acceptable and unacceptable behaviour, characterized as 'green' and 'red card behaviour' (see Figure 3.3). If someone flouted these rules then it was accepted that they might not be invited on to another assign-ment. However, sanctions were a highly problematic issue as they countermanded the democratic culture of the network, and there were few mechanisms in place to encourage accepted network behaviour outside of informal sanctions. For instance, the pharma network had no penalties for non-compliance by partner firms in the network. The European MCS Board only had the ability to change things through influence and interpersonal interaction; they did not have the power and authority to direct national firms.

Additionally, there was a history of local subcultures which persisted and which detracted from an integrated network. For instance, man-agement consultancy in general had grown out of accountancy and audit firms whose culture reflected the conservatism of some national partner heads, themselves accountants, with a strong risk-adverse cul-ture. This had the effect of causing distinct variations in the sharing of social norms within the pharma network and these social norms became more distant at the periphery, where social ties were weakest.

Pharmaceutical industry culture   At the level of the pharmaceutical industry, all pharma consultants brought with them a prior experience of industry norms and codes of practice. Many consultants had 10–15 years' experience working within the industry before joining C&L. They brought with them the industry's distinctive ways of doing things, its attitudes and norms of behaviour. Additionally, trade and scientific jour-nals and industry newsletters were important features of socialization, supplemented by the pharma network's internal databases, while

THE 'DO's (GREEN CARD BEHAVIOUR)

- **Do consult** always with the pharmaceutical network when pursuing cross-border opportunities – find the most relevant experience and the best people for the job
- **Do agree** and confirm in writing responsibilities and relationships for all the firms/offices involved (lead contractor, subcontractors, etc.)
- **Do plan** the assignment fully at the outset, particularly specification of deliverables from the parties involved
- **Do recognize** the value of **local understanding** plus **global expertise**
- **Do recognize** the **need for trade-offs** to ensure win-win situation for all participating firms
- **Do be** tolerant of **diverse views**
- **Do communicate, communicate, communicate** – keep people informed

THE 'DON'T's (RED CARD BEHAVIOUR)

- **Don't chase** a lead without checking with the appropriate key account person or country contact for the prospective client
- **Don't invade** another country, pursuing leads or doing work, without first consulting with the appropriate pharmaceutical contact
- **Don't assume** that you or your team are the best people for the job
- **Don't be insensitive** to other cultures and points of view
- **Don't disparage colleagues**
- **Don't reinvent** services locally
- **Don't ignore** the financial and billing arrangements – make sure these are agreed as part of the contractual arrangements up front

FIGURE 3.3   *Guidance on cross-border working (internal document, April 1997)*

industry events such as trade shows and conferences served to reinforce these experiences by providing role models, setting standards and exchanging information among participants.

Issues for the pharma network

Despite the overall success of the pharma network in Europe there still remained some unresolved issues in terms of effective and efficient networking. These issues were being actively debated and considered at the time that fieldwork was being carried out for this case study. The key issues resided at the level of the national firm which impacted on individual behaviour. As in the findings of Ove Arup (see Chapter 2 in this volume), motivation to join the network was uneven due to differences between national firms, in for example experience of networking, market structure and skills.

There was a strong perception that national firm requirements often took precedence over opportunities in the marketplace. For instance, firms were known to manage sectors so as to bring about their own success rather than that of the growing European business as a whole. This opportunism could be compounded by secrecy. One consultant experienced poor client account management in his country due to a lack of coordination and knowledge about the account. As he explained: 'I think that the partners want to protect their accounts and they don't share the information.' Naturally there was a degree of ambiguity both for those working within the pharma network and for their national firm. This manifested itself in divided loyalties: 'If I am not working for my partner and I am working for the network in another country, I will lose contact with people who decide my salary increase' (R&D Consultant).

In many respects the feeling was that they were still operating as a national organization rather than a European network. This is a similar situation to that of ABB's organizational paradox of trying to simultaneously manage internal competition and cooperation between subunits (see Chapter 4, Ruigrok et al., this volume). It was also felt that they needed to release and invest more resources, such as in language training. In terms of a more formal operation there were suggestions that there should be a formal European profit and loss (P&L) network. The European P&L would map into the complete team and take away the local requirements, thereby stripping out suboptimal agendas.

In general, differences in exchange conditions, internal capabilities and opportunism had led to a situation in the pharma network where there was a clear distinction between the hub of the network, represented by two or three country offices, and all other national firms on the periphery. As one consultant described it: 'The other countries feel like satellites and not really involved in the network.' The two means employed to discourage opportunistic behaviour had economic implications for national firms. The first was sanctions, then there was a levy (a percentage of turnover paid to a central fund, with additional charges for particular projects and other collective activities). A consultant described how these mechanisms worked: 'The levy is a mechanism for forcing behaviour in offices and also you don't get invited on to the next large job which comes up. So you hit them in the pocket.' This levy was due for reappraisal in terms of its scale and whether profits should be shared. Remuneration and performance measures, as touched on previously, had to reflect these changing roles and were seen as among the key mechanisms which had to be adjusted and changed in order to make the new organizational arrangements work. To this end the ability to monitor performance had to be improved.

There were suggestions that a greater normalization of revenue sharing was required between national firms if the network was to be truly European. This could only be achieved by creating a 'real' European firm and doing away with the national firm. Thus revenue and recognition of people would be decided only at the European level. One consultant felt that informal organizing was adequate for sharing knowledge and methodology, but that greater formalism was required when it came to sharing clients. Another consultant called for a need for a better framework to charge back the costs of fees and move to a system of fixed rates so that costs would not have to be renegotiated each time. In general he pointed to a need for working better together in the network in terms of sharing costs and profits across borders. In terms of differences in maturity at being a network player, the future was described by one senior consultant: 'It is a matter of time and also an issue of will. The individual partners need to be convinced of the necessity of working together.'

Social Controls in the Pharma Network

The effectiveness of integration in the pharma network may be assessed by considering the social controls which govern exchanges between national firms. At the time of this study, national firms were most implicated in the potential effectiveness of the pharma network as it was at this level that most of the unresolved issues lay. Understanding the influence of social controls upon national firms thereby provides a perspective on the network as a whole. However, it is also necessary to consider the individual components of the pharma network in terms of its division into functional subnetworks. Here three subnetworks – partners, consultants and project teams – are the focus. These will be analysed in terms of the social controls (restricting access to exchanges, culture, reputation and collective sanctions) outlined by Jones et al. (1997) which govern the exchanges within them. Finally we will turn to an analysis of the social controls governing the interactions between the leadership of the network and its other components.

Integration of national firms

National firms of the pharma network were independent profit centres which employed consultants primarily on the basis of their perceived market needs. They contributed to the pharma network by providing human resources to lead initiatives and financial resources by way of a levy to fund the infrastructure. They were also under an obligation to develop the pharmaceutical business (win contracts) in a way which aided the greater good of the network. National firms engaged in exchanges within the network by releasing resources for projects, sharing knowledge, information and clients; by the selection and coordination of multinational, multidisciplinary project members and promoting products and services to clients. Given the autonomy of national firms, we have shown how there was a temptation toward opportunism which threatened the safeguarding of exchanges. The social mechanisms responsible for guiding the cooperation and commitment of national firms were network culture, reputation and collective sanctions.

The large demand for consultancy services by the pharmaceutical industry ensured that the network was both lucrative and expanding. The success of the pharma industry programme helped to reinforce and develop the culture within the network. Since the pharma network's informal beginnings, it had worked to create widely shared assumptions and values, as Ouchi (1980: 138) has noted: 'common values and beliefs provide the harmony of interests that erase the possibility of opportunistic behaviour'. The code of conduct for cross-border working was one of the results of this effort. The network had also established routines for informal exchanges in the form of network meetings and events such as the pharma university. It was the structure of network members' social interactions which influenced the formation of a shared vision (Krackhardt, 1990). To aid formal and informal contact there was a database with all consultants' CVs, as well as a booklet issued to all consultants with the names and contact numbers of all pharma consultants.

Reputation is an important social control in deterring deceptive behaviour because it diffuses knowledge about reliability and skills through a network (Jones et al., 1997). The frequent exchanges and recombinations of consultants on projects meant that information about individuals and firms travelled quickly. Non-cooperation by firms, either in the interface with the client or with the network, would expose them to collective sanctions by other firms. Those firms which gained a good reputation for cooperation and skills would find that they were called on more often in multinational teams. It was particularly important to maintain a reputation with the client firm, for as clients became increasingly international, consultants' reputations spread across boundaries within the client firm to their other country subunits. Each national firm in pharma had to maintain the integrity of the network to ensure confidence in future assignments.

Despite a well developed culture and emphasis on reputation, we found evidence of opportunistic and deceptive behaviour (see pages 100–1) which impeded the development and integration of the network. The realities of different firm contexts meant opportunistic rewards often outweighed the benefits to be derived from a network culture. Another explanation for this may have been the few collective sanctions open to consultants of the pharma network, other than exclusion from lucrative assignments. No other recourse was open to the national firms which were independent profit centres. The available collective sanctions may have failed because they did not increase the costs of opportunism. In the first instance, transgressions were not always detectable. For example, it is not easy to know how thoroughly a firm consulted with the network when looking for resources for project teams. Secondly, if a firm had sunk few costs in people or IT, then it did not rely on large scale collaborative projects to recover that investment.

There had also been disincentives for cooperation, due to bad past experiences, for instance, where the fee scales of collaborating firms had caused embarrassment with the client, the project had not been profitable, or the other firm's consultant lacked expected skills. There were also other more subtle social forces which came into play and conditioned the willingness to cooperate. These were the more diffuse impressions that some national firms had of themselves as being on the periphery of the network. For instance, where some firms were perceived as having a critical mass of resources, smaller firms felt unequal in exchange relationships. Trust would not be elicited from national firms if they felt they were being exposed to high risk (Jarillo, 1988). Trustful behaviour could only be generated by showing that the firm would be worse off if it behaved opportunistically.

Finally, for those firms who did feel on the periphery of the network, there were few incentives to be a network player. The only mandatory investment required of firms was a small levy as a percentage of gross profits. This was possibly too minimal to encourage firms to seek a return on their investment.

Given the independent financial status of national firms, an alternative market focus from the pharma network, small opportunism costs, disincentives, social distance from other firms and few incentives for cooperative behaviour, the then available form of collective sanction did not prevent unacceptable behaviour. Further, it would seem that in the absence of well-developed collective sanctions, the force of culture and reputation were not enough to safeguard exchanges.

Integration of partners

The country leader or partner subnetwork was where the locus of power resided within the pharma network. In its management role it was the set of exchanges out of which the current and future coordination mechanisms were derived. The partners were the source of macro-network developments and initiatives. Traditionally, country leaders met to secure advantages for their firm, but over time the aim of the pharma network had been to give them responsibility at a European level, in this way encouraging European thinking first and country second. Critically, this subnetwork was responsible for the well-being, performance and reputation of the pharma network as a whole. These people had the longest experience of networking, some having been instrumental in the establishment of the pharma network. They also had the greatest expertise and experience in the pharmaceuticals sector.

The social controls which were particularly salient for, and successful in, safeguarding and coordinating exchanges within the partner sub-network, were restricted access, macroculture and reputation. The criteria for membership had a status-maximizing effect (Podolny, 1993) which created the conditions for restricted access to exchanges within the group. The status of members was based upon their seniority, expertise and reputations in consulting and leadership. Thus, reputation was also fundamentally intertwined with the status maximization strategy of restricting access to exchanges. The reliability, character and skills of a partner are going to be especially important during the establishment of a network, when novelty creates conditions of uncertainty. It would seem that reputation, in the form of a track record, and innovative capability, will also be critical as the pharma network enters a new stage of development. This new stage was set in the context of the merger with Price Waterhouse, which adds another dimension of uncertainty to the exchanges.

Finally, macroculture was a strong social bond in partner exchanges as the breadth of experience at different levels of the organization was very high in this group. We have indicated how all consultants had been socialized into the general C&L ethos which provided shared values and norms around professionalism in consulting. Additionally, their industry experience provided consultants with a shared language, standards and rules of conduct. This has been particularly influential in establishing the network where they attempted to mirror industry practices. Most importantly, as 'shapers' of the pharmaceutical network, they set the parameters for a network culture in which codes of behaviour and work routines were established, informal links encouraged and boundary-spanning roles with clients clarified.

This group were able to manage both strong and weak ties (Granovettter, 1982). Strong ties were important for the coherence of the partner network in their leadership role as policy makers and standard setters, while weak ties were necessary for interfacing with the rest of the network in consultancy and development roles. Partners may also be seen to have had boundary-spanning roles between subnetworks and with clients. It was these multiple roles and tasks in the context of a rapidly changing industry environment which prevented the management group becoming an inward-looking clique.

Integration of consultants

Consultants belonged to at least one and possibly as many as three specialist groups. These groups strengthened the knowledge base of the network. The specialist subnetworks were a forum for developing the skills of consultants and new methodologies for service delivery and for critically examining developments in their field. Specialist subnetworks had to be very forward thinking as the pharmaceutical sector was changing rapidly. Many of the members of the specialist groups had academic and professional training and so brought a critical mass of resource for development. The specialist group was a non-fee-earning exchange which was funded for its future resource potential to the pharma network. This made it a competing activity for time-constrained consultants. Members therefore had to believe that it would provide very positive outputs in terms of future resources. The key social mechanisms which facilitated within-group contacts were restricting access, network and industry culture and reputation.

The coordination of new and existing knowledge was facilitated by the creation of specialist groups through relational contracting via expertise. Specialist groups restricted exchanges and created identification between parties, they lowered the coordination costs of highly technical information and knowledge, and reduced opportunism by creating reciprocal exchanges. These subgroups were guided by industry-specific assumptions and values, gained from their professional knowledge and shared experiences. Many of these people had worked together on projects and so had strong relationships. As an original member and key leader of the pharma network saw it: 'The network essentially evolves from a clique – very often it is a core of individuals who know and like one another, who have shared experiences. By building up the social structure this draws people in, it is the social pull.' Thus quite a lot of networking occurred informally when people chatted out of hours and gossiped. Whereas the industry culture largely guided the content of their exchanges, the pharma network culture guided the conduct of exchanges, in terms of how information and communication protocols were shared.

The reputation of specialist group members was transparent from previous working experiences or the knowledge database. The specialist group was a forum for demonstrating knowledge and expertise and so membership of this group could enhance or expose reputations. There was a danger of the specialist subgroups being too restricted and self-involved, thereby leading to the formation of cliques. This was more likely to occur where the same group members worked together on specialist projects. The creation of multidisciplinary teams was required to avert this trend. However, for many groups their lack of development and/or time pressures meant they were far from overembedded

(Granovetter, 1992) to the extent that inward-looking cliques were formed.

Integration of project teams

Project teams were temporary groupings created for a specific task and made possible by the cooperation of national firms. The project teams were characterized by task complexity under intense time pressure (Jones et al., 1997). They were comprised of a number of specialized inputs resulting in behavioural interdependence requiring coordination. In addition, staff were usually under enormous time pressures to complete, requiring parallel working patterns, coordination through meetings and group work. As a consultant explained:

> we inceasingly look to involve as many staff areas as we can in a project team because the only way we can really justify our complex organization, high prices and fee rates to our clients, is if we can genuinely tackle the more complex problems which require multiple, multidisciplinary inputs.

The complexity of coordinating exchanges was likely to relate to the size of group, duration of project and task requirements. Where the project was small and/or specialized, the social mechanisms would operate in a similar way to the specialist groups. Where the project brief was large and complex, cooperation between multidisciplinary group members was more challenging. As expertise and experience are the focus of the exchange, the guiding social mechanisms were network culture and reputation.

The pharma culture was an important feature in creating strong ties through shared codes of working, both within the group and in boundary-spanning activities. Also, the accepted informal socializing enabled people to get to know each other, to estimate character and develop trust. In this way the reputations of individuals were confirmed or developed on the job. Reputation was also key for project selection and in most cases the individuals were personally known to the lead consultant. The more that network members worked on projects with different people, the more opportunity for their reputation to be dispersed throughout the network.

Reputation also had the effect of creating disharmony in the network where some groups were characterized as behaving badly, for example in high charge-out rates. The effects could be long term, leading to stereotyping of some country firms by others. In general it took time to build up a good reputation but required only one bad experience to be labelled with a bad reputation.

The diversity and frequency of large projects, and the unstructured process of team building, meant that cliques did not form, as network members were constantly recombining in different ways. The multidisciplinary team was therefore important in creating loose ties and diffusing information, knowledge and learning throughout the pharma network.

Leadership and social controls

The partner subnetwork interfaced with consultants by leading developments in services, and with project teams as leaders with expertise, or in coordinator roles. The social controls which guided exchanges between partners and other groups were restricted access to exchanges, macroculture, reputation and collective sanctions. Partners interfaced with not more than two or three specialist groups and mostly only with one. This form of relational contracting restricted access because partners worked with fewer parties more often. Thus the interaction frequency was increased, which reduced variance in skills, expectations and goals that parties bring to the exchange (Jones et al., 1997). Furthermore, partners would often interact with the same personnel, but in different combinations on projects.

Partners were pivotal in the diffusion of macroculture to the wider pharma network as they moved between groupings. In their exchanges with specialist subnetworks and project teams they imparted assumptions and values and contributed professional knowledge and expertise. In addition, partners created the mechanisms for the socialization of the wider pharma network, through funding HR development programmes, knowledge management systems and setting targets for performance. If the pharma network was to flourish, then it was crucial for partners to have the respect of the wider network and here the role of reputation was vital. The standing of partners within the pharmaceutical industry and their competencies within the network reduced uncertainty on projects by giving confidence to other members. It encouraged cooperation on projects because consultants relied on leaders to manage the client and sell the work of the team. Similarly, with the specialist subnetworks, partners often led the group in terms of new initiatives and developing methodologies, thereby acting as a valuable resource.

The use of collective sanctions by partners was rarely enforced but theoretically could involve ostracism of consultants and informal and formal feedback into their personal development reviews. The accepted codes for behaviour were very explicit, as in the guidance on cross-border working, for which there was the possibility of temporary exclusion from projects.

But there was no evidence from our fieldwork that sanctions had been enforced. Even more problematic was the use of collective sanctions at the interface with national firms where the lead partner may not be a part of the pharma network. Where partners of national firms were a part of the pharma network, exclusion from projects would increase the costs of opportunism but may not have outweighed the benefits, particularly if that firm had a very national outlook. Where the partners of national firms were not pharma members, then exclusion may not have seemed very onerous as they would have priority clients in other sectors. Additionally, as reward and assessment of consultants were carried out at the firm level, unless they belonged to a large pharma group, their appraisal would not be conducted by a senior pharma member. Thus collective sanctions had relatively little impact on behaviour, particularly where the consultant's employer was not a member of the pharma network and where individual consultants made up a very small group within that firm.

The Future for the Pharma Network

The pharma network was ahead of the C&L partnership in networking terms and so was facing pace limits in its development. However, the way the pharma network invested internally was seen as an area open to revision: for example, how cost and profit centres allocate and how costs and profits are shared across borders. There was a perceived need for additional investment in practical development jobs, client accounts and business and human resource development. Greater communication was also required, such as easier accessing to video-conferencing and voice mail. As one consultant expressed it: 'The one request I would make to the partnership is to expect to fund this kind of thing. Also maintain patience with the fact that it may take some time before you see the results. It may also be that the results are not quantifiable.'

One significant issue repeated in many interviews was that of the size of the network. This was also found to be a critical issue for the Rabobank Group in developing internal networks (see Chapter 5, van Wijk and van den Bosch, this volume) At the time of this study, the pharma network had around 200 people and was growing, which led some consultants to question the optimal size that informal allegiance could be sustained. This did not concern other participants, who suggested splitting the network if it became too unwieldy. One suggestion was in terms of specialization in functional areas, for example, R&D, marketing, manufacturing. There was also resistance from some participants to the idea of more rules to govern a growing network. As one consultant explained: 'I think one of the strengths of the way in which we behave is that our bureaucratic rules, as far as they exist at all, do not hamper us in our behaviour with our clients, which is a strong point with our client.' Certainly as size increased a greater number of social controls would need to be employed. For instance, culture was a very strong coordinator of exchanges but its utility was diminished in the face of the greater complexity brought about by size.

It was well recognized by the management of the pharma network that their model of cooperation overlaying an existing federal structure had reached its limits. As a consultant described it: 'Putting coordination mechanisms over a national structure is like building on shifting sands.' It was now accepted that pharma needed to make a significant change from a federal structure to a more integrated global business. This coincided with the thinking within C&L (UK) and so during 1997 there had been a firmwide programme to this effect. There was a lot of complexity in integrating national businesses and the aim was to shift the management power from national heads to people with international roles. This would mean combining business responsibilities with control of resources.

Most interviewees felt the drive for globalization was going to be a key change in future developments. This mirrored developments in the competitive environment, characterized by merger activity and internationalization, technological change and changes in national health care policy across many European countries. A specialist in technology transfer reported: 'What we are doing today will be totally irrelevant in 12 months' time. And I see us as being at the forefront of developing the new thinking.' This has implications both for the calibre of consultant required and for developing people capabilities. The merger with Price Waterhouse will accelerate this trend. The strength of the European base was seen as an advantage here. In the near future it will be necessary to restructure on a theatre basis, that is, a large geographical region or collection of geographies.

Discussion

The social mechanisms used in different parts of the network varied but there was also some consistency. For instance, the network as a whole used reputation as a governance mechanism to safeguard exchanges. Similarly, all parts of the network used cultural controls to coordinate exchanges, although the emphasis on the content of these varied slightly: partners seemed to rely on all three components of the macroculture: corporate, pharma network and pharmaceutical industry; national firms were driven to cooperate via network cultural controls, while the consultants and project teams were governed by cultural controls of both the network and pharmaceutical industry (see Figure 3.4). Collective sanctions had the least impact, being a social control which operated only at the level of possibility.

The different types of social mechanism within and between subnetworks gives insights into the interaction effects of social mechanisms. In this section we explore some of the more important interaction effects, discuss how social controls can provide resources and be a basis of competitive advantage for firms.

Social mechanisms of control	SUBNETWORKS			
	NATIONAL FIRMS	PARTNERS	CONSULTANTS	PROJECT TEAMS
Restricted access: Relational			✓	
Status maximizing		✓ ✓		
Macroculture Corporate		✓ ✓		
Network culture	✓	✓ ✓	✓ ✓	✓ ✓
Pharma industry		✓ ✓	✓	✓
Collective sanctions				
Reputation	✓	✓ ✓	✓	✓ ✓

Key: ✓ utilization of social controls ✓✓ strong utilization of social controls

FIGURE 3.4 *Social mechanisms employed in different parts of the pharma network (adapted from Jones et al., 1997)*

Interaction effects of social mechanisms

According to Granovetter (1985), when economic relations develop within a social atmosphere, the possibility of opportunism is reduced and the need for elaborate mechanisms of governance disappears. However, the social mechanisms which are used are both potent and complex in their interaction. This case of the pharmaceutical network of Coopers & Lybrand Europe shows social controls being used both deliberately, as a part of the policy framework, and implicitly, arising from the embedded set of relationships which make up the network. There are three ways in which social mechanisms may be seen to inter-act: by reinforcing, substituting and undermining one another (Jones et al., 1997).

Reinforcing effects of social mechanisms Social mechanisms may rein-force each other through their congruency (Jones et al., 1997) because the effect of implementing one social mechanism creates the basis for another. For instance, the reputation of partners within the pharma net-work was very important for their within-group interactions as well as interacting with the wider network. It was the very reputation of part-ners, that is, their influence, which formed part of the culture of the network and set the standards for ways of working internally and with clients. In this way reputation was inseparable from cultural aspects of control and the two effects reinforced each other. Similarly, restricting access to exchanges enhanced knowledge about individuals, thereby providing an estimation of their character and trustworthiness. Reputations of group members were fashioned out of restricted exchanges, which in turn increased the identification with the group, making them socially reinforcing.

Substitution effects   The substitution of one social control for another may occur where their roles in either safeguarding or coordinating exchanges are interchangeable. For instance, both reputation and collective sanctions safeguarded exchanges between group members. It is possible that in the absence of agreed-upon collective sanctions, the embarrassment of a poor reputation will serve as an adequate deterrent to opportunistic behaviour. This may explain the lack of collective sanctions to coordinate specialist and project groups because they were based upon consultants' experience, interests, skills and, ultimately, reputations. It must also be noted that small groups made the visibility of members' actions greater and hence increased the likelihood that deceptive behaviour would be detected.

Similarly, restricted access and culture both served to coordinate exchanges between members and may substitute for one another. While a network remains within a certain size, there may not be any necessity to restrict access between members because it is contained enough to be governed by cultural norms. The way in which national firms of the pharma network coordinated with each other raises questions of restricting access as the network grows larger. Thus for the purposes of winning and delivering assignments, it may be necessary in the future to divide the network up along further specialist or geographic lines.

Thus, reputation may substitute for collective sanctions in safeguarding, and culture may substitute for restricting access in coordinating exchanges, where the network size is not too great. These substitutions do not work in reverse because in the case of collective sanctions they implicitly give group members a bad reputation. In other words, one can't have collective sanctions without evoking reputation but it is entirely possible to utilize reputation (that is, the fear of a bad reputation) without collective sanctions. Restricted access alone will not coordinate exchanges without a shared understanding about norms and ways of working. For instance, a contained group which does not get on socially will not share information or cooperate and hence will underperform.

Undermining effects of social mechanisms   In the same way that social mechanisms may work to reinforce one another, so they can act to undermine relationships. The reinforcing effect of reputation and culture can have detrimental outcomes when they are incongruous. For example, were a partner's reputation to become tarnished, say through poor client management or withholding business information, this would undermine the cultural basis of the network by leading network members to regard the culture of professionalism and knowledge sharing with cynicism.

Undermining effects were evidenced in the lack of sanctions for opportunistic behaviour. The limited repertoire of collective sanctions open to the pharma network had few financial consequences. Further, the financial consequences of governance must be aligned with the expectations of the network. Where national firms have responsibility for their own profits, then they want to see rewards accruing from their own network solidarity as much as they would wish transgressors to be punished. If there is no profit sharing from collective network activities then activities at the firm level are going to take precedence over network activities. In other words, national firms resort to myopic behaviour (Loewenstein and Elster, 1992).

It would seem from the analysis of the pharma network that its success can be explained as a result of its highly developed social relations, based upon a strong culture, well defined subnetworks and leadership of good repute. Where the pharma network displayed non-cooperative behaviour was at the level of the national firms, which demonstrates that network governance, particularly for large size, may not be wholly successful when based purely on social mechanisms of control. Where there is a conflict between network activities and firm level activities then it may be necessary to introduce principles of fair division from collective effort, or more formal mechanisms of accountability and rules (Lindenberg, 1997).

Social controls as resources and competitive advantage

Network governance may provide organizational resources, as the three dimensions of social capital identified by Nahapiet and Ghoshal (1998) have shown. Applied to the pharma network, the structural dimension may be seen in the advantageous position of partners within the network. Social capital was gained by experience and reputation, which enabled them not only to access information and resources but also to facilitate the diffusion of knowledge throughout the network, thereby in turn acting as a resource. The relational dimension is captured in the relationships built up over the years within the pharma network. The resultant generation of trust between consultants enabled efficient working relationships, particularly in the intensive environment of project groups. The cognitive dimension is apparent in the culture of the pharma network which provided a mindset for consultants, governing their expectations and working behaviour.

In general it has been realized that self-enforcing mechanisms or social controls are more effective than third party enforcement mechanisms (Dyer and Singh, 1998). In their work on strategic alliances, Dyer and Singh (1998: 670–671) give four reasons for the effectiveness of social controls: contracting costs are avoided because the trust between parties means that not every detail in the contract has to be specified. Related to this, contracts fail to anticipate all forms of cheating. Secondly, the monitoring costs of the exchange are lower because there is no need to invest in costly monitoring mechanisms to ensure contract fulfilment. Thirdly, lower costs are associated with complex adaptation, thereby allowing exchange parties to adjust to agreements on the hoof in response to unforeseen market changes. Finally, self-enforcing mechanisms are not subject to the time limitations of contracts.

Dyer and Singh (1998) develop the work on the returns from relational organizing by identifying six mechanisms that preserve relational rents under conditions of self-enforcing contracts. The first, causal ambiguity, is where the development of goodwill and trust is a complex and situation-specific process which cannot be copied. We have seen that in the pharma network goodwill and trust arose out of the 'social pull' between consultants, derived from complex and long term interactions in the context of a shared macroculture.

The second is time compression diseconomies, whereby complex social relations governing exchanges take time to develop and cannot be bought or sold in the marketplace. It will therefore take time for some national firms in the pharma network to develop the necessary trust in this set of relationships. An emphasis on long term relationships is essential to the development of trust, because it makes it clear that the relationship itself is considered valuable (Jarillo, 1988). But once established, trust becomes an intangible asset underpinning network exchanges.

The third mechanism, interorganizational asset interconnectedness, occurs when initial relation-specific investments, such as the joint development of specialist methodologies in the pharma network, create conditions that invite subsequent specialized investments, such as training in methodology delivery, that are economically viable.

Fourthly, partner scarcity refers to the rarity of finding partners with complementary strategic resources and relational capability. For instance, partners in another network may lack relational capability or the relation building skills and process skills necessary to employ effective governance mechanisms.

Fifthly, resource indivisibility refers to the long term relationships which partners and consultants develop and the dedicated linkages, such as skill transfer and skill complementarities, that enhance the benefits from engaging in the joint relationship. This co-evolution of capabilities is not necessarily transferable to another firm.

Finally, there is the institutional environment as a whole, which is socially complex and therefore difficult to replicate with the necessary informal rules controlling opportunism and encouraging cooperative behaviour. The institutional environment of the pharma network was provided by MCS within CLE, which supplied the necessary impetus and marshalling of resources for the formation of networks. This environment also supplied the cultural signals for behavioural norms and routines.

There are also costs, however, in building a network like the European pharma network, and in motivating individuals' cooperative behaviour. In the first instance there are time costs to enable social mechanisms to emerge and develop. The network was here reliant upon an existing critical mass of leaders with networking skills to diffuse new ways of working. There were also resource implications in terms of developing human resources and creating devices for cultural homogeneity. Additionally, resources may be required to develop an incentive system where there is diminished motivation to cooperate when opportunism costs are low. Sharing mechanisms have to be perceived as fair (Jarillo, 1988). Further, there are the costs of success, for as the network grows, more formal mechanisms may need to be introduced to manage complexity. Thus management time will be required to develop formal mechanisms which complement and extend the governance power of the existing social controls. Finally, the fluidity and changing nature of the network requires constant adjustment and customization, with inherent development costs.

There are real competitive advantages to be gained from adopting relational and network forms of organizing. Relational governance lowers the costs of monitoring and is flexible whilst achieving gains in scale and core competencies. Relational rents are preserved due to the non-imitability of complex and time-related social structures which provide a virtuous cycle of investment and complementarities. The social controls employed by relational forms generate social capital (Nahapiet and Ghoshal, 1998) for organizations, providing process gains in coordination and cooperation. Given the right mix of social controls and the investment of time in relationships, the combination of assets and returns are non-imitable by other firms, thereby providing a unique competitive advantage.

Conclusion

The development of the pharma network was one of emerging formalization of coordination mechanisms and increasing complexity in scale and scope. From its origins as an informal network of independent national firms, the pharma network may be seen to have developed in terms of the character of its coordination mechanisms. During its informal stages, the pharma network relied upon a few social mechanisms of control to coordinate a European-wide network. This was based on intangible assets such as trust and the commitment of pharma professionals. Since its formalization in 1996, the pace of change increased within the pharma network with the development of IT, culture, methodologies for service delivery and the specialist subnetworks.

The success of the network in terms of growth and revenues demonstrated the feasibility of operating on a global basis, but it also led to a more complex situation which suggests different modes of coordination and resourcing. On the one hand there was a wide variation between national firms in their willingness to operate as a network. On the other, there was evidence of increasing expectations by members in terms of resourcing the network. The increasing size of the network may call for further subdivisions and formalization of exchanges. It would seem that the basis for future coordination mechanisms will be more in terms of tangible assets, such as investment by national firms in the network and in incentive systems for cooperation. Social mechanisms of control may need to be supplemented by more formal coordination mechanisms in terms of accountability and rules for behaviour.

The analysis of social mechanisms of control in the governance of the pharmaceutical network of Coopers & Lybrand Europe throws up further and deeper avenues of research enquiry. On the specifics of social controls is the question of the 'elasticity' of social norms, or their robustness in the face of increasing group size. At which point in the growth of the network are cultural controls no longer effective on their own as a coordination mechanism? For instance, in relation to restricting access to exchanges, at which point is it then necessary to subdivide the network, for example along geographical, functional or knowledge-based lines? Is there a time limit on restricted access to small groups, after which they become 'stale' and lose their capacity to innovate? More precise empirical research is needed into the whole area of network size and related contingent factors, such as the purpose and function of the network, the developmental stage of the network and its complexity.

Another crucial area for research is the role of reward and recognition in the governance of relational exchanges. In what way might reward and recognition provide complementary effects as a positive social control to balance the negativity of collective sanctions? One example of how this might work is provided by Guia and Camison (1998), who show how national firms pool the factors they own or use in their activities, and where the value of the capital and work pooled by each firm is not homogeneous a special incentive system is required. Each individual then receives a share of the common output corresponding to their contribution. This might suit the collective framework of the pharma network.

Similarly, what might be the effects of the introduction of formal coordination mechanisms, such as rules and procedures, into a previously relational contract? How far can collective costs be increased and apportioned fairly? How for instance might the introduction of collective profit and loss influence the myopia of national firms in the pharma network?

The role of individual motivations within the network is also an important but under-researched area. For instance the role of altruism and morals in governing behaviour is well understood at the individual level but little explored in the context of networking. Siltkin and Roth (1993: 368) maintain that trusting relationships are rooted in congruence between the individual's values and the values of the organization. This has important implications for criteria by which members are accepted into the network.

The implications for organizations in adopting social controls suggest at least four key issues. First, relational organizing has sunk costs in investment in time and relationships. The smooth and efficient working of a network may only be realized in the medium to long term. There are also development costs in human resources and in the cultural rules and norms which must be owned by individuals. Secondly, it is particularly important that a strong leadership team guides and directs the development of the network. Thirdly, organizations should be cautious in adopting social controls on at least two accounts: social controls must be congruent with one another and they should be appropriate for the size and complexity of the network. Related to this last point is the final issue of the appropriate mix of control mechanisms to ensure the coordination and safeguarding of exchanges. As the network evolves, it may be appropriate to consider what other forms of non-relational controls, such as rewards, rules and incentives, would be complementary to the relational foundation of the network.

Notes

We acknowledge the support of the UK Economic and Social Research Council, PricewaterhouseCoopers and the Consortium members of the Centre for Creativity Strategy and Change. Our thanks go to Paul Batchelor, Chris David, Bente Lowendahl and David Shaw, for very helpful comments on earlier versions of this work, as well as the participants in this study who gave so generously of their time.

4

ABB: Beyond the Global Matrix towards the Network Multidivisional Organization

Winfried Ruigrok, Leona Achtenhagen, Mathias Wagner and Johannes Rüegg-Stürm

If there is one European company that over the last ten years has managed to excite management consultants, scholars and business people alike, then it is ABB (ASEA Brown Boveri), the Swiss-Swedish professional engineering group. Repeatedly voted Europe's most respected company, ABB has become a textbook case of success over a short period of time: merging Swedish ASEA and Swiss Brown Boveri into one joint entity, reducing the head office role, implementing a global management development policy, and developing a highly effective international organization (cf. Barham and Heimer, 1998: 175ff.).[1] Bartlett and Ghoshal (1993) combined these elements and used ABB as their most prominent case to claim the rise of an organizational form beyond the multidivisional organization. A few years later, Bartlett and Ghoshal analysed ABB's global matrix structure (in place until 1998) as the appropriate form for companies to deal with the 'global–local dilemma' (Bartlett and Ghoshal, 1995b: 470).

The matrix organization had provided a highly successful model of internationalization for many companies over the 1960s and 1970s, and usually represented a *geographical, that is, international, extension of the multidivisional organization*. The main advantages associated with the matrix organization are its parallel reporting systems to geographical *and* product (and possibly functional) managers, allowing for a coordination of diverging internal company interests; its multiple information channels, enhancing the level of intra-company communication; and its overlapping responsibilities, creating a platform within the company for discussion and decision making. The matrix provided multinational firms with a model to deal with uncertain and diverging environments, especially in locally responsive industries.

Companies have applied matrix structures successfully in various kinds of activities, such as the development of new products and services (cf. Larson and Gobeli, 1987; McCollum and Sherman, 1993). However, as a model of *international organizing*, the matrix lost much of its appeal over the 1980s as integrating markets, converging standards and consumer tastes, increasing competition and the shortening of product life cycles forced companies to develop new solutions to manage their products *across* national borders. Peters and Waterman (1982: 49) even saw the matrix as the summit of complicated and ultimately unworkable organizational structures.

ABB's choice for a global matrix structure to manage the newly merged company was therefore far from self-evident. Yet in a widely read article in the *Harvard Business Review,* Bartlett and Ghoshal (1990) suggested that the main problem with 'matrix management' is not so much the need for companies to take into account different product and geographical dimensions, but the fact that 'organizational development has not kept pace (with strategic thinking), and managerial attitudes lag even further behind'. The challenge, they argued, was to focus not on creating the ideal structures, but on 'developing the abilities, behavior, and performance of individual managers' (1990: 145). Rugman and Hodgetts (1995: 250) derived three key criteria for a matrix to work well: *clarity* (how well people understand what they are doing and why they are doing it); *continuity* (the same core objectives and values); and *consistency* (of managers throughout the organization pursuing the same objectives). ABB, it has been implied by many authors, got this balance right and moved beyond the multidivisional organization (Bartlett and Ghoshal, 1993: 24ff.) to develop a 'dancing giant' (Kets de Vries, 1994; Barham and Heimer, 1998).

So more puzzling was the fact that ABB in August 1998 announced that it would reorganize into what appears to resemble a *multidivisional* organization. Dissolving its regional management layer, ABB established seven business segments which included a total of 33 business areas. Is this the end of ABB's acclaimed matrix structure, and has ABB become just like any other multidivisional organization? This chapter analyses the overall organizational transformations during the ten years after the ABB merger as well as its 1998 reorganization by asking the following questions: has ABB really departed from its global matrix structure, and if so, why? and has ABB really reorganized towards a conventional multidivisional organization?

In the summer of 1998, we conducted 25 interviews at different levels of the ABB Group. Seven interviews took place at the international head office and at the Financial Services department of the ABB Group, and 18 interviews were carried out at ABB Switzerland (ABB CH) with managers of the Swiss country holding and managing directors of the various front-line companies of ABB Switzerland. ABB CH is one of ABB's larger country holdings with a very international outlook. The interviews took place just before the August 1998 announcement of ABB's new organizational structure and were aimed at understanding the functioning and weaknesses of the ABB matrix organization. After August 1998, additional communication has taken place with ABB CH on the interpretations that we have drawn.

This chapter is organized as follows. The next section traces the history of the ABB group and the organizational structure that evolved over the ten years after the merger. After that we address the external and internal drivers for ABB's organizational change, and in the following section sketch the three stages of ABB's organizational development over the 1988–1998 period. We then touch upon the process sequencing of these changes, and identify the barriers to change at ABB. After comparing the official reasons for ABB's 1998 reorganization with the impressions that we gathered carrying out our interviews, we identify some management issues yet to be resolved. Finally, we summarize our findings and reflect upon the question as to whether ABB's reorganization reflects a move back to the traditional multidivisional organization.

History, Context and Organizational Structure of ABB

The history of generating and using electricity started in 1866, when Werner von Siemens invented the principle of the self-exciting generator (dynamo). In 1879, Edison developed the incandescent lamp. Around that time, Charles Brown, who was working at Oerlikon Machinery Corporation (Switzerland), and his colleague Walter Boveri started to think about establishing an electrical equipment factory, following the examples set by General Electric (US), AEG and Siemens (Germany) and a company called ASEA (Sweden).

Brown and Boveri founded their own factory called Brown, Boveri & Cie (BBC) in February 1892 with 100 factory workers and 24 office workers (Steigmeier, 1991: 4). From the very beginning, BBC had a strong export orientation and it gained a foothold in most leading European industrial countries before World War I. After 1945, new business areas, such as electronics and nuclear power, were opened up. In 1987, BBC listed 159 group companies on all five continents and employed about

100,000 people around the world (Catrina, 1991). At that time, BBC also showed low performance rates as a result of high costs, low levels of innovation and a weakness in developing new markets.

Swedish ASEA had been in a similar position in the early 1980s. Percy Barnevik had taken it upon himself to reorganize ASEA into 350 profit centres and to decentralize responsibilities. The profit centre managers were allowed to act highly autonomously, as long as they produced profits. Barnevik's attempts had been very successful and ASEA had subsequently begun to expand into the US.

When ASEA and BBC entered talks in 1987, both parties recognized the potential mutual benefits. ASEA contributed superior current profit performance, sophisticated management controls and marketing aggressiveness, while BBC brought a strong order book and high technical expertise. ASEA operated in geographic areas and in product spheres that on the whole complemented rather than competed with those of BBC, even though there were some areas, such as power transmission, where there was a significant overlap (Catrina, 1991).

On 1 January 1988, both companies transferred their activities to the newly founded ABB ASEA Brown Boveri Ltd. ABB became the world's largest producer of engineering products and services and a leading supplier of process automation systems, robotics, high-speed locomotives, and environmental and pollution control equipment. The ASEA Holding (former ASEA) and the BBC Holding (former BBC) each possesses 50 per cent of the ABB ASEA Brown Boveri Ltd. (ABB Group) shares. The two parent companies remained independent corporations and maintain their national identities as Swiss and Swedish companies.

ABB now faced the challenge of building one collectivity out of two companies from different countries that had long regarded each other as rivals. Spurred by the expectation that restructuring and post-merger integration efforts would initially hamper performance, Barnevik continued the pattern of reorganizations carried out at ASEA and set out the principles of decentralization of responsibilities and individual accountability:

> The only way to structure a complex, global organization is to make it as simple and local as possible . . . Our managers need well-defined sets of responsibilities, clear accountability, and maximum degree of freedom to execute . . . Our operations are divided into nearly 1,100 companies with an average of 200 people. These companies are divided into 3,500 profit centers with an average of 50 employees . . . We are fervent believers in decentralization. When we structure local operations, we always push to create separate legal entities. Separate companies allow you to create *real* balance sheets with *real* responsibility for cash flow and dividends.(Percy Barnevik in Taylor, 1991: 99, emphasis added)

It took ABB only two months to develop the main features of the new organization. Since both ASEA and BBC had had a matrix organization prior to their merger, the matrix structure was a logical choice for the new company as well. The matrix structure enabled ABB to 'think global, act local' – which was more than just a slogan to ABB. Dealing with large public and private customers, ABB had to negotiate at a local level, strike compromises on issues such as local content, while being able to draw components and services from a large and efficient global organization in the background. The ABB matrix was refined in 1993 and again slightly in 1996, before the new structure was announced in 1998. The details of these stages are discussed later in this chapter.

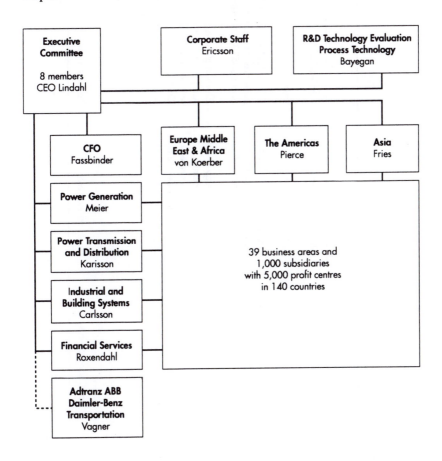

FIGURE 4.1   *Organizational chart of the ABB Group (1997)*

Table 4.1 ABB compared with its main competitors (1997)

Competitors	ABB	Siemens	GE	Mitsubishi Group
HQ	Zürich-Oerlikon/CH	Munich/Germany	Fairfield/USA	Tokyo, Japan
Number of employees	Group: 215,000	Group: 386,000	Group: 276,000	Group: 322,000
Consolidated revenues	Group: US$31,300 million; power related business: about US$29,500 million	Group: US$64,750 million; power related business: about US$20,500 million	Group: US$90,800 million; power related business: about US$23,300 million	Group: US$166,300 million; power related business: about US$28,000 million
Strategy	Focus on large key plant projects; efforts towards a solution provider; back-end vertical integration strategy; expansion strategy	Innovation strategy at high-end megawatt plants; product services strategy; International presence by acquisitions	Efforts in globalization (esp. in Asia) by acquisitions; product services strategy; TQM strategy (Six Sigma Quality programme); streamlining; portfolio of innovative services and products; strategy aims to be the No. 1, 2 or 3 in each business area	Expansion strategy by acquisitions; marketing strategy that focuses on strengthening customer relationships and immediate response to the market; streamlining its investments into areas that have the highest revenue-generating potential over the long term
Area of competition	Plant, components	Plant, components	Plant, components	Plant, components

Table 4.1 cont.

Competitors	ABB	Siemens	GE	Mitsubishi Group
In-house trends	Towards 'network multidivisional'; focus on product services	Restructuring (10-point programme to enhance profitability), cost problems, focus on (financial) services; efforts towards an integrative problem solver (general contractor)	Six Sigma Quality Initiative, leadership programme; pushing service activities	Efforts toward an integrative product line; trend towards a solution provider; create new businesses (e.g. product services); further investments in Asia and emerging markets
Organizational structure	Global matrix structure	M-form	(Financial) holding structure	Holding structure
Relative competitiveness	Medium; since 1996 declining revenues, profits and productivity; goal is to regain dominant position in this industry as in the beginning of the 1990s.	Low; lagging performance; profit declined to US$150 million in 1997; strong turnaround efforts	High; steadily increasing revenues and profits; Six Sigma Quality projects achieved US$94 million in savings	Medium/high; revenues and profit have increased between 1996 and 1998

Sources: Siemens Internet pages (1998); Siemens Annual Report 1997; General Electric Annual Report 1997; Mitsubishi Group Annual Report (1998); Merrill Lynch (1998)

ABB Switzerland (ABB CH), where most interviews were conducted, is one of the 140 national holding organizations of the ABB Group. The former BBC head office location was transformed into today's ABB CH and in the overall ABB Group, ABB CH plays an important role. ABB CH is one of the largest national ABB organizations and is well known for its advanced research and development and its highly skilled workforce. ABB CH is highly interconnected with ABB companies around the world, as indicated by its high degree of exports (80 per cent). It owns companies in all business segments as well as in financial services. With its line of products and services, ABB CH covers the entire power distribution spectrum from the generating plant to the wall socket. It also provides products and systems for applications in industry and transportation. At the end of 1997, ABB CH had 25 companies and employed about 12,000 people (ABB Switzerland, 1997).

ABB's major competitors are three other global players: Siemens, Mitsubishi, and General Electric (cf. Table 4.1). General Electric has been another highly admired company, led by another admired CEO (Jack Welch), which for many years has clearly outperformed ABB and which is expecting a continued profitable growth over the coming years. Recently, Siemens has started a 10-point programme in order to achieve a turnaround in its power division. Mitsubishi Group has also invested a lot in its power-related business activities. In addition, Hitachi and Toshiba – previous system providers – offer specialized components and single technologies or services. If one takes into account ABB's emerging activities in financial services (see below), investment banks can also be viewed as competitors. Finally, ABB's activities in the field of services and maintenance have produced a new type of competition (for example, privatized plant operating companies).

Drivers for Change at ABB

The basis of both ASEA's restructuring over the early 1980s and BBC's willingness to merge with its former arch-rival was a company crisis, leading to slowing growth and performance rates. Performance measurement remained an important tool at ABB and has been guiding change ever since, exposing problems at the business segment and country level. At the same time, as will be shown below, this emphasis on internal accounting at times led to suboptimal solutions.

Over the 1990s, there has been a worldwide trend towards deregulation and privatization in power supply markets, with formerly government-controlled utility companies developing into commercially thinking market partners. These 'new' customers now demanded complete turnkey plants with a full range of services, including financial services, operations, and maintenance. This raised the level of complexity of the business, making it more important for suppliers to manage in-house and external deliveries effectively, and posed a huge challenge for each firm to manage its internal knowledge effectively. It also implied that local differentiation (and local bargaining) was less important than a supplier's ability to offer a reliable solution at a reasonable price.

As a consequence, the international power generation and transmission industry has gone through a dramatic consolidation process. In 1990, firms such as Hitachi, Westinghouse, AEG and Toshiba were still playing a role as independent end producers. Since then, excess capacity forced Hitachi and Toshiba to leave the business and focus on specialized components; ABB took over Westinghouse's power transmission and distribution divisions in 1990; and in 1996, the rest of the Westinghouse corporation merged with Siemens.

In addition to these external factors, there were a number of internal drivers for change at ABB, *often resulting from the inherent weaknesses of the ABB matrix.* Despite a range of instruments to enhance internal transparency, and despite the numerous efforts to explain the ABB structure, many employees (as well as numerous external partners) still felt that they did not understand the matrix. Moreover, the internal negotiations between the small profit centres were occasionally difficult and frequently resulted in micropolitics.

Content, Scope, and Depth of Organizational Innovations

This section discusses the organizational innovations at ABB over the last ten years in terms of structural, process and cultural changes. They are analysed from their initiation within ABB by giving information about content, scope, and depth of change. The main features are summarized in Table 4.2.

Building the Global Matrix (1988–1993)

Just as he had done at ASEA, Barnevik began decentralizing the operations of most ABB subsidiaries into independent profit centres. The profit centre concept was to enhance internal financial transparency and customer orientation. A key element of the ABB matrix was to make the business area (BA) managers and country managers understand their complementary and different roles. The BA managers were to set the strategic framework, coordinate R&D and production, and monitor quality standards and performance. The country managers were to actively supervise the operating business, to foster local contacts and to

Table 4.2   History of ABB (1988–1998)

Evolution of ABB	Before 1988		1988–1993	1993–1997	1998—
	Pre-merger phase				
	ASEA	BBC			
PHASE DESCRIPTION			Development of global matrix	Global matrix with regional dimensions	'Network Multidivisional'
GENERAL CONDITIONS	• good economic conditions • growing market	• good economic conditions • growing market	• consolidation in industry • tough competition • chances in emerging markets	• deregulation and privatization of utilities • tough competition	• market saturation • declining economic conditions
PERFORMANCE/ INCOME*	• superior performance	• weak performance, but strong position in Europe	• performance affected by post-merger integration (income: US$1,150 million)	• highest income in 1995 (US$2,100 million). Income decreased over time (in 1997 US$850 million)	• in 1998 performance still declining • sales decreasing (in 1998)
SALES	• sales increasing	• sales decreasing	• sales increased up to US$28,750 million	• sales increased up to US$31,260 million	
IN-HOUSE TRENDS	• reorganized by Barnevik early 1980s • rather marketing oriented	• technology oriented • huge units • bureaucracy	• merger was viewed as an opportunity for implementing fundamental change and growth • merger integrating efforts	• growing awareness of insufficient customer and sales orientation • service business identified • region/country oriented	• restructuring efforts towards product/segment orientation
STRATEGIC CONCEPTS	• internationalization efforts (e.g. US market) • strategic marketing concepts	• technology-oriented strategy • product innovation strategy	• streamlining of corporate activities • enhancing regional presence by acquisitions • re-engineering of business processes	• continuing smaller acquisitions • outsourcing • implementation of regions • customer focus concept • focus on Eastern markets	• financial services strategy • solution provider strategy • attempts to achieve critical mass in each business field

Table 4.2 cont.

Evolution of ABB	Before 1988		1988–1993	1993–1997	1998—
	ASEA Pre-merger phase	BBC			
PHASE DESCRIPTION			Development of global matrix	Global matrix with regional dimensions	'Network Multidivisional'
CORPORATE STRUCTURE	• global matrix structure • profit centre structure (350)	• matrix structure, 6 segments and 8 regions/countries	• matrix organization, 6 business segments • profit centre organization • 12-member executive committee	• global matrix organization, 4 business segments • lead country concept • 8-member executive committee	• regional dimension eliminated, business segments dominant line of authority • 8-member executive committee (7 business segments plus CEO)
EMERGENCE OF NETWORK ELEMENTS	• small legal entities • strong decentralization	• focus on technological expertise • first initiatives to horizontal networking among segments	• small legal entities • strong decentralization • international network	• small legal entities • building of cross-boundary networks • stronger focus on people and culture	• networking among segments • horizontal communication
HR MANAGEMENT	• focus on people	• focus on people • high skilled engineers	• decentralization of HR responsibilities	• strong investment in HR • international personnel transfers	• growing awareness of need to enhance ABB-wide cohesion

* income before taxes

Source: ABB Group Internet pages (1998); BBC Group Annual Report (1987) interviews

carry responsibilities for human resources (HR) activities. Of these two dimensions, the balance was slightly in favour of the country managers, signified by the fact that the country managers of the most important ABB national organizations such as Sweden, Germany, USA and Switzerland, all had a seat on the executive board.

For the first few years after the merger, ABB focused on integrating their worldwide operations, restructuring BAs, outsourcing activities, acquiring companies and selling off other companies or parts of them. In the first five years after the merger, ABB was involved in more than 100 mergers and acquisitions transactions as well as joint ventures, various cost-cutting programmes aimed at avoiding duplicate tasks and resources, and reducing administration costs. As had been done with ASEA before, the ABB head office was trimmed down initially to just over 100 staff. Instead of having centralized corporate laboratories for R&D, ABB created a network of eight R&D centres of excellence, which were closely linked to front-line companies. Finally, a vital ingredient in managing worldwide activities, ABB developed a simple but very effective and transparent *internal financial controlling system*, called ABACUS. Its structure followed the matrix idea, by allowing one to analyse financial data in a business-oriented and in a country/regional-oriented way simultaneously.

In the early 1990s, ABB CH and various other country organizations were facing one similar problem: the quality of their products, services and customer orientation was too low, and costs were too high. ABB therefore launched its 'Customer Orientation Program', initiated at the group level, but managed by country organizations such as ABB CH. The programme aimed at enhancing customer satisfaction, connecting customer needs and innovation processes, and reducing service costs. Around the same time, some other smaller changes took place, such as a reduction of employees due to a European recession, and the establishment of a segment: 'environmental systems'. Finally, in 1992 ABB introduced its 'centres of excellence' concept, in which one company per BA was allocated worldwide leadership. ABB was one of the first to introduce such a lead country concept, which aimed at reducing costs by avoiding resource duplication in the ABB national companies, thus simplifying the matrix and providing clear responsibilities. On the downside, however, this approach also gave room to micropolitics and country rivalry.

Redefining the matrix: adding the regional dimension (1993–1998)

In 1993, after the establishment of the European Union and the North American Free Trade Agreement, ABB adjusted its organization by adding a regional dimension and by making the regional managers full executive committee members. This reorganization created three regions and five business segments (power distribution and transmission were integrated). In this set-up, ABB attempted to benefit from the fact that country borders became more permeable, allowing for lateral linkages within regional areas. This reorganization did not just reduce the importance of the individual country holdings, but in retrospect also enabled the business segments to attain a more dominant position in the organization.

Thus the ABB matrix from 1993 to 1996 combined five *business segments* and three *regions* (which also captured the *country* dimension). The business segments were split up into 39 business areas, each of them representing a distinct worldwide product market. A BA manager reported (1) to the executive committee member responsible for the business segment's overall strategy and performance, and (2) to the executive committee member responsible for the specific region, who supported and coordinated the operating companies within a world region. This global matrix structure has been ABB's organizational framework for some ten years (cf. Table 4.2, pp. 126/127).

After redesigning the matrix, ABB undertook another important effort to raise customer orientation. Its Customer Focus programme aimed at improving process orientation, customer relations, and quality management at the same time (Zoller, 1998). Customer Focus became an ongoing programme pursuing continuous analysis and improvement of internal processes on the one hand, and a continuous (re)orientation to the customer on the other. Though initiated by the ABB group, all ABB companies were required to have a Customer Focus manager put in charge of its implementation.

In 1996, the number of business segments was reduced from five to four. By this time, ABB had begun to recognize the scope for further *lateral linkages amongst its segments* to improve the project management for turnkey power plants and to increase economies of scale and scope. At ABB CH, various cross-company teams (CCTs) were installed to explore such networking linkages. The CCT team members are the Managing Directors of the various ABB CH front-line companies. This team composition, and the explicit support by the ABB CH top management, indicates the importance ABB CH attaches to these teams. By 1998, eight CCTs at ABB CH were exploring the networking potential in areas such as marketing, organization development, human resources, finance and controlling, etc., and were evaluating individually or jointly developed concepts or methods. Another example of ABB's attempts to cross business segments is the 'open spaces' concept. In this concept, employees in the same country but from different management levels and segments get together once a month to discuss current organizational issues. Other important tools to enhance networking across segments include joint database management, international personnel transfers, and numerous kinds of meeting. These efforts however are limited to the country level.

Finally, ABB identified that its global matrix structure also required a set of essentially non-structural features, i.e. a corporate culture based on *open communication and empowerment*. In 1998, various teams throughout ABB were re-evaluating the overall company mission, its values and the existing policies booklet (cf. Lindahl, 1999: 8).

The emerging problems with matrix management at ABB

Although the 1993 reorganization was intended to simplify the organization, several interviewees indicated that many employees actually had difficulty understanding the overall structure. Frequent problems arose in the fields of business segmentation, in the working of the internal market mechanism, and in the internal decision-making processes.

First, having only four business segments, there was a great *heterogeneity within business segments* in terms of front-line companies' size, customers, technologies and business logic. In 1998, ABB recognized that it had somewhat lost the balance between global efficiency and local responsiveness. An internal analysis showed that the horizontal differentiation of the four business segments was highly ineffective. A segment such as Industrial and Building Systems had deteriorated into an 'all-purpose division' whose products were in different phases of the life cycles, serving entirely different customer segments, therefore offering very little scope for meaningful central coordination. At the basis of this is one of ABB's long time dilemmas, i.e. how to seek both differentiation and integration. ABB is a company with numerous local, regional and global businesses alongside each other (cf. Barham and Heimer, 1998: 64). The diversity of its products, technologies and markets has made a perfect segmentation of businesses very difficult. As it was, the segment managers had *difficulties in boosting special growth areas* and pushed the restructuring towards a more optimal business segmentation. The country managers did not see the problem in quite the same terms, since their role was to ensure the company's market orientation and customer relations rather than worldwide efficiency in managing segments.

A second problem area emerged in the field of ABB's *internal market mechanism* – an area in which ABB also pioneered new organizational solutions. In order to coordinate the vertical and horizontal resource flows among the various profit centres, ABB developed a market-oriented transfer pricing system. ABB's transfer pricing system – undoubtedly one of the most advanced in the world – required a lot of time and energy. Within a single business segment this did not raise any real problems, because at the end of the day the profit centres all contributed to the overall performance of their segment. However, the cross-segment margin calculation in particular led to frequent conflict, because each business segment sought to maximize its own profits. As a result, profit centres from different business segments competed for resources and investment, leading to situations in which single profit centre objectives could easily override the overall group objectives.

With its matrix structure and profit centre philosophy, ABB had deliberately created an organizational paradox: *competition and cooperation* at the same time (cf. Van Wijk and Van den Bosch, Chapter 5 in this volume). The core dilemma was simple: how to create a spirit of internal competition while at the same time providing a cooperative internal environment to exploit the scale and scope advantages offered by the multinational organization? Several interviewees indicated that internal fights and competition were at times more important than fighting external competitors. Thus, the strong autonomy of the small front-line companies strengthened entrepreneurship and customer orientation on the one hand, while on the other obstructing inter-segment cooperation and corporate strategizing. This even led to a point where some front-line companies understood their role as owner of the business rather than as a business opportunity provider for the ABB Group. As one interviewee remarked: 'Everybody is seeking to increase his margin. It's not the overall success in the market that counts, but the performance of one's own profit centre. Therefore it's difficult to offer competitive prices to the final customer in the market' (Top Manager, ABB Switzerland, summer 1998).

A third fundamental problem was that individual managers found it increasingly difficult to live up to the expectations of the matrix. Particularly in Europe, the dynamism of the first years had waned, the number of staff members had increased and formerly flexible structures had become more rusty. As a result, several managers left the company (often to go to competitors), frustrated with years of pressure from above. Moreover, the regional dimensions in the company had effectively created *regional principalities* leading to long and complex decision-making processes and contributing to an increasingly political climate within the matrix. Many at ABB felt that the power of these regional barons had become disproportionately large in relation to the diminishing importance of the regional dimension, given the changes in the market indicated earlier (see also Bantel and Schär, 1998: 6). This was reflected in the following comment: 'One of the drawbacks of the matrix structure is that its problems are always a mix of region and segment problems. The company is highly political' (Assistant Vice-President, summer 1998).

In conclusion, while the matrix organization and the profit centre structure at ABB had long provided a useful organizational framework, ABB became confronted with some of the very disadvantages of the matrix organization that Bartlett and Ghoshal mentioned in their 1990 article: 'conflict and confusion; . . . international logjams . . . ; and over-lapping responsibilities produced turf battles and a loss of accountability' (1990: 139).

Beyond the global matrix: the 'network multidivisional organization' (1998—)

As a result of the above problems ABB announced in 1998 the decision to dissolve its regional layer and eliminate the positions of the business region managers and their staff. About 100 managers worldwide lost their jobs due to these changes. The country organizations will remain, continuing to represent ABB's 'multidomestic' presence in markets around the world. However, the business segments have become the dominant dimension within the company. By focusing on segments instead of regions, Göran Lindahl, the new CEO after Percy Barnevik left in 1997, particularly seeks to strengthen ABB's product orientation.

Various press reports have suggested that a fierce internal struggle at ABB preceded the reorganization (cf. Bantel and Schär, 1998: 6). In view of the changes that have taken place, this seems quite likely: Eberhard von Koerber, former head of Europe/Africa, saw his position elimi-nated and subsequently left ABB, and Sune Carlsson saw his industrial and building systems (all-purpose division) business segment being split up into three business segments (automation; oil, gas and petro-chemicals; and products and contracting).

Figure 4.2 shows the new organization of ABB as of 1998. The first change is that ABB now has seven business segments as the dominant structure. Each executive committee member carries the responsibility for one segment, with the CEO having overall responsibility. This prod-uct-oriented organization aims at promoting growth in areas where ABB has technology advantages and unique capabilities, and to cut myopic internal competition. The newly added financial services busi-ness segment is to help ABB provide complete solutions, including financing packages, to newly privatized customers and those in emerg-ing markets. The second change is the removal of the regional layer. As a result, country organizations now report directly to Zurich. Altogether, ABB expects to achieve shorter decision-making processes and greater responsiveness to deregulation and privatization.

However, ABB has made a point of ensuring *continuity in the organi-zation*. The group's head office is to remain small and focused on truly strategic activities. The business segment and business area managers maintain responsibility for worldwide product strategies ranging from R&D and investments to market allocation and sourcing, and business results. The country holdings will maintain the relationships with local stakeholders such as customers, governments, labour unions and

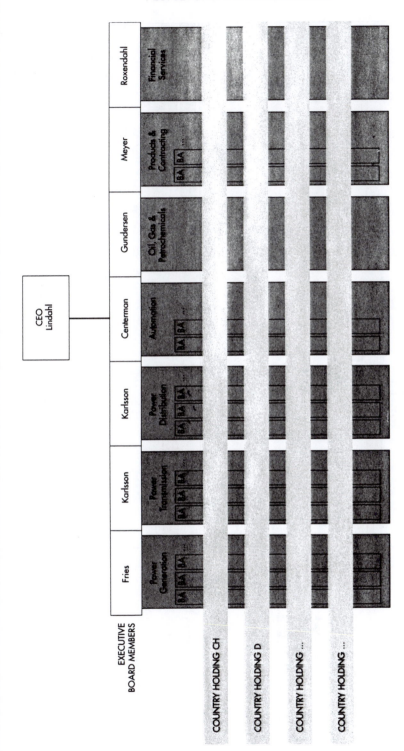

FIGURE 4.2   ABB's organization as of 1998 (ABB Group, 1998)

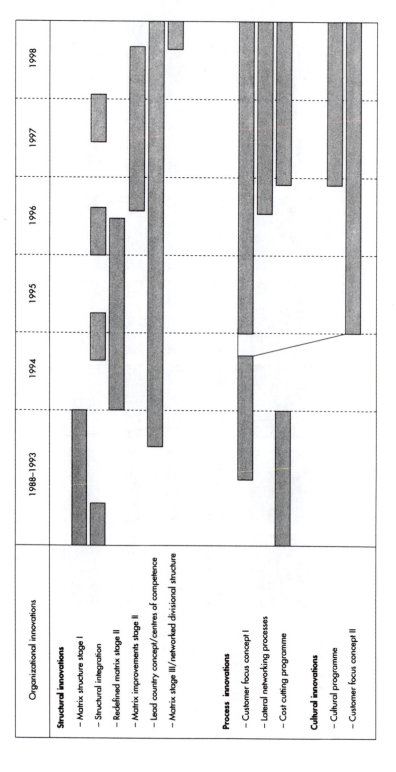

FIGURE 4.3 Organizational changes at ABB (1988–1998) (Source: ABB interviews)

media, and will remain responsible for local operations, marketing and human resource management within their country. Front-line managers will continue to have direct customer contacts and will be responsible for running the daily business. Indeed, the worldwide architecture of small front-line companies, the centres of excellence concept, the internal labour market, the importance of entrepreneurship, the search for cross-segment networking (at the level of country organizations), and the ABACUS information system will remain core elements of ABB's organization. This quote from CEO Lindahl sums up the situation within ABB: 'The end of the matrix seems to take place as fast as it was introduced in 1988, although the new structure is only about an improvement (instead of an elimination) of the matrix' (Roost and Meier, 1998: 58).

Thus, the 1998 ABB reorganization does not represent a full departure from the global matrix. Rather, it is an attempt to *transform the matrix from a geographical to a product bias, while maintaining the full range of existing internal networking mechanisms*. In our view, ABB has not returned to the classical Chandlerian multidivisional organization (Chandler, 1980). Rather, it seems to be transforming into what Richard Whittington and Michael Mayer (1997: 253ff.) have termed the *network multidivisional*: in their view, the network multidivisional is a flatter version with the emphasis on the lateral rather than the vertical, knowledge rather than scale and scope, and human resources and self-organizing rather than corporate planning and bureaucracy.

ABB has maintained three core features of the multidivisional organization, yet has transformed each of them. First, the overall ABB organization is based on strict managerial hierarchies, and it may be argued that the corporate centre has become more powerful since the 1998 reorganization (cf. *Wirtschaftswoche*, 1998). However, ABB has supplemented these hierarchies by systematically decentralizing operating and country-specific responsibilities, and by encouraging entrepreneurial behaviour. Secondly, ABB now has a divisional structure, yet at the country level ABB is deliberately cutting through divisional boundaries by combining operations in country holdings, by having senior management cross-company teams exploring scale and scope opportunities, and by creating a financial services segment which depends on cooperation with other segments. Thirdly, ABB has an internal capital market in place and closely monitors front-line companies' and business segments' performance, yet it has *added* an internal labour market as another key resource. As the head of human resource management explained:

> Our internal labour market really works like a market. Employees can be contracted by other ABB companies once they have been in their jobs for more than 18 months. The only rule is that the direct superior has to be

informed. Jobs are announced in the internal job market on the intranet. Previously, it was considered a bad habit to hunt people internally. The result was that many people left ABB, as they were recruited by external head hunters. This created a change of mentality.

Process Sequencing

In terms of sequencing, ABB used two types of change action: the first type was characterized by a short time frame, top-down initiated and closely managed, but rarely with a cultural impact; the second was characterized by a longer time frame, with various loci of action, managed more loosely with the aim to change modes of behaviour. Kanter et al., (1992: 492) referred to these two types of change actions as 'bold strokes' and 'long marches'. Bold strokes are strategic decisions, such as merger and acquisitions or designing the organizational framework, whereas long marches are more operational initiatives, such as transforming quality or customer relationships.

Thus, the last ten years at ABB may be interpreted as a pattern of *continuity and change*. Figure 4.3 summarizes the various change programmes at ABB over the 1988–1998 period. The combination of this continuity and change can be seen in the fact that many programmes were carried out in parallel, that many stretched beyond individual reorganizations, and that the number of change programmes has increased over time. The 1998 strengthening of the product dimension,

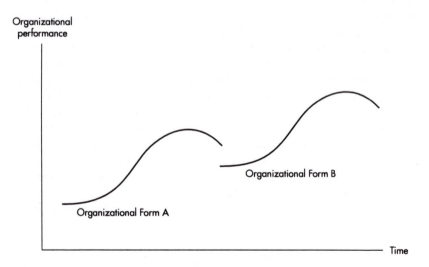

FIGURE 4.4   *Life cycle of organizational forms (Source: ABB interviewee)*

moreover, is in line with the fact that from the beginning, 'Barnevik [had been] more interested in the products and businesses' than in the country dimension (Barham and Heimer, 1998: 74).

At ABB, there is an explicit view on the sequencing and transition of an organizational form, described by Lindahl (Solenthaler, 1998) and restated by one of our interview partners. Given the environmental conditions, organizations develop a form that may enable them to improve performance for a number of years. However, in the view of ABB, *organizational life cycles are limited*: after some five years, the performance gains of a previously appropriate form have been exploited to the full, and performance begins to decline. At that moment ABB will have to adjust its form to the newly changed environmental conditions. An organizational form can thus be seen as a temporary optimal growth trajectory. Even if the performance benefits of such a new form will not be immediately visible, they will emerge in due course (see Figure 4.4).

Barriers to Change at ABB in the 1990s

To every corporation, change is a real challenge and often creates resistance (Hambrick et al., 1998b). Frequently, organizational change fails because of implementation problems and internal institutionalization rather than because of any inherent conceptual problems of the innovation itself (cf. Kanter, 1983: 301). Even if change at ABB may be interpreted as a combination of continuity and change, some real internal barriers have affected both the functioning of the matrix and ABB's 1998 reorganization. At the start of the chapter we referred to Rugman and Hodgetts' three criteria for a matrix to work well (1995: 250). Here we briefly evaluate these criteria:

- *Clarity* refers to how well people understand what they are doing and why they are doing it. Based on the views expressed by several interviewees, we have to conclude that ABB had failed to achieve sufficient organizational clarity for the 'matrix in the mind' to develop. Despite Barnevik's energetic attempt to communicate the nature and rationale of ABB's corporate structures and values, too many employees only saw financial clarity, based on the ABACUS system of monitoring profit centres' performance, not organizational clarity.
- *Continuity* refers to the extent to which the company has stuck to the same core objectives (including products) and values. This criterion has been fulfilled partly. ABB has not shifted its product range dramatically, apart from adding a new business segment: 'financial services'. The company has also remained committed to its

expansion into emerging markets in Central and Eastern Europe and in Asia, even when economic recessions hit these regions. However, in retrospect, adding three regional layers in 1993 (which Barnevik had seen as 'regrettable' but inevitable, see Barham and Heimer, 1998: 286) effectively sowed a seed of disintegration in the organization between the head office and the country organization. The three regional barons and the three segment chiefs had different views of the need to focus on the business dimension, and an equal weight in the executive committee.

- *Consistency* refers to the extent to which managers throughout the organization have been pursuing the same objectives. Perhaps the biggest weakness of the ABB matrix during later years was the internal rivalry and the micropolitics between the various profit centres, among the business segments and between the product and the regional dimension. For instance, the heterogeneity of front line companies in terms of firm structures, competitive environments and business logic (for example semiconductors versus plant projects) implied that concepts developed by ABB CH did not necessarily fit with each front line company. Likewise, some interviewees argued that reporting standards had been set to match the needs of the machine industry which did not fit their own business equally well. Inevitably, the front line companies' independence often hampered the implementation of such concepts.

An underlying barrier to the development of the matrix may have been that ABB's corporate culture has been based rather one-sidedly on achieving customer focus. Bartlett and Ghoshal (1993: 26) suggested that the *Mission, Values, and Policies* booklet provided a strong shared vision and corporate culture. However, we found that by 1998 its influence was rather limited. Various interviewees in fact criticized the lack of a corporate culture functioning as a 'glue' in the overall company, and indicated that it would be difficult to create a strong unifying culture for the whole ABB Group as this would contradict the principle of decentralization and unwavering customer focus.

The 1998 ABB Reorganization: Beyond the Authorized Motives

ABB has presented its 1998 reorganization as a logical and relatively minor organizational transformation, with the prime objective to improve customer focus by separating businesses with local and more global customers and with different product life cycles. The company has put great effort into communicating continuity rather than change. And for good reasons: despite some occasional incidents in Asia, ABB has long enjoyed a favourable press, which is reflected in the ABB brand reputation, its market capitalization and its ability to recruit talented engineers and managers. As one interviewee remarked: 'ABB is very successful in creating an external image of success' (Assistant Vice-President).

This section compares the official reasons given for the reorganization with the impressions that we gathered during our interviews at ABB CH. Table 4.3 summarizes the main points. The ABB case drives home some management truisms and points to the difficulties of building a network organization:

- It is possible to reduce managerial hierarchies and decentralize operational decision making, but this may easily be at the expense of company-wide coordination.
- Pushing for internal transparency, entrepreneurship and profit responsibility may produce a culture in which 'strong men win' (as ABB's culture is frequently described by employees).
- Establishing a regional management layer (as many large companies have done recently, cf. Laserre and Schütte, 1995) also implies inserting another power centre.
- Networking between divisions may be obtained *within one country* but is much more difficult to establish across countries (let alone regions).

Table 4.3 *Official reasons and interpretations of ABB's 1998 reorganization*

Official reason	Our interpretation
• Simplifying segment business activities	• Three original business segments were too differentiated; too difficult to manage the portfolio
• Creating new synergies	• Countries/regions were creating boundaries; few contacts among profit centres which were within the same segment but located within different countries
• Cost reduction by cutting one hundred management positions	• Eliminating 'regional princes'; more centralized power for the heads of product segments
• Promote growth area and focus along business segments	• Preparation for divestment activities (or even for splitting up the group); internal competition at international level
• Focus investor attention	• Transparency by publishing data on each of the eight business segments; creates legitimization for further action and integration of Swiss and Swedish shares
• Faster decision-making	• 'Strong men win' as ABB's *de facto* slogan led to slow decision making based on political power instead of market/product orientation

Source: ABB Group (1998), interviews

Unresolved Management Issues

In order to capture the full potential that the new organization offers, ABB needs to address some as yet unresolved management issues. These are summarized here.

The first challenge is to reduce the internal conflicts and micropolitics which are the unintended consequence of creating an internal market and calculating internal margins. In the view of various interviewees, the internal market has frequently led to myopic competition against other profit centres, hindering horizontal networking processes. It remains yet to be seen whether and how the new organization can help tackle that challenge.

A second problem lies in the field of *interface management*. ABB's lead country concept aims at improving the coordination of worldwide processes, yet several interview partners indicated that ABB did not assign clear enough responsibilities to the lead country organizations. ABB has often faced the problem of determining which country organization is to take the lead in which country/project. As a result, there has been too much duplication of work. Since adding or taking away country organizations' responsibilities in large international plant projects is inherently a critical and political issue, more clarity and central leadership is needed here.

A third challenge, mentioned by numerous interview partners, is that of *exploiting synergies within and across segments*, or, put differently, to make the 'network' element in the network multidivisional work. Many interviewees indicated that with increasing cost and time pressure, exploiting potential synergy represented a great challenge for ABB, though they usually did not have a very clear idea of how to achieve that. It is not immediately obvious whether and how such interdivisional networking between the seven business segments may materialize. One way may be by strengthening ABB's horizontal process focus – which would require a change in incentives and employees' behaviour.

A fourth challenge is to *develop an ABB culture beyond financial results, and beyond the front line company or the country organization*. While people are usually very proud to work for ABB, employees talk mostly about the corporate culture of their front line company or country organization, rather than referring to the ABB Group culture. We found that ABB managers perceive organizational culture as a strong coordination mechanism between head office and units. However, ABB managers do not perceive organizational culture as playing an equally strong role as a coordination mechanism between or within units. Thus, the influence of the *Mission, Values, and Policies* booklet seems to have worn off at last. Developing a horizontally unifying corporate culture is by no means a luxury for a company with such truly worldwide operations.

A fifth challenge resides in developing a *new understanding of management's role*. The management of front line companies needs to appreciate that, being assigned the responsibility to run a profit centre, they are not the single owner of a specific business, but rather the business opportunity provider for other front-line companies or segments. Only such an understanding will raise internal networking and ultimately improve service to the customer.

The financial implications of ABB's 1998 reorganization could not yet be assessed at the time of writing this case study, though it is obvious that ABB will have to go a long way to match General Electric's rates of return. Finally, it is worth mentioning that many of the above challenges have existed since the merger in 1988. It would appear that problems which are not solved during the first years after a merger continue to haunt the organization afterwards.

Conclusion

ABB has often been referred to by gurus and management scholars as a model organization for other companies. This chapter has depicted the transformation of the ABB organization over the 1988–1998 period, and analysed the nature of its 1998 reorganization into what at first sight would appear to resemble a classical multidivisional organization. The chapter described how ABB transformed from a global matrix with a strong country focus (1988–1993), through a global matrix with regional focus (1993–1998) to what Whittington and Mayer (1997: 253ff) termed a network multidivisional (from 1998).

During the first stage of the ABB organization, the key words were turnaround management of individual profit centres, infusing entrepreneurship, creating internal markets and enhancing local responsiveness. The second stage was characterized by the rise of regional trade blocks, fierce international competition, and the increasing importance of emerging markets in Asia and in Central and Eastern Europe, calling for enhanced regional coordination and internal networking. During the third stage, continuing tough competition and the need to offer relatively similar products plus a full service package to newly deregulated private sector players further boosted internal networking and strengthened the product versus the country dimension.

We arrived at two major conclusions. First, ABB has not entirely removed its global matrix structure, but rather transformed it by strengthening its product focus while maintaining the country dimension. Secondly, ABB has not 'regressed' to a classical multidivisional form but has supplemented this form with characteristics beyond its three defining features:

- *managerial hierarchies*: ABB has decentralized operational decision making to its network of profit centres, whereas strategic decision making is shared between the business areas and business segments, rather than concentrated entirely at the head office.
- *divisionalization*: ABB is deliberately and increasingly crossing divisional boundaries at the level of the country organizations, seeking to reduce costs and create company-wide synergies.
- *internal capital market*: ABB monitors the performance of its profit centres, its business areas and business segments primarily by financial controlling instruments. Adding a financial services segment in fact increased the importance of the internal capital market; yet ABB has also added internal labour markets to manage human resources and knowledge as another key internal resource.

The ABB 1998 reorganization seems to have resulted largely from the limitations of the 1993 global matrix organization, that is, the rivalry between the various profit centres; the internal politics between the business segments, the regions and the head office; the loss of sight of the global business dimension as a result of the introduction of the regions in 1993; and the use of only three business segments until 1998, combining very different businesses in one division. However, we interpreted the 1998 reorganization as a combination of continuity and change, since many structures, responsibilities and processes have essentially remained unchanged compared to the period before August 1998. This view is in line with more quantitative research which suggests that we 'do not see evidence of a new form supplanting the old, but we do see evidence of *new arrangements supplementing the old'* (Ruigrok et al., 1999: 59, emphasis added).

In our view, ABB continues to be a pioneer of innovative forms of organizing. Its global matrix enabled it to experiment and gain experiences that many other companies have yet to obtain. The openness that ABB employees displayed talking to us and their search for better organizational solutions reflect a strong commitment to the company and its products. And, frankly, we can't wait to learn about ABB's reorganization in the year 2003, and see the next stage in networking the multidivisional organization.

Acknowledgements

The authors thank Nikolaus von Bock for his research assistance and Norbert Lang at ABB Switzerland for enlightening us on ABB's history. Furthermore, the authors acknowledge the generous support by the HSG Grundlagenforschungsfonds.

Note

1 The story even goes that students at one of Europe's leading international business schools got to the point where they left the room as soon as a professor brought up ABB to illustrate effective management practices.

5

The Emergence and Development of Internal Networks and their Impact on Knowledge Flows: The Case of Rabobank Group

Raymond A. van Wijk and Frans A.J. van den Bosch

In recent years increases in environmental turbulence have transformed the competitive landscape. The new landscape has forced firms to increase their exploration of new opportunities (March, 1995) by managing knowledge creation and sharing as one of the most strategically significant activities (Grant, 1996a), and treating organization form as a 'new strategic variable' (Daft and Lewin, 1993: ii). These developments have required that firms challenge their internal mode of organizing (Bartlett and Ghoshal, 1993; Ghoshal and Bartlett, 1998; Van Wijk and Van den Bosch, 1998b). Recent research has pointed out that in a wide variety of industries across Europe, Japan and the United States, several leading firms have apparently recognized this need. Preliminary findings indicate that these firms have restructured and adopted new forms of organizing, or are currently in the process of transition towards new forms of organizing (Whittington et al., 1999b).

One such new mode of organizing is the *internal network organization*, alternatively labelled the N-form corporation (Hedlund, 1994; Pettigrew et al., 1995; Hedlund and Ridderstråle, 1997) or integrated network (Nohria and Ghoshal, 1997; Ghoshal and Bartlett, 1998). The internal network differentiates itself from traditional organizational forms in terms of structure, management and knowledge processes (Van Wijk and Van den Bosch, 1998b), with the proviso that complementarities between these and other organizational attributes must be present to achieve and sustain high performance levels (Starbuck, 1993; Whittington, et al., 1999b). Although an increasing number of firms seem to be involved in the transition towards this or alternative forms of organizing, empirical insight into the transition towards internal networks is limited. Apart from the study by Ferlie and Pettigrew (1996) on the British National Health Service (NHS), existing work is mainly cross-sectional rather than longitudinal in nature and focuses on the characteristics of internal networks once they are established (see Chapter 1 of this volume).

The purpose of this chapter is to provide new insights into the developmental process of internal network forms of organizing by applying a longitudinal case study methodology (Pettigrew, 1990). It briefly describes the history and evolution of Rabobank Group, a Dutch-based multinational financial services corporation, and assesses the change journey of the company towards an internal network form of organizing over the past decade. The focus of the case study is on the changes in structure, management and knowledge processes in particular, as well as the complementarities among them, that constituted Rabobank's corporate-wide transition. Analysing the transition process, we pay attention to progression and regression phases in the development of internal networks (Van den Bosch and Van Wijk, 1999), the differential pace of change that distinct units may find themselves in, and possible bipolarities in structure; as for example where both hierarchical and network forms are, and perhaps must be, present at the same time.

To illustrate the intricacies of change towards internal network forms of organizing, the case study is framed along the lines of an embedded case study design with *three units of analysis*, each focusing on changes in structure, management and knowledge processes. The first unit of analysis deals with the transition process of Rabobank at the corporate level. Alongside the drivers for change, we will analyse the pace, scope and depth of the change process towards internal network forms of organizing for different units within Rabobank. The second and third units of analysis focus on two organizational units of the group that have pursued different change trajectories to describe in depth the challenges involved in changing into internal networks. Local member banks are the second unit of analysis, at the start of the change process towards an internal network. This analysis describes how barriers of horizontal knowledge sharing among local member banks influences their change trajectory. The third unit of analysis involves a longitudinal analysis of the transition process of a facilitatory business unit, Spectrum, towards an internal network, which has functioned as a kind of template for creating internal networks for the rest of the Rabobank organization. This analysis pays attention to both supporting factors and barriers in creating internal networks.

In the next section, the theoretical background of internal networks is briefly sketched around three themes: an internal network's structure, management and knowledge processes. Next, the key analytical questions to be addressed, the longitudinal case study methodology and research design are explicated. In the three following sections, the case study findings are reported at the corporate level, at the level of the local member banks, and the business unit Spectrum. With regard to all three units of analysis attention will be paid to drivers for change, content and process sequencing, depth and pace of change, barriers, and the consequences of adopting an internal network. The chapter concludes with a discussion of the main findings.

Theoretical Background of Internal Networks

A key advantage of internal networks is the 'ability to create value through the accumulation, transfer, and integration of different kinds of knowledge, resources, and capabilities across dispersed organizational units' (Nohria and Ghoshal, 1997: 208). However, to capitalize on this ability and to benefit from the flexibility (Volberda, 1998), self-renewal and organic growth that are likely to accrue from it (Hedberg et al., 1976), a firm has to change a multitude of characteristics. What is more, Whittington et al. (1999b) found that a firm in transition needs to change organizational attributes concurrently to achieve the complementarities required for above-normal performance levels. Internal networks are different compared to traditional organizational forms with respect to *three themes*: structure, management and knowledge processes. Each of these themes will be elaborated on. Figure 5.1 depicts the organizational structure, management processes and knowledge processes of an idealized internal network and guides the following discussion.

Organizational structure

Hedlund (1994) has denoted the structure of the internal network as a heterarchy rather than hierarchy, which presumes that a dense set of dispersed, differentiated, but interdependent organizational units constitutes the structure of an internal network. Since units in internal networks are also decentralized at both the operational and strategic level, this suggests that they are not so much dispersed and differentiated in terms of geography alone, but more fundamentally in terms of resources, capabilities, activities and knowledge (cf. Tsoukas, 1996; Galunic and Rodan, 1998).

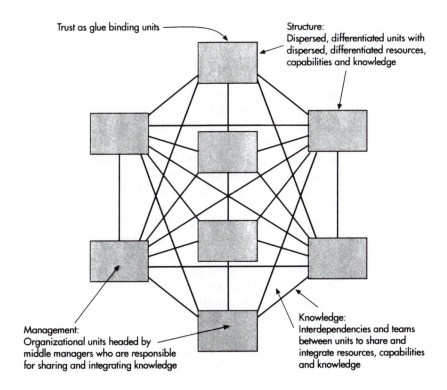

Trust as glue binding units

Structure:
Dispersed, differentiated units with dispersed, differentiated resources, capabilities and knowledge

Management:
Organizational units headed by middle managers who are responsible for sharing and integrating knowledge

Knowledge:
Interdependencies and teams between units to share and integrate resources, capabilities and knowledge

FIGURE 5.1   *An example of an internal network (based on Ghoshal and Bartlett, 1997)*

Due to constraints springing from bounded rationality, all knowledge relevant to firm behaviour and success is difficult to capture entirely at the corporate level (March and Simon, 1958). Those with the specialized knowledge and expertise most vital to the company's competitiveness are usually located far away from corporate headquarters (Bartlett and Ghoshal, 1993). Whereas in existing organizational forms, such as the multidivisional form, decisions are made on the basis of knowledge residing at higher levels, in internal networks each unit pursues its own decisions (see Figure 5.1). Operational and strategic decisions are based on localized knowledge and other resources such as geographical areas, markets, technologies, or even specific problems. As each unit is capable of performing different activities in congruence with market demand, this decentralization of activities also gives rise to a *differentiation* of actors, activities and resources.

Notwithstanding this differentiation, units remain dependent on the performance of other units, and are therefore required to collaborate

(Jones et al., 1997). These types of interdependency enable resources and activities to be integrated among units without the interference of the corporate hierarchy (cf. Lawrence and Lorsch, 1967b). In this vein, Baker argues that networks are '*integrated* across formal groups created by vertical, horizontal, and spatial differentiation for any type of relation' (1992: 424–425; original emphasis). A particular role in this respect is granted to teams and other temporal constellations of different people from varying organizational levels and units (Hedlund, 1994), not only to explore new opportunities but to expand on existing ones (Müllern, Chapter 8 in this volume). In this way, combinations result from interdependencies that move beyond the sequential and pooled, and include the reciprocal and team-based types (Thompson, 1967; Van de Ven et al., 1976).

However, hierarchy has not completely vanished in internal networks. A hierarchy fosters exploitation, whereas a network increases exploration (Hedlund, 1994: March, 1995). Both a hierarchy and a network are therefore required 'to engage in sufficient exploitation to ensure current viability and, at the same time, to devote enough energy to exploration to ensure its future viability' (Levinthal and March, 1993: 105). Likewise, a hierarchy remains indispensable when certain decisions must be reached swiftly, disputes are to be resolved, or allegiance to a firm's mission and objectives must be induced. Although in extreme cases the internal network may supplant the hierarchy in general, the structure of internal networks is likely to supplement hierarchy and may therefore be considered bipolar (see also Nonaka and Takeuchi, 1995; Sánchez-Runde and Quintanilla, Chapter 9 in this volume).

Management processes

Changing organization structure alone will not give rise to internal networks. Subtler changes in management are required as well (Hedlund, 1994). Bartlett and Ghoshal (1993) have observed at ABB (see also Ruigrok et al., Chapter 4 in this volume) that managerial roles and processes at various levels in internal networks are different from those in firms with more traditional organization forms. Indigenous to this change of management philosophy is to conceive of managers more as stewards 'whose behavior is ordered such that pro-organizational, collectivist behaviors have higher utility than individualistic, self-serving behaviours' (Davis et al., 1997: 24), rather than supposedly economically rational agents of the sort found in conventional organization forms (Miles and Creed, 1995; Ghoshal and Moran, 1996).

Instead of taking on the traditional roles of monitor and controller, top managers in internal networks are the architects of the organization. In that spirit, they are discharged from strategic planning and composing grand strategies, and instead are responsible for creating a shared context and vision for long term development and organic growth. Within this context, middle management's role is to link and leverage the distributed resources and capabilities, rather than implementing resource allocation decisions made at the top. By taking over this integrative and synthesizing role from top management, middle managers can circumvent the often long and tedious vertical path to and from headquarters. To substantiate the structural interdependencies that underlie integration, middle managers also need to create and maintain *trust* among organizational members by behaving as coaches and supporting the initiatives taken by front line managers (see Figure 5.1, p. 147). Rather than being restricted by decisions made at higher levels in the hierarchy, front line managers pursue the opportunities that crop up in the environment themselves, and generate and update knowledge as necessary (Bartlett and Ghoshal, 1993; Hedlund, 1994).

Based on such studies as the ones elaborated above, Van den Bosch and Van Wijk (2000) have argued that as managerial roles and tasks have changed, the nature of managerial knowledge and managerial capabilities at the different levels must have changed as well. In congruence with Hedlund (1994), they assert that 'know-what' and 'know-how' are no longer associated with higher managerial levels but have entered the domain of front line managers. Furthermore, due to the presence of interdependencies and collaboration between organizational units, 'know-who' and 'know-where' are doubtless becoming more important, especially for an internal network's middle management.

Knowledge processes

Environmental turbulence has induced firms to take the management of knowledge seriously, and to do so effectively, they must consider internal network forms of organizing (Bartlett and Ghoshal, 1993; Hedlund, 1994). But what do these knowledge processes look like in contrast to the ones in more orthodox forms of organization?

At the most basic level, two different types of knowledge process can be discerned. First, organizational units may create and accumulate knowledge with their own means and resources (cf. Nonaka and Takeuchi, 1995). This knowledge creation process is essentially the same as the type employed in traditional organizational forms. But, as mentioned above, in traditional organizations knowledge is subsequently transferred to and applied at higher levels, whereas in internal networks knowledge is retained at the unit level. Secondly, knowledge may be transferred and integrated among organizational units. This knowledge sharing capacity differentiates the internal network from other organization forms and gives internal networks the unique ability to take advantage of a distributed and dispersed knowledge structure (Hedlund, 1994; Van Wijk and Van den Bosch, 1998a).

Knowledge transfer and integration processes may be promoted by both vertical and horizontal knowledge flows (cf. Aoki, 1986). In more traditional forms of organizing, knowledge integration is preserved by hierarchy, where knowledge flows are primarily vertical and unidirectional between headquarters and divisions, business units, and operating units. In internal networks vertical knowledge flows are either supplanted or, where the hierarchy remains present, supplemented by *horizontal, multidirectional knowledge flows* which preserve knowledge integration and the embeddedness of the units in the organization (Fenton and Pettigrew, Chapters 2 and 3 in this volume; Hedlund, 1994; Quinn et al., 1996; Van Wijk and Van den Bosch, 1998a). What is more, horizontal knowledge flows in traditional organization forms are less frequent and largely informal. In internal networks on the other hand, while these knowledge flows may also be informal they are mainly formalized. This is reflected in, for example, the extensive use of teams where knowledge is shared and integrated (cf. Fenton and Pettigrew, Chapters 2 and 3 in this volume).

Method

Firms that wish to move from a traditional organization form towards an internal network form of organizing must undertake a change journey. However, scholarly enquiry into these journeys is still inadequately developed both in number and scope. To contribute to our understanding, processual and longitudinal research approaches are required to uncover processes of strategic and organizational change brought about by firms in transition (Pettigrew, 1990, 1992, 1997). Such an approach asks a number of key analytical questions that guide the investigation and requires an appropriate research methodology, and research design.

Key analytical questions

The foregoing theoretical outline triggered the formulation of four analytical questions to be addressed about the developmental journey to create internal networks. The questions are presented in Table 5.1. The first question focuses on the drivers for change, and the heterogeneity of the pace of change. Large firms are normally made up of various divisions, departments and units. Since these units may produce different products and services, each unit may pursue a different change trajectory, leading to a differential pace of change for the firm in its entirety. The second question focuses on the impact of the change process on the structure, management and knowledge processes of a firm in transition. As mentioned above, internal network forms of organizing are different from traditional organizational forms in terms of these three themes. Considering this, it is important to see what the effect of the change process on these three organizational attributes is, as well as the issue to what extent complementarities between structure, management and knowledge processes are required.

Horizontal knowledge sharing is the lifeblood of internal networks. Knowledge processes may constitute the greatest difference between the internal network and traditional organizational forms. So the third question relates to how changes in the configuration of knowledge flows may be used as an indicator of the transition towards internal networks. The fourth question concerns the enabling and restricting factors, specifically those relating to horizontal knowledge sharing, and those involved in the change process towards internal network forms of organizing.

Table 5.1   *Key analytical questions*

Key question	Addressed in
I Why and how do large multi-unit firms incorporate internal network forms of organizing? Do different paces of change towards internal networks exist?	First unit of analysis
II How are organizational structure, management and knowledge processes of internal networks different in comparison to traditional organizational forms?	Second and third units of analysis
III Why are knowledge processes important and how can these processes be used in assessing the progress of the change process towards internal networks?	Second and third units of analysis
IV What are the enabling and restricting factors for horizontal knowledge sharing in internal networks?	Second and third units of analysis

Longitudinal case study methodology

The case study methodology has been suggested as an appropriate method for examining in-depth phenomena of organizations in their real-life context. It serves the purpose of exploring contemporary issues, and of developing and expanding theory (Eisenhardt, 1989b; Yin, 1994). Since little is known about the transitional and evolutionary processes involved in moving towards internal networks, and their effects on structure, management and knowledge processes, the case study methodology seemed appropriate for current purposes. To bring time and dynamics centrally into the analysis (Pettigrew, 1992), this chapter employs a longitudinal case study methodology of the sort advocated by Pettigrew (1990). That is, we were in search of (1) the embeddedness of the case across a number of levels of analysis, (2) temporal interconnections of events, (3) an explanation of action in its context, and (4) the linkage of process to outcome. In that capacity, the research method is consistent with the contextualist research tradition, in which an event or phenomenon is investigated 'in its setting'; that is, not only the socio-economic, political and business context, but the intraorganizational context are of concern (Pettigrew, 1985b).

Research design and data collection

As the international financial services industry has become a highly volatile field worldwide (e.g. Crane and Bodie, 1996), many international banks have started to question the mode of organizing they employ, and as a consequence have initiated a move towards new forms of organizing. One example is US-based Banc One, which has become a prototypical example of replicating knowledge and best practices (Winter and Szulanski, 1998).

The case study in this chapter was carried out at Rabobank Group, a Dutch multinational financial services corporation employing about 44,000 people, which recently instigated a corporate-wide transition towards a new mode of organizing. The third largest financial services corporation in the Netherlands behind competitors ABN–AMRO Bank and Internationale Nederlanden Group (ING), Rabobank ranked 248th in terms of total revenues and 52nd in terms of total assets on Fortune's 1998 Global 500. Owing to its expertise in the agricultural, health care and food industries, Rabobank is the second largest player in these industries in many foreign countries such as Australia and the United States. Rabobank ranked 33rd in terms of total revenues and 28th in terms of total assets in the global financial industry rankings (*Fortune*, 3 August, 1998). Moreover, Rabobank is the sole financial institution in the Netherlands and one among the more than twenty in the global financial industry accredited the AAA rating for credit liability by US rating companies Moody's and Standard & Poor's.

Yin (1994) argues that a case study design can be either holistic or embedded. In spite of the holistic view that was maintained as a requirement for longitudinal case study research (Pettigrew, 1990), we employed an embedded case study design embodying *three units of analysis*: (1) the corporate level Rabobank Group, (2) the local member banks through which domestic clients are served, and (3) a facilitatory business unit called Spectrum (see Figure 5.2). The corporate level constitutes the first unit of analysis. Although Rabobank experienced a corporate-wide change journey, different parts of the Rabobank Group found themselves in different phases of change. Another rationale for adding two units of analysis was to provide the depth which the corporate level could not provide. The local member banks and the facilitatory business unit, each in a different phase of development, were therefore framed within two separate units of analysis. Since the

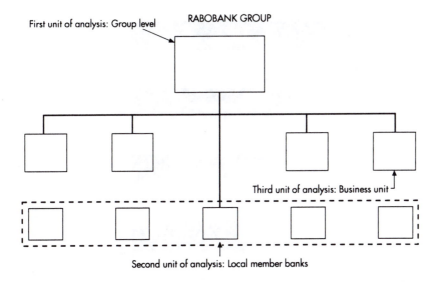

First unit of analysis: Group level

RABOBANK GROUP

Third unit of analysis: Business unit

Second unit of analysis: Local member banks

FIGURE 5.2   *Embedded case study design of transition process: three units of analysis*

two embedded units were in different phases of transition – the local member banks in the early stages of adopting an internal network, while Spectrum is well advanced into the challenges involved in being an internal network – they were also able to provide comparative data.

While these two embedded units of analysis allowed for a closer look at the transition processes to internal networks, the corporate unit of analysis was chosen to explore the questions involved in managing the differential pace of change. The two embedded units of analysis focused on the second, third and fourth analytical questions. These concern changes in structure, management and knowledge processes during transition and the barriers and supporting factors involved in sharing knowledge horizontally and moving towards an internal network. In addition to the key analytical questions to be addressed, Table 5.1 (p. 151) presents the units of analysis in which they are addressed. In this vein, the second and third units of analysis are contextually embedded in the first unit of analysis. Although the history of Rabobank is narrated to improve on the contextualist character of the case study (cf. Pettigrew, 1985), the major focus is on the period 1988–1998, which covers the entire change process in Rabobank's adoption of internal networks.

Data were obtained from a total of 40 pro forma interviews conducted during the period 1996–1998. Interviews were semi-structured to

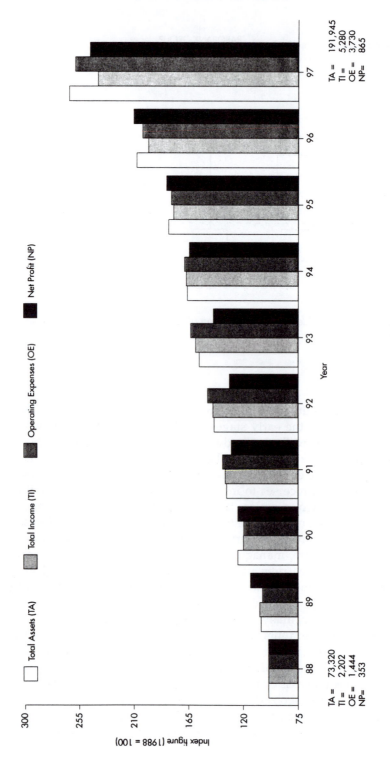

FIGURE 5.3 Performance index figures Rabobank Group 1988–1998 (1988 = 100) (annual reports)

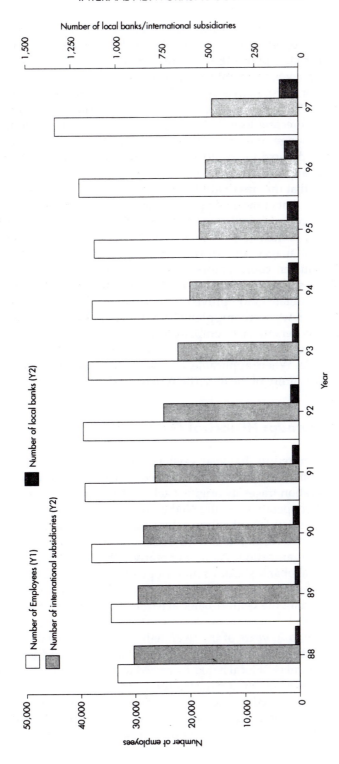

FIGURE 5.4   Number of employees, local banks and international subsidiaries Rabobank Group 1988–1998 (annual reports)

provide focus, reliability and increased validity (Yin, 1994), without passing by the opportunity 'to let people speak for themselves' in the shaping of their perceptions (Eisenhardt, 1989b; Starbuck, 1993: 887).

At the group level, seven interviews were conducted with managers and members of the strategy staff at the central organization Rabobank Nederland in 1996. In that same year, interviews were held with 18 general managers directing local banks to gain general insights into their processes of change and the management of knowledge. As local member banks differed in size (from a total balance sheet exceeding 1 billion ecus, to approximately 20 million ecus) general managers were approached so that the size distribution of the banks they directed was proportionate to that of the entire population of local banks. Data on the process of change and knowledge processes at Spectrum were obtained by interviewing 15 members in the period 1997–1998, ranging from the business unit manager and (former) management team members (N = 7) to cluster coordinators and project managers (N = 8). Additionally, a substantial number of informal talks with employees throughout the organization proved to be of value. The data obtained from the interviews were supplemented by (1) public information sources, such as generic and company-specific magazines and annual reports, and (2) company information sources, such as internal memos and archival data. Where applicable, all investigators were triangulated to increase the validity of the data (Pettigrew, 1990; Yin, 1994).

Rabobank Group: Historical Overview

Rabobank celebrated its 100-year existence as a cooperative in 1998. Although the name 'Rabobank' was adopted only in 1972, the financial services corporation traces its origins back to 1898 when 46 local agricultural credit cooperatives in the Netherlands were merged into two credit federations: Raiffeisenbank and Boerenleenbank. Simultaneous to the merger, the two credit federations decided in conjunction to establish a central organization. As a cooperative, the local boards also decided that Rabobank should remain operating as a decentralized organization. Thus the local banks remained completely responsible for their actions, while the central bank acted as an advisor to the local credit institutions.[1]

In the first 60 to 70 years of the twentieth century, societal developments led Rabobank to change the way in which it had traditionally operated. The number of local banks increased to a maximum of 1,324 in 1955 while the inclusion of non-agricultural customers in the clientele, including small and medium-sized enterprises (SME) and large firms, and the diversification of the branch, made customers more heterogeneous. As local member banks did not prove resourceful enough to deal with these changed circumstances, it was decided in 1972 to unite Raiffeisenbank and Boerenleenbank into one organization: Rabobank. In 1980, as the first international Rabobank subsidiary was opened, the name of the central organization was changed to 'Rabobank Nederland'. During the first century of its existence, Rabobank Group has thus evolved from a domestic agricultural bank, serving farmers with savings and loans products, to a high-tech multinational financial corporation offering the gamut of financial products and services to a broad range of customers. Still, the bank has continued to operate as a cooperative.

During the last decade, the financial performance of Rabobank has improved steadily (see Figure 5.3). In the period 1988–1997, total assets increased from 73,320 million ecus to 191,945 million ecus. Total income and operating expenses in 1988 multiplied by a factor of 2.5 to 5,280 ecus, and to 3,730 million ecus in 1997. Net profits rose from 353 million ecus in 1988 to 865 million ecus in 1997. Rabobank's domestic and international growth is also reflected in the development of the number of employees, international subsidiaries and local banks in the last decade, as displayed in Figure 5.4. Except for a small decrease in the period 1992–1995, the number of employees has increased from 33,200 to 44,667 in the past decade. The number of international subsidiaries also increased markedly, from 24 to 112, while the number of domestic local banks almost halved from 906 to 481 in the period 1988–1997. Although not indicative of a growth process, the decline in the number of local banks resulted from a concentration in which smaller banks were merged into larger ones. This, together with international expansion and the other performance figures, was an integral part of the change journey towards a new form of organizing that Rabobank instigated in 1988. Besides dealing with the environmental dynamics that impinged upon it, Rabobank has undertaken this corporate-wide change process to revitalize the cooperative identity of Rabobank Group.

First Unit of Analysis: The Change Journey of Rabobank

The cooperative identity that Rabobank Group adheres to has always been a strong intraorganizational contextual variable that has guided its development. Rabobank has a culture in which the client is placed centrally; everything starts with the client. As its CEO stressed in 1996, Rabobank's strategy is that it 'unremittingly seeks to link-up with the changed and changing societal circumstances' (Wijffels, 1996). Because local banks are responsible for their actions at both the strategic and operational levels, most market knowledge is retained by the local banks. In contrast to Rabobank's competitors who rely on the corporate hierarchy, the local member banks aim to exploit a competitive edge through continuous assessment of what clients expect from their bank.

In the earlier years, when the mass market for products prevailed, it was difficult for Rabobank to differentiate itself from its main competitors. But in the late 1970s and the 1980s, more demanding customers, and corporate clients in particular, started to ask for more integrated financial products which, because of legislative changes, could provide tax benefits. Consequently, banks were compelled to bring All-Finanz (or Universal Life Products) to the market. These combine products, such as insurance, mortgages, savings, investments and loans which were offered separately, into one package.

This development led to an industry-wide concentration movement in which some of Rabobank's competitors merged, and others followed an acquisition trajectory, or did both. Whereas Algemene Bank Nederland (ABN) merged with Amsterdam–Rotterdam Bank (AMRO bank) to form ABN-AMRO Bank and remained in the banking industry, Nationale Middenstandsbank (NMB) merged with insurer Nationale Nederlanden (NN) to form the banking-insurance combination Internationale Nederlanden Groep (ING). The latter also acquired Postbank in 1992, formerly known as Rijkspostspaarbank, which was Rabobank's main rival in the first half of the twentieth century. These two financial conglomerates that emerged from the concentration wave have continued to be Rabobank's main competitors since the mid-1980s.

To implement its strategy, Rabobank also took part in this wave by acquiring cooperative insurer Interpolis in 1990, and after a collaboration of seven years, global top ten investment banker Robeco in 1997. In addition, Rabobank entered the large cooperative alliance network UNICO, comprising Austrian RZB, Belgian CERA, German DG Bank, Italian ICCREA, Finnish OKO Bank and Swedish Förenings bank, to provide its international clients with tailored products and services. In this *external network* Rabobank became the nodal bank together with French-based Crédit Agricole, with which it started to cooperate in 1990, and with total revenues of US$34,015 million and with total assets of US$417,975 million listed 67th and 9th respectively on Fortune's Global 500 in 1998 (*Fortune*, 3 August, 1998). These developments formed an integral part of Rabobank's change journey.

Drivers for change at Rabobank

The blurring of product boundaries in the financial services sector has challenged financial institutions to change and integrate their products and services. Rabobank's competitors ABN-AMRO and ING pursued, in the words of a member of Rabobank's strategy staff, a strategy tied to the extended product function. These competitors offered a broad range of products and services, and by 'taking these off the shelves' integrated and combined them. Rabobank's traditional competitor Postbank on the other hand maintained its focus on selling mass products.

Although 'Rabobank could not entirely live up to the environmental dynamics during those years', according to a member of Rabobank's strategy staff, these developments stimulated Rabobank to change even further. It was felt that only by means of this strategy could Rabobank differentiate itself from its competitors. The CEO of Rabobank, Herman Wijffels, commented on Rabobank's transformation caused by the individualization of society: 'the change that had to be made . . . is the transformation in capabilities. Client wishes constitute the full guiding principle, the bank possesses the expertise to fulfill these' (external document, 1996). Based upon such a strategy, Rabobank aimed to be a completely customer-driven organization, and to offer clients fully tailored products, rather than the semi-tailored products that result from integrating products off the shelves. However, this strategy required that Rabobank adopt a new mode of organizing, one in which the expertise and knowledge of its employees could be more easily created, integrated and used. Apart from this strategic intent, a second and related driver made Rabobank adopt a new form of organizing.

As the central organization Rabobank Nederland grew both in size and influence, due to the mergers and acquisitions of the mid- to late-1980s, Rabobank Group, just like its competitors, came to resemble a large hierarchy rather than the decentralized organization that it had been since its founding in 1898. As a result of this gradual evolution to a centralized organization, the subunits began to complain that Rabobank Nederland did not know what happened at the periphery of the organization. At the same time, corporate headquarters began to dictate strategy to the subunits, thereby diminishing their autonomy. In addition, the local units themselves did not know where and from whom to get appropriate knowledge. The hierarchical organization form that gradually emerged was considered inappropriate to implement Rabobank's new strategy. As the CEO explained:

The hierarchical, pyramidal structure, with its tendency to uniformity, belongs to the past. The present era demands differentiation and specification, and with that, units with a large degree of autonomy. They have to serve the market and clients in a differentiated fashion. Adapting to client needs forces responsibilities at the level where contacts with the clients occur . . . Traditional organization concepts start from a concentration of knowledge at the top, to be directed downwards via the hierarchy. Owing to the distribution of knowledge, it has become impossible and unnecessary to manage organizations from the top. An inversion of that organizing principle is necessary. Basically, the pyramid has been inverted. But that is not a stable organizational form. Hence, it is better to think in terms of *the network concept*. The organization as a system of relations between people, who collectively want to realize a shared idea . . . Central to the network concept is that all

cells, call them expertise centres, in the network have their own responsibility. One cannot speak of subordination, but of mutual service rendering
based on equivalence. It is a living organism, in which every cell performs its
own function, without getting formalized instructions. The core notions of a
network are 'working together' and 'environmental awareness'. Only by
realizing that your behaviour affects other cells in the system, will you make
good choices. (Wijffels, 1996:b; italics added)

With the individualization of society increasing the concentration of the
financial industry, the developments in information technology and All-
Finanz products, top management in 1988 began to see the necessity of
restructuring. Furthermore, as Rabobank needed to broaden its scope to
remain competitive, the inclusion of yet more corporate clients and a
regrouping of tasks, competences, and responsibilities' (*Annual Report*,
1988) was in order. Less emphasis should be laid upon the local member
banks, traditionally the mainstays of Rabobank, while other units at
Rabobank should receive more attention in order to serve corporate
clients more effectively. After some initial discussions, the executive
board gained sufficient support in two to three years to move towards
this new mode of organizing. Later this proved to be an internal network form.

According to its CEO, Rabobank's transition was largely the result of
'the changes "on the outside" [that took] place quicker than ever'.
However, Rabobank's CEO still accredits the largest part of the change
to an *internal driver*, as he talks about the 'line of fracture' that constituted the start of the transition process Rabobank was about to undergo:

For we operate on the basis of continuity, there was no external factor, such
as a merger, a privatization, or an introduction on the stock exchange, that
symbolized the line of fracture. In the shape of a new style, we deliberately
created and symbolized such a line of fracture, and as such, marked the transition from a product-driven to a customer-driven organization. (Wijffels,
1996, 7)

The new style Rabobank attempted to adopt involved two important
complications. First, although Rabobank aimed to be customer-driven,
it could not abandon selling mass products, for there was still a large
market for such products in the form of standard mortgages, savings,
loans, and so forth. As mentioned above by Rabobank's CEO, such
products can only be exploited by means of the economies of scale
which a hierarchical organization generates. Thus, Rabobank needed to
maintain at least some of its hierarchical form to preserve the exploitation of mass products, while introducing an internal network-based
form of organizing to preserve the exploration of new, client-tailored
products in line with market demand. Secondly, in 1988 Rabobank was
made up of three major divisions: Wholesale Banking, Support Services

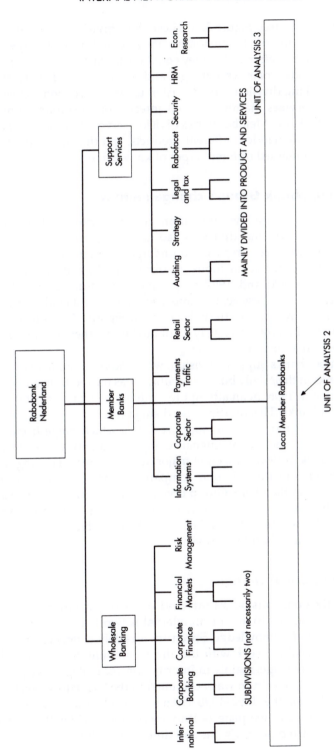

FIGURE 5.5 *Organizational structure Rabobank Group 1988 (annual report)*

and Member Banks (see Figure 5.5). These three divisions were so differentiated in terms of the customers they served and the type of products which they offered that they could not be part of the same network to integrate their knowledge and resources. Whereas the Wholesale Banking division served corporate and international clients and Support Services mainly serviced internal organizational units within Rabobank, the Member Banks division served domestic clients. All these clients demanded different products, and thus the units that served them maintained different types of knowledge.

Scope of Rabobank Group's change journey

Although the corporate-level transition process started in 1988, the change journeys of distinct divisions had different years of departure. Some divisions were not prepared to undergo such an encompassing change in 1988, or like acquisitions insurer Interpolis and investment banker Robeco (1990 and 1997 respectively) post-dated the 1988 changes. Before 1996, these acquisitions were normally included in the corporate hierarchy as a fourth division (as in Figure 5.5). As of 1996, each acquired company, previously combined with others in the same division, formed a separate division.

The Member Banks Support division, which advises and helps local member banks in their daily business routine, was moved from a line to a staff position in 1996, in an attempt to facilitate networking between local member banks. This division was distinct from Support Services, which carries out more general support duties which range from IT support to coffee machine maintenance. Figure 5.6 depicts the structure of Rabobank in 1998, with eight major divisions created during the corporate-level transition. If one compares Figures 5.5 and 5.6, it becomes clear that Rabobank Group became less centralized. The year in which Rabobank's corporate structure underwent the largest change was in 1996 (this was reflected in the *Annual Report*, which did not contain an organization chart for that year).

Differential pace of change

Of all the divisions, business units and other organizational units, Spectrum was the first to initiate an internal network. In line with the strategic demand for knowledge, Spectrum was deliberately created in 1992 as an internal network with the aim to provide the group with cutting-edge knowledge, mainly in Information Technology. As a services business unit, Spectrum was positioned in the facilitatory division Rabofacet. During the 1992–1998 change period described below, Spectrum constituted a template, or learning platform, within Rabobank Group, from which other divisions and units tried to learn.

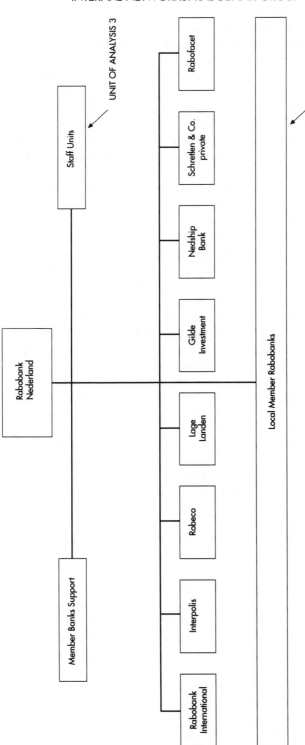

FIGURE 5.6   *Organizational structure Rabobank Group 1998 (annual report)*

In 1996, Rabofacet underwent the change to an internal network form of organizing. It moved from a hierarchy with two divisions to a flat organizational structure with 14 business units, in order to increase collaboration among units. Rabobank International's change programme to internal network forms of organizing also commenced in 1996, the year in which Wholesale Banking was renamed Rabobank International. Currently, Rabobank International even advertises with the claim that because of the network structure adopted, clients of, for example, the office in Sydney or London can benefit from knowledge generated in the office in Hong Kong.

The transition of the local member banks was preceded by two change programmes: FOCUS and EDLB. The corporate change programme FOCUS was instigated to increase customer responsiveness at Rabobank, by establishing two different business templates, one for standard and one for tailored products. The local bank change programme EDLB (Efficiency Drive Local Banks) was designed to increase the efficiency of local banks by sharing the best practices of some high-performing local banks. Furthermore, in 1991 an internal labour market was created to abolish the regional recruitment procedure that had been in place, and to benefit from the knowledge which employees had gained working in different parts of Rabobank. In the context of the two corporate change programmes FOCUS and EDLB, the successive change journeys at the local member banks and the Support division were based on what was called Vision '98. An extension of FOCUS, this programme was initiated in 1995 with the formal incorporation of a new banking style and a new corporate logo. These moves alongside the adoption of a network form changed Rabobank's position in the financial services industry. Nevertheless, the actual change process at the local member banks started in 1997–1998. In 1998, the Member Banks support division launched an initiative for a 'flexible network organization'.

Figure 5.7 tentatively illustrates the phenomenon of the differential pace of change in five parts of Rabobank, by showing the change processes of each in terms of organizational differentiation and integration, and in particular horizontal integration. Two of these five parts, the local member banks and the business unit Spectrum, relate to the units to be discussed below. Except for their size, local member banks were much alike. As a result, most local banks offered similar products based on a similar knowledge base. The degree of differentiation was relatively low. At the same time, since they operated largely autonomously without consultation with other local banks, the local banks were not tightly integrated at the horizontal level. This is reflected in Figure 5.7: the starting point of the change process is in the bottom left corner. Therefore the change process of the local member banks, starting in 1997–1998, was initiated to increase the local banks' position on both

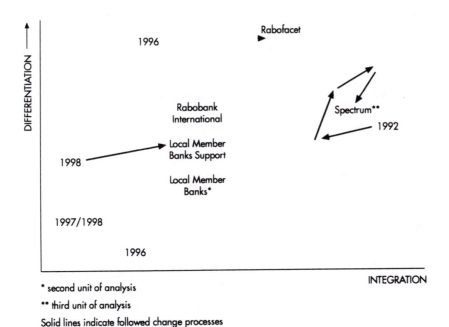

FIGURE 5.7   *Differential pace of change of five parts of the Rabobank Group*

dimensions. The knowledge stocks of local member banks were envisaged as more differentiated, while increasing horizontal knowledge flows would preserve the integration of these knowledge stocks.

Rabofacet's change process, started in 1996, was intended to increase the integration of its already differentiated business units by increasing the collaboration between them. Also starting in 1996, Rabobank International's change process was a trajectory in which the differentiation of the international subsidiaries increased, followed by a gradual integration of these subsidiaries by emphasizing the knowledge sharing between them. Since 1996 Rabobank International has been systematically implementing a knowledge-driven strategy with a focus on customers and a focus on sectors that 'put firmly in place a networked approach which brings together all available expertise within the Rabobank Group'. Only the Member Banks support division was less horizontally integrated, partly due to its functional structure. In 1998, this also began the change to a 'flexible network organization' in order to increase internal integration. Finally, Spectrum was created with the intent of developing an internal network. Notwithstanding the minor shifts that took place as a result of the problems associated with evolution and the high growth it faced, Spectrum has always been differentiated while being integrated. That is, units in Spectrum were decentralized and had discretion to perform a variety of activities, while they worked closely together.

Second Unit of Analysis: the Local Member Banks

The local member banks serve domestic clients with the products offered by Rabobank. We focus particularly on the knowledge process characteristics of the local banks to describe the degree to which they constitute an internal network. The three themes of structure, management and knowledge processes guide the analysis.

Organizational structure

In almost all of the interviews, the general managers stressed that each local bank is largely autonomous. Although the central organization involves itself in affairs that are best handled by a central actor or those that are of concern for the entire organization to keep it on track, both operational and strategic matters are almost completely at the discretion of the local units. That is, within the confines of the industry Rabobank is operating in, what the name Rabobank stands for, what it purports to be, and within the products and services offered, local units act upon local developments using their own resources and discretion. Despite the autonomy of the local units, some linkages exist between them in the form of management meetings, seminars, national and regional consultative structures, interpersonal networks and Information Technology networks. In the interviews it was revealed, however, that local banks make no use of teams of employees originating from different local banks.

The interviews also indicated that differences exist among local banks in the commonality of this consent. An important cause of this is that the central organization develops most products and services to be distributed through the local banks. Moreover, a few of the general managers felt that the central organization involved itself more in their local units than it did in others. As a corollary, they argued that the local banks they lead are dependent on the central organization rather than on themselves and other local banks, and that the central organization exerts too dominant a role to call Rabobank a network organization. At the other extreme, a few of the general managers perceived their local units as operating in a 'market with the name Rabobank pinned on it'. That is, they felt they were loners in a 'market' where local units, rather than collaborating, competed with each other to gain the best clients.

Management

Managers and employees at different levels within the local banks have different responsibilities both for the creation of knowledge within the local bank they work for and the sharing of knowledge with other organizational units of Rabobank. Differences in responsibility for the creation of knowledge are not significant across general management, supervisory management and employees. The specific roles exercised at each level vary substantially, though. As a general manager illustrated in an interview, 'my role is more one of making sure that knowledge gets created and used properly, whereas the supervisory managers and, even more, the employees are the ones who must do it. They are closest to our clients.'

In interviews general managers adduced arguments in support of the importance of sharing of knowledge across local banks. Since general managers generally have longer tenure and therefore know more people in Rabobank, it appeared they have the primary responsibility for their local units, and are usually the ones who participate in seminars and meetings. As one of the general managers mentioned, the person in such a position 'is the one designated to share knowledge with colleagues'. Heavy responsibility for sharing knowledge with other local units is put on the general managers. The role of supervisory management, and to a greater extent employees, is limited in that they hardly participate in events that transcend the boundaries of local banks.

Knowledge processes and flows

In Figure 5.8, the two types of knowledge flow that occur in the local member bank setting are depicted: (1) vertical knowledge flows from the central organization Rabobank Nederland to the local banks, and (2) horizontal knowledge flows between the local member banks. The interviews revealed that flows of knowledge at Rabobank are primarily *vertical and unidirectional* in the sense that the central organization, or one of its affiliated subsidiaries, is the main source of new knowledge for the local banks. Horizontal knowledge flows between local banks are less important. Furthermore, the interviews made clear that the general managers of the local banks tend to perceive the central organization as 'thinking for them', and that most knowledge is retained at and obtained from, this central point. It appeared that most local banks rely on knowledge obtained from the central organization. Examples of how knowledge was transferred vertically are the use of advisors of the central organization, products and services, seminars or company documents. The central organization and affiliated subsidiaries invent and develop the core and related products and services respectively. Advisors help local units comply with the wishes of the client at the local site when the matter is too complex to be locally organized. These mechanisms facilitate the vertical transfer of explicit knowledge while mechanisms for the horizontal dissemination of tacit knowledge are not widely used. These products and services are distributed via the local units. Market knowledge and knowledge of the local context, however, are mostly created and obtained within the local bank itself.

In line with this finding, a manager at the central organization observed that Rabobank 'focuses increasingly on systems'. Consequently, the locally embedded distinction between two different local banks in two different geographic areas is becoming blurred, in the sense that the local banks are 'nothing more than an interface between client and system', making cooperation and knowledge sharing between them unnecessary.

Corroborative evidence: supportive instruments and barriers

Although extremely useful for sharing knowledge horizontally, the formation of interfunctional and interunit teams and the transfer of employees and management between local banks are among the less frequently used instruments for horizontal knowledge sharing. The 'horizontal' mechanisms of management conferences and informal talks are more popular, but are not used to intentionally share knowledge. The interviews clarify that *horizontal knowledge sharing* is inhibited to the

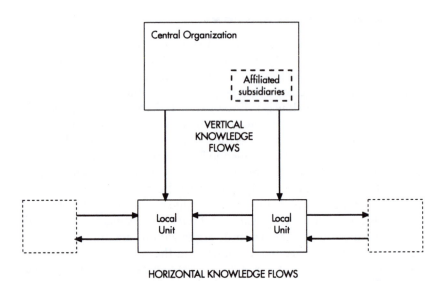

FIGURE 5.8   *Knowledge flows in the local member bank setting (adapted from van Wijk and van den Bosch, 1998)*

degree that each local bank, partly because of its relative autonomy, is perceived by its management to be a separate organization rather than a unit serving the entire organization of Rabobank Group.

To a large extent, the local banks compete with each other within the organization. Furthermore, the boards of local banks are comprised of local inhabitants, who do not have an interest in their local bank sharing knowledge with others. This was reflected in the case of rival home appliance shop owners, who being on the boards of their local banks, had no interest in sharing knowledge. Another barrier to the horizontal spread of knowledge is the observation, revealed in an interview, that many units do not realize what they know, and moreover, do not know where to find the appropriate knowledge. To a large extent, apparently, Rabobank's local banks are not transparent enough to share knowledge effectively and efficiently.

Although the local member banks look like an internal network form of organizing from the outside, a closer look at structure, management, and in particular the knowledge flows between local banks, reveals that the 'network' of local member banks is not yet a network. But, as mentioned above, a change journey was instigated in 1997–1998 to bring the local member banks closer to an internal network form of organizing, the consequences of which still have to be seen.

Third Unit Of Analysis: Spectrum During 1992–1998

This embedded case study illustrates the change process and evolution of Spectrum in the period 1992–1998. Spectrum, a business unit within Rabofacet and the facilitatory division within Rabobank (see Figures 5.5 and 5.6), was created to provide Rabobank Group with cutting-edge knowledge, particularly in the area of Information Technology (IT) in order to improve Rabobank's competitive position.

Structural transition of Spectrum 1992–1998

The structure of Spectrum underwent substantial changes in its short history, which are illustrated in Figure 5.9. The major transition occurred in 1994–1995 when the previous mode of organizing was completely recast. At its founding in 1992, Spectrum employed 30 people and was organized along two explorative product units (PUs) that stood in close relation to each other. Shortly after its founding, Spectrum obtained a number of groups of Information Technology experts from other parts of Rabobank and incorporated them as three new PUs in the existing organizational structure. With their inclusion, the number of employees rose from 30 to 60. This increase in organizational size triggered a process of compartmentalization, which was strongly evident in the dress code of the different PUs. As a management team member observed, 'People in one product unit wear T-shirts, whereas people in another wear suits. This illustrates the difference in culture between the product units, and the resulting lack of communication and knowledge sharing between them.'

As these developments inhibited the creation and sharing of knowledge horizontally across PUs (as illustrated in Figure 5.9), the structure of Spectrum was completely reconceived by Spectrum's management team during 1994–1995. They sought to regain the internal network structure and the explorative focus of the years right after founding. The five PUs were abolished, and instead three 'areas of attention' (AoA) were conceived to change the rhetoric used in Spectrum. Partly because the number of employees increased to approximately 100, each AoA housed a variable number of interdependent, fluid 'clusters' to retain, as the business unit manager of Spectrum referred to it, 'the subtlety of small groups'. The number of clusters in an AoA was deliberately variable in order to be able to tailor Spectrum to client demand and technological advancements. That is, in one period of time there could be five clusters, whereas in a subsequent period there could be three or eight clusters, possibly with entirely different names.

1992
30 employees
2 Product Units

1993
60 employees
5 Product Units

1994–95
100 employees > 120 employees
3 Areas of Attention
15 Product Clusters

1996
220 employees
4 Areas of Attention
13 Clusters

1997–98
350 employees > 550 employees
6 Areas of Attention
29 Clusters

FIGURE 5.9   *Spectrum's transition process towards an internal network: 1992–1998*

By the end of 1996, the number of employees had increased to 220. As in the previous period, there was only one formal management layer. The number of organizational layers, however, had increased with the establishment of projects and teams cutting across clusters and AoAs to ease collaboration. Although the increase in number of employees led to tighter time schedules, in particular on behalf of the managers, and, moreover, to creating an additional AoA, the way of organizing remained intact in the period 1997–1998. However, the number of employees has grown to approximately 350 people (partly because of the inflow of people from another business unit of Rabobank), increasing the total number of AoAs to six, and consequently the number of clusters.

Transition of management processes in Spectrum 1992–1998

The structural transition process of Spectrum towards an internal network also had implications for management processes. The increase in employees had a substantial impact on the managerial function in that the 'span of control' of managers increased rapidly over time. During the main transition period in 1994–1995, an extra layer of coordinating personnel was added to free up the management team, who could no longer oversee the activities of all employees in the AoAs which they led. These cluster coordinators were not appointed with formal management positions and tasks (for example, execution of performance appraisals, authority to sign for contracts of more than $5,000); rather, they came to be, as the BU manager of Spectrum called them, 'the functional feeders' of Spectrum. Their task was limited to overseeing and leading the activities in the clusters so that the goals of Spectrum were adhered to. They also served an important role in establishing new linkages across clusters and AoAs. Thus, although there were *three organizational layers* (management team – cluster coordinators – employees), there was only *one formal management layer*.

In 1996, the number of organizational layers increased by one with the establishment of project managers heading the projects and teams of persons in different clusters and AoAs. These project managers originated from one of the clusters participating in the project, and if the project was traversing AoA boundaries they came from the management team. As the number of employees increased from approximately 220 to approximately 350 over the period 1996–1998, the demands on managers' time had substantially increased. As a management team member said, 'If I do all my performance appraisal talks with the employees, I will be busy for one to two months.' This development has currently led to extensive discussions about giving formal management functions to the cluster coordinators. Discussion has centred around the need to maintain only one formal layer of management in order to preserve Spectrum's flatness with concomitant agility and flexibility; while recognizing that the increasing size of Spectrum requires additional management resources.

Currently, the management team of Spectrum appears to favour maintaining one management layer. As the BU manager of Spectrum recognized, 'the *way* of dealing with things matters, no matter what kind of structure you have. The processes are important.' Emphasizing collaboration, communication, informality and fluidity has always been an integral part of the vision of Spectrum. All the changes in Spectrum have also occurred in line with this vision of the BU manager, who has been with Spectrum since its founding, and throughout Rabobank is recognized as the champion of Spectrum. Almost all changes in the transition process of Spectrum have been at the discretion of the BU manager and the management team.

Knowledge flows in transition within Spectrum 1992–1998

Over its seven-year existence, Spectrum has witnessed different developments regarding horizontal and vertical knowledge flows. These have been both the result and the cause of the managerial and structural changes that took place to reconceptualize the business unit. This reconceptualization stems from continuous threats to Spectrum's transition to an internal network form. Shortly after its founding, the two PUs stood in close relation to each other and were able to share both explicit and tacit knowledge on a horizontal basis, either by face to face contacts or via Information Technology systems. With the incorporation of another three PUs in 1993, the increasing compartmentalization quickly led to increasing differences among the PUs, inhibiting the process of horizontal knowledge sharing across PU boundaries.

The main transition period of 1994–1995 was instigated to reconfigure knowledge flows, in particular horizontal knowledge flows. With renaming of product units as areas of attention and the incorporation of clusters, the aim was to maintain close links within Spectrum and, as a result, the sharing of knowledge across boundaries. Clusters remained small in order to ensure that employees could consult each other to solve problems. This worked by both formal and informal routes, as the Chief Executive described: 'unintended meetings at the central coffee machine'. As the number of employees increased constantly, however, the AoAs also became 'islands' within Spectrum in terms of knowledge sharing. This doubtlessly resulted in fewer innovative efforts to generate new products and services.

The incorporation of projects as a structural mechanism was executed in 1996 to ameliorate the transfer of knowledge across boundaries within Spectrum. However, as more employees started working for

Spectrum, projects were increasingly established within the confines of the AoAs, not crossing the boundaries of them, thereby leading to a decrease in horizontal knowledge flows. The relative increase of vertical knowledge flows was strengthened by the incorporation of a substantial number of employees from another business unit of Rabobank. This unit had a hierarchical tradition, which was internalized by its members. As a result, these employees had substantial difficulties in adapting to Spectrum's internal network characteristics.

Discussion and Conclusion

Although change at the corporate level is still going on, it has become evident that in the period 1988–1998, Rabobank Group increased its effectiveness in creating and sharing knowledge throughout the organization. Knowledge creation and knowledge sharing constituted an important external and internal driver for Rabobank to introduce internal network forms of organizing. Rabobank aimed to differentiate itself from its main competitors by providing fully tailored products to its customers which required a strong capability in creating, sharing and integrating knowledge (cf. Van Wijk and Van den Bosch, 1998a). However, the case study also illustrated the *bipolarity of structure* that remained, due to the imperative to accommodate all customer requirements. A hierarchy was needed for mass products, while a network was imperative to capitalize on the management of knowledge.

The first analytical question aimed to provide insights into the *differential pace of change* when a firm moves towards internal network forms of organizing, and the drivers for such change. It appears that a large corporation's organizational parts may exhibit differential paces of change when they develop new forms of organizing. During Rabobank's change journey towards an internal network form of organizing, several internal networks developed concurrently and at different paces, in distinct divisions and organizational units. Three antecedents to these differential paces of change can be observed: all deal with the heterogeneity a firm exposes. First, the size of Rabobank restricted the development of one large internal network. Secondly, since different divisions and organizational units served different customers, it was necessary to pursue different change processes for each division or unit. Thirdly, the nature of the products, mass or tailored, proved a large determinant of the change processes pursued.

These antecedents also relate to the drivers for change at Rabobank. Although strong external pressures were present in the shape of environmental dynamics such as the individualization of society, and changes in the nature of products and services offered, the most important driver at Rabobank was an internal one. While its competitors were mainly offering mass or semi-tailored products, Rabobank decided to differentiate further and provide its customers with fully tailored products. As a first mover in the industry Rabobank recognized it needed to restructure and adopt a new form of organizing: an internal network.

It was difficult to assess the consequences of adopting internal network forms of organizing at the local member banks, for they are still beginning the process of change. It was apparent, however, that because the central organization developed the bulk of the products, the local member banks continued to rely heavily on vertical knowledge flows. Furthermore, tailoring products to client needs at the site of the local member bank was done primarily without consultation with other local member banks and the knowledge stocks these held. As decreases in horizontal knowledge flows indicated a decrease in the degree of internal networking, the *knowledge perspective* seemed a good indicator of whether a firm, or organizational unit, operates as an internal network.

This relationship, earlier suggested by Van Wijk and Van den Bosch (1998b), was also illustrated at Spectrum. In addition, in the case of Spectrum it has been illustrated that internal networks increase the effectiveness by which knowledge can be created, shared and integrated. In this way, new combinations of knowledge were possible that led to the exploration of new products and services. The impact of size on the evolution of Spectrum, however, is still an unresolved issue. In 1996, Spectrum found a solution by introducing 'areas of attention' and clusters. However, as size continued to increase, Spectrum could not continue to include organizational and managerial levels as this unequivocally led to an increase in the degree of hierarchy and a decrease in the degree of internal networking. It would seem that size plays an important role in the development towards, and evolution of, internal network forms of organizing.

Besides indicating the importance of the knowledge perspective, all units of analysis also illustrated the fact that *complementarities* are needed between structural, managerial and knowledge attributes of organizations during change (Starbuck, 1993; Whittington et al., 1999b). The case evidence of the local member banks highlights the problem of removing the structures and managerial hierarchies of traditional organizations. Without changing structures and management processes, substantial horizontal knowledge sharing will not take place. The Spectrum case provided evidence of the complementarities between structure, management and knowledge processes as well. For instance, it appeared that when horizontal knowledge-sharing opportunities were threatened, deliberate structural and managerial changes were aimed at restoring these opportunities.

As horizontal knowledge flows may be considered the lifeblood of internal networks, understanding the *enabling and restricting factors* of this knowledge-sharing process is of great importance. Our case evidence contributes to this understanding in several ways. From the complementarities argument made above, it is obvious that organizational structure and management processes can both enable and restrict horizontal knowledge sharing. The more organizational structure and management processes are in line with those of an internal network, the more an enabling influence will be exerted. Although the effect of size is a significant attribute of organizations that has been widely researched, the study at Spectrum has underscored size as an important factor, as it impinges strongly on the development and evolution of internal networks. Although Spectrum found a solution to this problem in 1996 with the inclusion of areas of attention and clusters in the organization, this also meant an increase in the degree of hierarchy. The same solution may not be available when the next threshold of size is reached, for that would mean an increase in the level of hierarchy that could threaten the formation of internal networks. Nevertheless, while hierarchy proved indispensable in providing mass products to customers, it appeared to have important side-effects in terms of the knowledge flow configuration used among the local banks.

Besides providing insights into the key analytical questions that were addressed, the case study also illustrated some other issues that may be important for future research. First, the change journey of Rabobank illustrates the possibility that an organic element is involved in moving towards internal network forms of organizing. In the first instance, top management recognized the need to adopt a new form of organizing. It was only at a later stage that the form of organizing culminated in an internal network. Whether Rabobank has managed to move towards the internal network form of organizing visualized by Rabobank's CEO is difficult to assess. At the time of the investigation, the local member banks appeared not to be functioning as an internal network. However, many parts of the organization were still in the process of changing in 1998. Spectrum, on the other hand, was created as an internal network, but experienced the difficulties of being a high-growth firm. As its size increased, operating as an internal network became more problematic. With the efforts of the business unit manager and the intermediate changes in the structure of Spectrum, however, it has managed to overcome these problems to some extent. The developments at Spectrum are also evidence of organic evolution.

Secondly, this case study indicates that internal networks are not confined to *multinational operations*. Much of the literature on new organizational forms stems from scholarly work done in the fields of international management and MNCs. In the context of the MNC, new modes of organizing emerge because of environmental turbulence which requires both local responsiveness and the maintenance of a global, integrated profile (Bartlett and Ghoshal, 1989, 1993; Hedlund and Ridderstråle, 1997). The international business literature, stresses MNCs locally responsive and differentiated, while remaining integrated as a whole (cf. Lawrence and Lorsch, 1967b; Baker, 1992).

Thirdly, there are important *contextual measures* in the case study that have to be taken into account in future research. The failure of the local banks to operate as an internal network may be ascribed partly to the fact that Rabobank is a cooperative. The very autonomy derived from a cooperative structure may reduce the motivation to share knowledge between subunits, as was shown with the effect of the involvement of local people on the boards of local member banks. Thus, while the cooperative structure certainly facilitated the development of internal networks with the absence of a strong hierarchy, it also provided Rabobank with some barriers to the development of its internal network.

In conclusion, the analysis of the change towards new forms of organizing in a large corporation revealed that different parts of the corporation appeared to have differential paces of change, and were subject to a bipolarity in forms of organizing. These differential paces influence the configuration of knowledge flows both at the corporate level and at the organizational unit level, and consequently, the opportunities for knowledge creation and sharing. Strategies aimed at increasing these opportunities have to take these findings into account.

Acknowledgements

The authors are indebted to managers at Rabobank for their valuable support. The authors also greatly appreciate the constructive criticisms of the editor Andrew Pettigrew and other collaborators in the INN-FORM project on new organization forms: Leona Achtenhagen, Chris David, Evelyn Fenton, Leif Melin, Tomas Müllern, Simon Peck, Winfried Ruigrok, Carlos Sánchez-Runde and Richard Whittington. These people certainly improved our thinking and helped clarify our ideas. The authors are furthermore thankful to Marco Huygens, who read through various earlier drafts of this chapter and provided us with comments and suggestions.

Note

1   Invented by German Mayor Friedrich Wilhelm Raiffeisen (1818–1888), the cooperative principle was grounded in the establishment of credit institutions of which farmers became members by depositing their savings and excess financial resources in the form of earnings and profits. Coordinated by representatives chosen from and by the members, these local banks, pooled financial resources

from many different sources. When farmers were short of financial resources, the credit institutions could remedy shortages at lower interest rates than when farmers contacted traders and shopkeepers for loans, giving their harvest as security. The profits made are explicitly used to preserve the continuity of the cooperatives, rather than paid out as dividends to stockholders. Another essential part of the cooperative principle is that major decisions are made on the basis of democratic governance; that is, in meetings where associates from both the local banks and the central organization discuss, and occasionally vote for, the strategies to be implemented.

6

Hilti AG: Shared Leadership and the Rise of the Communicating Organization

Winfried Ruigrok, Leona Achtenhagen, Johannes Rüegg-Stürm and Mathias Wagner

An inspiring literature emerged in the early 1990s which claimed that there was a rise of new forms of organizing (for example, Bartlett and Ghoshal, 1993; Ezzamel et al., 1994; Hedlund, 1994). According to this literature, some innovative companies were moving beyond traditional hierarchies and compartmentalization, and towards strategic and operational decentralization and intra-company networks, seeking to repair some of the disadvantages associated with the Chandlerian multidivisional organization (Chandler, 1980). In themselves, the company structures and processes referred to in this literature were not really new, as they had been developed by functional specialists in areas such as IT, logistics, marketing and human resources. However, what made this literature interesting was the attempt to address the *combined* implications of the many isolated changes.

Recently, it has been suggested that an important characteristic of newly emerging modes of organizing is the intensity of communication (Rockart, 1998). Traditional organizations were designed to simplify and *reduce* the need for communication because the exchange of ideas and information was very expensive. The advances in information technology, the dispersion of knowledge across organizations and international competitive pressures have changed this logic altogether:

'In today's world of intense competition, the benefits of both economies of scale and local innovation are necessary. Thus, a federal approach is appearing more and more today. Its only drawback is that it requires better management and more coordination than the older forms. It is much more communication-intensive' (Rockart, 1998: 417).

The shift towards such a communicating organization may arise with a fundamental change in leadership and management roles (e.g. Bush and Frohman, 1991). Traditionally, managers spent a great deal of their time planning, budgeting, and reporting back variance in subordinate behaviour for intervention, as employees were not trusted to take charge or resolve discrepancies themselves (Tersine et al., 1997). In a federal and communicating organization, employees are more likely to be *expected to take charge* or resolve dilemmas themselves; managers will need to *encourage* and reward employees' cooperative behaviour; and subsequently *new measures* will be needed to evaluate individual inputs, group performance and linkages to suppliers or customers.

Unfortunately, few detailed process studies of such comprehensive organizational innovations are available. This chapter pursues three questions, in its analysis of the case of Hilti AG, a company based in the Principality of Liechtenstein, and a world leader in its field, supplying fastening and demolition systems to the construction industry. The first question refers to the issue of *process sequencing* when moving beyond the Chandlerian organization: did Hilti first move beyond hierarchies or beyond divisions, or were these parallel or even complementary changes? The second question addresses the role of *communication* in the post-Chandlerian organization: what communication needs and solutions emerged as Hilti shifted away from established corporate structures towards new and unfamiliar internal linkages? The third issue this chapter explores is the role of *leadership* in organizational transformation: how and to what extent did Hilti's top management shape the changes that took place, and how and when did Hilti employees assume leadership themselves?

This case is a prime example of a company experimenting with new modes of organizing, as it goes beyond the implementation of empowerment, which has often been cited as one of the key characteristics of new organizational trends in the area of human resource management. Within Hilti, the notion of empowerment is considered to be still too hierarchical – instead the company searches for ways to really share its leadership, rather than 'empowering' by hierarchically imposing a certain behaviour. All employees 'take charge' in the company's tasks – by actively seeking responsibility instead of being asked to take it on. The means for creating the spirit of shared leadership throughout the organization is extensive communication, fostered by multiple communication channels, as well as by courses for every employee in which the freedom to communicate and to take charge are promoted. This focus on communication to support the idea of shared leadership led us to the notion of Hilti as a 'communicating organization'.

Hilti has been experimenting with organizational innovations for decades, and in doing so has proven to be a restless organization always searching for an even better way of doing business. The dynamic character of this restlessness and continuous stretching of organizational routines fits Hilti's idea of actively searching for new modes of *organizing* rather than having an organization (cf. Chapters 1 and 10 in this volume).

Hilti is located in Schaan in the Principality of Liechtenstein, which is a small (160 square kilometres and 31,500 inhabitants) state between Austria and Switzerland. It offers professional users in the construction industry a comprehensive programme of drilling and demolition, powder-actuated fastening, anchor, diamond and construction chemical systems. Hilti considers its core competency to be high quality innovation, resulting from close contacts with its customers. Two-thirds of its 12,000 employees work in marketing organizations, that is, in direct sales, engineering and customer service functions. In 1998, Hilti achieved sales of 2,630 million Swiss francs ($ 1.9 billion).

During 1997 and 1998, a total of 55 interviews were conducted at all levels of the firm. The interviews focused on the evolution of the Hilti organization and the logic of the various organizational and managerial innovations introduced in the company over the 1980s and 1990s. The interviews had a duration of 1–2 hours, and 16 of the interviews were with members of the executive board and the extended executive board, the so-called corporate management group. The interviews dealt with a broad array of topics, to allow us to explore numerous issues in the company. At first, the interviews were aimed at gaining an overall picture of the organization, but soon we began to focus on leadership, interaction and communication issues as these appeared to be the distinguishing elements within the company. We have carried out a number of internal workshops over the 1997–1998 period to test our findings. In this chapter, we shall occasionally refer to other articles on Hilti published in German-speaking academic and popular journals.

This chapter is organized as follows. In the next section we describe the company's evolution until the early 1980s and analyse its main competitors. We then identify the external and internal drivers for change. The following two sections constitute the core of the chapter: they cluster and analyse the various changes at Hilti starting in 1983 and examine their process sequencing. We go on to address the barriers to change in the Hilti organization, before reflecting on the consequences of the changes described for both top management and other employees. The next section identifies some management issues yet to be resolved. The final section summarizes the main findings and reflects upon the three guiding questions of this case study.

Evolution of the Organization and Major Competitors

The evolution of the Hilti organization until 1983 may be divided into four stages: establishment and growth (1941–1961), internationalization (1962–1972), Hilti Management Model (1973–1976) and restructuring (1977–1982). These periods constitute the formative years of the organization and provide the setting for the changes over the 1980s and 1990s.

Establishment and growth (1941–1961)

The history of Hilti is especially the story of one entrepreneur: Martin Hilti. In 1941, Martin Hilti joined his brother Eugen to work in his Schaan mechanical workshop. This workshop, with five employees, specialized in contract manufacturing but gradually also began to develop some fastening products of its own. Since it was difficult to find skilled workers, Hilti engaged in intensive training and early on started offering special master craftsmen courses, thus putting a focus on people at an early stage of the company's development. By 1945, employment had risen to 100 – although this number declined over the next few years following the post-war business decline (Hilti, 1995).

Despite this recession, the Hilti brothers were convinced that in Europe's post-war reconstruction, fastening technology had great chances of succeeding in the market. After the war, Hilti was commissioned to produce a high-velocity fastening tool as well as special studs to go with it. Even though the tool did not function properly and the studs broke frequently, Hilti purchased the tool's patent from the Swiss company that had developed it and further developed both tool and studs. This decision for *in-house product innovation* was to become the first leg of the organization. Hilti focused on developing a safer fastening method based on the power of a hammer blow. These hand-driven tools were safer but still not very efficient. In 1950, Hilti launched its first in-house-designed powder-actuated tool, Perfix, and the first Hilti-designed hand-drive tools appeared on the market in 1951. By 1950, sales volumes reached 3.8 million Swiss francs, and by 1954 this had risen to 6.7 million Swiss francs. In the following years, priority was given to minimizing the risks of uncontained driving power. The 'DX principle', using a driving piston, further reduced the risk of severe injury through improper use. In later years, this care for the well-being of its employees led to the nickname of 'Mom Hilti'. In 1958 Hilti began the serial production of its DX 100 in Schaan, and the tool became the star of the Hanover 1958 Trade Fair.

With sales of the DX 100 rising steadily, safety concerns remained an issue. After witnessing a fatal accident that showed how dangerous high-velocity tools could be if used improperly, Martin Hilti realized that he needed to provide a highly trained sales and support staff, and on-site demonstration. This led to the creation of the second leg of the Hilti organization: the introduction of *direct sales and marketing*. Between 1954 and 1961, several national market organizations were founded in Europe and North America. By 1961, 20 years after Martin Hilti had joined the family workshop, sales had reached 40 million Swiss francs ($9.3 million), and 420 people were employed.

Internationalization (1962–1972)

Following the establishment of direct sales through the national market organizations, the 1960s were dominated by the drive to decentralize marketing activities. This was boosted by the fact that during the 1960s the sellers' market turned into a buyers' market: customers began to demand high-quality products tailored to their specifications, at a reasonable price. In these years, Hilti sales representatives became frequent visitors to building sites all over the world: the red Hilti tool box became a symbol of quality among construction workers, and the sentence 'Pass me the Hilti, please!' is still often used for any brand of drilling machines.

By the mid-1960s, it became obvious that running a product line of only hand-drive and power-actuated tools imposed clear boundaries to further growth. Therefore, Hilti decided to diversify into products for fastening heavy loads by adding drilling and electric tools. In 1967 Hilti achieved a second breakthrough innovation when it introduced the TE 17 electro-pneumatic rotary hammer drill.

By the late 1960s, when it had also begun to penetrate the Southeast Asian market, Hilti ran into the limits of decentralizing market activities. The need was felt to make it easier for the market organizations to represent their views to headquarters and to ensure information flows between the various market organizations. Therefore, five market region departments were created at Schaan. Additional changes also took place at Schaan: nearby production plants were acquired in order to enhance capacity; top management was professionalized after the creation of a board of directors which was to serve as an advisory body to Martin Hilti; and a number of Research and Development (R&D) departments were relocated abroad in response to scarcity in the local labour market and the strict Liechtenstein immigration policies. Thus, a development office for steelworks equipment was opened in Glasgow in 1971, and a Hilti Development Corporation was founded in Munich in 1973 to develop drilling technology and mechanical as well as chemical anchor systems.

The 1960s had been a hugely successful decade for Hilti. By 1971, sales reached Swiss francs 376 million ($99.8 million) and 4,720 people were employed, 65 per cent of whom were in international sales and distribution. However, in this period the seeds were sown of an organizational dilemma that was to return constantly in the decades to come: how to reconcile the occasionally conflicting views of product innovation and market orientation.

Hilti Management Model (1973–1975)

In 1973, Hilti took a giant step by launching the Hilti Management Model, which had been developed in cooperation with the University of St Gallen. This model – a systems approach based on the work by Hans Ulrich (1970) – provided a *framework for understanding* what had become a complex network of intrafirm relationships and potentially rival views. The Hilti Management Model identified the interdependences of the various parts of the organization, especially between the two legs of production and marketing. Most importantly, the Hilti Management Model modified the decision-making process: top management decisions now required a form (*Entscheidungsantrag*) indicating not just the problem and the decision's objectives, but also how the decision would affect other parts of the organization. This procedure, while intellectually challenging and time-consuming, helped immensely to raise organizational transparency, and was still used at the time of writing this case study (January 1999). In line with the model, Hilti also altered its corporate structure, introducing a management committee with members from finance, marketing and engineering, with Martin Hilti acting as Chairman. In retrospect, developing and implementing the Hilti Management Model may be seen as an attempt to help the corporate brain to better understand its own legs, and to upgrade internal networking mechanisms in the company. In 1976, sales reached Swiss francs 550 million ($224.7 million).

Restructuring (1976–1982)

The new management committee had an unfortunate start. It increased capital expenditures and investments by 140 per cent within one year at a time when sales growth rates had just begun to decline, forcing Hilti to borrow large amounts of capital. However, Hilti succeeded in averting a financial crisis and began to invest in computer applications for 'Total Quality Management', long before the term became fashionable.

Since production had continued to internationalize, manufacturing facilities increasingly began to serve their markets directly, creating a stronger need for local expertise in functions such as production and logistics. In 1976, therefore, product managers were assigned to the market organizations – which remained the linchpin of Hilti's international strategy. In 1980, an integrated cost and contribution margin calculation system was established, to enhance the financial transparency of the market organizations. In the same year, Martin Hilti pooled his Hilti shares in a family trust. With the formation of this trust, all family members waived their inheritance rights to Hilti shares, securing the future of the company independent of family involvement. In 1982, sales reached Swiss francs 750 million ($373.8 million).

Hilti's competitors in the early 1980s

By the early 1980s, Hilti had come to face a diffuse group of competitors, which were active in one or two of Hilti's businesses (see Table 6.1). By far the two most important competitors were (and are) Bosch and Würth.

Bosch was founded in 1886, and today has a family trust as its main shareholder. It is a highly internationalized company represented in 131 countries (early 1999) with total sales of almost DM 47 billion ($26.2 billion) in 1997. First and foremost, Bosch ranks amongst the world's largest and most innovative automotive suppliers (1997: DM 28.7 billion, $16.0 billion). Furthermore, Bosch is a supplier of fixed network and mobile communications equipment (1997: DM 5.3 billion, $3.0 billion) and of capital goods (1997: DM 2.1 billion, $1.2 billion). Its consumer goods business sector (1997: DM 11.1 billion, $6.2 billion) accounts for 23 per cent of total sales. It includes a joint venture with Siemens producing household appliances such as white goods; a thermo-technology (gas-fired heating) unit; and the power tool business. Bosch is the world's largest producer of electronic tools. Its devices are aimed at professional and non-professional users alike. Bosch tools are less expensive but (according to Hilti sources) also less durable than Hilti products and are sold via different distribution channels, including do-it-yourself markets.

Würth is Hilti's main competitor in the area of fastening technologies. A family-owned company founded in 1945, Würth presents itself as one of the success stories of post-war German history. Würth is a direct marketing enterprise, using regional sourcing centres and doing business through 189 companies in 72 countries (January 1999) with sales of just over DM 6 billion ($3.4 billion) in 1997. While Würth offers a range of over 50,000 products and sizes, only 10 per cent of these are produced in-house. Until 1997, Würth sold its products exclusively to professional users via direct sales channels. Recently, the company has begun to acquire do-it-yourself markets. Unlike Hilti, growth by acquisition has been an important element of Würth's strategy. Würth also puts a strong emphasis on its people, e.g. through its 1997 'Grow to be great' programme. Employee salaries are largely based on sales.

Table 6.1 *Hilti compared with its main competitors (1998)*

Company	HQ location	Market segments	Type of competitor	Employees	Competitor of Hilti BU	Comments
Hilti AG	Schaan, Principality of Liechtenstein	drilling & demolition; new businesses (positioning); construction chemicals; direct fastening; diamond systems; anchors	–	12,000	–	products of its six business units sold worldwide; Hilti has no single competitor active in all its businesses
Bosch	Stuttgart, Germany	automotive; communication technology; consumer goods; capital goods	global player, competing in two of Hilti's BUs	180,000	drilling & demolition; direct fastening	world's largest independent automotive supplier and major whitegood producer; successfully produces good quality drilling machines and sells them worldwide through retail outlets
Würth Group	Künzelsau, Germany	automotive; electro; metal; industry; wood	becoming a global player, competing in two Hilti's BUs	27,600	anchor system; construction chemicals	main competitor in anchor business, very innovative and imitative; only 10% in-house production; while expanding direct sales globally, still 92% of sales in Europe
Heseding GmbH	Lohne, Germany	anchor systems	regional player, competing in one of Hilti's BU	n.a.	anchor system	'Fischer' brand is leading competitor in fastening technology
Berner Group	Künzelsau, Germany	automotive; metal; electro; industry	regional player, competing in one of Hilti's BU	6,000	anchor system	Very dynamic competitor in anchor business, focused on Europe
Makita	Japan	saws; drills; cordless tools; routers and planners; shears; outdoor tools	main Japanese competitor, active in one of Hilti's BU	n.a.	drilling & demolition	products sold worldwide, i.e. through Grizzly Ind., a US mail order company founded in 1983, and through the internet

n.a. = not available
Source: numerous interviews at Hilti, annual reports, company websites

By 1998, other Hilti competitors included Makita (Japan) and AIM (US) in the drilling and demolition business; Heseding and Berner in anchor systems; Rupert and Göltz in the diamond business; and Spitz in the direct fastening business.

Drivers for Change

The early 1980s were a time of paradoxes for Hilti. On the one hand, expansion continued with the opening of production facilities, and in 1982 and 1983 Hilti service centres were opened in Canton and Beijing with the aim of establishing the company in a large-volume and high-growth market. On the other hand, a recession in the US and European construction industry slowed down sales considerably. However, not all of Hilti's competitors were equally hit. Both Bosch, which sells its products partly to non-professional users through retail outlets, and Würth, which positions itself as a trading company, are less vulnerable to business cycles in the construction industry. Nevertheless, it was crucial for Hilti to keep up its expensive innovation efforts, since its demanding customers tended to be early adopters of technological innovations. Innovation, however, was often hampered by the circumstance that the construction industry was, and still is, a rather fragmented industry. Many countries have maintained their own building, materials, quality and safety standards, meaning that professional customers across the world may demand different products and may require a different marketing and instruction approach. The existence of these heterogeneous customer segments and country-specific circumstances explains why concentration levels amongst Hilti's competitors are limited, and why small competitors may be in a good position to supply specific geographic or product markets.

Triggered by these external problems, Hilti was confronted with a *company crisis*. As indicated, Hilti's two legs had been its product innovation and its market orientation. By the early 1980s, Hilti was in dire need of another breakthrough innovation. Moreover, Hilti had never developed a strong process orientation, and began to experience problems managing its international production network. Communication between R&D, production and marketing was less than optimal. More critically, a number of problems emerged in its direct sales and marketing departments: the ratio of sales and distribution employees fell to below 60 per cent of total personnel – a very unfavourable ratio for a direct sales organization such as Hilti – and the five marketing departments dating from the late 1960s did not prove very effective. On top of that, Martin Hilti, still the driving force of the company, had turned 65 in 1980, and steps had to be taken to prepare the company for a life after Martin Hilti. Unfortunately, an extensive company review revealed that the corporation and its management displayed a rather low propensity to change. It was felt that, while many employees did feel committed to the company, employees no longer felt sufficiently responsible for emerging problems or failures. Eventually, top management understood that Hilti's strong initial values, based on 'Mom Hilti' and the 'Happy Valley' (referring to the Rhine valley of Liechtenstein), were not necessarily widely shared in the company any more, and that it had become necessary to build a new company-wide corporate culture.

Change at Hilti after 1983: Content, Scope and Depth

In Hilti's development after 1983, three periods may be identified, each with its specific organizational issues. Table 6.2 summarizes the entire history of the company.

Three-dimensional matrix (1983–1986)

In reaction to the 1982 problems, four product divisions were introduced to be responsible for product innovation and market supply: drilling and demolition; direct fastening; diamond systems; and anchors. Each division was put in charge of its own development, production, marketing, logistics and controlling. The former Research Department was renamed Innovation Department and was given the responsibility to explore new fields of technology and basic technologies. Market innovation teams (MIT) were created to maintain the flow of information among the development departments of the divisions, the market organization and the newly created Innovation Department. Furthermore, plants specialized their roles to form an international production network, leading to extensive intra-company (product and money) transfers. In 1986, Hilti finally achieved its third breakthrough innovation and entered the construction chemicals business, leading to the creation of a fifth division. This segment turned out to be an ideal supplement to the existing product mix.

In the area of marketing, three corporate market regions (Western Hemisphere; Europe; Near, Middle and Far East) were created, enabling the company to reorganize top management at the national organizations and to integrate regional production units. Three strategic business units (SBUs) were also introduced based on customer segments: mechanical and electrical, industry and construction. Each was headed by a market segment manager who reported directly to the board. They had the strategic task of identifying future growth potential in their areas, ranging from new technologies to products and customer segments. The SBUs were to facilitate the flow of ideas from the market to

Table 6.2 *The evolution of Hilti AG (1941–1997)*

	1941–1961	1962–1972	1973–1976	1977–1982	1983–1986	1987–1992	1993–1996	1997 to date
Phase Description	Establishment and growth	Internationalization	Hilti Management Model	Restructuring	Three-dimensional matrix	Changes at all levels	Team focus	The communicating organization
Environmental conditions	• post war constructing boom	• favourable economic climate	• declining economic conditions	• recession, company crisis in 1982	• good economic conditions	• increased competition • exchange rates problems	• increased competition	• increased competition • globalization
In-house Trends	• product orientation • acquisition of patent for a fastening tool • first breakthrough innovation: DX principle for powder-actuated fastening	• decentralized marketing activities • shift from product to market orientation • second breakthrough innovation: electro-pneumatic drilling • increased internationalization	• Hilti Management Model • shift from technology to market orientation continued	• increasing internationalization • period of crisis led to fundamental change of organization	• weaknesses in product innovations revealed • Executive Board and Corporate Management Group as extended board • unfavourable cost structure	• re-orientation of Hilti Group necessary • not sufficient marketing and sales orientation • Martin Hilti cedes chair to son Michael	• new E.B. • Michael Hilti cedes chair to non-family member • new role of the E.B. • sales growth higher than profit growth	• profitable sales development • strategic thinking at all levels • challenging employees
Strategic concepts	• direct sales and marketing, but product orientation • specialization in fastening technology • first internationalization efforts	• diversification in the constructing sector, i.e. into fastening of heavy loads or entering the drilling market • regionalization of sales • integration of market organizations	• diversification • internationalization • TQM	• establishment of family trust in 1980 • reduction of overhead costs	• focus on competencies • competence-oriented diversification (entering construction chemicals market) • marketing strategy	• 'Strategy 2000' • new marketing strategy • strategic move to concentrate on core business	• 'Strategy 2000' concept • Factor Time • reengineering of business processes	• 'Champion 3C' strategy, based on customer, competence and concentration • new strategy development process • locally adapted strategies

Table 6.2 cont.

	1941–1961	1962–1972	1973–1976	1977–1982	1983–1986	1987–1992	1993–1996	1997 to date
Phase Description	Establishment and growth	Internationalization	Hilti Management Model	Restructuring	Three-dimensional matrix	Changes at all levels	Team focus	The communicating organization
Corporate structure	• functional organization	• restructuring of sales and distribution system, five regional departments report to Martin Hilti • internationalization of production and R&D • supervisory board of directors	• improving the links between marketing organization, R&D and production • introduction of new hierarchical level • management committee with members from marketing, finance, engineering, Martin Hilti as Chairman	• restructuring the marketing organizations and production • establishing of product managers • corporate management services • marketing managers replace region managers, 3 market regions	• three-dimensional matrix (customer segments, market regions and product divisions) • creating four product divisions responsible for product innovation and market supply • central corporate departments	• reorganization of sales and distribution according to market segments • strategic specialization of plants	• organizational institutionalization of sales agents within market organizations • improvements within the three-dimensional matrix organization	• simplifying corporate structure to two dimensions (markets and products) • networking aspects dominate • strengthening of BU • centralized corporate functions act as service provider for MOs and BUs.
Emergence of internal networking features	• focus on developing people	• increasing importance of networking between production and marketing organizations	• first attention to information flow and corporate-wide networking	• international production network, production and distribution linked • need for corporate culture discovered • team work	• team-work, awareness for individual responsibility • facilitating more communication between all areas	• team-oriented working models • HIPS • outsourcing	• emergence of some key characteristics of an internal network organization (e.g. internal labour market, IT) • improved inter-unit communication within Hilti • TTM	• high interdependence of units • horizontal linkages • flattened hierarchies and decentralization of responsibilities • bottom-up planning • E.B. only strategic role • dotted lines principle in the whole company

Table 6.2 *cont.*

	1941–1961	1962–1972	1973–1976	1977–1982	1983–1986	1987–1992	1993–1996	1997 to date
Phase Description	Establishment and growth	Internationalization	Hilti Management Model	Restructuring	Three-dimensional matrix	Changes at all levels	Team focus	The communicating organization
HR-management	• intensive training and courses for employees	• institutionalization of employee committee • social and financial benefits • investment in HR	• intensive training and courses	• seminars for personal development to prepare employees for changes and enhance team spirit • inter-personal skills	• 'Leadership programme' introduced in 1985, seminars for thousands of people	• empowerment • cross-functional teams	• empowerment • worldwide HR-activities • CIP • Semi-autonomous work groups	• Inno compact • Competencies model • Inter-personal communication

the business areas. Within this customer segmentation, the sales support structure was also modified: the direct sales staff now received support from call centres (named 'customer service'), and Hilti centres as points of direct sale.

Effectively, this restructuring led to the formation of a three-dimensional matrix. The *regional axes* focused on sales, the *divisions* on technological innovation and production, while the *strategic business units* focused on strategic marketing issues for the different customer segments and identified new business opportunities. The three-dimensional matrix, conceived as a mechanism to secure internal communication and coordination, remained in place until 1997.

Besides these organizational changes, Hilti had learned that open-mindedness to change was critical to the company's future success. In 1985 it introduced its *Leadership programme*, which aimed to spread its ambition to be the leading company in its product areas and in customer services. It was also aimed at fostering a team spirit among the workforce, an awareness of individual responsibility, a creative and innovative approach in all aspects of work, and a willingness to strive for ongoing self-improvement. The following internal statement was given on the leadership programme: 'Leadership means to view permanent change as an opportunity. It means to have shared values and goals, to show personal commitment and to cooperate. To live leadership requires a behaviour based on openness, creativity, fairness and the will for constant improvement.'

The leadership programme was introduced under the slogan 'Leadership makes the difference – our corporate culture', and led to a strong and never-receding *focus on people*. However, the programme was more than just a slogan. Effectively, it constituted an important step towards *sharing leadership in the organization*. Using a cascade principle of training the trainers, thousands of employees participated in these one-day seminars over the following years (cf. also Hummel, 1990: 11). In 1986, sales reached Swiss francs 1,200 million ($744.4 million).

Changes at all levels (1987–1992)

After Hilti had reorganized both legs of its organization and had sought to infuse a new spirit into the company, the following years were dominated by a series of smaller but significant changes at all levels of the company.

At the top, an executive board was created in 1987, consisting of the company's executive management. In addition, a corporate management group was set up which also included the levels just below the executive top managers, in order to ensure the flow of information and enhance both the continuity and the quality of decision making. Late 1989, at the age of 74, Martin Hilti ceded the chair of the executive board to his son Michael. The partial delegation of decision making to the corporate management group aimed to ensure continuity, but also reflected the participatory ideas of Michael Hilti. In 1992, the structure and composition of the supervisory board of directors and the executive board were further revised in order to separate the functions completely (cf. Hummel, 1990: 15).

Late in 1989 Hilti introduced a new slogan: 'Strategy 2000'. This term mostly reflected the emerging management jargon at the time, since its main idea was to identify and communicate direct sales, direct fastening, innovation and quality as *Hilti's core competencies*. In 1991 Hilti launched its Hilti integrated production system (HIPS) as a follow-up programme to Strategy 2000. With HIPS, Hilti restructured its plants into units with reduced hierarchies and higher employee responsibilities. The aims of HIPS were to raise employees' identification with Hilti products and to reduce time-to-market cycles. Key technologies and processes were identified, and substantial parts of production were outsourced. In the late 1990s, Hilti only produced some 30 per cent of its products in-house. As Martin Hilti used to put it: 'owning the market is more important than owning production'.

The new market segments established standardized sales concepts and steering tools on a worldwide basis. Sales staff now focused on segmented customers, whose needs, language and buying patterns were well traced. While the goal was still for every buyer on a construction site to have only one *contact person* at Hilti, *different sales people* could be responsible for different customers on large sites. In 1991, sales surpassed Swiss francs 2 billion ($1.37 billion) for the first time.

Team focus (1993–1996)

In 1993 Michael Hilti assumed the position of Chairman of the board of directors with Martin Hilti as its honorary President. At the same time, non-family member Pius Baschera became CEO. In terms of its top management structure and role divisions, Hilti now resembled a publicly held company. In the Liechtenstein corporate governance system (which corresponds to the Swiss one, since Liechtenstein has long been in a monetary union with Switzerland), the executive board is responsible for the daily management of the company, while the board of directors is the body which needs to decide on appointments and strategic issues. One year later, the market region of Asia was relocated from Schaan to Hong Kong, reflecting a decision to grow geographically rather than to diversify into different businesses (cf. Werner and Hügli, 1995: 20). Standard software packages were introduced in the national market organizations and supranational logistics centres were established. In production, Hilti moved towards increasingly capital-intensive facilities, demanding ever more highly skilled people.

While Hilti had begun to introduce all kinds of teams back in the 1970s, the 1993–1996 period marks the *maturation of Hilti's team orientation*. The top management team was affected in terms of its composition, the team processes and its role definition. The executive board and corporate management group composition became increasingly international: by the end of 1996, six out of 23 corporate management group members were non-German speakers. Many company executives felt this heterogeneity raised the level of discussions and helped the company deal better with its complex environment (cf. Hambrick et al., 1998a). As an executive board member explained: 'We work together as a team, in a very creative way. We take decisions as a group, and our different skills turn out to be very complementary.'

In parallel, top management adopted a new role 'to live the example'. As Michael Hilti put it: 'The fish starts smelling at the head' (Werner and Hügli, 1995: 21). Top managers now had to act as facilitators, recognizing and eliminating structural and personal barriers, and enabling as many employees as possible to be involved in shaping the organization. Staffing key positions and developing high potential were seen as of utmost strategic importance – which also included the outplacement of people who were unable or unwilling to accept the new rules of the game. The following principles explicitly stated top management's new role (Oertig, 1996: 17):

- developing and realizing corporate policies
- living the corporate culture
- integrating employees into the company processes, and motivating them
- developing employees
- supporting intra- and inter-unit communication
- fostering teamwork
- taking responsibility for resources
- increasing organizational efficiency

A marketing assistant gave some concrete examples of this new role in action:

> Top management is very visible in the company. They eat in the same canteen as the employees. The corporate management group has parking lots in front of the entrance but it is part of the corporate culture that they do not use them but use the regular parking lots instead. Managers now make their own coffee and photocopies to show the new role of management.

In 1995, semi-autonomous units were set up in manufacturing. This was not always easy, as some employees had difficulty in coping with the new uncertainties that went with these teams: mistakes were accepted as long as appropriate lessons were drawn from them. Each unit is headed by a management team rather than exclusively by the head of the unit, and task forces can be created spontaneously for specific problems. While introducing these units, it emerged that despite years of decentralizing the company, many decisions were still made too high up in the hierarchy (Werner and Hügli, 1995). In order to ensure team commitment, a team-based bonus system was introduced with individual and team performance measures that flexibly influence the annual bonus received by every employee (which, depending on the job, may range from 10 to 50 per cent of the annual salary).

At the same time, a continuous improvement process (CIP) was introduced in the plants. According to this system, CIP problem collection spaces were created where every employee can post a note with a specified problem which cannot be solved by a single individual but which requires the involvement of different people in the company. Any individual may subsequently set up a task force for solving this issue. It must be reported how many people have spent how much time, and eventually the solution is assessed by the direct superior. Depending on the nature of the solution, the task force may for example, go out for dinner – the only stipulation is that the prize has to be spent together. In the plants the CIP system has worked very well, and other parts of the organization have begun to introduce it.

In 1994, the 'factor time' programme was initiated with the objective to speed up the three core business processes: product development, order fulfilment and sales. Hilti's so-called Time-to Money (TTM) projects seek to integrate cross-functional knowledge and customer needs in the product development process. Each division usually runs five to six TTM-projects at the same time. In total, around 20 are run internally, and an additional 15 projects are run with external partners.

The communicating organization (1997–)

With the TTM projects, the need for extensive communication became evident, not only from management to employees but between all units and across all hierarchical levels. Early in 1997 Hilti's organization was restructured, directing the entire organization towards the customer, and minimizing hierarchical layers:

- The three-dimensional matrix had proven too complex to ensure clear responsibilities and organizational transparency and therefore was *reduced to the two basic dimensions*: the business units and market organizations. Corporate headquarters' functions were simplified, and a small corporate staff (for example, corporate research) were to support the newly created business units and the market organizations (MOs).

- The product divisions and the marketing responsibility of the former SBUs were integrated into business units (BUs). The existing BUs (drilling and demolition systems, anchor systems, direct fastening systems, chemical systems and diamond systems) expanded: a sixth BU was added: new businesses. BUs enjoy a relatively high degree of autonomy and are fully responsible for *individual product line strategies*, including marketing, product line development and customer liaison.
- The market organizations received full responsibility for *selling in their region* the products developed by the BUs and for the customer segments. The MOs were to serve as distribution channels and as strategic information filters to the business units. Sales organizations in more than 100 countries (some 50 fully owned MOs and some 70 sales partners) were grouped into seven market regions (Central and Southern Europe, Germany, Northern and Eastern Europe, North America, Latin America, Near/Middle East and Africa and Asia). These market regions (headed by a regional manager whose role is best described as a coach and coordinator) need to seek market expansion, increase profitability and sales, and develop employees. In each MO, teams of engineers and product specialists provide in-depth product knowledge to end users. Many MOs have introduced extensive inventory systems of products and services, and provide a telephone advisory system to customers who require solutions for problems or wish to order products. Two-thirds of Hilti's 12,000 employees worldwide are working in the MOs.
- The seven-member board of directors was to supervise the company, while the four-member (and quite internationally composed) executive board effectively manages the group. The heads of the different units plus the executive board form the corporate management group and together count as the top management team. Figure 6.1 shows Hilti's 1997 organizational chart.

FIGURE 6.1 *Hilti's organizational structure, 1997*

Alongside these structural changes, the post-1997 period marks the rise of the *communicating organization* at Hilti. A package of far-reaching communication programmes was started over this period, jointly developed with external consultants and the University of St Gallen.

The first component of the communication programme was the *Champion 3C* strategy, which was implemented across all units of the organization. '3C' stands for 'customer, competence, and concentration', and attempted to take the Strategy 2000 concept one step further. The Champion 3C strategy stands on three main pillars:

- *increasing market reach:* seeking further international growth, winning new customers more quickly and offering better service for existing customers;
- *revitalizing product leadership:* strengthening Hilti's position as a leading supplier of first-class products and services, by concentrating (both in the sense of focusing on and condensing) the processes of applying know-how resulting from contact with customers and of introducing new products into the market;
- *improving the cost position:* by simplifying various structures and processes, and changing the organizational architecture.

The Champion 3C strategy decentralized important parts of the strategy development process to all different units. Initially, pilot projects were run in the French, North American and several Asian MOs in order to gain experience in implementing such a decentralized strategy development process, and to draft guidelines on how to pursue it. Subsequently, each BU and MO identified its own objectives and implementation trajectories, which were presented to the Hilti board and decided upon. Occasionally, this led to proposals that top management did not welcome. For instance, the French MO proposed a drastic reorganization along entirely different lines from the other MOs. After clarifying that delivery and service standards and corporate values would be upheld, the French MO received permission to implement its proposed structure. Hilti management realized that if they were to achieve shared leadership and enhanced identification with the company, they should not impose their own structures and ideas on single units. As the head of a business unit explained:

> We really have reached empowerment. Every unit decides its own targets. The only general target is to make profit, but every unit is in charge of deciding how much and how. Before, rough targets were given, e.g. growth of 10 per cent. It is incredible how well these new targets are met – usually deviation is 1–3 per cent.

The second component of the communication programme was the culture programme *Innovation 1 Compact*. Starting in 1997 and lasting for five years, all 12,000 employees in 100 countries are to participate in a seminar aimed at raising awareness of the importance of innovation for Hilti, and at creating the right corporate culture to foster communication and innovation. Reaching beyond the objectives of the leadership programme, Innovation 1 Compact communicated five principles to which all employees in the company have to agree:

- *Tolerance:* to respect the opinions of others, to think globally beyond one's own areas of responsibility, to be able to question one's own view through differentiated reasoning;
- *Change:* to accept change, to be prepared to take new challenges, to take risks and to benefit from opportunities;
- *Self-responsibility:* to be aware of and identify responsibility as a personal task and to stand up for everything one does or does not do;
- *Freedom of choice:* to recognize the freedom to go one's own way and to accept certain situations (for example, the businesses that Hilti is in), change other situations (for example, where performance may be increased) or ultimately leave a situation or even the company (for example, if you cannot identify with the company's principles). In Hilti jargon there are: 'accept it', 'change it' and 'leave it' situations;
- *Learning:* to gain new experience through knowledge, capabilities and motivation, to regard mistakes as learning something new, and to use positive and negative experiences as the basis for learning processes.

The seminars were developed by the corporate training and development department. They are to be led by Hilti people, based on the train-the-trainer principle. When formulating the seminars, the following conditions were specified: the enabling of intercultural use, simple and clear language use at all levels, ease to remember, the fostering of discussions; and that they should be provocative but not extreme, humorous and with a ten-year perspective.

All newly developed courses are first attended by the top management, both to ensure their agreement on the courses' content and to live the example to the other employees. Subsequently, existing teams from every unit participate together with their boss or coach with the aim of providing joint experiences and a common language, and thus to facilitate interunit relations. The interactive seminars take three whole days, spread over a nine-month period. The second day takes place three months after the first, and the third day again three months later. This third day is moderated by the team manager, with the objective to reflect jointly upon the team's development over the past six months. In 1998, Hilti employees were talking a lot about the seminar and the

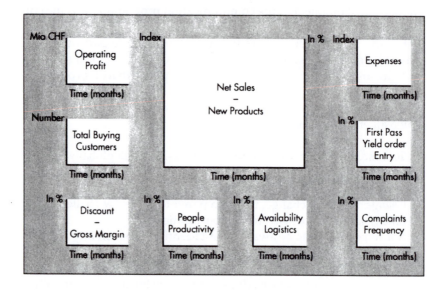

FIGURE 6.2   *Example of a Hilti cockpit chart*

values it transmits, and many indicated that the seminars reflected a high degree of respect and appreciation of the individual employee, regardless of the position held. The seminars have created highly effective platforms for open communication in the organization and have led to an increased willingness to cooperate across units. The head of press/information explained the new approach:

> With Champion 3C, communication has been hugely intensified. Communication channels have been standardized e.g. the *Team* company-wide newsletter is now translated into all major languages and sent home to every employee. This way, the families can understand the company better and employees don't have to read it during work time. The changing role of communication has improved job satisfaction and linkages with foreign units.

A third component of the communication programme has been the introduction of the *cockpit chart*. These charts graphically show performance from team to corporate level based on pre-defined targets, using both quantitative and qualitative figures. The cockpit charts are openly displayed on blackboards in all units. Their impact has been enormous: they have dramatically increased the transparency of each team's objectives as well as the motivation of individual employees to contribute to these joint objectives. Team-based annual bonuses are largely determined by meeting the targets. Figure 6.2 provides an example of a cockpit chart.

Process Sequencing and Analysis: Why did Hilti Develop towards a Communicating Organization?

It has taken Hilti at least 25 years to develop as a communicating organization – and many steps are yet to be made. Here, the two relevant questions are: why did this kind of organization emerge, and could it be copied by other organizations?

Hilti has been facing an odd mixture of tough and enabling external conditions. It is not easy to define the population of firms Hilti belongs to, since even its leading competitors are active in only one or two of Hilti's businesses. Notwithstanding its specific business portfolio, Hilti faces constant pressure in each business and in both legs of its organization, either from rivals with a track record in product innovation (for example Bosch), or from firms with an aggressive and successful process orientation (for example Würth). Environmental conditions have been far from ideal, since Hilti is more vulnerable to business cycles than many of its competitors. Furthermore, Hilti faces a highly demanding and heterogeneous group of customers, forcing the company constantly to rethink how communication between the MOs and the BUs may be improved. Finally, located in the Rhine Valley and surrounded by the Liechtenstein, Swiss and Austrian Alps, the company has a strong culture based on family values and paternalistic care, fostering mutual expectations and a high degree of trust. Walking around in this company, one can literally sense these values. As a marketing assistant explained: '"Mom Hilti" cares for you. The employees in turn are proud to work for Hilti. The culture tolerates making mistakes and supports initiatives of one's own.'

More important than these external circumstances have been a series of internal factors which coincided to trigger the organizational changes described above. The following points may summarize these internal triggers:

- *system thinking*: ever since the introduction of the Hilti Management Model in 1973, top management has adamantly sought to comprehend the organization in its entirety and to perceive individual linkages within the company as part of the whole. This holistic view has guided top management into setting up the company-wide seminars, spurring job rotation, and seeking to improve the MO–BU links;
- *direct sales*: most employees easily understand that to a company which depends on dealing directly with its customers not only to sell its products, but also to instruct in their use and identify market trends at an early stage, clear and smooth internal communication is a must;
- *continuous change*: after the early 1980s' company crisis, Hilti went through a series of far-reaching transformations which many employees found stressful and difficult to grasp. Hilti had to make

sure its employees could function properly in these new structures and processes as well, and realized it had to explain the backgrounds of these changes in order to retain the loyalty of its employees;

- *leadership change*: over the 1980s Martin Hilti, the company founder, gradually withdrew from the company. This opened up prospects of a change of leadership;
- *shared leadership*: Michael Hilti, the founder's son, firmly believes in participation and shared leadership at all levels of the organization. Paradoxically, shared leadership was injected into the organization *top-down* – but was subsequently picked up at all levels of the organization. The head of R&D explained the change in management style:

> The company has changed a lot over the past decade – not in a revolution, but in an evolution. Previously, when issues were tabled during executive board meetings, Martin Hilti used to ask whether anybody had any objections. But nobody really discussed the matters. Frequently, two teams worked on the same topic to then choose the better solution. Michael Hilti changed this top down through the Inno seminars [to enhance open communication], but then again employees would now no longer accept such a management style.

- *recruitment*: having consistently sought to hire the best people in their fields, Hilti needed to maximize these people's contribution to the company, by communicating their expectations and opportunities to every individual. Thus, they attempted to maximize the company's return and to retain its talented workforce (cf. Quintanilla and Sánchez-Runde, Chapter 7 in this volume, who argue that one of the success factors of Freemap is hiring very talented people and acculturating them to the corporate values);
- *information technology*: the changes at Hilti have been enabled by IT but have not been IT-driven. IT helps units and teams to monitor progress against a number of self-imposed targets, and to recognize at an early stage the discrepancy between their targets and the actual situation. However, no interviewee regarded IT as the backbone of the recent changes – in fact some indicated that Hilti was comparatively weak in this area;
- *two-legged organization*: in an organization with one leg (and two-thirds of the employees) rooted in the national markets offering customers tailor-made solutions, and another leg in product innovation seeking to develop generic products, conflicting views between MOs and BUs are inevitable. Indeed, conflicting views between the MOs and BUs have been a leitmotiv of Hilti history – as have been efforts to create platforms and bring these views together in order to allow some synthesis to emerge. 'At Hilti, communication

is understood as the ability to see, understand, and evaluate the motives of other individuals and teams within the company and to see how the company and these individuals can interact to foster entrepreneurial action'(Ciucci, 1996: 38).

Barriers to Change

If there have been individuals resisting the changes at Hilti over the last ten years, we have not met them. We also talked to former employees who said that they had left the company for other reasons than the numerous reorganizations. It would appear that Hilti's efforts internally to communicate its strategic and organizational objectives, the reasons behind these objectives, the chances it gave to employees to take leadership in pursuing these objectives, and the clear line to either accept, change or leave difficult situations have helped to sustain a highly cohesive organization.

Nevertheless, there is only so much change an organization can handle within a given amount of time, and Hilti has occasionally stretched its people. A major structural barrier to change throughout Hilti has been the three-dimensional matrix, which, until it was changed back to a two-dimensional matrix in 1997, was a constant source of confusion and non-essential complexity in the organization. Designed as a vehicle to *facilitate* company internal communication, instead, the three-dimensional matrix *frustrated* communication: the three dimensions and the differentiation of market regions and customer segments were difficult to understand and forced employees to sit in many long coordination meetings. The three-dimensional matrix (of which two dimensions were focused on the customer) moreover shifted the balance of power in the organization in favour of marketing and sales – yet contrary to the expectations of the marketing and sales people, customer satisfaction did not rise as a result of it. In retrospect, the three-dimensional matrix was an intermediary stage between the old and the new organization, like an Echternacht procession in which the participants take two steps forward, followed by one step back and two steps forward again.

Finally, as in any company with most employees working abroad in sales organizations, Hilti's challenge has been to explain to the MOs why the organizational changes and communication programme were necessary. As in most such companies, the direct sales force had not shown a particularly strong interest in what was going on in the rest of the company. However, as the company came to rely on customer and market information for introducing new products or services, it became important to extend the communication programme to the entire company, so that people in the market organizations understood and were directly involved in the product development process of the various business units.

Consequences of the Rise of Shared Leadership and a Communicating Organization

The rise of shared leadership does not imply that centralized leadership has disappeared in Hilti. On the contrary, top management (in the case of Hilti, the corporate management group) often walks a tightrope. First, top management needs to make sure that delegation is not perceived by employees as an indication of uninterest or indifference. Top management needs to be highly visible, communicating and 'living the example' by energizing employees. Secondly, sharing leadership does not mean discarding leadership. At Hilti, hierarchies have been maintained *within* teams and units, and reporting structures (such as the cockpit charts) to top management have remained intact. What has changed is that reporting structures have become based on *transparent measures*: the progress and results of one's own unit as well as of other units are visible to all. Thirdly, top management needs to communicate which direction the firm is going in, while at the same time involving its people in the strategy process (cf. Kim and Mauborgne, 1997). That is, top management needs to *set the strategic and organizational parameters* in order to allow the employees to take leadership within their own domain. Fourthly, the system of shared leadership and communication may perhaps be put to the real test only at the next company crisis. When times are hard, 'tough' financial considerations often overshadow 'softer' organizational projects (cf. Truss et al., 1997). We do not believe, however, that the many organizational innovations and the principle of shared leadership can easily be reversed.

Social competencies have become essential factors for all managers to be successful at Hilti. By the mid-1990s, Hilti had put a comprehensive strategic manpower development (SMD) process in place. Hilti is seeking to attract intellectually agile, innovative, and truly international employees. The company has long been an active corporate member of CEMS, the Community of European Management Schools, an alliance of leading business schools in every European country. CEMS graduates spend a considerable time abroad at a foreign university and at a foreign company, and can speak at least two foreign languages, meaning that there are few linguistic barriers when discussing important issues with internal or external stakeholders. Employees are the object of extensive job rotation: eight out of ten positions in the organization are internally staffed with Hilti employees, facilitating knowledge transfer, enhancing awareness of other parts of the organization and offering interesting career chances. Another reason for internal rotation is that recruiting externally is much more expensive – although obviously some external recruiting is necessary to bring in new ideas and skills. Once they are in the system, employees and their superiors are jointly responsible for developing employees' competencies and ambitions, using a variety of in-house training programmes and monitoring progress via feedback and coaching sessions. The company considers it essential to identify those employees who have performed well in their jobs and who require new challenges – even if every employee carries the explicit responsibility for his/her own development. Hilti tracks the careers of a pool of talented people throughout the worldwide organization, and directly communicates with them about their strengths, development needs and personal as well as career aspirations.

As a result of the numerous changes, many managers feel the organizational charts no longer reflect the actual organization. Traditionally,

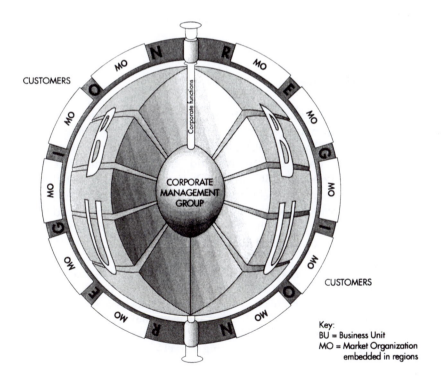

FIGURE 6.3   *Redrawing Hilti's 1997 organizational structure (based on interviews)*

organizational charts have been based on structural dimensions of hier-archy and subordination. As leadership processes are shared, these dimensions no longer fully reflect the content of internal relationships. The head of a business unit explained his perceptions of the organiza-tion: 'The role of top management has definitely changed. I would not mind if the organizational charts were changed, using a different approach of depicting the organization, not with me on top and the others subordinated. It could for instance be round, showing the team structure.' Figure 6.3 shows an attempt to reflect Hilti's current organi-zational structure.

The organizational chart is shaped like a globe, reflecting Hilti's worldwide presence. Top management is in the centre of the globe and not at the top, as it only provides strategic guidance. The other units are interlinked and have permeable borders. Market organizations are grouped into different regions but again show points of contact between each other and with the business units. The market organizations are at the exterior of the globe, as they have contact with the customers. The functions are depicted as the pole in the middle, because they support all other units.

Unresolved Issues

There are two major issues at Hilti that remain to be resolved – and that have had full top management attention since the 1997 changes. The first is to improve the BU–MO interface. Many feel that market infor-mation is not used effectively, and that communication and coordination between the BUs and MOs is suboptimal. A first step to resolve this problem has been to delegate MO representatives to the BUs. However, over the next months and years further efforts need to be made to get the two legs of the organization to move in the same direc-tion at the same pace. As the Head of Logistics explained:

> There is still too little customer orientation, and the rate of innovation is too low. Too much effort is put into cutting time and too little into customer ori-entation. Hilti products are often too high-tech oriented, even if the markets want to use a machine only 10–15 times and they would buy a machine with a shorter life cycle. There is still potential for further development within increasing market orientation and using market knowledge.

The second unresolved issue is related to the first. Many interviewees indicate that the time-to-money process is not effective enough. Too much effort and resources are wasted in order to meet *internal* deadlines and milestones, rather than *external* market demands. While people in the organization regard this as an area for further improvement, it is worth recapping that Hilti's success rates are well above those of many industries. Müllern (Chapter 8 in this volume) reports similar findings from the team-based structure within Saab Training Systems, where the internal focus on production deadlines prevailed over market-driven development issues.

Key Empirical Findings and Conclusion

At the end of the second millennium the Hilti organization displays many of the features claimed by various authors as constituting, or leading towards, a fundamentally new form of organizing. Hilti has made particular progress in decentralizing its organization, modifying its hierarchies, and innovating its HR policies. Interpreting these changes, the terms 'shared leadership' and 'communicating organization' have been introduced to indicate that leadership has deliberately been distributed throughout many parts of the organization, and that the company increasingly depends on *hierarchical as well as lateral communication* in order to clarify to employees the logic of the reorganizations and their opportunity to take charge within the newly created settings.

At the start of this chapter three questions were raised. The first question referred to the *process sequencing*: did Hilti first move beyond hierarchies or beyond divisions, or were these parallel or even complementary changes? We found that while Hilti did change its leadership processes and transformed the nature of its hierarchies, it made much less progress in moving beyond divisions. Transformation at Hilti occasionally took two steps forward, one back and two forward again. Hilti succeeded in clarifying the importance of each leg of the organization to the other, but it has struggled to find the appropriate balance between its direct sales and its product innovation orientation. Even in 1999, internal networking between these two legs of the organization was widely considered to be suboptimal.

The second question asked what *communication* needs and solutions emerged as Hilti shifted from established corporate structures towards new and unfamiliar internal linkages. We have seen that Hilti has deliberately communicated its organizational and strategic objectives, as well as the opportunities and expectations these created to individual employees, as a means to shape its culture and 'glue' the organization (Schein, 1984). Since its leadership programme in 1985, Hilti has carried out a series of programmes with the aim of transforming the organizational culture and the attitudes of individual employees. These programmes have been highly effective, not least because they were attended by large numbers and eventually by every employee of the organization. However, the Hilti case also suggests that it may be easier to change top managers' and employees' attitudes at headquarters and let them take responsibility, than to make functionally and geographically distinct parts of the organization understand each other.

The third question referred to the role of *leadership*: how and to what extent did Hilti's top management shape the changes that took place, and how and when did Hilti employees assume leadership themselves? Our conclusion is that Hilti actively distributed leadership and decentralized a lot of operational decision-making power to lower levels of the organization. Yet at the same time, top management maintained a central role by setting the strategic and organizational parameters to allow the employees to take leadership within their domain. They achieved this by communicating this internally whenever and wherever possible, and by living the example. Moreover, when decentralizing operational decision-making, hierarchies were maintained *within* teams and units, and reporting structures – while made transparent to all – remained intact.

The case of Hilti shows how top management may successfully transform an organization while averting the classical organizational dilemma of employees knowingly limiting management's influence on their work through informal social control (e.g. Etzioni, 1961). The *communication programmes* and the *rise of shared leadership* both created cultural cohesion and have helped Hilti employees see how they may contribute to their company's success. These may represent important steps in democratizing the organization (Mintzberg, 1983: 544ff.; Gastil, 1994) and in establishing a 'new moral contract' and a 'shared destiny' for management and employees (Ghoshal and Bartlett, 1997: 285).

The remaining problem of integrating the product and the sales legs of the organization raises the question of the *places* where communication is transmitted and knowledge is shared (Nonaka, 1998), and the ways in which geographically or functionally distinct groups and individuals communicate (e.g. Watson, 1995). The latter problem areas will be the topic of further research at Hilti.

Notes

The authors acknowledge the generous support by the HSG Grundlagenforschungsfonds and thank Johanna Hertel for her drawing of the organizational chart shown in Figure 6.3.

Appendix 1: Hilti's Financial Results (1992–1998)

Group Results (Swiss Francs millions/%)	1998	1997	1996	1995	1994	1993	1992
Net sales	2630	2580	2211	2025	2275	2175	2113
Depreciation	139.8	136.4	128.2	115.9	131.9	138.9	131.8
Operating result	226.1	193.6	140.1	171.4	219.1	147.0	141.6
Net financial result	69.2	55.1	84.1	47.7	(20.3)	69.4	20.4
Result of ordinary activities	295.3	248.7	224.2	219.1	198.8	216.4	162.1
Net income of the group	262.2	225.7	204.2	192.5	168.0	172.8	117.3
Cash flow	400.6	362.1	332.4	310.3	300.3	311.6	252.2
Return on operating capital in %	11.7	9.7	7.3	10.7	13.36	9.2	9.1
Return on total assets in %	9.4	8.3	8.1	8.1	7.6	8.6	6.6
Return on equity in %	12.5	11.7	11.7	12.2	11.3	12.4	8.9

7

New Forms of Organizing through Human Resource Management: The Case of Fremap

Javier Quintanilla and Carlos J. Sánchez-Runde

The structural and organizational developments observed within Fremap since 1992 may be described as a configurational process (Miller, 1986) towards a new form of organizing (NFO). Fremap, a medium-large firm leader within the Spanish mutual insurance industry, has moved rapidly from a highly centralized and bureaucratic organization to a decentralized structure, with semi-autonomous teams, characterized by an agile and dynamic management style. The aim of this investigation is to identify and explain the logic and the driving forces behind this configurational process through a case study approach. Specific attention is given to the role of human resource management (HRM) and the corporate culture, which are considered to be the key drivers of Fremap´s organizational evolution.

This case study analyses the introduction of a distinctive organizational structure within Fremap´s territorial branches, whereby each employee now performs practically the full range of both administrative and commercial activities. The previous organization was functionally arranged with employees performing a very small number of specialized tasks. This meant a radical change in the conception, managerial processes, and employees' tasks and responsibilities within the territorial branches, which comprise around 95 per cent of the firm's total workforce. Nevertheless, as analysed below, Fremap's entire structure and all its systems have been challenged by this project.

This experience, along with other plans such as a creative information technology scheme, made Fremap a truly pioneering firm; both within the Spanish insurance industry as a whole and within Spanish business circles. A recent academic approach, which sees the firm as a learning organization, stresses the industrial relevance by pointing out how an organization can learn the multiplicity of strategies, practices and technologies employed by other successful organizations in its own industry (Ingram and Baum, 1997). In the Fremap case, the new organizational developments are mainly the result of their internal features and capabilities, instigated at headquarters level, not a direct consequence of market pressures. Fremap has become an influential model, not only within the mutual insurance sector, but in the Spanish insurance industry as a whole.

A major finding of the Fremap case study is related to the critical role that HRM issues may have played in the instigation and successful implementation of NFOs. As has been pointed out in the personnel literature, companies need to use HRM 'high performance practices', which enhance intensive professional development of their employees, if they are to become innovative firms and achieve long-term success in today's highly competitive business environment (Ulrich, 1997; Pfeffer, 1998). Our chapter argues that firms introducing NFOs may also be developing very proactive and innovative HRM strategies. A European survey on NFOs shows the impressive growth in the use of these HRM practices over 1992–1996 (Whittington et al., 1999b). The Fremap case illustrates how a firm incorporates the management of its personnel matters into the company credo and explicit corporate culture, to a point where it becomes the driving force behind the firm's organizational innovations.

This case study also confirms recent studies (Milgrom and Roberts, 1995; Nohria, 1996) which adopted a systemic approach to the analysis of NFOs. This means that organizational features interact, becoming configurations or systems which are more than the sum of their parts (Meyer et al., 1993a). Therefore it is essential to analyse the whole phenomenon as one single unit. Supporting the holistic view, evidence from the INNFORM survey reveals that high performing firms develop a dense set of complementarities by establishing strong ties simultaneously among variables such as: operations decentralization, information technology systems, proactive HRM arrangements, project-based work and horizontal linkages. In Fremap most of these variables arose within a short time, all with the same aim: to reshape the organization and its processes to achieve its corporate goals more effectively.

The chapter is organized as follows. Following this introduction, there is a brief description of what is understood by NFO within the current academic literature and its HRM implications. The method-ological approach used in this research and the features of the fieldwork conducted are explained in the third section. Later, the key features of Fremap, its historical organizational development and the Spanish busi-ness context within which this evolution had been taking place are analysed. The critical elements underlying the process of development of Fremap towards a NFO are then highlighted, together with an analy-sis at three separate organizational levels. A set of conclusions is also provided.

Literature Review

New forms of competition and internal pressures demand new ways of organizing company activities. Various authors (Powell, 1990; Baker, 1992; Nohria, 1996) have written about the dissolution of traditional forms of organizing as a way to manage in rapidly changing environ-ments (Meyer et. al., 1993b; D'Aveni, 1994; Brown and Eisenhardt, 1998). Leading firms are responding to the new challenges by redefining the organization of their activities and their internal processes and systems, with less formal and hierarchical structures (Miles and Snow, 1994).

Although studies of new forms of organizing have been steadily growing in the 1990s, there has been little research in this area, and even less research into the connection between NFO and HRM (Kanter and Eccles, 1992). While authors recognize the need to revise traditional structures to help companies adapt to their competitive challenges, there is no consensus on the best way to analyse the development of NFO initiatives.

To understand the differences between the traditional organizations and NFOs, scholars have highlighted their different structural and sys-tems configuration. In relation to their structures, the organizations differ on their basic operational logic. Traditional companies enforce the logic of division and differentiation (Hedlund, 1994) which is enforced by internal regulations (Powell, 1990), while NFOs follow a logic of combination and integration differentiation (Hedlund, 1994) on the basis of complementary strengths. Traditional and newer forms of organizing also differ in their system configurations. Traditional firms develop interunit coordination through 'vertical' means such as multi-player planning, top-down resource allocation, and formal performance evaluation from headquarters (Nohria, 1996). In contrast, NFOs coordi-nate informally by using 'horizontal' mechanisms like cross-functional research and development teams, mutual support and participatory activities through quality management, decentralization, and flexible work arrangements, all of which result in decision-making power being pushed down through the organization (Hastings, 1996). Furthermore, as Osborn (1998: 481) emphasizes, 'new-form organizations are likely to organize more explicitly around processes than traditional-form organizations that emphasize functional hierarchy'.

Similarly, while control and conflict resolution in traditional firms tends to be based on hierarchical supervision and enforcement (Powell, 1990), NFOs rely more heavily on self-discipline based on norms of reciprocity, reputation, trust and legitimacy (Powell, 1990; Hastings, 1996; Chakravarthy and Gargiulo, 1998).

In relation to personnel matters, authors have also pointed out that changes in firms' structures and systems can be paralleled by changes in the way the organization manages its personnel (Wright and McHan, 1992; Lado and Wilson, 1994; MacDuffie, 1995; Milgrom and Roberts, 1995). For example, Allred et al. (1996: 17) argue that 'the evolution of organizational forms has always driven the ingredients and paths of managerial careers'. More specifically, introducing NFOs requires a different view of the foundation upon which personnel policies and practices rest.

Recently, evidence has shown that innovative firms are departing from some of the common personnel trends of the 1990s, such as downsizing, extensive reliance on external labour markets, outsourcing employees and high rates of turnover, as they grapple with organizational restructuring (Beatty and Schneier, 1997; Ulrich, 1997; Pfeffer, 1998). These authors have remarked on the critical role of the HRM function as a key agent in corporate transformation and change, with employees being trained in such a way that they can constantly adapt to new requirements. Ghoshal and Bartlett (1998: 142) emphasize that 'there is one central truth in corporate transformation that is often overlooked: companies cannot renew their business unless they first revitalize their people'. Whittington and Mayer (1997) state that HRM function has become central to the process of making new forms of organization work, and found two distinct types of HRM practice in the emerging NFOs: those related to supporting horizontal networking, and those concerned with maintaining organizational integration.

This brings us to the familiar 'decentralization versus centralization' debate (see Storey and Sisson, 1993: 80–109). It is difficult to strike a perfect balance between making a clear statement of HRM strategy at the centre of an organization and its implementation at the periphery. The need to simultaneously integrate and differentiate in managing NFOs can significantly affect personnel matters. The dichotomy can be particularly pronounced in multinational companies (Rosenzweig and Nohria, 1994). Pettigrew (1999a) gives evidence as to how the management of such dualities is common within NFOs experiences in connection with HRM issues, in relation not only to the dichotomy of strategy centralization and operational decentralization, but to the coexistence of holding the ring at the centre and empowering employees as well.

Snow and Snell (1993: 471) argue that staffing, as the act of recruitment, selecting and appraising and promoting individuals, must drive the formation of firms' competitive strategy which is indispensable 'in dynamic network organizations that are regularly reconfigured to pursue shifting market opportunities'. Chakravarthy and Gargiulo (1998) point out that one of the key behaviours required for the success of NFOs is employee empowerment. Furthermore, these authors remark on how an empowering organization requires its front line employees both to take the primary lead in driving its strategy and to have a genuine commitment to the firm's culture and management vision. In relation to job design, NFOs, in contrast to traditional firms which are based on the strict division of work, are becoming more 'de-jobbed' (Brousseau et al., 1996). They adapt more easily to change and the management of knowledge work, thus enhancing the use of teamwork.

Similarly Bahrami (1992: 43) remarks that compensation cannot be linked to organizational positions because NFOs are less hierarchical in nature: 'An individual's effectiveness is based on results and credibility, rather than on formal authority, job descriptions, and position in hierarchy.' Instead, pay needs to be related both to performance – at the individual and, especially, group level – and to the acquisition of new skills (Brousseau et al., 1996). Or as Lawler (1992: 168) argued: 'skill-based pay encourages people to learn horizontal skills. This allows these individuals to see things from other people's viewpoints, which is especially important in a horizontal oriented organizational structure.'

The scarcity of detailed case studies specifically focused on understanding HRM and NFOs is notorious. Recently, a longitudinal study of people management issues in complex organizations has provided some evidence of HRM change creating new ways of working (Stiles, 1999). This study explains how Glaxo-Wellcome broke up a long-established hierarchical organization, setting up numerous project and task teams. Looking to anticipate and influence the strategy of the firm's major customer (the UK's National Health Service), internal barriers were broken down and replaced with horizontal working systems to enhance knowledge transfer and encourage entrepreneurial behaviour. The redesign of job roles, the flattening of hierarchies and the shortening of reporting lines are highlighted as some of its most immediate consequences (Stiles, 1999: 163).

Nevertheless much of the previous literature lacks prescriptiveness, due to its emphasis on merely describing the required features of the HRM practices of new organizational arrangements. Discussing how Fremap is introducing a new form of organizing, we will analyse both the role of the HR function as a driving force and the direct implications of the new organizational pattern for HR policies and practices. By so doing, we aim to break new ground in a relatively unexplored area (Kanter and Eccles, 1992).

Methodology and fieldwork

The methodological approach chosen for this investigation is case study research. This case study focuses on the context (in order to explain *what)* and on the process (to explain *how*) with the aim of explaining *why* something is happening. The study, however, does not depart from any previous, formal and explicit hypotheses with the final purpose of testing and building theory. Our research is of a more exploratory and explanatory nature, fundamentally concerned with the underlying interaction among a set of organizational factors over a period of time.

Various scholars have written about the possibility of theory building through case studies (Eisenhardt, 1989b; Pettigrew, 1990; Yin, 1994), a distinctive feature of which is the capacity to make adjustments during the data collection process (Eisenhardt, 1989b: 539). The research process can take into account findings from previous investigations, adopting changes to data collection instruments. This type of research approach, in grounded theory (Glaser and Strauss, 1967), is well suited for complex organizational phenomena such as NFO and its HRM implications, in which solid constructs are unable to be rigorously defined a priori.

A key issue is the practicality of finding and gaining access to companies with this extensive organizational development within each specific business community. After a detailed analysis of the Spanish business community it was decided to focus on the experience of Fremap due to its recent reorganization of work, which affected around 90 per cent of its activities and processes and most of the employees. Furthermore, Fremap is changing the formal structures within the territorial and branch organization, as well as the control system and coordination between them and headquarters. This firm offers an excellent opportunity to study both the critical role played by the HRM function and policies, and the company culture as major driving forces behind the process of organizational development.

Fieldwork was conducted from autumn 1997 to autumn 1998, mainly in Fremap's headquarters (HQ) in Madrid and in two territorial branches (one of which is also a territorial HQ). From the outset, it was considered essential to develop the fieldwork in both parts of the organization in order to obtain a more detailed view of the dynamics and interaction between the HQ and the territorial branches. It was also essential to avoid possible bias produced by a partial perspective.

It was decided early on that in-depth, open-ended and semi-structured interviews with managers would be the most suitable method for investigating the underlying process in the NFO configuration and its managerial and HRM implications. Other techniques, such as studying the firm's public and private documentation, the mutual insurance sector and newspaper-documentary sources, and visiting some of its premises and HQ, were also used in order to enhance, triangulate and validate the interview information.

The fieldwork was done at different time intervals over a one-year period. The Personnel Director was interviewed on four separate occasions. This allowed improvement and clarification of the data obtained, enriching previous information (Jones, 1991; Seidman, 1991). Triangulation with internal and newspaper data was an important and useful method, confirming the reliability and accuracy of the interview information (Yin, 1994: 92). A total of 16 interviews were carried out with 13 different people, the average interview lasting over 90 minutes. Half of them were conducted at HQ level. The General Manager and the Medical, Information Technology and Quality Directors were all interviewed. The Personnel Director was asked systematically about managerial issues and other managers were also asked about HRM and industrial relations. We placed special emphasis on understanding the organization of work, the process of decentralization and its implications, the role of the personnel function, staffing policies, training, information and communication, compensation, and management development. In the branches and the territorial headquarters interviews were with 'integral agents', as well as with the branch and territorial directors. All the interviews were tape-recorded.

Data analysis and interpretation is the most critical and difficult element of qualitative research (Miles and Huberman, 1994; Yin, 1994). It was decided to organize and structure all the information by writing an extensive chronological case study. These write-ups are often purely descriptive, but are central to the generation of insights (Eisenhardt, 1989b: 540). A draft of the case study was sent to the firm, prompting both oral and written feedback, which helped to clarify some data and validate the accuracy of the information, enhancing construct validity of the case study by respondent validation (Yin, 1994).

In order to avoid traditional criticism regarding the validity and reliability of case study research in the social sciences, we (1) used multiple sources of evidence; (2) followed a systematic method in the within-case construction; and (3) obtained permission from the informants to publish the information once it had been checked.

The Spanish Business Context and the Organizational Evolution of Fremap

In this section, the key features of Fremap and its historical development are analysed. A broader picture of Spanish business is also given, to show the context in which the organizational evolution of Fremap has been taking place.

The Spanish context

The Spanish economy and the industrial infrastructure remained underdeveloped into the 1950s, later initiating an accelerated transformation and modernization of the productivity and economic structures. This has led to a rapid change in the profile of firms over the past two decades (García Delgado, 1995). The interventionist role of the state in business matters, the traditional failure of educational and training systems, the small size of firms and their family ownership, are some of the reasons behind the relatively slow professionalization of Spanish firms until recently. Only since the 1960s has personal capitalism begun to be replaced by professional management cadres.

The Spanish business community is heavily dominated by small and medium-sized firms (Costa, 1995). The development of large companies had been constrained, among other influences, by the effects of late industrialization, the difficulties of obtaining financial resources, the lack of proper competition produced by decades of isolation and the small size of the business market. Despite the spectacular growth of the private sector in recent decades, the presence of public enterprises remained significant until the privatization programme of the 1990s. The Spanish economy is now a highly internationalized market. After the restrictions on foreign capital were abolished in the 1960s, a large number of MNCs set up in Spain in the period 1970–1990.

Institutional limits such as the failure of the vocational training system and the regulated legal nature of job and skill classifications are still strongly influencing the patterns of work organization in Spain (Pérez Díaz and Rodríguez, 1995; Köhler and Woodard, 1997). However, changes in recent years due to more relaxed labour legislation, the influence of the multinationals' practices, and their spread through collective bargaining at firm and industry level, are developing new models of work organization based upon the search for labour flexibility. The lack of any extensive cadre of professional managers until recent decades is another reason behind the centralization and concentration in large companies of the decision making in a small group of directors.

The role of the law is one of the key characteristics of the Spanish labour system (Martínez, 1998). Labour regulations apply to practically all spheres of employment, with labour courts and the administrative authorities playing a major role, despite the introduction of alternative judicial bodies and major legal reforms in 1994 and 1997 which slightly relaxed the regulation of the labour market. The impact of this reform on work organization will be considerable, since it implies the transformation of the traditional professional categories into new professional groups, aiming at developing more functional mobility, flexibility and multiskilling, and also modifying the compensation structure. As in other European countries, the introduction of modern HRM practices in

Spanish companies, which began slowly during the 1980s, is acquiring more importance in the larger firms. However, the scope of their implementation and results is patchy and even contradictory (Pérez Díaz and Rodríguez, 1995; Baruel, 1996).

Spain is a good example of a country in which the business system, despite undergoing a radical modernization in a very short span of time, is significantly imprinted by its past institutional legacy (Crouch, 1993).

Fremap profile

Fremap, founded in 1933, is a mutual insurance company that provides its associated firms' employees with insurance coverage for work-related accidents and occupational diseases. It also manages health centres and four hospitals for the treatment of work-related accidents and illnesses.

There are two sides to the activity of a mutual insurance company for industrial accidents and occupational disease: insurance and health care. Affiliated companies insure their employees against any accidents or diseases they might suffer in the course of their work and, in addition, the mutual company organizes its own medical centres, where it attends insured workers who have suffered work-related accidents or diseases. It also establishes prevention programmes, including regular medical check-ups and follow-ups for employees of affiliated companies, as well as accident prevention training and awareness-raising activities. Mutual insurance companies were created in Spain at the turn of the century at the request of employers, to cover for claims resulting from industrial accidents. Since the enactment of the Social Security Act of 1966, they have cooperated in providing sickness benefits and health care (Andreu and Ricart, 1995: 2).

In recent years there has been a clear trend towards the concentration of mutual insurance companies covering industrial accidents, owing to the government requirements set forth in the 1990 National Budget Act. Inabilities to meet legally mandated minimum requirements (50 affiliated employers and 30,000 protected workers) forced a large number of mutual insurance companies to embark on a process of mergers and takeovers which is not yet complete. Thus, whereas in 1990 there were 95 mutual insurance companies in Spain, by 1997 there were only 32 (*Cinco Días*, 1997).[1]

Fremap is, therefore, a non-profit organization within the framework of the Spanish Social Security system. However, company management is autonomous and independent of social security, reporting directly to its owners, the mutual associated firms. The company is the leading mutual insurance company in Spain with 119 branches or centres across the country, employing more than 2,200 people. Its revenues from employers' contributions in 1997 amounted to 122,304 million pesetas (around $790 million), with 319,306 associated firms and covering more than 1,950,000 employees. Its operating surplus was over 12,500 million pesetas (around $80 million) in 1997 (*Annual Report*, 1997 and *Guía del Empleado*, 1998).[2]

Key organizational characteristics and development

From its inception Fremap has always stressed the importance of offering its customers high quality service. This is, as observed within the sector, the underlying explanation behind the success of this firm, which is the outstanding leader with a 16.5 per cent market share in 1995 (Alonso, 1997). In this sense, Fremap has a long history of fostering a strong internal culture. The summary which follows affirms the importance of excellence of service and employee empowerment in the company credo.

Basic principles of Fremap's corporate culture

- Fremap, Mutua de Accidentes de Trabajo, is a *common project* bound by ethical principles which tends towards continuous improvement.
- *Fremap believes the individual is the centre of social relations.* Consequently, all our activity is focused, in the final analysis, on the service provided to workers and on our own employees' professional and personal fulfilment. Thus, the organization is built around the individuals, with a profound respect for both their dignity and freedom.
- The basic objective of Fremap is *Quality*, as the maximum expression of our organization's culture, which is manifested, with our own personal style, in a job well done and whose ultimate purpose is the full satisfaction of the user of our services.
- The members, as the service's sole source of finance, must receive an adequate response to their need for cover against occupational risks among their workforce. Fremap encourages suggestions and provides for their implementation through the participation channels set forth in its articles of association: General Meeting of Members, management board, business advisory board and regional advisory board.

  The employees affiliated to Fremap are aware of the effectiveness of the initiative undertaken in the management of the Social Security system, and wish to *extend* the mutual society's *area* of cooperation to other contingencies of the system.
- The organization's employees are the ones directly responsible for providing the service and *it is an ongoing goal of Fremap to develop their personal and professional skills within a favourable framework of human relationships.*

- The recruitment of new employees to Fremap will be carried out in accordance with *objective selection criteria*, verifying that the candidate has the right personal and professional qualities for the position to be filled.
- Promotion in Fremap is understood as an individual project that evolves in accordance with each employee's abilities, desire to improve and capacity to take on responsibilities, within a suitable framework that ensures *equality of opportunity for promotion*, helping the employee to adapt to his or her job and providing training.
- In order to provide the best service, all of the personnel must receive *ongoing training;* thus, an annual training plan, applicable to the largest possible number of employees and encompassing both professional and cultural aspects, will be drawn up for each province.
- *Information* makes participation possible within the company and ensures that the company is accurately represented to the outside world. It is for this reason that Fremap makes information available on two levels: first, providing employees with monthly information on the organization's progress, excluding only data that affect personal privacy. Secondly, promoting openness and building trust, *vis-à-vis* its members and society as a whole, by submitting its balance sheets and income statements to external audits.
- *Decentralization* generates efficiency and favours creativity and initiative. It is our company's policy to promote actions that increase the autonomy of the decision centres, so that they can find their own solutions to their own particular problems.

Five historical stages can be identified in Fremap´s development. *The first one was initiated in 1970* and involved the introduction of what is known as 'integral treatment of industrial accidents', with the aim of *improving service quality* to affiliated companies. This treatment is defined in Fremap as 'the coordinated application of all available preventive, therapeutic, reparative and restorative techniques in the fight against occupational hazards and their physical, mental, social, human and economic consequences'. To achieve this, branches' medical centres and annual corporate goals were set up. The introduction of this service implied a new focus in seeing the relationship with clients as a whole, a unique perspective that required enhanced coordination of the various departments and units of the organization.

In the *second stage*, between 1985 and 1988, Fremap decided to initiate a slow process of *decentralization*, transferring decision making to the branches. To accomplish this, special efforts were made in training, mainly during 1986 and 1987. Corporate goals were also defined in order to enhance customer service, thus generating initiatives and creativity throughout the company.

In 1988, the *third period*, two major developments took placed. First, the process of *decentralization* began to have a direct impact in the organ-ization, mainly because of the responsibilities transferred to the branches and the territorial headquarters. Secondly, a decision was made to *define formally*, through a company-wide effort, *the corporate goals and culture* to be spread across the organization (see above). During a period of several months the whole workforce actively participated in this process through seminars, surveys and workshops. Two values became the guiding principles of Fremap: ethics, and the idea of the individual as the centre of social relationships.

During the *fourth period* (1990–1991), 'Quality' was defined as the cor-porate goal for these two years. A *Total Quality Plan* was launched, with an action programme for each work centre and the direct participation of most of the personnel. The idea behind this plan was to enhance and sys-tematize something that had always been a corporate feature of Fremap. It was also realized that the high level of quality reached without a spe-cific effort was the result of holding fast to ethics and the individual, now explicit in the company's written organization culture.

In 1992, a *fifth period* started. All the previous experiences crystal-lized into an ambitious scheme that would have far-reaching organizational consequences. This period provides the focus for the analysis of NFO and HRM in Fremap.

The 'integral agent' scheme   This section focuses on the process involved in the introduction of a new organization of work in Fremap´s territorial branches. We will also analyse its managerial and HRM impli-cations at three internal levels: employee, territorial and HQ.

Since 1992, Fremap has undergone a radical change in the way it organizes the operations leading to the delivery of customer services. A persuasive decentralization process from HQ to the territorial organi-zation was set up. The territorial organization is constituted by the aforementioned 119 branches or medical centres. They comprise around 95 per cent of the firm's total headcount and provide the whole service to Fremap's customers, the affiliated companies. Fremap's General Manager described the situation of the company before 1992 and the aims of the decentralization process as follows:

> That old structure led to an excessive degree of specialization, created rigid hierarchical divisions, and divided areas of activity with niches and bound-aries that served no useful purpose. The corporate goal in 1992 was to improve management. We were confident that we knew what we wanted and that we were serious about attaining maximum quality, but in practice we never seemed to achieve the progress we had been hoping for. Something was holding us back. And we suddenly realized that it was the organization, and the distribution of tasks mainly within the territorial branches. That is why we decided that there had to be a change . . . Which was not so much of a change really, since the basic values and the culture were already there in

Fremap; they had been developing in the company since its inception. (Andreu and Ricart, 1995: 4)

Fremap's administrative structure based on departments and well-defined job categories, following the Spanish insurance sector tradition, had remained practically unchanged since 1933. The associated management systems had not changed substantially either, even taking into account the previous decentralization efforts described above. This structure (as shown in Figure 7.1), partly determined by legal requirements for mutual insurance companies, had effectively prevented the company from operating in accordance with its own objectives and values.

It was realized that in the relationship between Fremap's employees and its customers, too much importance was being given to resolving bureaucratic issues, to the detriment of customer service. Customers were treated like mere dossiers handled by several different employees

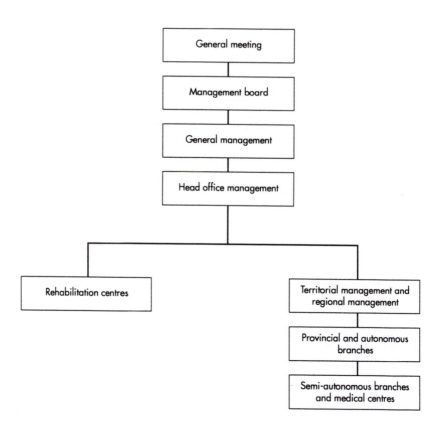

FIGURE 7.1 *Fremap's organization chart*

within the same branch, not individual case histories. In short, the internal structure worked against the integration of insurance claim processing. The need to place more emphasis on interpersonal relationships and to integrate the tasks was obvious to all.

HQ decided to implement a new form of work organization whereby each employee within the territorial branches had to perform the full range of administrative tasks, and most of the commercial activities involving customer service. They departed from a highly departmentalized functional specialization to a new position called the *integral agent*. The General Manager explained the previous organizational arrangements within the territorial branches and its transformation as follows:

> Each branch comprised a number of departments integrated by several employees with different job categories. This traditional structure, under a Taylorist conception, determined that each employee acquired a great deal of knowledge in some specific areas and, simultaneously, they were thoroughly unaware about their fellows' tasks. This represented an important problem in integrating the employees into the firm's activities and, even more importantly, in developing their own professional and personal competencies as, in most of the cases, the decision making was concentrated in the hands of a few people. Under the circumstances it was decided to abolish the departmental and functional divisions within the territorial branches.

The key achievement has been that now all Fremap's territorial employees approach their tasks in a completely different way. They now understand, and practically all of them can perform, the various activities involved in their daily work. *The final result may also be described as being a team-based structure, somewhat in line with the Saab Training System experience* (see Müllern, Chapter 8 in this volume). The introduction of this distinctive work organization within the Fremap branches clearly constitutes an NFO experience as it implies the substitution of a very hierarchical structure for a new, flat and horizontal one, the introduction of managerial systems emphasizing knowledge coordination and the replacement of bureaucratic processes, and enhancement of delegation and employee empowerment. This new approach has brought a number of important organizational and cultural changes. The major move was an ambitious decentralization process, coordination becoming HQ's key task.

The implementation process of the new organization of work

In June 1992, under the impulse of the General Manager and as a compulsory headquarters mandate, the project that is now known as the *integral agent* scheme was presented. The basic idea was that every employee within the territorial organization should be able to solve all of any particular customer's problems, whether the customer was a company or a worker. This implied a dramatic change in the conception, structure and organizational systems of the territorial branches. Figure 7.2 shows both the previous and the current organizational structures of Fremap´s territorial branches. As the Personnel Director pointed out: 'This change implied the complete abolition of the organizational pyramid within the territorial organization, as currently only one hierarchy level exists, between the Director and the rest of the employees.'

The new organization gave rise to the concept of the integral agent, who reported only to the Branch Manager. The idea was that job categories and departments would be wiped out and that all the clerical employees would be able to conduct all relations between Fremap and a particular customer. In the way things were organized before, in some branches up to eight employees had been needed, depending on the problem. An integral agent would not supervise any other employees; the agent would be directly responsible for carrying out whatever activities might be necessary to solve the problems of the customers assigned to him/her.

The implementation process was initiated by assigning customers to agents on a territorial basis: in any given territory, the agent dealt with all aspects of the relationship between Fremap and its customers. At the head office, whose customers were in fact the branches, the effects of the change were less dramatic. A detailed plan was developed in which Catalonia was chosen to pioneer the project implementation. The process was conducted in phases. The first one was to *inform* the personnel specifically chosen, in greater detail than the general information communicated to the whole workforce through different channels. The second step was to provide training.

Training was a key element in establishing the new work organization, within which the previous structure of the branches by specialized departments just disappeared. By definition, the introduction of the concept of the integral agent meant that a lot of people had to take responsibility for a number of activities that had previously been carried out by others. At the same time, certain coordination of tasks became unnecessary because all the activities that needed coordination were now in the hands of one single person. Depending on its size, there might have been anywhere between three and 12 people in a territorial branch who had to abandon their very differentiated areas of specialization to become integral agents. To do this, intensive training programmes have been developed for the employees, instilling a new management culture where people provide quick and effective solutions to clients.

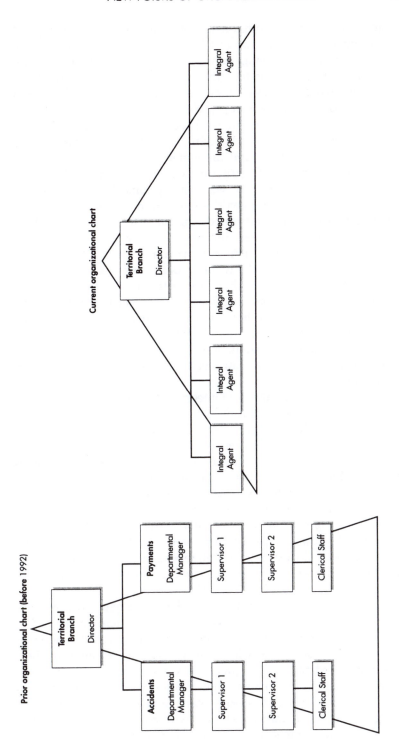

FIGURE 7.2   Structural organizational changes in Fremap's territorial branches

Together with specialized tutors to assist integral agents, and support tools designed by HQ, the project began to be operational in some branches. After the systematic training and mock simulations by computer-assisted teaching models, the integral agents took qualifying examinations in order to check if they were able to perform all the tasks of the new position. This is also requisite if employees are officially to obtain the new internal job category – integral agent – and get a pay increase.

The much-needed change in Fremap's *technological infrastructure* was a critical aid to supporting and implementing the whole process. In 1992 the technological infrastructure was becoming obsolete. It is argued within the firm that this was a lucky coincidence. Most of the computer applications had been designed from a functional point of view and had been poorly integrated. This made it much easier to think about a new structure for new information systems in line with the basic philosophy of the new organizational approach. In other parts, the technology became part of the whole process, and the transition was considered normal. A new technology, with client-server structures, which fits with the new organization of work conception, was introduced. New applications have been developed, integrating the information used into a user-friendly interface at workstations, thus allowing several tasks to be simultaneously carried out. Employees now have personal computers, creating electronic desktops from which they perform most of their duties.

The aim was to decentralize and integrate, making sure that each integral agent had the technological system support to perform all their new needs and responsibilities. Moreover, despite the critical importance of the information technology system in implementing the integral agent scheme, the stress was put on its design. Having the right systems is simply a technical issue, a matter of choosing the technology and putting it to work. In the information systems area Fremap is a pioneer firm, which has obtained an international prize from such a prestigious institution as the Smithsonian (see details in http://innovate.si.edu/smith/1996).

In addition, the *management systems* were adapted to the new situation. In particular, the existing control, reporting and incentive systems were now clearly inappropriate. The new systems needed to be coordinated to provide information to a highly varied and widely dispersed group of people, tasks and systems to achieve the new structural and organizational challenges. The new technology system has helped to make the organizational structure more flexible, and to create a horizontal management system in which the 'integral agents' are more qualified, intensifying coordination throughout the whole organization. For example, readily available information at any point in the health-care network has facilitated the work of integral agents and medical workforce by helping to decrease treatment periods, with a direct reduction in lost workdays due to accidents at work and occupational diseases.

Likewise, transaction times have become considerably shorter. As one of the integral agents says: 'It makes our work much easier, since now we can do several tasks at the same time and also provide a much better service to clients, who no longer have to be transferred to other people. Nor do we have to make them wait or call them later.' The branch management systems are also based, as explained below, upon teamwork: all of the agents share the same management criteria and follow the same calendar of tasks.

This Fremap scheme was not only a pioneering breakthrough at an internal company level but also a unique experience within the Spanish insurance industry as a whole. Within the insurance sector, as well as in the Spanish business context, the 'integral agent project' is a 'revolutionary' experiment.

The three levels of analysis

The process of introduction of the integral agent and its managerial implications are analysed at three different levels within Fremap: the individual or employee level, the branch and territorial level (including territorial headquarters), and the company's headquarters level.

The individual or employee level   The organizational transformation of Fremap revolves around the integral agents. The key issue was to concentrate all the activities previously performed by the branch team on a single person, who could solve all of a particular customer's problems. This involved a major acquisition of new knowledge and skills. One single job category was introduced: the integral agent, who had to demonstrate both knowledge and experience. Those who passed the relevant examination were rewarded with significant incentives. Furthermore, *permanent training* became an activity inherent in the performance of the integral agent position. Health workers have not been directly affected by the change, although they may benefit indirectly due to improved coordination with clerical personnel and a greater degree of support.

The new organization brought with it some tension at the individual level. Some employees felt uncomfortable with these changes, particularly those who had joined before the new organization was defined and thought that they could make a good career for themselves in Fremap by becoming specialists. Management accepted this from the start. The Personnel Director expressed the situation in this way: 'Of course, we realized that several employees were suffering with these changes. We recognized that we changed our mind and that we made a mistake with all those that joined Fremap with the idea of becoming specialist as a professional career.'

The main remedy was to respect the job categories and task activities of the people who expressly did not want to become integral agents. For them a new position of *agent* was created. Nevertheless, a recent internal survey provided evidence that around 48 per cent of all branch employees assumed the role of integral agent relatively promptly. The majority of the employees also seemed more satisfied and motivated than before. Users have adapted gradually to their new way of working. One integral agent stated: 'Even if they offered me a 20 per cent salary increase to do the job I was doing before, I would not accept it.' The number of people not performing well in the new position has declined greatly over the last few years. It was less than 10 per cent in 1997 and continuing growth in headcount and the profile of new employees will cause this figure to continue to drop over the next few years.

The branch and territorial level   The integral agent project brought many crucial changes in the structure and organization of the branch and the territorial headquarters. As the new administrative organization is based upon the individual, the departmental and functional divisions of the territorial branches were abolished. The consequence was the total rupture and demolition of the formal functional and departmental boundaries of the previous organizational structure.

Despite the fact that all integral agents act independently in their own area of influence, they also receive specific training in teamwork. There are certain tasks, such as cash control or reception, which are rotated among them. This kind of teamwork is made possible by the way the branch is now organized. The layout of the office is designed to facilitate interaction and contact between the members of the team. Each workstation, even though it has its own style, has the same physical layout and organization (Andreu and Ricart, 1995: 5). All of the agents share the same management criteria and common data-processing tools (see Figure 7.3).

In addition, all the agents follow the same calendar of tasks (see Figure 7.4). These allow for a degree of standardization, so that one can easily be substituted for another without affecting the service quality or affiliated companies' expectations. This may be considered an innovative form of knowledge management (Stewart, 1997) that allows the integral agents to work both individually and as a network simultaneously.

In the branches there are now only two job categories: those of integral agent and branch director. The branches have a very flat and lean organizational structure. The director's role has also changed. The director now works as coordinator of the branch activity, supporting the work of the integral agents and facilitating commercial activity. While everyone has direct access to the whole organization, the director is the link between the territorial level and HQ.

Management tasks
1. Daily branch supervision (no more than one hour, first thing in the morning and one hour at the end of the day's work, to bring oneself up to date on the developments). Management tools: • Discharge pending listing • Report pending listing • Serious injuries listing • Payment to representative, referrals, fakes, membership • Budget control (detail of accounts) • Reservations • Issues • Cancellations • Accounting (daily reports)
2. Weekly meeting with all the components (management, medical service, etc.). Items to be discussed: • Assessment of injured with sick leave • Complicated cases • Duration • Political cases • In general, all those cases that affect the branch's progress
3. Sales management • New customers • Study of cancellations • Strategies for winning and retaining customers

FIGURE 7.3   *Guidelines for unifying management criteria*

The major territorial branches now play a more dynamic role. The director of the most important branch in each of the 12 territories is also the territorial director, coordinating the territorial branches, defining commercial strategies and developing projects of common interest.

After the integral agent scheme was introduced, the role of the directors became much more important. The territorial directors now meet formally and informally without direct representation from the headquarters. They discuss shared problems in the branches, making direct decisions on some issues and asking HQ to introduce others. On occasion, they are required to attend the meetings of some of the HQ's functional directors.

The initiatives by HQ are seen to have had very positive effects, and ones which are characteristic of the decentralization process, reflecting

CALENDAR OF TASKS

	DAILY	WEEKLY	MONTHLY
LIST AGENDAS	GUIDE	ISSUE	PAY REPRESENTATIVE	SCHEDULE CLAIMS & ISSUE TC-1

	DAILY	WEEKLY	MONTHLY	
LIST AGENDAS	GUIDE	ISSUE	PAY REPRESENTATIVE	SCHEDULE CLAIMS & ISSUE TC-1
	GADEA	DISCHARGE PENDING LISTING		CAPTURE TC-1 AND TC-2
	CONTRIBUTIONS	REPORT PENDING LISTING	CODE 91 LISTING (11)	
CAPTURE	SICK LEAVES	REVIEW SERIOUS CASES	REFERRAL LISTING (30)	
	DISCHARGES	OPEN SERIOUS CASE FILES	FAKES LISTING (40)	
	REPORTS-GUARENTEE CONTROL	MONITOR INJURED PERSONS IN OTHER CENTRES	MEMBERSHIP LISTING (2,4,5)	
CODE REPORTS			RESERVATIONS LISTING	
CALL 5 COMPANIES FROM THE PORTFOLIO			SERIOUS CASES LISTING	
INVOICES	CODE		PREPARE SICK LEAVE PAYMENTS	
	RETURN		REVIEW TRAFFIC RECOVERIES	
CORRESPONDENCE			CLOSE (LAST DAY)	
EXPEDITE REPORT				
REVIEW CONTRIBUTIONS BY COMPANIES				
REVIEW MILD CASES				
CENTRALIZATIONS				

FIGURE 7.4   Calendar of integral agents' tasks

the emergence of new horizontal networks and linkages within Fremap and revealing the true structural and organizational configuration of the firm.

The company's headquarters level Despite the previous changes affecting the activities of company headquarters, changes in its organization were minimal compared with those in the territorial organization. After a long debate, it was finally decided that functional organization by departments should be retained. The logic behind this decision was the role of HQ in giving support to the branches' activities through specialized departments. The shift to more integrated departments was considered to be an inefficient response.

The real change within group headquarters was the acquisition of a more developed role for coordinators, enabling them to respond rapidly to the needs of the branches. Many of their previous competencies and responsibilities were transferred to the branches and the integral agents, who obtained higher decision-making responsibilities. This development has replaced the former pyramidal system of control in which HQ needed to authorize practically all of the territorial branches' activities by a flat structure, an agile support procedure and permanent assistance. The crucial new task was to develop the framework and shared guidelines that the branches need to perform their activities: in short, a new coordination pattern. A relevant piece of data is that the headcount of the central organization is less than 5 per cent of the total workforce, and it became an unwritten rule not to increase the central headcount above this figure. This aim was fixed before the decentralization process began in 1985.

HRM implications and some unresolved management issues

Fremap operated without a personnel director for many years. Only after 1989 was an experienced manager in this field hired from outside. The idea that presides over Fremap's personnel approach is that line managers, specifically branch directors, are the ones with personnel responsibility. As the General Manager argues: 'I have as many personnel directors as Fremap has branch directors.' The personnel function was decentralized (Hall and Torrington, 1998), being put into the hands of the territorial and branch directors, who were in charge of most recruitment. Only a few common guidelines about training and recruiting university graduates were made explicit. This was also the case with regard to the career path to becoming branch director, that is, by acquiring experience in various regional branches. The compensation policy had always been centralized at HQ level.

Despite not having a proper personnel department in Fremap until recently, many of the corporate principles are HRM policies. Most of the current HRM policies and practices had been performed in the same way since the company had been formed, mainly due to the smaller size of the organization and the smaller number of employees. The main change following the appointment of the new Personnel Director, and the further development of the decentralization process in 1992, was the centralization of the personnel policy: the aim was to create a workforce that shared a common culture. The true glue in Fremap that facilitates the much-needed coordination and integration, since it is now a very decentralized organization, is a shared corporate culture and the feeling of belonging. As discussed in the ABB case study (see Ruigrok et al. Chapter 4 in this volume) the Fremap managerial team perceive organizational culture as a strong coordination mechanism between head office and territorial units. The General Manager explained this: 'The problem of how to make the new organization actually work will be less of a problem if people are ready and the culture is in place – as was true in our case' (Andreu and Ricart, 1995: 5).

Therefore common employee profiles and systems were needed to ensure that all new employees could internalize the current Fremap management style. It was realized that decentralization of selection was a problem because every branch or territorial director chose a different personal profile. The Fremap case demonstrates that one of the critical resources of the new forms of organizing is the creation of a corporate human resource strategy based upon mutual trust and a common identity (see also Whittington and Mayer, 1997).

Selection, acculturation and management development, together with permanent training, became the cornerstone of the newly centralized Fremap personnel policy. Despite this, the role of the territorial division and branches is crucial in all personnel decisions because, for example, the final selection decision is their responsibility. The key aspect is to follow the process designed for the whole organization, and after an interview with the company Personnel Director, every branch director must decide who to select among a group of candidates. The selection process is quite refined, looking (particularly in the case of the integral agents) for profiles that match the values embedded in Fremap's corporate culture. One essential feature is social responsiveness due to the fact that the firm serves employees who have suffered either accidents or occupational diseases. Candidates with experience working with non-profit organizations are highly regarded. It is said within Fremap: 'We will never recruit MBAs, we are looking for another kind of person. We want people who share our principles, with special sensitivity to serving the society and not just worried about their own professional career.' There is also a sophisticated induction programme over a long period, with intensive training activities. This entails all the new candidates living together in a hotel for several weeks. This programme is held in the central HQ in Madrid to help employees identify with a highly visible whole organization.

The Fremap case exemplifies how innovative firms are managing dualities (Pettigrew, 1999a), in this case simultaneous HRM centralization and decentralization, as a way of supporting the implementation of new organizational arrangements. Another relevant example of the need for carefully managing dualities in NFOs is the co-existence in Fremap of two different types of workforce: those that readily accepted the new work system and those that preferred the old 'rules of the game'. Despite the fact that this latter group, as explained above, comprises less that 10 per cent of the territorial headcount, its existence is unquestionable. A similar situation was reported in the aforementioned study of Glaxo-Wellcome (Stiles, 1999). The greater the number of employees and their identification with the old set of beliefs and value systems implied by a hierarchical organization, the more difficult it would be to effect change by introducing NFOs' experiences.

At the end of 1997 Fremap's workforce numbered 2,203 (64 per cent men, 36 per cent women; mean age, 38 years; average seniority in the company, 11 years; 84 per cent are permanent employees). Over 64 per cent of Fremap's employees are university graduates.

Employee satisfaction is quite high, as monitored by ongoing employee surveys. We also directly observed the strong commitment and identification of Fremap´s employees with the firm's values and goals. Fremap has made employee involvement the critical HRM policy and the pillar upon which it builds the implementation of its integral agent scheme. Furthermore, it facilitates the transition from a 'bureaucratic' organization to an 'entrepreneurial network' (Chakravarthy and Gargiulo, 1998). Industrial relations in Fremap are peaceful, with a harmonious relationship with unions and no industrial conflict.

Fremap, therefore, has a very people-centred strategy (Pfeffer, 1998) and a relaxed atmosphere which generates flexibility, customer service, productivity, and learning and skill development through a number of high HRM performance practices, such as employment security, selective hiring, self-managed teams and decentralization, extensive training, reduction in status differences, and information sharing. The HRM policies and practices of Fremap can be described as being very sophisticated and innovative within the Spanish business environment and the mutual insurance sector.

Nevertheless, some future question marks have been observed in relation to the current configuration of personnel policies such as professional career, compensation and performance appraisal practices. These policies – and the way by which they have traditionally been managed – reflect a certain paternalism. They do not resolve all the expectations of the people, and in this they could be incompatible with the level of development, professionalism and commitment of the

Fremap workforce. An example of an unresolved management issue of this new organization of work is the negative factor that once the integral agent job category has been achieved, further professional progress is very limited.

In recent times, initiatives to find solutions and alternatives to these unresolved issues are mainly generated and led by the territorial organization. The new horizontal network in Fremap, which comprises the territorial and branch directors, has proven to be a powerful forum that is actively proposing solutions to HQ. Territorial and HQ directors are now working very closely to generate new solutions to their organizational and market challenges. It can be argued that the new coordination pattern between HQ and the territories has also proven to be effective.

Conclusions. The Driving Forces Configuring a New Form of Organizing in Fremap

This case study presents an interesting example of a process of configurating (Miller, 1986) a new form of organizing. The Fremap case is a distinctly novel example of the introduction of a distinctive work organization within its territorial branches which constitute a unique NFO experience. The key features of the new arrangement are the substitution of a hierarchical structure for a new lean and horizontal one, the introduction of managerial systems emphasizing knowledge coordination and replacing previous bureaucratic processes, and the permanent enhancement of employee involvement and delegation.

Without neglecting the importance of external environmental pressures (new government regulations, the mutual insurance market competition, the greater client expectations and the evolution of the Spanish business environment) in accelerating the introduction of the decentralized organization in Fremap, the key driving forces behind the process of a NFO configuration are Fremap´s internal features. Changes were instigated at headquarters level with the aim of overcoming the organizational limitations that had restricted the natural development of Fremap's capabilities.

This company realized after a process of self-examination that the problem of achieving its own corporate goals resided within its structure and work organization. The measures taken were the natural result of the combination of a strongly imprinted corporate culture and a personnel approach led by top management and well operationalized through a coherent set of systems and procedures. The two crucial driving forces behind this organizational development are: corporate culture and some appropriate and sophisticated HRM policies and practices.

The General Manager, with several decades of experience, is the figure visible behind the current organizational elements that characterize Fremap. Within Fremap, and in much the same way as evidenced in Ove Arup Partnership (see Fenton and Pettigrew, Chapter 2 in this volume), the *General Manager's leadership not only articulates the new strategy and structure but also provides the role model to be followed and inspiration for all*. The values and managerial guidelines of the founders and subsequent top executives of this company became operationalized in a particular management style. This style includes a permanent search for better ways of meeting customer needs, and an overall attitude of putting the individual first and foremost at the centre of the business relationship (Beer, 1997; Pfeffer, 1998). The business activity of the company in providing a higher quality of life and health to employees has also encouraged this management style. Nevertheless, this feature of Fremap is not seen in many other mutual insurance companies.

The results of the programme of organizational change initiated in 1992 include the effective consolidation of a corporate culture that had been latent in Fremap since its origin and facilitated the consolidation of the *Integral Agent* project. As Ghoshal and Bartlett (1997: 142) argue: 'rather than focusing on individual behaviors, the more important challenge is to change the internal environment that in turn influences people's behaviours. To reshape it, managers must transform their own behavioral contexts.' The previously described leadership and its inherent values and features became institutionalized throughout the whole corporation, acquiring an autonomous role independent of top management. This corporate culture provides the necessary mobilization in search of innovative organizational forms and managerial systems that enables Fremap to achieve its goals and values. Corporate culture became the key driving force in the development of Fremap towards a NFO. The main role of top management in this new organizational form is primarily providing the context to help in its realization (Chakravarthy and Gargiulo, 1998).

The above programme of organizational change includes several simultaneous initiatives highlighted through the case study, such as quality plans, operational decentralization, information technology systems, project-based work, horizontal linkages, etc. This illustrates the need for adopting a systemic approach (Milgrom and Roberts, 1995; Nohria, 1996) in investigating NFOs due to the constellations of variables behind this type of experience. The Fremap case confirms that several organizational features and special projects interact, enhancing the implementation of the individual agent scheme. The final result is much more than the aggregation of the individual components (Meyer et al., 1993a).

Equally, the overall personnel approach of Fremap, as well as the selection, management development and training policies, has had a direct influence in facilitating the process of decentralization, and reinforcing the company's corporate culture. Customers and employees are the cornerstone of Fremap's organization. The use of sophisticated HRM practices to recruit, train and develop young university graduates as the base of the workforce has proven a very successful strategy. Fremap's approach towards personnel can be described as green-field. This means looking for employees with a solid education base, and, if possible, without professional experience, to be acculturated into an explicit corporate culture and management style. Fremap, rather than selecting candidates that fit a certain job description, is aligning its selection and management development with the firm's corporate culture and strategy (Snow and Snell, 1993), by looking for people that can implement both. The clearest HRM implication of the introduction of the integral agent scheme, a NFO experience, has been the need to centralize personnel policy at headquarters, decentralizing only its implementation, under tight monitoring from central management. This confirms the existence of clear dualities in managing new forms of organizing (Pettigrew, 1999a).

This analysis of the experience of Fremap's organizational development brought interesting new insights, such as how powerful internal forces within an organization can become the driving force of organizational development and evolution. The case also highlights the important role of HRM policies and practices within a decentralization process, as both facilitator of the process itself, and in self-transforming to provide the necessary consistency and alignment with corporate strategy (Ulrich, 1997; Wright and McHan, 1992). Furthermore, this case study provides interesting evidence on how a proactive and solid HRM approach can become a truly driving force in the conception and design of NFOs experience, playing a part in the formulation of Fremap's strategy, not just playing a facilitator role in its implementation.

Another key insight from the Fremap case analysis is the necessary contextualization that this investigation required. It is well observed in the literature (see Sisson, 1994) that HRM is inextricably linked with the cultural and institutional environment in which the firms' activities take place. Fremap´s integral agent scheme was a breakthrough in its industry and in the Spanish labour market and HRM experiences of the 1980s. This case demonstrates that despite the fact that managerial choices relating to personnel are constrained by institutional and industry constraints, Fremap discovered enough freedom within the highly restricted Spanish industrial relations of the 1980s and the regulated mutual insurance sector, to forge its own path.

The role of the HRM function in NFOs developments, as well as the implications of these arrangements for both the personnel policies and practices, require the use of more in-depth and longitudinal case studies to allow a proper understanding of the multiple variables and dynamics that may intervene. This research approach offers a promising avenue for further studies aiming at testing the generalizability of our findings and refining theoretical models of the processes leading to organizational innovation.

Notes

Several managers and employees of Fremap made possible this investigation. To them, and specially to Juan Gabriel Fernández, we express our most sincere gratitude. We also gratefully acknowledge support from the Research Division of IESE, University of Navarra.

1   *Cinco Días*, 25 November 1997: 'Las Mutuas también se suben al carro de la prevención': x.

2   Fremap, *Company Annual Report 1997* and *Guía del Empleado 1998*, Dirección de Recursos Humanos, Fremap, Madrid.

8

Integrating the Team-based Structure in the Business Process: The Case of Saab Training Systems

Tomas Müllern

This chapter describes the radical, company-wide, organizational change in Saab Training Systems from 1992 up until 1998. Saab Training Systems is a high-tech company working in the defence industry, and it is characterized as a prime mover in its industry when it comes to organizational renewal. The company is a fully owned part of the Saab group, but with a considerable degree of freedom. The Saab group is made up of a number of companies developing and producing both military and civil products. This case focuses on the change from a traditional functional structure to a team-based structure with a number of features relevant to the theme of this book: innovating forms of organizing. Following a strategy of concentration on core competence, the company, as a whole, is structured in a number of teams organized along business processes. The chapter is theoretically based on literature on team-based structures (and similar concepts) and the organization of business processes. It argues that the literature on new forms of organizing needs to focus more on team-based concepts and on how teams, projects or other small groups can be adapted to the business process. We have a fairly detailed knowledge of the transformation from functional to divisional, M-form structures (Chandler, 1962). The case of Saab Training Systems illustrates another form of radical transformation, from a functional principle of organizing to a process oriented structure organized in a number of teams. Even though the case cannot function as a role model for company-wide change in bigger, and more complex organizations, it shows how radical change ideas can be implemented in small and medium-sized organizations, as well as in parts of bigger organizations.

The chapter has eight sections: next, a literature review introduces a number of important theoretical concepts to the case, followed by the methodology used. The case study is then presented, first with a focus on the industry and drivers for change, followed by a description of the company and its business philosophy. Following this, the organizational change is presented and analysed using concepts from the literature review. The change process is then analysed with a focus on aspects of learning and barriers to change. The chapter concludes with a summary of theoretical issues in the case.

Team-based Structures and New Forms of Organizing

The literature on organizational forms and archetypes has for a long time been troubled by the inadequacy of traditional structural forms (functional, divisional and matrix structures) to capture the richness of today's organizational world. The literature has started to develop new metaphors for at least some of the features of new and innovative forms of organizing. Examples of such metaphors are networks (Miles and Snow, 1986, 1992; Nohria and Eccles, 1992; Fulk and DeSanctis, 1995), projectified organizations (Hastings, 1996; Turner, 1999), process organization (Fulk and DeSanctis, 1995), virtual organizations (DeSanctis and Staudenmayer, 1998), and the cellular form (Miles et al., 1997). As argued in many places in this book, any attempt to capture new forms of organizing needs to adopt a holistic view of organizations, integrating structures, processes and boundaries (Whittington et al., 1999b). The results from the INNFORM project survey (see Fenton and Pettigrew, Chapter 1 in this volume) indicate that finding the right balance between different aspects is crucial for the success of the organization. This review, primarily based on the structural and processual aspects, argues that a team-based structure, arranged to support the business process, is a good example of a new form of organizing (Jarvenpaa and Ives, 1994).

The literature on new and innovative forms of organizing, as well as the human resource management literature, often stresses the use of decentralized, group-based structures. Concepts like team-based structures (Keidel, 1990; Hirschhorn, 1991; DeMent, 1996; Hastings, 1996; Baldwin et. al, 1997; McHugh, 1997; Sewell, 1998), project forms of organizing (DeFillippi and Arthur, 1998; Lundin and Midler, 1998), organizational learning (Bouwen and Fry, 1991; Dodgson, 1993; Boudès et al., 1998), are often used to describe the features of organizational innovation. It is argued in this chapter that the team, as a basic building block in the organization, is one promising starting point for understanding how organizations manage to combine horizontal and vertical coordination and communication.

When reviewing the literature on team-based structures, one is faced with a problem. As noted by a number of writers, the use of words like team-based management, TQM, BPR (Business Process Reengineering), virtual organizations and HRM, reflect fads and trends in the management industry, rather than genuine innovation. The claims made in the normative management literature are often totalizing (De Cock, 1998), with a strong tendency to close the discourse using ideological arguments (Sinclair, 1992). The empirical evidence is also weak, with few valid propositions put forward and tested in the literature (Jaffe and Scott, 1998). The perspective taken in many studies on team-based structures and other group-based structures is internal, focusing on the group as such, instead of on the team-based structure as a key organizing principle for the entire organization (Campion et al., 1996; Little and Madigan, 1997). The case described here is an example of how such company-wide organizing can be implemented. It addresses a number of theoretical issues connected to new forms of organizing in general, and internal network organizations in particular.

The literature on team-based management and other forms of group-based management has a marked intra-group perspective. The focus is more on the group's functioning and less on how teams can be organized to form bigger units. This also means that less emphasis is put on the integration of teams. This chapter will argue that it is important to describe and understand the arrangements for integrating teams. The case of Saab Training Systems shows how this can be done on a company-wide scale.

A second marked trend in the literature is the focus on processual and dynamic aspects. From an HRM perspective Mirvis (1997) argues that leading companies focus on organizing for innovation by involving employees, conducting training and mentoring programmes, using flexible work arrangements and team-based work redesign. In the field of project management it is often argued that companies organized by projects are an important arena for innovation (Anderson and Larsson, 1998). The notion of the projectified society with an increasing number of companies organized by projects, or other forms of temporary organization, draws attention to processes in companies (Lundin and Sôderholm, 1998), how they organize innovation and the ongoing business processes. Or to quote Hastings (1996:107): 'The resulting organization can be conceived of as a constantly changing kaleidoscope of teams, forming, delivering work and dissolving as required.'

A key question which is addressed later in the chapter is how a team-based structure can be combined with a strong focus on processes in order to achieve company-wide innovation. The case of Saab Training Systems illustrates how a team-based structure is organized to follow the core business processes of the firm, and how this has helped Saab to re-engineer its operations, making it very successful in its industry (defence). The new structure of the company can be described as a cross-functional heterarchy (Maccoby, 1991), where teams are organized to support key elements of the business process (the design phase of projects, contacts with customers, logistics, deliverance and innovation). Miles and Snow (1995) use the metaphor of a sphere to describe an organization with an ability to 'rotate' resources depending on market demands by using internal project organization and external alliances to build flexibility.

An important theoretical issue concerning team-based structures is how company-wide coordination and communication is achieved. The network organization, with its delayered and decentralized structure, cannot rely on the hierarchy to provide coordination (Nohria and Eccles, 1992). Coordination is instead created by horizontal means (IT-solutions, management-by-objectives, meetings, HR development, and by building a corporate culture). This confronts top management with a dilemma – how to build on the strengths of team-based structures, in terms of specialization, motivation and knowledge sharing (Little and Madigan, 1997), at the same time as company-wide coordination is achieved. The case presented below will show how Saab Training Systems has tried to solve this dilemma.

This case will focus on three analytical themes. The first has to do with the restructuring of the company – the transition from a traditional functional structure to the present team-based structure, and towards a more project-oriented company in the future. A second theme has to do with how to organize both innovation and an effective business process. A third theme is that of the different processes in the company (planning, business and innovation). The key research questions addressed in the chapter are:

- How can a team-based structure be organized to reflect the basic business process in a company?
- What are the advantages and disadvantages of a team-based structure in a highly competitive environment?

Research Methods

This case was chosen to illustrate an innovative organizational design that had also proved to be highly effective (in its industry). The Saab case has a number of interesting features. The company has built a consistent team-based structure with a strong focus on horizontal principles of organizing. Virtually the whole company is organized in teams for different purposes. This is combined with a strong market orientation involving many teams and a strong focus on knowledge management. The team-based structure has recently been further developed by a wider use of projects for innovation purposes. Needless to say, the company also has a high degree of decentralization and delayering.

This company is an excellent example of a company in transition, and there are good opportunities to evaluate different organizational experiments. It also provides a managable research unit (primarily in terms of company size with 260 employees), even though the company is part of a group with more than 5,000 employees. By choosing a medium-sized company we had the opportunity to acquire considerable detail about its features and organizing principles. A clear contribution of the Saab case is the description of microprocesses of organizing, with a strong focus on how the organization works operationally. The case study method provides a good opportunity for developing a thorough understanding of the processes of organizational change within a company (Yin, 1984; Bryman, 1989; Pettigrew, 1990).

In total, 14 interviews were conducted with respondents representing the important parts of the company. Two of the key respondents were interviewed three times over a one-year period. The selection of respondents was made in dialogue with the Managing Director and the Personnel Manager. Special care was taken to avoid biased respondents. To avoid that we interviewed two persons representing each type of function. The method used was qualitative, and focused on the respondents' descriptions, or stories, of their company and its radical change processes (Reason and Hawkins, 1988).

All interviews were made using an interview pro-forma agreed upon in the INNFORM research group. The interviews, lasting between one and two hours, were tape-recorded and transcribed. Field notes were also taken during interviews and informal discussions with the Managing Director and Personnel Manager. The case description is also based on secondary material (including company descriptions, brochures and annual reports) and has also been thoroughly checked by all respondents to ensure that it provides an accurate description of the company.

Drivers for Change in the Defence Industry

Saab Training Systems started its operations in the mid-1940s producing range equipment for military training purposes. In the mid-1970s the company started the production of laser-based simulators, the most successful of the present business areas. The company is operating in the defence industry (more specifically army material) which is characterized by a number of broad trends.

Despite the fact that a number of wars are going on, the trend during the 1980s to 1990s has been disarmament, with political ambitions to reduce military budgets. The collapse of the Soviet Union and the end of the cold war led to a drastic reduction of military spending at the same time as the peace movement has been growing stronger.

The industry is also characterized by a severe overcapacity which has forced it into extensive structural changes. One study of the aircraft industry (Eriksson, 1995), describes the structural changes that took place from the 1960s to the 1980s. One main trend is the rapid closure and merger of companies. During the 1990s this trend accelerated and complicated networks and alliances of subcontractors have emerged. Eriksson points to military demand (with a pronounced arms reduction in the Western world) as a clear driver for change (with mergers and international collaborations as the obvious responses).

Compared to other industrial markets it is hard for this industry to receive national support and it also has strong protectionist tendences. This causes a political environment affecting the business process (negotiations with states rather than other companies) and protracted decision making. The ambition to reduce military budgets has resulted in fewer repeat orders.

All these trends make the industry very different from more traditional consumer and industrial markets. The sales process too is very different, with long and complicated negotiations with military and political counterparts. Taken together, this makes it hard to predict future sales. As a market leader in its niche, Saab Training Systems has attained a strong position, with long-term contracts with major customers in the US, UK, Germany, Norway and a number of other countries. However, the company is very exposed to national policy changes, economic crises and changing procurement policies. The decision taken by individual customers to buy training equipment can be affected by a number of factors in society. In Saab Training Systems this uncertainty is reflected in a flexible team-based structure that can respond quickly to customer demands. The company also invests heavily in developing new applications and exploring new markets.

The defence industry (as a whole) is often described as an industry in deep crisis. The 1990s was marked by intensive restructuring of the industry and a stronger reliance on strategic alliances. Since the new military policy programme (adopted by the Swedish government in 1996) the Swedish defence industry has entered a number of international collaborations. The Saab Group, for instance, has started a formal collaboration with British Aerospace to market the JAS 39 Gripen fighter in a global arena. The Eurofighter project is another example of the trend towards international collaboration (between the UK, Spain, France and Germany). Mergers are numerous, with Boeing's takeover of McDonnel Douglas in the mid-1990s as the most spectacular example. Saab Training Systems is obviously affected by the trends described above, especially the competitive situation with reduced national budgets for military spending. Their products, though, are special in a number of ways. The company has so far not entered into any formal collaborations with external partners (apart from the regular agents and consultants used in the different countries where they sell their products, and subcontractors for production), either for marketing or for technical purposes (product development and production).

The high degree of uncertainty in the industry, and the need for flexibility in the marketplace, has nevertheless forced the company to react. Instead of entering external alliances, the company has chosen a strategy of concentrating on their core competence, with a focus on laser-based simulation. The products are, in a sense, much more cost-effective for the customer. The realistic simulation technique decreases the need for using 'sharp'ammunition and other equipment. The products are 'lightweight' and easy to handle, reducing the need for advanced support systems.

Another important reason for the success of the company is its close contacts with customers. Not only marketing but members of different product and application teams frequently visit the customers. This is also a key aspect of organizational learning in the company.

The trends in the defence industry described above are clearly drivers for the organizational change in Saab Training Systems. At the beginning of the 1990s the company faced a very difficult situation with productivity problems and a very turbulent market. As one team manager stated: 'The big focus we had during that period [1992–1993] was to keep up with delivery times.' The Managing Director similarly argued: 'The purpose of the proposed change ideas was to strengthen our competitiveness by a radical lowering of throughput times in both development and production.'

To deal with this situation decisions were taken to focus on the company's internal operations – how to gain efficiency by creating a more flexible team-based structure that could be integrated with a more process-oriented view of doing business – and concentrate on their core competence (laser-based simulation).

Compared to the main part of the defence industry, Saab Training Systems can be described as a prime mover when it comes to organizational renewal. While the trend in the industry has been to build competetive strength by strategic alliances, Saab Training Systems has focused on adding to its own strength. The flexible organizational design is unique not only to the Saab group, but to the industry as a whole: 'We would not be competitive if we followed the rest of the industry. They tend to build in too much administration in the companies' (team leader).

Saab Training Systems and the Saab Group

The Saab group consists of a number of independent companies (Saab, Saab Aircraft, Saab Dynamics, Saab Ericsson Space, Ericsson Saab Avionics, Saab Combitech and Saab Training Systems). The major product in the Saab group is the fourth generation combat aircraft JAS 39 Gripen. During 1998 Saab adopted a new structure with five business areas: Military Aerospace, Space, Training Systems, Commercial Aircraft and Combitech. This chapter focuses on Saab Training Systems, a company that has been transformed from a traditional functional structure in the early 1990s to a highly effective team-based structure. No other part of the Saab group has made such a significant change in organizational design.

Saab Training Systems' annual report for 1997 reports a turnover of 668 million Swedish kronor (£52 million sterling), with 260 employees at the end of that year. The company has experienced rapid growth in terms of turnover figures, from £15 million to £50 million from 1992 to 1997 (the number of employees during that period increased from 200 to 260). This rapid growth is partly due to the fact that the company received two major international orders in 1992 (followed by a number of successful deals in subsequent years). But it should also be stressed that 1992 was the year when the new team-based structure was implemented on a large scale.

Although the company is formally a part of the Saab Group (Saab AB), it is generally acknowledged in the company that the links to Linköping (where the corporate headquarters is situated) are loose. Saab Training Systems is given a lot of operational freedom (both in financial and organizational terms), with the Managing Director (Mr Hans Robertsson) enjoying a very good reputation in the Saab group. The formal corporate governance structure (with Saab Training Systems being completely owned by Saab AB and the Investor group, the dominant shareholder in Saab AB), does not reflect the strong informal position which the company has in the group.

The Saab Group consists of fairly independent companies, with Saab Training Systems holding a strong posititition. The companies, though, are interrelated in various ways. As well as sharing a number of central administrative resources, there are also examples of transfers of knowledge between the companies. This transfer, though, should not be overstressed, at least not at the group level. The technologies applied in the companies differ, and it is generally agreed in the group that the ideal of transferring knowledge has not reached its full potential.

Transfer of knowledge is an issue that is frequently discussed as a disadvantage of the team-based structure in Saab Training Systems. The respondents argue that a lot of tacit knowledge is embedded in the teams (and members of the teams) and the products they represent, and that it has been problematic to transfer experience between teams. One of the team leaders described this problem: 'We keep files for all documentation and descriptions, but they are not distributed among the teams. If you don't know what has been done before, and by whom, it's difficult to search for that information in the current filing system.'

Major Business Activities in Saab Training Systems[1]

The company's special niche is computer aided training equipment for military purposes, using visual simulation of different types of terrain and situations, and laser based simulation. The laser-based systems are the core competence of the firm (with a number of patents showing the high technical profile of the company and its employees). The laser simulator BT 46 is by far the largest product area in the company. A second product area is virtual simulation. The Saab BT 61 is a graphics-based simulator that uses authentic photographic environments and three-dimensional moving targets for virtual simulation. The BT 61 accounts for about 20 per cent of the company's turnover. The company is also involved in producing range equipment for live firing. Although this was the founding product of the company in the 1940s, the product area is a minor part of the company's current operations.

The business idea was to give the customer state of the art training systems using experience-based learning. Training Systems is a world leader in its area of simulation equipment, based on laser technology for aimed weapons. The largest markets for the present products are the UK, USA and Germany. The company is truly international in its operations. More than 90 per cent of manufactured goods are exported.

The economic stability of the company is guaranteed by a number of long-term contracts with a predictable planning horizon. These contracts are reflected in the internal organizational structure in the form of project teams for five of the major contracts: for example, a team for adapting the laser simulator BT 46 to the US army's Tank Weapons Gunnery Simulation System (TWGSS) and to the British army's Direct Fire Weapon Effects Simulators (DFWES). In addition to these established contracts (and negotiations for new contracts) the company also invested a lot of resources in developing new applications without a customer ordering a development project (the normal procedure in the defence industry is that development is customer ordered). The innovation process in the company thus bears more resemblance to that of 'normal' manufacturing companies than to other companies in the defence industry.

Company Philosophy

When visiting the company one is struck by a commonly held philosophy. This goes back to a very strongly formulated vision by the company's Managing Director. A key concept often used by the Managing Director is learning. A founding idea of the team-based structure is that the organization should reflect the learning ideals of the products. Some of the key principles of learning in the company are described below:

Experiential learning   One important aspect of organizational learning is to create opportunities for the individual to learn by doing. A significant arena for feedback is direct contact with the customer: product and application teams often meet the customer to discuss various issues concerning the product. The team itself is also an important factor in the feedback to individuals. The Managing Director stresses the fact that the teams should have access to all necessary information and that work results should be made visible and available. All respondents also mention the weekly meeting between all team leaders and the management team (including the Managing Director).

Cross-functional teams   The teams are organized to be an environment for individual learning. To achieve this goal, teams are organized around objects (subsystems of the products) rather than functions. The teams are in most cases cross-functional, bringing together people with different competences. They are thus specialized in terms of products but not in terms of competence.

Problem solving   The product teams are responsible not only for production but also for construction and product development. This includes both developing products and production processes. A major ambition is to solve problems in the group rather than individually, thus encouraging creative thinking.

Information   The explicit policy of the Managing Director is that information should be free and available. Each team should have access to all the information they need. The information issue also has another aspect, the need to make work results visible and available. An ambition in the company is to develop a system for storing knowledge in the organization rather than with the individual. The company has a well developed network of personal computers, giving the different teams access to the planning system LOTS, and to the control system. This intranet is also frequently used for internal communication in Saab Training Systems.

Individual growth   Growth of individuals is a strong value in the company. Individuals are encouraged to try out new ideas and to take risks. Individual growth is also stimulated by an emphasis on trial by error, to use not only intellectual but also emotional capacities.

Accumulation of experience   The Managing Director stresses that experience must be accumulated in the organization. This is achieved in a number of ways. The products in themselves are obviously a key factor, with a lot of knowledge stored in the current line of products. The business process (described below) has a well developed logistic of the three product areas (when they come to production). A clear ambition is also to accumulate experience not only in the individual but also in the team and the company in general.

The Transition from a Functional Structure to a Team-based Structure

In the early 1990s the company faced a difficult situation around meeting delivery times in both production and development. The relations between production and development seemed to be especially crucial for the overall effectiveness of the company: 'We have identified the difficulties with development issues, and creating new products with insufficient resources' (team leader). The company also felt a need to respond more quickly to environmental changes and stressed the value of communication between different parts of the company. The managing director of the company had for some time been troubled by the ineffectiveness of the company. In 1992 he took the initiative to start an experiment with a team-based organization. The underlying idea was to create a more flexible structure: 'All this requires that we develop new flexible processes, communication patterns and a new organizational structure' (Managing Director).

When the company received two major orders at Christmas 1992, a decision was taken to implement the team-based structure on a company-wide basis. Even though the idea for this had grown for some time among the members of the management team, market pressure forced the company to rapidly implement a new and more effective structure. Most respondents identified these two major orders as the incident that triggered the implementation of the new structure.

The philosophy behind the team-based structure is very much based on the ideas of the Managing Director. All respondents in the study agreed that he is the innovator and clear leader of the organizational change. The rhetorical skills of the managing director are extraordinary and they were a decisive factor in the success of the change project. The opinions of the employees concerning the managing director are homogeneous: he is depicted as visionary (and with the communicative skills to share his visions with the employees) and at the same time authoritarian and very demanding.

The radicalness of the change can best be understood if we compare the old and the new structures. Before 1992 the company was organized into functions with two construction departments (one focused on customer ordered development and the other on internally ordered development) and one production department, with an internal hierarchy in each department. The company also had a marketing and a purchasing department (see Figure 8.1 below).

The old structure was marked by an inadequacy to deal with more market-driven production processes and had problems in meeting delivery dates. One significant reason for that was the hierarchical and functional structure that created cross-functional problems of coordination and communication. This became a crucial problem when new contracts demanded that technical development was rapidly implemented in the production process. The old structure had severe problems in achieving this.

In the new structure of the company a total of more than 40 teams report directly to the managing director and the management team. The number of hierarchical levels has thus been reduced from three to two. The ideal size of a team, mentioned by a number of respondents, is 6–8 persons. When a team grows bigger it is split into two or more teams.

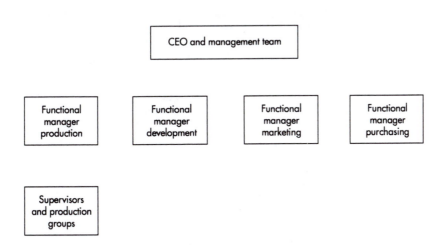

FIGURE 8.1   *The has team-based structure in Saab Training Systems*

There are also some examples of such 'cell-division' among product teams (Miles et al., 1997). The purpose of this organic growth of the organization is to increase flexibility and adaptability to environmental change.

The team-based organization is structured according to basic business processes. At the beginning of the business process we find five business teams and the market organization of the company. Each business team is responsible for one or more products, and one or more geographical areas. The business teams are responsible for negotiating contracts with the customers, and for monitoring contracts (the business teams have financial responsibility for each contract).

When a contract is signed they place a production order with a delivery team which plans the logistics of each order (using a Materials Planning System called LOTS).[2] In addition, the delivery team is responsible for the final testing of the product before shipping to the customer. The production planning process also involves a purchasing team (it is more correct to describe this team as a central function with an overall responsibility for purchasing).

For each contract an application team is involved in adapting the company's products to the needs of the customer. The business team

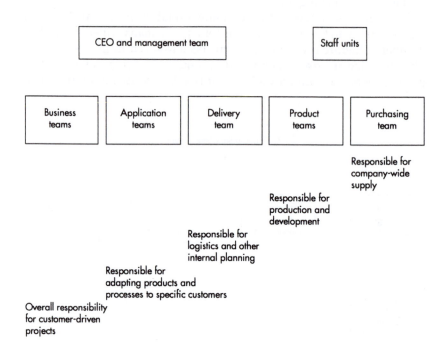

FIGURE 8.2 *The new team-based structure in Saab Training Systems*

responsible for a contract orders an application, and the application study by the application team then functions as a blueprint for the different product teams involved in the order (the business team places the formal production order with the different product teams).

Design and production of the different units in a project is carried out in one or a number of product teams (there are 14 product teams in the company, with 12 of them working in the product area of laser simulators). The product teams are organized according to products (subsystems), that is, optics, laser simulators, sensor modules. In addition to these teams involved in the business process there are a number of central functions – personnel, quality, purchasing and finance. The new organizational structure is depicted in Figure 8.2.

A Process Perspective on the New Team-based Structure

The business process is characterized by two different processes. The first is the production process: driven by contracts with customers, this primarily involves the delivery team and different product teams (the delivery team being responsible for production planning). The second process is that of construction and development. This is either customer driven (construction and development needed for specific contracts) or internally driven. Construction and development primarily involves application teams and product teams.

Coordination of the different teams involved in an order is a very important issue, due to the fact that the structure created for an order is temporary. The mix of teams involved in an order is dissolved as soon as the system is delivered to the customer. Any product team can also be involved in a number of different projects at the same time. The responsibility for the process coordination is split between a business team (having the commercial responsibility for each project) and the delivery team (responsible for production planning).

Since neither the business team nor the delivery team has the detailed knowledge necessary to place orders with the product teams, they need application teams to define the need for different parts in a system. This means that the application teams fulfil a key coordinating role in the business process, and they have a lot of contacts with different product teams. The work of the application teams is often contingent upon development in product teams, and especially when it comes to new applications (where the need of process- and product development is higher). Some applications, though, only require repetitive production of more standardized parts. The relations between application and product teams are therefore interdependent rather than sequential (DeSanctis and Staudenmayer, 1998).

The basic idea behind the team-based structure is to create an innovative and learning organization. The product teams, for instance, are responsible not only for producing their goods but also for construction and product development (including process development). One reason for building this organization in 1992 was to foster a more entrepreneurial spirit. To quote the managing director: 'Each team should be capable of becoming their own company.' It should be stressed though that the teams are not profit centres in the full sense, but are better described as cost centres with a high degree of operational freedom.

The descriptions in this section indicate a number of characteristics of new forms of organizing in Saab Training Systems. Below I summarize a number of these characteristics. The list is based on the survey variables of the INNFORM-project (see Fenton and Pettigrew, Chapter 1 of this volume).

Decentralizing   When the new structure was implemented in 1992, the five type of team were given a lot of operational freedom compared to the former structural arrangement, in particular operational decisions on production and development by the product teams. This freedom was balanced by a strong planning process in the company, with business teams responsible for the overall planning and the delivery team responsible for the production planning. The Managing Director has a very strong position in the company, and plays a crucial role in organizational integration.

Delayering   The number of hierarchical levels between top management and operating teams has decreased from three to two as a consequence of the team-based structure in 1992.

Communicating horizontally and vertically   The production and development processes in the company have forced the different teams to intensify cross-functional communication. Communication has also increased between different teams and the customers (especially application and product teams).

Information technology   The need for more efficient planning in the new team-based structure forced the company to introduce an up-to-date computerized planning system. This system was introduced when the team-based structure was implemented and it has been gradually refined. The use of IT has grown in importance as throughput times have been shortened, and where customers require more frequent contacts with different teams.

Practising new HRM   When the team-based structure was introduced, the company started an incentive system based on the overall results of the company, the team performance, and the results of each individual. This is done according to an elaborate scheme developed since 1992, where performance on the company, team, and individual level is measured on a number of dimensions. Some respondents argue that this incentive system has been vital to the success of the team-based structure. One central aspect of the incentive system is that it is transparent. The principles are clearly stated and open for discussion and improvement.

Downscoping   The decision to change the structure was accompanied by a change in the overall strategy of the company. A decision was taken to focus more on the core competence of the company, the laser-based training systems. This strategy has been successful so far in terms of growth in that business area.

Project forms of organizing   The experiences from the first five years of the team-based structure show a need for the project organization of development issues. During 1999 the company moved to a more project-based structure including development issues. The major difference between the team-based structure and the new project-based one is the temporary nature of the project groups formed in the new organization (Turner, 1999). It should be remembered that a team, even though it is depicted in the literature as a highly flexible organizational structure, is still a form of departmental structure, with the teams being organized for long term operations (compared to the project, which is organized for temporary operations).

The change initiative taken by the managing director in 1992 was very radical (in the context of the company and the industry). The major changes took place at the end of 1992 and during 1993 (including establishing the team-based structure, and building a planning system to deal with the production process). The period from 1994 until 1998 was characterized as a period of implementation and refining of the new structure. During 1998 the change activities increased, partly due to the building of new production facilities and partly due to an evaluation of the team-based structure. After the summer of 1998 a new structure was presented and discussed in the company. Even though this new structure is not as radical as the change in 1992, it still presents some organizational development challenges. At the beginning of 1999 it was also announced that the managing director had decided to leave the company, to start a new company and focus on developing new product ideas.

Process Sequencing – Learning from Experience

The team-based structure was an attempt to increase effectiveness in the construction and production process. The relations between the former construction and production departments were considered a major problem and throughput times for customer projects were considered to be too high. This was due to the functional structure, with two different departments responsible for crucial parts of the projects.

This team-based structure has been working for more than five years and was evaluated in 1998. This evaluation shows a mixed picture. The structure's main strength is effective production (in terms of time and cost), or as some respondents described it: 'They are effective in doing more of the same thing.' The teams are delimited in terms of objects (products), and responsibility and authority. They have achieved a high degree of expertise and specialisation in their area of responsibility. It is generally acknowledged that the product teams are highly effective when it comes to production.

The major weakness of the team-based structure is in achieving the same level of effectiveness when it comes to development issues. As mentioned before, each product team is responsible both for production and construction/development. It seems production issues have been the major focus for many of the product teams. As described by one of the team leaders: 'When it comes to production the team has very distinctive deadlines, you have to deliver at a certain date. The team members tend to give priority to production issues at the expense of development.'

The accumulation of experience is another issue that is frequently discussed as something that needs to be developed. A major problem is that experience is very much coupled to the individual teams. One ambition is to create a setting for both documentation of projects/products and for development. In order to deal with this a new library was built where all projects in the company are stored and are easily accessible.

A third problem discussed is the coordination of different teams, where it was argued that more effective coordination could bring down costs. It is hoped that this will be achieved by bringing together all personnel involved in production in one team, and by creating project teams for development issues. As noted by one of the team leaders: 'The teams behave like individuals. The consequence has been that we have not achieved the coordination between teams that we had hoped for.'

Conclusion

The team-based structure has been very successful in meeting the demands of the customer in terms of delivery deadlines and budget restrictions. A common opinion in the company is that this effectiveness has been at the expense of new product development and radical innovation. The focus in the product teams has been on delivering products on time. A general feeling in the company is that more emphasis must be put on development tasks if the company is to keep its position as an innovator in the market. If we follow the argument of Miles et al. (1997), the market situation pulled the company towards a stronger focus on innovation, making the integration of production and development even more urgent. In the emerging era of innovation, the capacity of the firm to rotate resources, create organizational learning and constantly change is crucial (Miles et al., 1997).

During the second half of 1998 the company gradually adopted a new structure for production and development issues. One large team was created for serial production (approximately 25 persons) in the established product areas. This new team (or department) is strictly focused on production issues (including a strong focus on continuous improvement in production processes and quality issues). It should be mentioned though that serial production still means customer-ordered production and not mass production. The ambition is that the team has total responsibility for production, planning, purchasing (taken over from the purchasing department and including contacts with subcontractors), logistics and test functions.

The team for serial production is supposed to be focused on building an effective production process. Compared to the former product teams, the new team can utilize resources in a more effective way (remember that the sharing of resources between teams was a major problem in the team-based structure). They can achieve a higher degree of specialization, without having to deal with new product development. Whether this will be the case or not is a matter of dispute in the company. Some respondents fear that the positive side of the team-based structure (a high degree of motivation among team members) will be lost in the new serial team. It is important to stress the fact that the new production team will still function as a cross-functional heterarchy with extensive contacts with customers and an extensive bridging of resources internally (Maccoby, 1991).

A pool of people was created for development issues, primarily to develop new products. This pool is organized into project teams for different development projects. The responsibility of each project team is to develop products or parts, not only as concepts or prototypes, but as products that could go directly into the team for serial production. The focus here is not only on developing new products but also on testing the products.

The new project-based structure presents some interesting leadership challenges, compared to the more fixed departmentalized structure (Hastings, 1996; Lundin and Söderholm, 1998). The team-based structure is still a form of departmentalized structure, with the team as the basic building block (in the form of small departments), while the project-based structure for development issues introduces a temporary form of organizing in parts of the company. From a top management perspective one problem is how to handle a portfolio of projects in different phases of the project life cycle (Jessen, 1996).

This management problem took on another dimension when it was announced that the managing director had decided to leave the company. The timing of this decision was probably deliberate, since he very much personified the team-based structure. In the interviews he stressed the fact that he wanted to 'move on' to new challenges. The company history (during the 1980s and 1990s) is very much connected to him, making him a 'critical node in the organization' (Baker, 1992: 399). He had a strong technical interest and kept a tight control over development issues. The dilemma now is how to deal with the organizational vulnerability arising from a reliance on his technical skills and strong control.

The analysis so far in this chapter shows that a team-based structure can be a very effective way of organizing activities. However, it is still a form of departmentalized structure. Each team tends to build its own culture and creates boundaries between itself and other teams. The challenge in the team-based structure is thus to enhance cooperation between teams. This challenge is most apparent in relation to development issues. The teams are highly effective when it comes to production, where cooperation is ensured by the formal planning system of the company. The planning system, though, is less effective when it comes to managing development and innovation. The expectation is that the new project organization will deal with this in a more effective way.

From a theoretical perspective, the results from the evaluation of the team-based structure are interesting. The assumption in the literature on team-based management is that the team-based structure, *per se*, is flexible and with a high motivation to innovate. As the case of Saab Training Systems shows, the truth of this assumption is far from evident. In fact, innovation seems to be the crucial problem in the team-based structure. This paradox can be understood from a cultural perspective. The single team gradually develops into an arena of identification for the individual. As the company has moved into a looser configuration the importance of this arena for identification has grown. This factor of cultural belongingness is evident in the interviews, where a number of respondents argue that the teams fulfil key roles for the individual, being 'the only stable place in a world that is constantly moving'.

This case has shown that the teams have given priority to meeting production deadlines rather than focusing on development issues. The respondents argue that this is due to the internal focus developed in each team. It has also been shown that the team-based structure has to be balanced by a strong focus on the business process, creating an understanding of the whole process between the teams. Frequent contacts between customers and different product teams have been one way of doing this.

One obvious question that can be raised, based on the analysis in this chapter, is why the company has not entered into any strategic alliances to build competitiveness. As argued by Miles and Snow (1995), among others, a major trend among innovative companies is increased reliance on an external network to build competitive strength. Saab Training Systems deviates from this trend. Even though the theoretical arguments for external networking are clear-cut (in terms of enhancing organizational capabilities and increasing flexibility: Perrow, 1992), the company has, so far, not realized the need for external networking.

Notes

1   The description in this section is based on technical descriptions of the products and on interviews.
2   The system is integrated with the purchasing system and is used for schedule control and for preliminary calculation and cost accounting.

9

Initial Steps on the Path towards New Forms of Organizing: Two Experiences within the Group Aguas de Barcelona

Carlos J. Sánchez-Runde and Javier Quintanilla

In this chapter, we illustrate the introduction of new forms of organizing (NFOs) within the group Aguas de Barcelona (AGBAR), a large organization and a major provider in the international market for water services. We discuss two very recent experiences within the AGBAR Group that constitute instances of new organizing arrangements.

The first experience is linked to the creation of the AGBAR Foundation, a unit in charge of coordinating all the firm's environmental research and development (R&D). The AGBAR Foundation experience – and herein its novelty as an organizing form – presents important insights into processes of knowledge management and virtual teamwork through informal, non-hierarchical, coordination mechanisms. The second experience concerns the need for a new equilibrium between centralizing and decentralizing in the purchasing function. This occurred with the introduction of a corporate purchasing unit in charge of coordinating purchases by the group's units. Both experiences show the subtleties of balancing seemingly opposing dualities, such as reinforcing formal and informal coordination and control devices, and simultaneously centralizing and decentralizing decision making authority.

The new organizing arrangements described in the AGBAR

Foundation and Corporate Purchasing Unit experiences operate within the larger AGBAR organization. We argue that these experiences constitute the beginning of a fully developed set of new organizing arrangements at the level of the larger AGBAR Group. Thus, the AGBAR case illustrates a cautious approach to solving another apparently contradictory duality characterizing the new arrangements: that of managing stability and innovation through gradual change processes.

Selected Literature on New Forms of Organizing

New challenges seem to continuously haunt companies operating in what have been variously referred to as 'hyper-turbulent' (Meyer et al., 1993a), 'high-velocity' (Eisenhardt, 1989a), and 'hyper-competitive' (D'Aveni, 1994) environments. For these firms, gone are the times when they could approach organizational strategy and structure in terms of 'clear industry boundaries, predictable competition, or a knowledgeable future' (Brown and Eisenhardt, 1998: 7).

Pioneering companies are beginning to address the new challenges. They improve on the limitations of hierarchical and bureaucratic forms by transforming the liabilities of firm size – be it large or small – and redesigning internal processes – making them less formal and hierarchical (Miles and Snow, 1994; Ghoshal and Bartlett, 1997). More specifically, some of the benefits that have been posited to accrue to firms following the innovation path include superior learning, enhanced legitimation and prestige, greater control over the external environment, and reduced overall costs (Podolny and Page, 1998).

While many scholars acknowledge the need to revise traditional arrangements to help organizations compete, there is no clear agreement on how to think about some of the NFOs that those companies introduce. This is complicated by the fact that research into this area of organization studies is still scarce (Kanter and Eccles, 1992; Daft and Lewin, 1993).

Alternative positions in the literature can be defined in terms of the objectivity of the structural characteristics of the new arrangements. At one extreme, Burt maintains that networks – a particularly popular exemplar of NFOs – are in the eye of the beholder when positing that 'two managers can do the same work in the same firm, but one can experience the firm as a traditional hierarchy while the other experiences the firm as a network organization' (1997: 361). At another extreme, some authors distinguish the substantive identity of network arrangements as fundamentally different from that of more traditional forms (Powell, 1990; Miles and Snow, 1994). Between the two extremes, still other scholars realize that part of the difficulty lies in what can be defined as the *dual nature* of the new modes of organizing.

This duality manifests itself in multiple ways. First, new arrangements are perceived as 'a matter of degree, not an absolute' (Burt, 1997: 360). Secondly, NFOs are both about content – or structure – and a process which is 'continually shaped and reshaped by the actions of actors who are in turn constrained by the structural positions in which they find themselves' (Nohria, 1992: 7). Thirdly, NFOs represent a generic tool for analysis, in the sense that 'all organizations are networks – patterns of roles and relationships – whether or not they fit the network organization image' (Baker, 1992: 399), so that 'to say an organization is a network form is a tautology' (Nohria, 1992: 12). Fourthly, the innovative arrangements should be best characterized as bi-modal 'in that they could accommodate opposing tendencies and yet function as coherent and cohesive concerns' (Bahrami, 1992: 43). With regard to this last point, Pettigrew notes that organizational innovation often requires mastering apparently contradictory dualities like continuity and change, hierarchies and networks, upwards and horizontal integration, empowering and holding the ring, centralizing and decentralizing, and identifying and sharing knowledge across units that both collaborate and compete (Pettigrew, 1999a).

Researchers and practitioners are also beginning to struggle with the conviction that analysis cannot proceed along single dimensions. Rather, there is need for a holistic understanding of all the features of NFOs. This is important for two reasons. First, organizational characteristics tend to interact among themselves, thus resulting in systems or configurations (Meyer et al., 1993b) that are more than the sum of their discrete components (Helgesen, 1995; Milgrom and Roberts, 1995). However, because that kind of systemic study is rare, the final analysis is fragmented, piecemeal, and concentrated on single features that do not explain the whole phenomenon (Nohria, 1996). Secondly, ignoring the interdependencies of the dimensions of the NFOs proves fatal when attempting to transform traditional firms, since 'it is necessary to work on changing all aspects of an organization simultaneously in the same direction. In practice, it is necessary to start somewhere; and yet the full rewards of making this start are unlikely to be reaped until substantial changes have been introduced elsewhere' (Ezzamel et al., 1994: 457). Of course, the systemic viewpoint also allows a more sophisticated understanding of the dual nature of the new arrangements to which we have just referred.

We illustrate these issues by studying two recent organizing experiences within the AGBAR Group. AGBAR, a major Spanish player in the Spanish and Latin American utility sector, is currently undergoing what can be characterized as both the initial stages in the process toward NFOs and the ordinary complexity of a traditional organization successfully adapting to rapidly changing environments.

Our case examples show the following structural elements of the

NFOs: knowledge management and diffusion, blurring of internal and external organizational barriers, brokering of a new equilibrium of opposites between centralizing and decentralizing, establishment of informal coordination mechanisms to supplement traditional means of control, and development of information and communication platforms aimed at encouraging virtual teamwork.

Research Methodology

New theory can be developed from case study research with rich accounts of issues of content and process. Eisenhardt suggests building theory from case studies: 'when little is known about a phenomenon, current perspectives seem inadequate because they have little empirical substantiation, or they conflict with each other or common sense'. Under such circumstances, Eisenhardt adds, 'the conflict inherent in the process is likely to generate the kind of novel theory which is desirable when extant theory seems inadequate' (1989b: 548).

Further, case studies represent an extremely effective way of looking at the phenomenon in its wholeness, thus allowing for a more systemic understanding which, we have argued, this kind of research requires (Pettigrew, 1985b). In this way, data gathered through questionnaires at an earlier stage of the INNFORM programme are further developed and enriched by means of the in-depth qualitative research to which this case study belongs.

The AGBAR Group is a large Spanish company undergoing rapid international expansion in its core business. AGBAR has also entered – and is still entering – new markets, related and unrelated to its main line of business. As a result of this growth, AGBAR experiences an urgent need to keep control over quite diversified operations while allowing business units substantial decision-making power. Because of this, and because of the potential tensions between hierarchical, command and control type of mechanisms on the one hand, and more integrative and informal coordination devices on the other, the AGBAR Group presents an ideal opportunity for analysing change and evolution toward newer forms of organizing. Therefore, this case study truly reflects the dual nature of NFOs, and the principle that new organizing modes supplement, rather than supplant traditional ones (Galbraith, 1995; Ferlie and Pettigrew, 1996).

Data have been gathered from personal interviews, company documentation and archival records. Eleven executives – at both the corporate and business level – were interviewed between September 1997 and February 1999, with a total of 16 interviews. The interviews followed an open format. Engaging in fluid conversation and discussion might have been hampered by strict adherence to a more structured pro-forma. At the end, basic patterns of responses may have been more revealing than specific answers to concrete questions (Piore, 1979).

To increase the reliability and validity of the study, a case study database was formed following Yin's method (1989). The research is based on 'explanation-building' as the mode of analysis. Explanation building is an iterative process that goes back and forth from the initial theoretical statements to the data at hand, thus revising theory statements against new evidence from the case (Yin, 1989). We minimized reliability threats by documenting the major steps, procedures and techniques used in data gathering and analysis. We also minimized validity threats. We relied on multiple sources of evidence. By following the explanation-building process, we established a chain of evidence in moving from extant theory to analysis to conclusions. Finally, we had the results reviewed by five company informants.

Profile of the AGBAR Group

The AGBAR company was founded in 1882 to provide water services to the city of Barcelona. Since then, it has become a major player in the Spanish economy by expanding the territory where it provides water services and entering new arenas, related and unrelated to its original business.

Ownership of the group reflects the following distribution. Forty-eight per cent of the shares are owned both by a holding controlled by Suez Lyonnaise des Eaux (51 per cent) and La Caixa (the leading Spanish savings bank, 49 per cent). Suez Lyonnaise des Eaux directly owns 1.5 per cent of the stock. Endesa, the largest Spanish producer of electricity, controls 11.5 per cent of the shares. The remaining 39 per cent 'floats' in the Stock Exchange (1).

The consolidated turnover in 1997 was 194,391 million pesetas ($1,296 million, over 15 per cent higher than in 1996), with consolidated profit before taxes of 16,447 million pesetas ($110 million), and a payroll of 13,617 employees. Aggregated operating revenues totalled 329,663 million pesetas ($2,200 million) in 1997, making AGBAR one of the ten largest Spanish business groups (1).

Fields of activity

The integral water cycle   AGBAR's principal activity is drinkable water and sewage services, which represent 45.6 per cent of the business of the group (1).

Because of the public nature of the service, the evolution of the group in this business parallels that of the public regulation of water. In Spain, potable water is a municipal competence. Each municipality decides whether or not to privatize the provision of the service. In December 1997 less than 20 per cent of the municipalities had privatized thus. However, those municipalities comprise 42 per cent of the Spanish population (Vergós, 1998: 46–47). AGBAR dominates the Spanish market, with 54 per cent of the privatized water service and serving on average more than 11 million people (accounting for seasonal up and downs). The French companies Vivendi and Saur control 13 and 12 per cent, respectively, of the privatized market. Smaller Spanish companies share the remaining 21 per cent.

The strong presence of French companies is due to the know-how and prior development of French water policy, a model closely followed by Spanish legislators since the last century. Following the French system has allowed Spain to be among the world leaders in effective ways of managing such a scarce resource as drinkable water. A joint venture dominated by companies from France (Suez-Lyonnaise des Eaux with 35 per cent and Vivendi with 8 per cent), Spain (AGBAR with 25 per cent) and Britain (Anglian Water with 5 per cent), for instance, recently won the bid to serve the water needs of the greater Buenos Aires, Argentina.

AGBAR's international expansion in the water business covers successful bids in Colombia, Argentina, Chile, Cuba, Uruguay, Portugal and Morocco serving over 16 million people altogether. There are ongoing projects to invest in other Latin American countries as well (2).

AGBAR's service to municipalities has recently led to a new, unrelated activity: collection of levies, consisting in the management of the collection of miscellaneous municipal taxes, in both Spain and Latin America. By mid-1997 this new business affected over one million inhabitants in several cities (1).

Health insurance   This line of activity involves the production, management and distribution of private health insurance, individually and collectively, along with the management of proprietary health centres (hospitals, analysis centres, and so on). It serves over one million people in Spain and Argentina. It grew over 15 per cent in 1997 and constitutes 29.4 per cent of AGBAR's consolidated turnover (1).

Solid waste   This sector of activity basically includes the treatment of solid urban waste, sewer building and maintenance, urban and highway cleaning, tending of parks and gardens, industrial cleaning, depuration of chemical and sanitary waste, and environmental and waste consulting and auditing. Several subsidiaries serve over seven million people in Spain and Portugal. This sector grew 35 per cent during 1997 in terms of the contracted portfolio (thus becoming Spain's second major operator) and represents 17 per cent of AGBAR's consolidated business (1).

Computing services and electronic commerce In 1997 a multimedia network unit was created, gathering all the activities of the group in computing and network management and enabling the creation of integral services in this field in Spain and Portugal. It comprises 5.6 per cent of AGBAR's consolidated business, having grown 13.5 per cent in 1997. In mid-1998 AGBAR also created a new unit in charge of developing sales activities through internet and electronic catalogues, an area that is expected to grow very heavily in the near future (1), (3).

Other services This category comprises two groups of activity. The first, technical assistance consultancy, has grown noticeably in recent years by introducing the technical development of real time monitoring systems for hydrological variables and water quality in Spain, South America, France and Portugal (4). The second is the market for the technical inspection of vehicles, in which the group has become the Spanish leader. AGBAR also owns stations for the inspection of vehicles in Portugal, Argentina and Costa Rica. This business is expected to grow very rapidly in the near future. In 1997 these services comprised 7.8 per cent of the group's consolidated business (1), (3).

Organizational Goals and Values

AGBAR prides itself on being a highly innovative group aiming at excellence in technical development and care for the natural environment. As the Executive Chairman of the group put it in a widely circulated document in 1995:

> [AGBAR maintains an] exceptional commitment to serving the community . . . together with our aim to achieve the highest levels of quality in all our products . . . [This] commitment keeps us constantly on the alert, interested in any innovation . . . at the vanguard of any new technological application that allows us to improve our products and to ensure the proper management of natural resources and the protection of the environment. (4)

Indeed, it could be argued that an engineering culture of excellence and continual challenge pervades the group. Anecdotally, this is illustrated by small symbols. For instance it is common for engineers in the group to disclose their engineering degrees on their business cards (this is seen less, if at all, with regard to other professional titles).

Care for the natural environment has always been a main concern of AGBAR's out of both a humanistic commitment to improve people's quality of life and a business interest in minimizing the problems related to pollution in general and water pollution in particular. As a top executive explained:

We suffer from pollution from two viewpoints. First, because nobody really wants to live with all that dirt. Secondly, because we cannot provide polluted water to our customers. And it is easier for us to make sure that customers receive healthy, non-polluted water, if that water is not already heavily polluted when it flows into our system in the first place.

The environmental policy of the group is based on the following principles (4):

1   development of new methods and models to improve the environment by means of research, both within the group and in cooperation with other institutions, specially with universities and public administrations;
2   use of environment-friendly technologies and methods;
3   open communication with consumers and administrations on environmental issues;
4   employee sensitivity and awareness training on environmental issues;
5   promotion of environmental education outside the group;
6   periodic environmental evaluations of all the group's work centres.

Activities supporting the group's commitment to environmental awareness include regular commissions at all levels to discuss environmental issues and alternatives, newsletters addressed to all employees (quarterly) and group managers and public administrations (biannually) on firm initiatives and research.

Of course, the company serves the interests of very diverse stakeholders, among which shareholders and employees rank first. However, with regard to pursuing innovation through commitment to technical expertise and respect for the environment, AGBAR indeed ranks above and beyond the average company in both its geographical markets and sector.

Organizational structure

Structure of the lines of business   AGBAR is a large and potentially very complex organization (5). Because of the highly varied array of businesses in which the group competes, specialization by sector is seen as the most sensible organizing principle. The nucleus and the heart of the group, around the integral water cycle business in the city of Barcelona and a major portion of its surroundings, constitutes what is internally called the 'matrix company' (6). The rest of the businesses, including the companies of the integral water cycle outside Barcelona, are organized in sectors comprising different companies which are mostly fully owned, direct or indirectly, by AGBAR.

By mid-1997 the integral water cycle business comprised 15

completely or substantially owned companies (apart from the matrix), nine of which own (totally or partially) between one and ten other companies. Similarly, the international expansion in the water business comprises six companies, completely or partly dominated by AGBAR (two of them participating in between three and five other companies in the same business), plus eight other companies with minority participations (ranging from 5 to 46 per cent of the stock).

The health insurance sector is dominated by a fully owned head company controlling all or the majority of the shares in 13 companies which in turn completely own or dominate ten other companies. This head company also owns minority portions of three other companies in the sector. The international expansion of the health business comprises five companies, one of which is owned 40 per cent by the group while the other four are fully owned.

Two companies which are dominated by the group in the solid waste business own seven other companies and partially control five other firms. The international expansion in Portugal is headed by one company of which the group owns 76 per cent of its shares.

The computing services and electronic commerce sector is led by three companies with complete or majority group control, which in turn dominate eight other firms. AGBAR also controls 62 per cent of its Portuguese company.

This pattern of company ownership and structure is basically the same for the other service sectors, but with much smaller participation in the consolidated turnover of the group.

Structuring philosophy   Despite the natural complexity of its diverse and international businesses, AGBAR is managed with extremely simple and clear policies combining centralized controls and delegated autonomy. A top executive defends the appropriate mix of centralization and autonomy, comparing the structural approaches of AGBAR and the Catholic Church:

> Many times I think we should be paying more attention to the way the Church operates. There you have the most successful organization of all, at least in terms of survival, centred around two basic ideas. One, final authority remains with Rome, and everybody knows it and accepts it. Two, within each territory, bishops – and even pastors – fully develop their own practices, with very high degrees of freedom. Of course, part of the trick is that there is a clear, overall philosophy and sense of finality. But they also know that the Pope simply cannot get involved with the specifics of each parish: there are thousands of them! I certainly look to the Church for inspiration even on how to operate the company. Maintaining a common culture and sense of goals, with central and final authority over the very basic issues, and letting local managers develop their own policies and implementing them. Otherwise, we would be completely lost. We have just become too big and diverse.

Of course, maintaining 'a common culture and sense of goals' is increasingly challenged as new companies are acquired and new lines of businesses evolve. This, in turn, is related to the fact that most of the group's recent growth has been of the revolutionary, rather than evolutionary type (Kagono et al., 1985; Chang, 1995). Accordingly, an executive in a top financial position explained that:

> There is a clear need for a more centralized practice in the financial and economic area. We still need the different companies in the group to really breathe together. We may have gone too far in allowing idiosyncratic modes all around the group. We need the pendulum to swing a little bit more in the direction of centralizing decision making at headquarters' level.

However, there is still a strong view that decentralizing operational decision making is a must in a group as diverse as AGBAR. One of the very top managers puts it this way:

> We have, and need, a light head with strong arms. Our control structure is based on lots of autonomy for the different parts of the sectors. Of course, we have centralized some functions, but even in those cases, we want and keep our minds open to allowing deviations from headquarters. I always tell the head of the different companies: 'If you have a reason, do it your way. Unless you miserably fail again and again, I will back you up.' How could we do otherwise?

As a matter of fact, this kind of statement does not only come from the top of the group. It is also shared by most of the people that we interviewed in this research.

Management structure At the group level, an executive chairman and his chief executive officer figure as the top two executives. Both of them, along with three other general managers form the top management team (TMT). The TMT is the place where major strategic decisions are made. Besides some initial specialization among the three general managers, tasks within the TMT are shared in flexible terms, and according to the specifics of each situation.

Immediately reporting to the TMT are 16 other executives. Of these 16, ten are responsible for different areas within the matrix, and the other six are responsible for the other activities of the group. Therefore, 21 people form the higher management of the group and are clearly set apart from the rest of the executives and managers in terms of their strategic and operational responsibilities.

In the next section, we present two recent experiences illustrating the tensions, dilemmas and processes involved in the transition from traditional to newer organizing arrangements. While so far those experiences operate at the periphery of the main productive and commercial activities of the group, we think that they constitute the initial steps towards a more fully developed set of new organizing modes.

New Internal Organizing Arrangements: Initial Steps

The AGBAR Group is an extremely successful organization in terms of growth and profitability. This reflects the very able management strategy and operation, with strong and committed leadership at different levels.

When asking the management about the challenges the future may bring to the group, one double-sided issue stands out time and again. This issue relates generally to the increased complexity in the management of a growing group in a changing and extremely competitive environment.

One side of the new complexity refers to the maturation of the group's core business, the integral water cycle. Because of heavy entry barriers into the mature water business, existing competitors are in a strong position in relation to AGBAR. These are other similarly successful, large, and competitive corporations struggling for excellence in their home markets. A top manager explained:

> There has been a change in the group's culture in that we used to say 'We have a good business. We are in the business of selling water. And we are the only [private group] in the [Spanish] market.' We grew up a little bit too complacent. Now the ground has moved under our feet. Foreign companies, also with very mature domestic markets, settled here, right amongst us. Soon, our domestic market matured. And there we go, they and us, looking for greener pastures in less developed markets. That is why we keep meeting each other in all the bids in Latin America, for instance.

The other side of complexity for AGBAR has to do with its diversification strategy, which is related to the need for markets with high growth potential. One of the managers in charge of corporate strategy put it this way:

> We finally realized that we simply were not in the water service business. We are in the service business. Having successfully delivered water services showed us that we could also succeed at delivering other services, be they garden tending, tax collection, technical vehicle maintenance, electronic commerce, you name it.

Of course, complexity here is compounded by the need for tolerance of more diverse ways of managing in new related and unrelated businesses. This, as we have seen, puts even more pressure on keeping control while allowing for differentiated management of different business through decentralized, autonomous decision making at local levels. In the end, as a top manager in charge of diversification said:

> Everything is now both easier and more difficult. Easier because we are growing stronger and resourceful. More difficult because each time that we enter a new market, we have to 'let go' a little bit more. You cannot keep a short rein on everything or else you put yourself on the verge of inaction.

Maturation of the traditional water business and diversification into new activities led to four dilemmas. First, managing – and leveraging on – diverse and dispersed personal and organizational knowledge. Secondly, escaping from the rigidities of barriers between intra-organizational units – group companies, sectors and functions – and extra organizational actors – competitors, public governments, academic and research institutions and the like. Thirdly, finding ways of addressing relationships with internal and external stakeholders on the basis of informal, lateral, even spontaneous coordination, away from hierarchical, traditional 'command-and-control' mechanisms. These three issues lie at the heart of developing NFOs. A fourth dilemma is the complexity of managing the 'equilibrium of opposites' between centralizing and decentralizing purchasing decision making.

Knowledge Management and Virtual Teamwork: The AGBAR Foundation Experience

The CEIA, or Centre for Water Research and Studies (7), was founded in the 1950s to promote research, publications, and industry gatherings related to the integral water cycle. It served an important role until the mid-1970s, when an independent national water association was created. Since most of the functions of the CEIA were then increasingly being performed by the national association, the Centre virtually disbanded. It was only marginally used for promoting research partnerships between the group and academic and research institutions. This was the situation of the CEIA prior to the creation of the AGBAR Foundation (AF).

In January 1997, the top management at AGBAR decided to revamp the role of the old CEIA by creating the AF. The AF was created as a means to achieving the following goals:

- coordinating all the group's environmental R&D;
- developing a database for the diffusion of technical and commercial know-how;
- providing a technological platform for virtual teamworking from separate functions and distant locations.

By improving the coordination of environmental R&D, AGBAR aims to exploit the efficiencies within its current processes. By developing a database to enable the diffusion of technical and commercial knowledge among units, and by allowing virtual teamworking by people from distant locations and functions, AGBAR is exploring avenues for adding value through new activities and processes. This is consistent with the new arrangements aimed at improving organizational capabilities by both transferring current knowledge among units (Hamel, 1991), and creating future knowledge within increasingly networked operations (Powell and Brantley, 1992). To date, however, there is a lack of research documenting the processes and structural arrangements for creating and managing cross-unit linkages to share, transfer and develop organizational knowledge (for an exception, see Ichijo and Nonaka's (1998) work on the Advanced-I Group at Toshiba).

Coordination of environmental R&D

A group as large as AGBAR, with as many dispersed establishments for water services as municipalities served, is bound to duplicate functions that simultaneously or sequentially take place at different locations. The duplication of functions that provide productive operations – like building and maintaining the water distribution system in each geographical area – is absolutely necessary for the provision of the service. That is not the case, however, with regard to the content of what can be generally construed as staff functions, like R&D which, because of AGBAR's decentralizing philosophy, each and every territorial unit might consider worth pursuing. An executive at the AF explains:

> One day, I realized that our plant in Mallorca, let us say, is developing a new system for reusing the sludges produced in water treatment. And I suddenly remember that one of our plants in Barcelona has been previously involved in a similar study. I would immediately call the Mallorca people and discover they had no idea of that study. A few days after I send them the report, they call me back thanking me. They could benefit from some of the research already done in Barcelona, with obvious savings. This kind of situation kept happening all the time. We realized we needed a system to make people aware of all the technical (and, later, commercial) know-how dispersed in separate units. This became a first priority for those of us at the AF.

Coordinating environmental R&D went beyond avoiding unknown duplication. Soon, the top management agreed to channel all future environmental R&D proposals through the AF, so that each unit willing to undertake them could benefit from the knowledge and experience of the rest of the group's units. However, to effectively accomplish this, two issues had to be solved. First, the role of the AF itself. Would the AF simply become a hierarchical structure in charge of approving and channelling the group's environmental research? Or would the AF rather act as a formal provider of information and knowledge so that informal coordination could emerge among different units interested in similar projects? Secondly, what is the appropriate operational means by which the AF would actually make all the unit's expertise available to people interested in accessing it? By addressing these two issues, the top management set the basis of a 'knowledge management infrastructure' (March and Garvin, 1997: 4). This infrastructure consists of a specialized unit – the AF – to manage the storage and diffusion of knowledge, with defined roles and responsibilities to coordinate all the group's environmental R&D. It is equipped with the appropriate technology and tools, like an intranet communication system and a Lotus Notes groupware platform. A similar knowledge-sharing infrastructure is found in the case of the pharmaceutical network in Coopers & Lybrand Europe (see Fenton and Pettigrew, Chapter 3 in this volume).

On the issue of the unit's role, it was decided that the AF would not be vested with formal authority over the units engaging in environmental R&D. It would remain each unit's prerogative to decide on the kind of R&D that they would be performing. The AF would become an informal promoter of collaborative ventures between different units by providing them with two services: a database with the R&D already performed in the group and a software package for teamworking through an intranet system specially developed for that purpose.

In sum, by charging the AF with becoming the informal coordinator of environmental R&D, with no formal, hierarchical authority to bind the units directly engaged in research, AGBAR opted for a NFO consistent with modern internal network governance designs (Heckscher, 1994). Further, the AF experience, as we shall illustrate in the next section, nicely fits the pattern of knowledge management projects aimed at creating knowledge repositories, improving knowledge access, enhancing a knowledge environment, and managing knowledge as an asset (Davenport et al., 1998).

Development of a repository of technical and commercial how-how

The second issue just underlined, how to operationalize the coordination of environmental R&D, was answered by the development of what is internally known as 'Proyecto BITA' (Bank of Water Information and Technology Project) (8). The project has two parts, a library application and a tool for remote teamwork. The library application is a database including the reports and materials on all the research taking place within the group, so that it can be accessed for reference by all the units. It also incorporates bibliography and documentation – some in full text – from external sources (journals, books, conference materials, and so on) on the integral water cycle. This part of the project is also intended for the benefit of interested parties outside the group (like researchers and public administrations). As the AF Director explains:

> We have organized the AF as a foundation, so that parts of the BITA will be available to people outside the group through the internet. We are also beginning to consider how to extend the focus of the AF to include activities unrelated to the water cycle but still relevant for the other businesses within the group. Thus, we plan to expand it both vertically – to allow more people to benefit from it – and horizontally – to introduce material in fields other than water.

This same executive added: 'We are also working on how to link with partners from other companies with whom we have developed joint ventures in Latin America so that we can share our technological know-how.' Not surprisingly, the extension of AF's stakeholders to include people from inside and outside the group, nicely fits another characteristic of NFOs, that of helping the focal organization move toward more inclusive governance arrangements by breaking internal and external boundaries (Ashkenas et al., 1995).

In sum, the BITA project represents an important effort towards adopting new organizing arrangements by doing two things. First, integrating and fostering the diffusion of technical and commercial knowledge heretofore anchored along strict functional demarcations. Secondly, relaxing organizational boundaries by allowing access to the databases of third parties, including joint-venture partners, researchers and public administrations.

Virtual teamworking

The second part of the BITA project includes the development of computer applications to facilitate teamwork by people from different locations, both geographical and functional. A first step included moving from sharing information between different units to elaborating that information together, especially between the main R&D units in Barcelona, Alicante and Madrid. A second step evolved from that cooperation between the main R&D units, so that experts from different locations and functions (commercial, technical, legal, financial, and so on) could work together in creating new business opportunities. So far, those new projects have worked on bids for managing the water services in newly privatized markets. But the AF experience is now at the stage of being extended to other business areas and projects. As the AF Manager put it:

We designed the BITA so that a project manager could look for collaborators without restrictions derived from where those people are physically located. In this way, we become more flexible not only in terms of where people are located, but also in our ability to work at the same time on several projects with very different groups of people.

By facilitating virtual teamworking among functionally and geographically distant units, the AF leverages the benefits of flexibility which have been posed to accrue to those introducing NFOs (Podolny and Page, 1998).

Controlling and Letting Go: The Corporate Purchasing Unit Experience

In January 1997, at about the same time that the AF was charged with its mission, AGBAR created a corporate purchasing unit (CPU) in charge of coordinating all the group's purchases and other related services, including travel arrangements and security. The goal was that by the end of 1998 the new corporate purchasing unit should be coordinating somewhere between 40 and 50 per cent of the group's purchases (9). This represented a major change, since before 1997, prior to the new CPU arrangement, purchasing and related services were handled autonomously by each local unit.

The CPU reports directly to the TMT and operates at three levels. First, at a corporate level, the CPU defines broad policies and regulations on how purchasing and related services are to be managed by the group's units. At this level, the CPU negotiates broad arrangements with major suppliers so that the different units may enjoy an advantage in dealing with those suppliers. Secondly, the CPU has led the division of all the group's purchasing activities into three geographical areas in Spain and Portugal – each of which is called 'CAMS' (10) these three leading purchasing centres for materials and services – regulate, store, and manage the stock and miscellaneous materials that different units need (this basically applies to building and maintenance material). Thirdly, at the establishment level, in each location wherever a unit or group company operates, communication with the respective CAMS is fostered so that a fluid delivery of materials can reach the establishments as needed. In sum, by working at these different levels – corporate, CAMS, establishments – the AGBAR Group develops three types of efficiency: (1) it minimizes the costs of purchases by the units (by negotiating special conditions with fewer suppliers); (2) it diminishes the amount of stock needed at any point of time (by concentrating stock in only three main storage centres, one per CAMS); (3) it reduces the incidence of obsolescence for any given type of material in stock (by reducing the amount of stock that is needed in any warehouse).

Immediately after establishing the CPU, AGBAR's top management realized that there were three risks involved in such a move towards centralizing the purchasing function. First, it would go against the basic philosophy of allowing local managers to take the initiative on matters of their most basic competence. Secondly, it would make it more difficult for managers at the different – and physically dispersed – establishments to keep in touch with suppliers. A manager at the CPU explained: 'To many managers, specially those in charge of small units, keeping in touch with suppliers also meant keeping in touch with new products and new product applications. Therefore, we had to devise a way of keeping the communication avenue opened between those managers and the suppliers.' Thirdly, it would introduce some rigidities – and inefficiencies – in some processes that could be difficult to standardize by the CPU. As a top manager recognized:

> To some extent, we cannot completely centralize the purchasing function. There are cases where you need to buy from local suppliers just to maintain the kind of relationships with the local community that makes the whole business flourish. Even if this means having to eventually pay a higher price for a product, you still win in terms of local relationships. Of course, this is also the case with other services, like banking, when we develop joint ventures with local partners or even with a public administration.

How has the group responded to these challenges? Basically by recognizing the need to centralize while at the same time, decentralizing the purchasing activity of the local establishments. This seemingly contradictory situation translates into initiatives like 'allowing local management to decide the extent to which they want to be centralized', as a top financial manager put it. Also instituting regular gatherings between local managers, suppliers and corporate purchasing staff to discuss each other's views and exchange experiences. Those meetings have a strong organizational and technical orientation, and keep the communication between the participants from stopping.

The recent CPU experience, which initially appears as somehow contradictory (centralizing while letting local management *escape* central guidelines; constraining relationships between purchasing parties while developing mutual gatherings so that those relationships are kept in place), incorporates basic traits of the NFOs such as flexible ways of arranging the purchasing function both centralized and decentralized, and expanding the flow of exchanges between the parties to the purchasing relationship. The CPU further illustrates the proposition that new organizing arrangements need to be thought of as supplementing, rather than supplanting more traditional ones.

Discussion

At this point, we can look back at the two basic issues posed in Section A.

The first issue deals with the alternative positions on the ontological objectivity of the characteristics of the NFOs. Whereas, as we have seen, Burt maintains that networks are in the eye of the beholder and Nohria adds that to say an organization is a network is a tautology, other authors argue for the separate structural characteristics of internal networks as distinctive NFOs. What can be concluded from the AGBAR experiences?

The AGBAR case is a clear example of the need for NFOs to incorporate apparently opposing organizing principles. Internal network arrangements are posited to go further than the mere requirement to operate in environments that demand both local responsiveness and global integration (Nohria and Ghoshal, 1997). The dual nature of NFOs is also manifest in the need to bring about an equilibrium between centralizing and decentralizing firm activities, as well as in being simultaneously excellent at seemingly contradictory competencies such as flexibility, efficiency, innovation, quality and cost (Hill, 1988a; Snow and Ottensmeyer, 1990) or, as Dean and Sussman put it, 'pursuing more than one generic strategy without being "stuck in the middle"' (1989: 312). This equilibrium between opposing tendencies is, in turn, the structural manifestation of the insight that NFOs are characterized by supplementing existing organizational arrangements rather than by tendencies to supplant existent ones (Nonaka, 1994; Galbraith, 1995; Ferlie and Pettigrew, 1996; Pettigrew, 1999a).

The duality of organizational arrangements is also derived from the principle that 'the purpose of the integration process is to ensure that the learning organization overlays and supplements the entrepreneurial organization instead of supplanting it' (Ghoshal and Bartlett, 1997: 199–200). Indeed, we have seen how the CPU experience provided increased responsibilities for local managers, who are expected to balance the need to achieve purchasing efficiencies by following the corporate procedure while at the same time attending to the idiosyncrasies of the local environments in which each unit operates.

Is that enough to consider the AGBAR Group as fully developed around new organizing principles? Certainly not. Although the areas covered by the new organizing experiences are substantial – environmental R&D and purchasing – there is still a lot of activity within the group which is subject to traditional governance forms and procedures. However, there is also the view within the group that the point of the new experiences goes beyond solving specific R&D or purchasing concerns. In this sense, the top management pays close attention to how these experiences evolve so as to consider whether to extend them to other areas.

In sum, the AGBAR Group is most probably right in the middle of the road between the tautological and ontological characterizations of the concept of the NFOs. The more the group introduces similar experiences and keeps testing those new ways of organizing, the more the group will have to be characterized as a clearly distinctive exemplar of a new type of organizing arrangement. Otherwise, we will be confronting a hybrid form, more in line with the tautological characterization.

The second issue from the literature review poses adopting a systemic view of organizational change, and asks how this view confronts the reality of having to start somewhere before reaching a fully blown configuration. In this respect, the AGBAR experiences provide a nice illustration of an organization cautiously testing the waters before completely changing towards NFOs. This constitutes a clear exponent of an exploration–exploitation sequence of organizational innovation and learning (March, 1991). This sequence is also seen in Rabobank (see Van Wijk and Van den Bosch Chapter 5 in this volume) where a separate unit – Spectrum – constitutes a learning template for other organizational units.

To the extent that the AGBAR experiences are successful, and so far they certainly are, a momentum for change may press the organization toward similar experiences on a larger scale. In fact, there is research evidence indicating that once new organizing arrangements are in place, inertia acts to deepen and extend them (Gulati, 1995).

In this regard, we have seen the AF experimenting with the boundaries of its organizing logic vertically and horizontally. Vertically, by broadening the number of external parties with access, under limited restrictions, to the tools and means of knowledge management and virtual teamworking. Horizontally, by introducing subjects other than environmental R&D into its knowledge management infrastructure. Of course, similar points can be made on how to solve most of the group's centralizing versus decentralizing dilemmas by learning from the CPU experience.

Let us summarize the major points from this study. The AF and CPU experiences do constitute NFOs. First, the AF demonstrates a way of structuring the complexity derived from knowledge management processes with regard to the integral water cycle and the group's environmental R&D. Before creation of the AF, that knowledge was widely dispersed across units separated along functional and geographical lines. Thanks to the AF's infrastructure, that knowledge is now available for use by all units, regardless of their physical location.

Secondly, due to both the new ways of knowledge management and virtual teamworking capability, AGBAR has increased the joint capabilities of people internal and external to the organization. Being able to cross internal and external group lines lies at the heart of truly becoming a boundaryless organization.

Thirdly, the AF illustrates a solution to the tension of formally and informally controlling and coordinating different units engaged in environmental R&D. This was done by not configuring the AF as a hierarchical link for the management of R&D. Rather, in accordance with new organizing principles, the AF is expected to perform its control and coordination functions by means of informal, rather than bureaucratic processes. In this way, the AF leverages the benefits of both establishing weak ties among units for purposes of knowledge capture and creating stronger linkages among those engaging in virtual team-working for purposes of knowledge transfer (Hansen, 1999).

The CPU also shares characteristics of the new organizing concept. The CPU formalizes a dual equilibrium between centralizing and decentralizing pressures regarding the group's units purchasing processes. It also tightens control of the organization by establishing clear guidelines at the corporate level for negotiating with suppliers. But the CPU also distributes authority by developing two initiatives: (1) allowing local units, at their own discretion, to deviate from the corporate guidelines; and (2) promoting and enlarging the network of contacts between suppliers and local unit personnel.

Finally, we need to underline once more the dual nature of the NFOs as shown in the AGBAR case. We have referred to the continuous equilibrium between centralization and decentralization as operated by the CPU. This equilibrium is enacted by another duality, that of stability and innovation within the purchasing function: AGBAR maintains its structuring philosophy of decentralization by giving local units decision-making authority on how to apply, if at all, purchasing guidelines promulgated at the corporate level. Another duality relates to the dynamic tension between traditional means of control through hierarchical lines of command and the informal means of control fostered through lateral and diagonal processes of influence – as shown by the AF experience. Still another duality, seen both in the AF and CPU experiences, is found in the way AGBAR both keeps and dilutes organizational barriers. All these three dualities lie within the framework of two other ones. From a structural viewpoint, AGBAR changes both radically – by diversifying and penetrating new lines of business – and gradually – by cautiously testing the new AF and CPU arrangements before extending them across the organization. AGBAR's change initiatives may be viewed from two different perspectives: both radical and revolutionary – if viewed from the perspective of the units affected – or gradual and incremental – if from the viewpoint of the group as a whole.

Implications for Practice and Research

From a practitioner's point of view, our analysis is useful in presenting a way to confront challenges related to the processes and outcomes of change. Change processes cause upheaval and tensions that need to be managed. Successfully managing the processes, however, does not necessarily translate into successfully achieving the intended outcomes. Population ecology scholars cautioned long ago against the 'liability of newness' arising from introducing both new organizations and NFOs (Stinchcombe, 1959: 148–150; Hannan and Freeman, 1989). The AGBAR experiences provide an example of a large organization minimizing the liabilities of newness by cautiously limiting the introduction of NFOs to two strategic business units – the AF and the CPU – and waiting for the outcomes of the change processes in those units before considering the posibility of introducing larger-scale, corporate-wide transformations.

That AGBAR's gradual change approach has not created major internal tensions might be a function of the relatively low weight of the activities of the AF and the UAC when compared to the total activity of the group. Therefore, managers are cautioned not to dismiss problems beforehand, that may only surface after major change. This is especially critical given the emphasis in the literature on the need for a consistent set of governance arrangements across the whole organization.

Another implication of our research derives from the dual nature of the new organizing processes. Very often when dealing with innovation, one tends to overvalue the newer forms while undervaluing the more traditional ones. As a result, older arrangements which may actually provide valuable services risk being replaced by newer, untested ones. Whenever that happens, performance is likely to decrease. Managers need to evaluate the pros and cons of both the old and the new, knowing that only under extremely rare circumstances may superior performance be achieved by merely supplanting, rather than supplementing mechanisms. Once again, practitioners are encouraged to make up their own minds on what really needs to be changed in their organizations. In the long run, a cautious, even sceptical, approach may serve them well.

One promising area for further research lies in the analysis of the conditions under which organizations are likely to follow either the *cautious* or the *bold* path towards the introduction of NFOs. Among others, contingencies like degree of legitimation and institutionalization of the NFOs, level of internal consensus on the desirability of renewed ways of organizing, and extent of organizational slack and resources – to risk and foster innovation in processes and structures – may affect the likelihood, the speed of adoption and development of innovative forms of organizing. We feel this is an extremely promising line of research for theory development and testing.

More research is also needed on the locus of non-local, corporate-wide organizing innovations. Both the AF and CPU experiences in AGBAR were initiated – and still remain – at the group's headquarters. This is consistent with the design of the Advanced-I Group created at

Toshiba for purposes similar to those of the AF (Ichijo and Nonaka, 1998). Flexible and networked organizations, however, might also consider establishing units in charge of corporate-wide knowledge management and general services at different organizational levels, especially when their organizing principles depart from hierarchical, command-and-control modes.

Another question that calls for extended research relates to the challenges of the coexistence of traditional and new governance arrangements in firms: such firms may be alternatively characterized as in a transitory stage toward fully blown innovative forms or as hybrids containing older and newer ways of organizing. A natural extension of the study of design alternatives between pure and hybrid forms calls for the discussion of their performance implications. In the AGBAR experiences, the fact that, so far, no major tensions have arisen from currently maintaining traditional and newer arrangements needs to be tempered by the fact that the innovations only affect two strategic units of the group. Therefore, further research on performance effects requires not only long term, longitudinal analyses – among other reasons, so that the difference between transitory stages and hybrid states can be clearly ascertained – but also different mixes of the extent and prevalence of the newer arrangements *vis-à-vis* the more traditional ones.

Acknowledgements

We thank the management of the AGBAR Group, and particularly Mr Fernando Porta, for sharing information and insights. The opinions and interpretations expressed in this chapter do not necessarily represent the views of the AGBAR Group. Feedback from the book editors and the other members of the INNFORM programme improved this chapter a lot. We also gratefully acknowledge support in research time and expenses from the Research Unit of IESE, University of Navarra.

Notes

1 *Grupo AGBAR*. Noviembre 1998. Barcelona: Gabinete de Presidencia.

2 *La Vanguardia*, 23 Agosto 1998. Crisis en los mercados latinoamericanos: España, primer inversor en la zona. pp. 64.

3 AGBAR. Abril 1995. El Grupo AGBAR y las nuevas tecnologías. Madrid: Delegación General.

4 AGBAR. Octubre 1995. Actividad medioambiental del Grupo AGBAR. Madrid: Delegación General.

5 Due to AGBAR's organizational complexity and dynamism, chances are that by the time this chapter reaches the reader, some data on the number and ownership participation of the group's companies will already be dated.

6   The usage of *matrix* should not confound the reader, since it in no way refers to what the organization theory literature defines as a matrix (Davis and Lawrence, 1977). The term *matrix* within the AGBAR Group relates to its common etymological origin in *mother*, meaning that this company within the group has somehow come to be seen as the mother from which the other companies and businesses were born. The phonetical resemblance of the matrix–mother binomial is even greater in Spanish (*madre–matriz*). From now on, whenever we refer to *matrix*, we mean the *mother* company of the group, thus adhering to AGBAR's internal adoption of the term.

7   In Spanish, 'Centro de Estudios e Investigaciones del Agua'.

8   In Spanish, 'Banco de Información y Tecnologías del Agua'.

9   The goal of having the CPU coordinate somewhere between 40 and 50 per cent of the group's purchasing by the end of 1998 was certainly achieved.

10 In Spanish, 'Centro de Aprovisionamiento de Materiales y Servicios' translates as 'Purchasing Centre for Materials and Services'.

10

Complexities and Dualities in Innovative Forms of Organizing

Andrew M. Pettigrew and Evelyn M. Fenton

The study of innovative forms of organizing is itself a new field of enquiry. As such this field carries with it the liability of newness. Although there is a burgeoning corpus of writing, as yet there are few empirical studies to underpin what has been written. In preparing the review and synthesis of the field in Chapter 1 of this book we could find no other comprehensive scholarly assessment of the literature on new forms. In this rather incomplete and scattered intellectual terrain it is difficult to make an appraisal of what is known and not known.

One thing that is clear is that it is easier to find patterns in the drivers for change in forms of organizing than in the pattern of effects arising from those drivers. The principal drivers of the new competitive scene are globalization and information technology. Competitive pressures in many industries are demanding more rapid response times, greater flexibility and lower management costs, often alongside the sophisticated development and application of intellectual capital. The assumption is that this new competitive landscape renders anachronistic traditional, efficiency-oriented vertical structures and triggers the search for new organizational practices in which flexibility, knowledge collecting and connecting and horizontal collaboration are essential characteristics.

So far, so good. But then we begin to run into one of the prime liabilities of an emerging field, the fallacy of misplaced concreteness. Half-revealed and understood trends are conveniently and crudely captured as ideal types. Thus we are variously informed about the rise of the 'federal', (Handy, 1992) 'network' (Castells, 1996), and 'cellular' (Miles et al., 1997) forms and even the appearance of the 'boundaryless organization' (Ashkenas et al. 1995) and the 'individualized corporation' (Ghoshal and Bartlett, 1998). Such terminology is not, of course, always either misplaced or unhelpful. Language is an important attention director and energizer. The myopic and the sceptical may have to be persuaded that the world is indeed changing if only they would avert their gaze from their immediate horizon. But the present condition of management thinking and practice with its repetitive cycling of fads and fashions and a management research community often excited and deluded by novelty makes it difficult to be sceptical of revelatory language.

Important claims have been made for the rise of federal, network and cellular forms of organizing. Such claims warrant serious investigation but thus far empirical analysis has often rested upon accounts of exceptional organizations such as ABB, General Electric or 3M (Handy, 1992; Bartlett and Ghoshal, 1993), or atypical sectors and regions, for instance, West Coast American high tech (Bahrami, 1992). Theory is still struggling to keep up with the plethora of language and experiment (Daft and Lewin, 1993) and the performance benefits of these new organizations have barely been tested (Nohria, 1996). It is not surprising that some have doubted the extent to which these changes have so far diffused among the firm population (Hoskisson et al., 1993; Gummer, 1995).

Few can be amazed that there are disputes in making sense of emergent changes. All contemporary scholars of new forms of organizing share the same problem of trying to make sense of a moving target. Even if the changes in organizational practices are as radical as some authors believe, it will be some years before we can adequately understand just how profound these innovations have been. In the meantime, it may be circumspect of us not only to map the organizational terrain broadly through large sample studies, but also to systematically follow changes through time. We should be open to the possibility that innovative forms of organizing may emerge incrementally and radically, involve progression and regression, and be better characterized as the new supplementing the old, rather than the new supplanting the old.

It was these analytical considerations which influenced our choice of a large scale survey methodology to map the extent of organizational innovation over space (Europe, Japan and the USA) and at two time points, 1992 and 1996. Given the empirically limited, linguistically imprecise and often apocalyptic tone of much of the writing on innovative forms of organizing, it was not a straightforward issue to decide on the variables to capture in our survey instrument. What was undeniably consistent in existing literature was that organization design no longer involved choices just about structure and form, but needed to incorporate issues of structure and process. Furthermore, much of the new forms literature was now augmenting an interest in network formation and use inside the traditional boundaries of the firm with a new interest in various forms of interorganizational networking and collaboration. These developments led us to focus our survey investigation on change in organizational structures, processes and boundaries. Within these three broad areas of change we measured nine indicators of perceived change. Figure 10.1 captures the nine indicators of change in our survey and also emphasizes what our review of literature had hinted – that these innovations may be mutually reinforcing. Flatter structures may demand more horizontal interaction processes within the firm; interaction may be concentrated within more tightly drawn organizational boundaries as firms outsource and downscope; and reduced strategic focus may curtail tall hierarchies of control.

In Chapter 1 we summarized the key patterns of change from our European survey of innovative forms of organizing. We also noted that only 4.5 per cent of our sample adopted System 1 change and thereby were simultaneously changing their structures, processes and boundaries. While only a few companies carried out the full multidimensional raft of innovative practices, these System 1 firms enjoyed significant performance benefits, with a performance premium of more than 60 per cent.

On the other hand, those firms that combined only parts of this full system of theoretically complementary practices tended to obtain no significant performance pay-offs from such incomplete efforts. Indeed, just combining structural and boundary changes without complementary process changes was found to have negative effects on performance. IT is the only innovation taken singly which offered

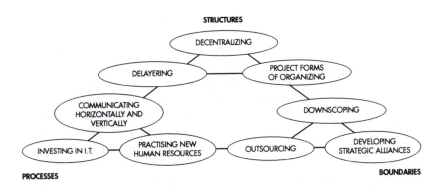

FIGURE 10.1 *New forms of organizing: the multiple indicators*

positive performance benefits over and above those available to the full system.

These are noteworthy findings, which in time we shall be able to confirm or disconfirm from our Japanese and US surveys. Mapping studies have the potential to pin down emerging trends of innovation across space and time. Where they also feature a dependent variable such as performance, it is possible to examine the consequences of innovative activity. However, mapping studies have their limitations. They can tell us much about the what of innovation, but because of their distance from managerial process and action they inform us little about the how and why of change. For this reason we decided to add to the progress and performance aims of the INNFORM programme a third objective. This required us to explore the transition process as firms moved from more traditional forms of organizing. This additional objective meant using a complementary method – the comparative longitudinal case study. The INNFORM programme of research has carried out 18 case studies in European firms (eight in the UK, four in Switzerland and Germany and two each in the Netherlands, Spain and Sweden). These case studies have been designed with two main purposes in mind:

- to analyse the practices and processes of the emergence of new forms of organizing; and
- to examine how and why the subset of our case study firms who attempted complementary change managed that process over the time period from the late 1980s to the late 1990s.

The eight case study chapters in this book offer the first exposure of our findings on practice and process in innovative forms of organizing. Pettigrew's (1999b) recent paper on complementarities in action in BP Amoco provides a detailed analysis of that firm's attempt at holistic change and an assessment of the performance consequences of an avowedly complementary innovation strategy.

In this final chapter two tasks remain. In the section which follows we examine patterns in the practices and processes of innovation across our eight case studies. Our analysis is focused on four main questions. What was the content and scope of innovation in the forms of organizing attempted in the eight organizations? What combination of external and internal drivers precipitated the innovation pathway? What patterns are discernible in the processes of initiation and development of the organizational innovations? And finally, what were some of the continuing management challenges, resolvable and perhaps unresolvable management issues, which these firms faced as they attempted the movement from more traditional organizational arrangements?

The third and final section of the chapter then explores the management of dualities as organizations attempt simultaneous and complementary innovations in organizing. Our survey findings suggest considerable complexity in the content and process of innovation. One notable pattern in our statistical results is that many firms are making simultaneous and apparently contradictory changes. Thus they appear to be building hierarchies and networks; seeking greater performance accountability upward and greater horizontal interpretation sideways; and attempting to both centralize and decentralize. These dualities may be a particularly interesting feature of modernizing firms and in the final section we explore them both for their analytical interest and for managerial challenges.

Practices and Processes in Innovative Forms of Organizing

The authors of the eight case study chapters in this book have been working collaboratively for three or more years on the INNFORM programme. In some cases working relationships pre-date the INNFORM involvement. These links have made it somewhat easier than would otherwise be the case to agree on the character and style of case study work – including important issues such as appropriate frameworks for analysis, study questions and rules of evidence. In preparing this volume the INNFORM network met and debated the analytical structure which might guide all the chapters. Thus we agreed each chapter would begin with a brief, customized literature review which would reflect the character of the organization under study and the particular content area of innovation explored in the chapter. Thereafter each case study chapter would analyse the sectoral, business and organizational context of the innovation; the external and internal drivers for change in new forms of organizing in each company; the content and scope of the relevant innovation; the process and dynamics of changing in each case example; some of the barriers to and facilitators of innovation; and any unresolved management challenges in each firm occasioned by the innovation journey. By and large the authors have followed this brief although there are obvious differences in emphasis and style of writing case by case.

We now engage in some pattern recognition across the eight case studies, reflecting in turn on the content and scope of innovation; the drivers for change and the process dynamics evident across the cases; and finally the continuing management challenges faced by the eight organizations as they experiment with and exploit innovative forms of organizing. In Chapter 1, Fenton and Pettigrew developed the theme of organizing as a dynamic and continuous process. This is a recognition of the early intellectual leadership provided by Weick (1979) in suggesting we should stamp out nouns such as organization and bring in verbs such as organizing. It is also a reflection of a much wider concern to bring processes of becoming centre stage in organizational analysis (Pettigrew, 1990, 1997) in a world where the static metaphors of fit and alignment so loved of contingency theorists seem now so much out of place (Pettigrew and Whipp, 1991).

More recently Whittington et al. (1999c) and Melin et al. (1999) have extended this argument to juxtapose organizing and strategizing. The use of the verbs organizing and strategizing emphasizes not just organizational strategies and forms in themselves, but the change journeys and continuous processes involved in moving towards and sustaining such strategic positions and forms. Linking organizing and strategizing also acknowledges the misplaced fallacy of treating these as two discrete practices, and a new concern with their inseparability. In the world of strategy post-Porter, static notions of positioning may have been superseded by a view of strategizing as an innovation contest where the inflexible and non-responsive firm may not survive. Indeed for some organizations (the professional service firms analysed in Chapters 2 and 3 of this book) the form of organizing used to deliver client services may be virtually synonymous with the strategizing of the firm. In this spirit, we now examine organizations not as end states but as the continuously re-created and ever precarious product of human activities.

The content and scope of innovative forms of organizing

A constant riddle in the literature on new forms of organizing is the what of change. Throughout this book we have mentioned a desire to balance structure with process, internal network formation and coordination with external mechanisms of collaboration and a new appreciation of how the hard infrastructure of IT development needed to be considered alongside a softer agenda of human resource innovation. Our focus on structures, processes and boundaries was then operationalized in our survey instrument in the nine variables detailed in Figure 10.1. This broad notion of newness was quite appropriate for the analysis of innovation in a survey-based mapping study, but what was to guide our operational definition of newness as we approached the micro context and processes of our case study organizations?

We used four instances of innovation as guidelines for our case studies. In the first instance, innovation may refer to the widespread adoption by organizational populations of an organizational innovation. Our literature review suggested that various types of organization may be appearing in the 1990s (examples include the network and cellular form). However, their appearance is untested in any large database and in any case the emergence of any prototypical organization may as yet be only partial and substantially uninstitutionalized. This may not, of course, inhibit a management system from claiming novelty. Indeed the Rabobank chapter in this book (Chapter 5) chronicles executive intent to build an internal network organization as yet with only partial success.

Newness may not need to encapsulate delivery of a new type of organization but merely some novel combination of organizational processes and structures not previously associated. A third instance of innovation could refer to some novel recombination of previously associated structures and processes. A fourth kind of newness could be an organizational innovation which is new for that industry sector in that particular economy, but may not be more generally new. The overarching consideration was that the changes which the organizations adopted were both perceived as new by their members and established as novel through the independent assessment of the research team working on the case study. All the case studies comfortably met this final interpretative criterion.

So what was the content and scope of the innovations in organizing in the eight case studies reported here? Five of the eight (Ove Arup – Chapter 2, ABB – Chapter 4, Rabobank – Chapter 5, Hilti – Chapter 6 and Saab Training Systems – Chapter 8) were aspirational to achieve company-wide organizational innovations. The other three (Coopers & Lybrand – Chapter 3, Fremap – Chapter 7, and AGBAR – Chapter 9) had more limited ambitions to change some important part of their organizational practices. Without exception, experimentation involved changing a bundle or set of organizational practices, thus requiring structure and process changes and in some cases structure, process and boundary changes.

Professional service organizations are often portrayed as exemplars of new forms of organizing. The professional is seen as the archetype of the new knowledge worker whilst the professional firm (whose principal product and resource is knowledge) is considered emblematic of the new knowledge-creating organization (Cooper et al., 1996; Pettigrew and Fenton, 1999). A closer look at some of the defining organizational characteristics of professional organizations makes it clear why Ove Arup and Coopers & Lybrand were chosen as receptive contexts for new forms of organizing. Such professional firms operate on a global scale with high profile, demanding clients. Their business is problem solving, sometimes involving complex and novel tasks and on other occasions quite structured and routine tasks. There is a requirement to create high quality standards for a common brand throughout the world and yet increasingly there are strong client pressures to customize services to meet local needs.

There is a predominance of fluid project structures, and work activities appear chaotic and emergent. Knowledge creating, collecting and sharing are all critical for project and corporate success. There is a high reliance on professional expertise which is guided by norms of professional conduct. Finding, keeping and motivating talent is a crucial business success factor. And there is now accumulating evidence that the partnership mode of governance so characteristic of such firms is being challenged by an emerging archetype – the managerial professional business (Cooper et al., 1996).

Ove Arup and Coopers & Lybrand well illustrate some of the organizational experimentation to meet the requirement of the knowledge-creating firm in a knowledge dominated sector with global reach. Both firms are moving from a loose federation of national practices towards an integrated global network form. This is being done through successive experimentation in both firms, with the move from national to global networks being staged through regional networks, sometimes with a skills focus and sometimes with an industry or sector focus. Both firms have attempted to centralize strategy and decentralize operations. Both have increased vertical levels and strengthened vertical communications whilst simultaneously constructing horizontal networks to share knowledge and better satisfy client needs. Both firms have invested greatly in IT to facilitate such vertical and horizontal linkages. They also have both professionalized and formalized their human resource activities and are constantly innovating to handle their common strategic issue of finding, keeping and motivating talent.

The special feature of the Coopers & Lybrand case is the development of the pharma network within the regional European organization – CLE. The pharma network illustrates the relational challenges of building and formalizing network ways of working alongside the complexities of the traditional and more hierarchical national organizations. The case shows the value of social mechanisms of control in networks and demonstrates the crucial importance of friendship, trust, reputation and power in making networks work in the service of complex and fluid problem solving under time pressure.

The theme of building internal networks and horizontal coordination is also a key feature of the Rabobank case in Chapter 5. Here the initiation of network forms was triggered in 1988 by the aspirations of the CEO. But it was the illustrative example of networks in action in the Spectrum part of the company – an IT internal consultancy operation – which made this innovation real. Progress in Spectrum encouraged the Rabobank CEO in 1996 to aspire to build an internal network throughout the whole of Rabobank. This aspiration led to a 1998 initiative to 'build a flexible network organization' amongst the local member banks in the Rabobank Group. The case illustrates differential pace of change in building internal networks in a large business, issues of progression and regression in network development and some of the problems of reconciling the traditional with the novel in organization development.

ABB is probably one of the companies discussed most often in the management literature in the 1990s and its former CEO Percy Barnevik is one of the most visible leaders in the worldwide business scene (Taylor, 1991; Bartlett and Ghoshal, 1993). Our ABB case in Chapter 4 exemplifies the danger of thinly researched accounts of management best practice which are rapidly dissolved by the passage of time. The St Gallen team who prepared the ABB case have taken a much deeper and more considered look at the progression of the ABB matrix organization throughout the 1990s. Their chapter brings out some of the continuing tensions in making the ABB matrix work. These included frequent problems in the mid-1990s with business segmentation, internal decision-making processes and the fallibilities of ABB's internal market mechanisms. ABB thus moved from a global matrix with a strong country focus in 1988 to 1993, through a global matrix with a strong regional focus in the period 1993 to 1998, to what the chapter authors call a networked multidivisional post-1998. In this latter period the matrix was tilted again with the product as the primary focus, the country as a secondary emphasis and the elimination of the regional focus created in the mid period of the 1990s. Leader effects in new forms of organizing were as evident in the ABB case as they were in Rabobank. Barnevik was the clear architect of ABB's organization development in the period 1988–1998 and it was his successor Lindahl who triggered the reorganization of 1998.

There are many process parallels between the Hilti, ABB and Rabobank cases although the content areas of innovation were quite different. In Chapter 6 we again find a long progression of organizational experimentation in the Hilti case, but this time involving, sometimes sequentially and at other times in parallel, innovations in top governance, structure, process, network development and human resource innovation.

The smallest of the corporate-wide innovation cases is Saab Training Systems – a medium-sized high-tech defence company. In the early part of the 1990s Saab had delivery time issues for both production and development activities. These problems and the pressure created by two very big orders precipitated the desire to create a more team-based form of organizing. The aspiration was to create greater flexibility and lateral working in teams with both production and development aims. Again this experimentation encouraged further innovation in organizing as it became clear that the new practices were delivering successes in production but at the cost of weakening the developmental capability of the company.

The two Spanish companies in Chapters 7 (Fremap) and 9 (AGBAR) are both early adopters of new forms of organizing in their sectors of the Spanish economy. The Fremap case illustrates moves from a highly centralized, bureaucratic and functionally designed organization to a decentralized structure with new integral roles performing more integrated tasks for the clients of the business. This was a radical change in organizing for the Fremap branches which had substantial human resource implications in areas such as selection, training, compensation and patterns of working. These innovations at the client-facing part of the organization had knock-on effects for the corporate centre and the role of territorial directors, but the experience of the new patterns of working was felt most strongly at the branch level.

The AGBAR case reveals careful experimentation with new forms of organizing in a rapidly growing, internationalizing and diversifying Spanish utility. The AGBAR Foundation restyled and reorganized the company R&D capability so it could meet the knowledge management requirements of a much more complex business. The purchasing department was also chosen as a demonstration site for innovation, this time by altering the balance of centralization and decentralization in its function. Again there are attempts in both AGBAR examples to alter the patterns of hierarchical and horizontal communication and knowledge flows, more effectively and efficiently harness geographically dispersed skill and knowledge, and encourage teamworking between previously separated businesses.

These cameos of organizational innovation show clearly that the 'new' in new forms of organizing can mean quite different content areas of change for firms of different sizes, in varying sectors, at different stages of their organizational development, in different economies. Nevertheless there are some constant themes across the cases. Drives to build stronger hierarchies which will support more performance oriented cultures in tougher global competitive conditions; a need to create stronger strategic frameworks at the centre and more customer-sensitive behaviour at the periphery of the organization; pressure to build more flexible firms where information and skill previously locked up either in geographical or product or skills silos can move more easily across the organization. The cases also reveal the explicit development of internal and external networks and teams to share knowledge and solve problems that much more flexibly, efficiently and quickly. But what are the common drivers of these innovations in organizing and were there any patterns in their development over time?

Patterns in the drivers for and development of the innovations

Explaining why changes occur in organizational settings is a complex subject. The term 'organization design', so characteristic of contingency thinking in organizational analysis, now seems over-simple and far too rational to capture the processes through which innovations emerge and are institutionalized. This is not to say there are not local efficiency-driven choices for changing organizational practices. Most innovations of substance have to be legitimized in their setting and efficiency-driven arguments will have to be constructed to satisfy whatever local governance pressures are in place. Many years ago, Pfeffer (1978) highlighted the significance of internal political factors in shaping the design choices of firms. More recently Pettigrew (1985a) and many others have documented the role of crises in triggering changes in organizational structure. Most recently the institutionalists are having their say. The rise and fall of management ideas and practices are now portrayed as imitative behaviour as firms compete for visibility, security and reputation in the worldwide fashion industry of management (Abrahamson, 1991, 1996). The reality, of course, is that there is likely to be a variety of motives for firms experimenting with new forms of organizing. Our eight case studies reveal a mixed bag of motives driving change. Some of these drivers come from the external context of the organization and others tend to spring from circumstances, people, and politics inside the firm.

None of the innovation pathways in our case studies were crisis driven, though company crises did play a role in the history of Hilti and ABB. Indeed there is substantial evidence that the self-concept and behaviour of some of our sample indicates that their innovation pathway was internally driven, even habitual. Hilti has a long history of organizational experimentation which is revealed through action and not just rhetoric. Fremap and AGBAR are early adopters of new forms of organizing in their sectors and in their economy. Ove Arup has a long history of successful innovation in engineering design and construction and this heritage appears to have spilled over into its organizational practices. ABB has been widely portrayed in the 1990s as a management innovator and its former CEO, Percy Barnevik has become a business icon. Our case study sample is not representative. But it was never meant to be. To explore process and dynamics in an emergent set of organizational practices it is helpful to have some outlier case studies. Some early adopters, or as March (1991) would argue, explorers are very helpful in understanding innovation processes.

Some of our cases can be seen as receptive contexts for change where there was a momentum and culture for innovation (Pettigrew et al., 1992). Within these contexts, leader effects were sometimes quite significant. We have already mentioned how the changing of the guard at the top of a business can precipitate innovations in organizing. This certainly happened in ABB as Lindahl succeeded Barnevik and in Hilti as the founding technical entrepreneur Martin Hilti was replaced by his son Michael. Leader effects in championing new modes of organizing were also evident at the corporate level and Spectrum level in Rabobank, and in the Saab, AGBAR, Fremap and Ove Arup cases. Sometimes, as in Rabobank, Saab and AGBAR, these leader effects were highly value laden; in other cases the values of the CEO were intermingled with strong competitive pressures for change, as in Saab and Ove Arup.

Leading change should not just be portrayed as an individually driven process. The evolution and development of innovation in all our cases was intimately tied in with the history, culture and politics of each firm. Nowhere was this more evident than in the rather special governance arrangements to be found in professional service firms. The rise of the European organization of Coopers & Lybrand (CLE), and the particular part of that we studied in detail (the pharma network) illustrate well the importance of bottom-up and organic processes of organization development. The precursor to the pharma network was a group of senior consultants (some of whom were partners) who built on their strong personal relationships to form a 'voluntary society' which eventually was institutionalized as the pharma network.

All these examples of internally generated innovations should not distract our gaze from the equally pertinent observation that innovation journeys are often initiated and sustained by cocktails of internal and external pressure. We have already commented on the strong customer and competitive pressures facing global professional service organizations such as Ove Arup and Coopers & Lybrand. There is no doubt that ABB's passion for organizational innovation in the 1990s was based at least partially on the disjuncture between its rising profile as an innovator in the management literature and serious press and its continuing failure to match the relentless performance improvement of its major competitor General Electric. ABB's move to fortify the regional side of its matrix at the same time was also shaped by its market moves into emergent regional economies such as Eastern Europe and China and, of course, the ever rising significance of the European Union. Our Hilti case also shows how leader effects were enabled by constant pressure from Hilti's two main competitors Bosch and Würth. Saab's move into the novel team-based structure and processes was undoubtedly triggered by its 'visionary CEO'. But his vision was sharpened by historical failures in meeting production and development deadlines and the strategic importance of two very large new contracts where failure was non-contemplatable.

The innovation journeys in our eight case study chapters also reveal a judicious desire to manage risk. Saab and Fremap both used demonstration sites to test and learn from their organizational experiments before diffusing the changes more widely through the organization. AGBAR carefully used two less than central parts of its organization

(R&D and purchasing) to explore the strengths and weaknesses of new forms of organizing. In this way AGBAR minimized risk and encouraged a learning process which avoided major internal tensions. Given the speed of growth of AGBAR in recent times and the rate of internationalizing and diversifying it had taken on board, this incremental approach was well suited to its capability to manage further change.

Most crucially the time series data in our case studies have revealed the more or less continuous process of organizing and reorganizing faced by our eight firms. None appeared to be thinking and acting about innovation as a move from one state to another. The innovation journeys were always incomplete, always in process, never quite there. ABB appears to have rationalized this sense of unfinished business by articulating a view of five-year cycles of organizational innovation. The hard fact may be that with an ever changing internal and external organizational context, organizations may be resting uneasily on a cusp between order and disorder. In this situation verbs such as organizing and strategizing must take precedence over the old nouns of organization and strategy. We will shortly explore these dynamic and uncertain qualities of modern organizing in an extended discussion of the dualities present in new forms of organizing. Before then we should explore some of the more concrete unresolved management issues faced by our case study firms as they dealt with anticipated and unanticipated consequences of their organizational innovations.

Unresolved management issues on the innovation journeys

All actions have their consequences. Some of these appear abruptly in the short term, others may brood for a time, be fanned by an ever changing context and arrive both as friend and foe of innovation initiatives. Changes by definition provoke unexpected effects which may be accommodated, even managed, but are rarely controllable. There is also the issue of perspective and perception. Initiators of innovations may feel the positive exhilaration of tackling a just cause. For others the change may mean a bruising encounter with the devil. All these dynamics are likely to be magnified by the almost continuous processes of innovating discerned in our eight case study organizations. Living with constant change means there are always multiple loose ends. This experience of wrestling with perpetual order and disorder is likely to be heightened by the upward and downward spirals of psychological success and failure as immediate objectives are met or otherwise. Tangible experiences of business success can provide a comforting balm for the tensions of innovation processes. This was certainly a factor in sustaining the innovation journeys of our firms – all of whom were at least moderately successful in the period of our case study investigations.

The character of organizational innovations is an important contributor to these process dynamics. Although ultimately shaped by local perceptual considerations, the extent to which innovations are incremental and radical is another key factor in chains of effect. We have demonstrated from our survey and case study data that for many organizations, new forms of organizing imply innovating in sets. Simultaneous and complementary change (Pettigrew, 1999a, 1999b) will create its own special burdens, but in the area of new forms of organizing special dynamics are in play. These involve the management of a series of dualities in areas such as centralizing and decentralizing and building hierarchies and networks. Our evidence about new forms of organizing shows firms evolving towards greater organizational complexity. Struggles to find highly customized and simple innovation journeys represent a constant management challenge (Pettigrew, 1999b).

A theme running through our eight case studies is the attempt to build and sustain effective internal networks. The Ove Arup, Coopers & Lybrand, Rabobank and AGBAR cases were frontstage examples of network building. ABB, Hilti, Fremap and to a lesser extent Saab also revealed innovations to build and improve horizontal collaboration across international boundaries, business divisions or functions. These cases all reveal some of the special management challenges in creating and sustaining networks, but the Coopers & Lybrand pharma network offers the deepest microprocess analysis of why networks work and what are the issues in keeping them working.

The adoption of a network mode of organizing by both Ove Arup and Coopers & Lybrand Europe (CLE) was a strategic response to market conditions with the objective of leveraging core competencies across both firms. In CLE their form of organizing represented a set of coordination mechanisms overlaid upon a federal structure of dispersed and independent partner firms. The pharma network was one of four industry networks and was the most advanced in terms of integration and coordination. The development of the pharma network formalized coordination mechanisms and increased the scale, scope and complexity of a pre-existing informal network. The network had begun informally, almost as a voluntary society of like-minded consultants. At this stage of its development the network relied upon a few social mechanisms of control to coordinate its European-wide activities. These included established relationships of trust and experience, together with a common belief in the virtues of working across Europe with a client set of pharmaceutical firms. These strong beginnings, with the network innovation being championed from the bottom up, albeit by senior partners with long experience in the pharmaceutical sector, ensured the right kind of energy and commitment. The early business success of the network fuelled this sense of psychological success and drew other like-minded individuals into the voluntary society. The pharma network illustrates well the importance of fateful beginnings triggering an upward spiral of success. By the time the pharma network was formalized and institutionalized as company policy in 1996, it was already seriously in business and delivering tangible outcomes for Coopers & Lybrand. Thereafter the pharma network grew in size, took on board further facilitative IT developments, built on its pre-existing strong culture and methodologies, created specialist subnetworks and continued to expand its services.

The pharma network's success can be explained at least partly by the availability of Nahapiet and Ghoshal's (1998) three elements of social capital – structural, relational and cognitive. Structural provision was accessible through the positional power of partners in the network. Social capital was attainable through the experience, reputation, skill and knowledge of early network members. And the cognitive dimension was made available by building a strong pharma mindset which shaped the problem-solving behaviour and expectations of the pharma consultants. Layered on top and around this social capital were effective leadership and brokerage of the network, a strong culture which was actively built and sustained, and a well formulated and explicit normative order exemplified in the green card and red card behavioural guidance for cross-border working (see Fenton and Pettigrew, Chapter 3).

Precisely because of their strong relational character, networks can be precarious forms of organizing. Successful as it was, by the time of the closure of our Coopers & Lybrand investigation, it was already clear that the pharma network was facing a number of management challenges. These challenges were caused by increasing size; problems of linkage between the network form and the more established national organizations in Coopers & Lybrand where profit was still counted and careers were made; and also problems of 'unbalanced integration' of the different national organizations who supplied participants for the pharma network. Size appears to be a crucial variable in network development and impact. As the pharma network grew, so it appeared the original social mechanisms that kept the network together were increasingly powerless. There was pressure to complement the original social mechanisms of control with more formal coordination mechanisms which provided sharper accountability and new rules for behaviour.

Increased network size may also precipitate adjustments in the number of subnetworks, the flow of people between networks to prevent intellectual staleness, and a rebalancing of the incentives and disincentives for sustaining energy and commitment to network purposes. It was noticeable that the pharma network was able to use neither strong collective sanctions to inhibit opportunism nor strong positive incentives to encourage collaborative behaviour. The emotional and social characteristics of the pharma network earlier in its life cycle meant that little formal action was needed in the design of incentives and disincentives. Greater size and complexity now challenged this lack of foresight. Latterly it also became clear that the strong social relationships which had been a great boost to network development at the pharma's pioneering phase, were now sometimes seen as cliques which were limiting the flow of ideas and people across the growing network.

Some of these management challenges in the pharma case are echoed elsewhere in our sample of case studies. Ove Arup also had problems with unbalanced integration as they sought to build regional and global networks from their national firms. The national organizations had different histories, were operating in widely different market conditions, had varying interests and capabilities to think and act collaboratively in networks, and had individuals who were more or less comfortable in operating as dual citizens with a foot in two or more organizations. The sheer scale of Rabobank was a major inhibitor of the corporate aim to build an internal network organization, and when attempts were made to encourage cooperative behaviour between the local member banks, it was soon apparent that the disincentives for collaborative behaviour were a good deal more real than the incentives. Hilti also had problems making horizontal coordination work. There the fulcrum of organization development was the business unit/marketing organization interface.

The ABB case illustrated the constant tensions in making global matrix organizations work. As they tilted their matrix regionally to mirror the refocusing of their businesses to regional economic blocs and emergent economies so they created a new set of roles and new power blocs in the company. These were eventually felt to be getting in the way of sufficient product and national focus, so in 1998 some blood was spilt on the carpet as the regional barons were swept out of office. Meanwhile Saab's attempt to build a team-based structure combining production and development purposes foundered on the predisposition of team members to privilege production matters over development considerations. Post-1998 these tensions were resolved by separation. Production teams were retained, but development activities were hived off to a pool of development employees. Fremap, for all its evident success in building integral roles to better satisfy client needs, and its sophisticated use of human resource strategies to support this new form of organizing, also found that when you delayer you reduce career opportunities. And when you limit careers you demotivate a set of people whose expectations and aspirations at work you had raised by providing them in the short term with more challenging jobs.

Managing Dualities in Innovative Forms of Organizing

There is a long tradition in the social sciences and in management and organization theory of using bipolar modes of thinking. The bipolar concepts are variously portrayed and used as dichotomies, paradoxes, contradictions and dualities. Dichotomies are remembered. They are powerful simplifiers and attention directors as the influence of Burns and Stalker's (1961) mechanistic and organic systems and March's (1991) exploration and exploitation in organizational learning testify. Dichotomies also tease. They may promise much analytically but deliver very little when applied in empirical analysis. Dichotomies may thus conceal as much as they reveal.

As Janssens and Steyaert (1999) have persuasively argued, although these various bipolar concepts all imply two distinct and indissoluble parts, they have slightly different meanings. Thus although a paradox is an apparent contradiction, no choice may be called for because the contradictory elements are accepted. A dilemma is often seen as an either–or situation in which one alternative must be preferred over the other attractive alternative (Hampden-Turner, 1981). Dualities, on the other hand, 'reflect opposing forces that must be balanced, properties that seem contradictory or paradoxical but which in fact are complementary' (Evans and Doz, 1992: 85). This view of dualities is highly consistent with the complementarities treatment of innovative forms of organizing and performance in the INNFORM programme (Pettigrew, 1999b; Whittington et al., 1999b). But what does 'balanced' mean in the resolution of tensions and dualities?

In a recent discussion of his exploration–exploitation duality, March (1999: 5) notes that 'balance is a nice word, but a cruel concept'. He rightly argues that defining an optimum mix of exploration and exploitation is difficult or impossible. It involves trade-offs across space, time, people and levels in a system. In other words, the experience of dualities and their management is likely to be highly context sensitive. Balancing centralization and decentralization (or to return to our theme of verb forms) centralizing and decentralizing, is likely to require quite adroit customizing. And if we add one duality to another and contend that the experience of new forms of organizing implies exposure to multiple dualities (see Figure 10.2), then the art of managing dualities becomes even more sensitive to local dynamics, uncertainties and complexities.

The survey and case study findings of the INNFORM programme have already established the dualities present in many of the innovations taking place in the modern organization. Figure 10.2 summarizes nine key dualities.

This research shows that our sample of firms are simultaneously

Living with and managing hierarchies *and* networks	The discipline to identify knowledge *and* the good citizenship to share knowledge
Greater performance accountability upwards *and* greater horizontal integration sideways	Balancing continuity *and* change: 'To change the world one must live with it'
Empowering *and* holding the ring	Continuous innovation requires some platforms of relative stability
Centralizing strategy *and* decentralizing operations	Delivering a complementary *and* contextually appropriate set of innovations and not the latest management fad
Standardizing *and* customizing	

FIGURE 10.2 *Managing dualities in the modern organization*

building hierarchies *and* networks; seeking greater performance accountability upward *and* greater horizontal integration sideways; and attempting to centralize strategy *and* decentralize operations.

Sophisticated leaders are aware that attempts to devolve authority and relax some controls in order to encourage creativity and build commitment can only occur when a firm has a clear and well communicated strategic framework. Empowering is only wise when the centre firmly holds the ring. Firms experienced in change management know also the virtues of simultaneously standardizing the broad vision for change and permitting degrees of freedom to decentralized units to customize the pace, sequencing and even the language of the change journey.

Increased global competition, the speed of technical and market change and the rise of information and communication technologies are all driving the knowledge economy and firm. Those changes are in turn encouraging greater networking and collaboration in firms and more alliances and partnerships between organizations. In these processes, knowledge transfer is a pressing requirement. But knowledge management creates its own dynamic and its own duality: the discipline to identify knowledge and the good citizenship to share knowledge. Our case study findings show that the incentive systems of most organizations are often remarkably misaligned with corporate attempts to build good citizenship in organizations where competition and collaboration have to coexist.

One of the sounder aphorisms in the practice of managing innovation is that 'to change the world one must live with it'. Although the high-performing organizations in our survey were innovating in sets, there are always strategic choices to be made about the scale, pace and sequencing of changes. Managerial judgements about where to start the innovation process and how to balance continuity and change are often critical to longer term success.

Our research results signal the dangers of precipitate action buoyed up on the latest management fad or fashion. Beware of attempts to improve performance through simple and singular changes. Leading innovation and performance is about delivering a complementary and contextually appropriate set of innovations and not the latest management trend.

The quantitative results from the INNFORM survey show that in making simultaneous innovations in their structures, processes and boundaries, many of our firms are exposing themselves to a range of dualities. We can see an even richer picture of these dualities in action in our case studies. Thus in Ove Arup and Coopers & Lybrand there were successive attempts to encourage dependence on the centre and independence from the centre; to promote the centralization of strategy and the decentralization of operations; to empower whilst holding on to power. Both professional service organizations were attempting to build strong global brands with all that involved in terms of coherence of identity and standardization of quality, whilst at the same time permitting customized client offerings in national and regional markets. The development of innovative forms of organizing in the Spanish-based utility AGBAR is a further clear example of the incorporation of dual principles of organizing. Organization development in AGBAR involved finding new balances between centralization and decentralization, continuity and change, and building the hierarchy whilst encouraging horizontal coordination. The other Spanish case Fremap illustrated well the human resource management complementarities which may be needed to support new forms of organizing. Fremap also demonstrated that the implementation of these complementarities had to acknowledge and reflect the new balance of centralization and decentralization. Thus the new human resource policies and practices were simultaneously centralizing and decentralizing people-related matters. This recognition that the complementarities in new forms of organizing are not just about multiple 'whats' of change, but also involve multiple 'hows' of changing, is a novel feature of our research findings and adds a further twist to our thesis that innovative forms of organizing are creating new levels of uncertainty and complexity for management.

Complexity building and routes to simplification in organizing

Our research findings on innovative forms of organizing paint a picture of greater organizational uncertainty and complexity. Although it is now well acknowledged that the new competitive landscape of firms is a great driver of change, we suspect that the more potent cause of complexity in firms lies in the responses firms make to the accumulating external pressure. Through space and time we have discovered a variable tendency for firms to be changing their structures, processes and boundaries. These often simultaneous and complementary innovations trigger the bipolar systems of thinking and acting we have characterized as dualities. The dualities are multiple and interdependent and promote highly customized action in local contexts which create further variety through time which has to be managed. All this is happening on a moving platform where the outcomes of action are washed up on a shore which itself is moving. Innovations which may have been conceived as solutions may end up being perceived as problems. Actions may be more localized than their effects.

Customization may thereby promote local short term successes, but unwittingly drive unexpected outcomes some distance in space and time from the immediate changes. In this context, contingency-based theorizing about fit or alignment seems peculiarly out of place (Evans and Doz, 1992; Gresov and Drazin, 1997). In organizations which are both seeking flexibility, learning and responsiveness and reacting to effects of their own and others' actions, tight fit or consistency may only breed maladaptivity and rigidity.

Some authors are already speculating on how organizations can accommodate to these emerging pathways of complexity. Following Evans and Doz (1992), Janssens and Steyaert (1999) catalogue six different strategies for managing dualities. These range from sequencing the innovations, to layering new capabilities to meet the multiple challenges of the several dualities. Janssens and Steyaert prefer what they call a trialectics solution where third parties are brought into the process of organizing to help achieve 'a balanced equilibrium' between the polar forces in the dualities. They suggest this can be achieved by creating a multivoiced dialogue among the several parties involved in the process of organizing. However, they do not offer a concrete illustration of their trialectics solution.

Our research cannot yet provide a clear empirical pattern of how firms that are attempting to develop new forms of organizing cope with any accelerating levels of complexity. However, there are undoubtedly emerging signs in our case studies of organizations responding to increasing complexity by instigating balancing routes to simplification. Looked at on a meta-level, these possible routes seem to require various forms and indicators of holistic thinking and action. Thus in the BP Amoco case (Pettigrew, 1999b), there was explicit executive recognition of the need to balance complexity and simplification.

In BP Amoco drives to create cross-business and cross-functional networks and teams as an exploratory pathway for innovation were curtailed when it became clear that the scale of these networks was inhibiting action. Interestingly, the main criterion used to cull what were perceived to be an excessive number of networks was their relative success in driving performance outcomes. So an exploratory move with longer term innovative purpose was then curtailed by an exploitative move which satisfied shorter term performance considerations.

Strategic leadership is undoubtedly important in defraying excessive ambiguity and complexity. Percy Barnevik is widely portrayed as the glue which held ABB together in the 1990s (Taylor, 1991; Bartlett and Ghoshal, 1993). The ability to deliver clear, simple and evocative messages which balance future goals with present needs seems to be a crucial simplifying routine in times of tension and change. Thus after the trauma of the exit of his predecessor, David Simon the new CEO of BP both challenged and relaxed the troubled organization. Here was 'the great communicator' 'Mr Everyman' who brought the essential simplifying message – 'from now on it's all about Performance, Reputation and Teamwork: PRT', was the simple slogan (Pettigrew, 1999b). Through this simple slogan was communicated purpose and priority – another key route to simplification.

Balancing order and disorder is intimately tied up with the management of continuity and change. Emotionally another route to simplification is finding zones of relative comfort in what may feel like relentless eras of continuous change. It is important to remember how many dualities come into existence. The two polar opposites in dualities such as centralization and decentralization or hierarchies and networks rarely appear at the same time. One pole probably already existed and the other arrived later. So the duality is triggered by novelty and it is the novelty which creates the potential disorder. But this novelty can be painted into the local scene in many ways. The new need not be reified or overstated. One simplifying routine is to link the future with the present and the past. In Chapter 2 (this volume) we showed how continuity was important to Arups. At the initial stages of their Reformation initiative they were careful to reaffirm the values which had been outlined by their founder Ove Arup in his 1970 'key speech'. Most successful leaders of change keep one foot firmly in the present, whilst launching forward with the other (Pettigrew, 1985a). The AGBAR case in this book is an excellent example of the balancing of continuity and change.

Although the implementation of IT systems is a notoriously complex and fractious process (Galliers and Baets, 1998), our case studies demonstrate the enormous potential of common IT operating environments for enabling the development of innovative forms of organizing. The internal networks and teams described in the Ove Arup, Coopers & Lybrand, AGBAR, ABB and Rabobank Spectrum cases would not have been possible without complementary IT changes. Without a common operating environment IT changes can promote complexity and inhibit cross-company communication. Where the common operating environment is in place and working (as now in BP Amoco), the communication and simplifying possibilities are enormous.

This discussion of simplifying routines in the modern organization is tentative and incomplete. Innovative forms of organizing are still emerging. The INNFORM programme is the first global attempt to collect quantitative data to map trends in organizing. In this book we have done some important pattern recognition in Europe, and other publications will emerge comparing Europe with Japan and the USA (Pettigrew et al., 1999). Our case studies have carried us beyond the aggregative trends of survey results and taken us into some micro-pattern recognition in the practices and processes of organizing in eight firms. But whilst a process of organizing is still appearing we can see neither the emergent trends clearly enough, nor the consequences of the still evolving patterns. What is clear is that there are big new challenges in understanding and managing the dualities and complexities in innovative forms of organizing. There is a learning process going on in firms in how to manage these dualities. Some of this may involve balancing the new relationships between complexity and simplicity in organizing. In this balancing, the simplifying options of ignoring the existence of the dualities, or privileging one pole of the duality over the other, are unlikely to meet the demands of the kinds of complementary innovation that organizations are now making.

References

ABB Group (1997) *ABB Annual Report*. Zürich.

ABB Group (1998) *ABB Press Release*, 12 August. Zürich.

ABB Group Internetpages (1998) http://www.abb.ch/abbgroup/introduction/aboutabb.html., 26.11.1998.

ABB Switzerland (1997) *ABB Switzerland Annual Report*. Baden.

Abrahamson, E. (1991) 'Managerial fads and fashions: the diffusion and rejection of innovations', *Academy of Management Review* 16: 586–612.

Abrahamson, E. (1996) 'Management fashion', *Academy of Management Review* 21 (1): 254–285.

Adams, S. (1980) 'Interorganizational processes and organization boundary activities', *Research in Organization Behaviour*, 2: 321–355.

Alavi, M. and Yoo, Y. (1995) 'Productivity gains of BPR: achieving success where others have failed', *Information Systems Management*, 12 (4) Fall: 43-47.

Aldrich, H. (1979) *Organization and Environment*. Englewood Cliffs, NJ: Prentice Hall.

Allred, P. S., Snow, C. C. and Miles, R. E. (1996) 'Characteristics of managerial careers in the 21st century', *Academy of Management Executive*, 10 (4): 17–26.

Alonso, V. P. (1997) 'Las Mutuas también se suben al carro de la prevención', *Cinco Días*, 25 November: 10.

Anderson, E. and Weitz, B. (1992) 'The use of pledges to build and sustain commitment in distribution channels', *Journal of Marketing Research*, 29 (February): 18–34.

Anderson, H. and Larsson, A. (1998) 'Projects as an arena for innovation: images of projects and their implications', in R. A. Lundin and C. Midler (eds), *Projects as Arenas for Renewal and Learning Processes*. Boston: Kluwer Academic. pp. 145–156.

Andreu, R. and Ricart, J. E. (1995) *Fremap*, DG–1127, IESE Research Division, Barcelona.

Aoki, M. (1986) 'Horizontal vs. vertical information structure of the firm', *American Economic Review*, 76 (5): 971–983.

Argyris, C. (1972) *The Applicability of Organizational Sociology*. London: Cambridge University Press.

Armour, H.O. and Teece, D.J. (1978) 'Organizational structure and economic performance: a test of the multi-divisional hypothesis', *The Ranch Journal of Economics*, 9 (1): 106–122.

Arndt, J. (1979) 'Towards a concept of domesticated markets', *Journal of Marketing*, 43 (4): 69–75.

Arup Bulletin (1995) *News from Ove Arup Partnership,* issue 145, November.

Ashkenas, R., Ulrich, D., Jick, T. and Kerr, S. (1995) *The Boundaryless Organization: Breaking the Chains of Organizational Structure.* San Francisco: Jossey-Bass.

Axelrod, R. (1985) 'An evolutionary approach to norms', *American Political Science Review,* 80: 1055–1111.

Bahrami, H. (1992) 'The emerging flexible organization. Perspectives from Silicon Valley', *California Management Review,* 34 (4): 33-52.

Baker, W. E. (1990) 'Market networks and corporate behaviour', *American Journal of Sociology,* 96: 589–625.

Baker, W.E. (1992) 'The network organization in theory and practice', in N. Nohria and R.G. Eccles (eds), *Networks and Organizations: Structure, Form, and Action.* Boston, MA: Harvard Business School Press. pp. 397–429.

Baldwin, T.T., Bedell, M.D. and Johnson, J.L. (1997) 'The social fabric of a team-based MBA-program: network effects on student satisfaction and performance', *Academy of Management Journal,* 40: 1369–1397.

Bantel, A. and Schär, M. (1998) 'Wir wollen allen zeigen wieviel Power wir haben', Interview with Göran Lindahl, *Cash,* 33, 14 August: 6–7.

Barham, K. and Heimer, C. (1998) *ABB – The Dancing Giant: Creating the Globally Connected Corporation.* London: Financial Times/Pitman Publishing.

Bartlett, C.A. (1986) 'Building and managing the transnational: the new organizational challenge', in M.E. Porter (ed.), *Competition in Global Industries.* Boston, MA: Harvard Business School Press. pp. 367–401.

Bartlett, C.A. and Ghoshal, S. (1986) 'Tap your subsidiaries for global reach', *Harvard Business Review,* November–December: 87–94.

Bartlett, C.A. and Ghoshal, S. (1989) *Managing across Borders: The Transnational Solution.* Boston, MA: Harvard Business School Press.

Bartlett, C.A. and Ghoshal, S. (1990) 'Matrix management: not a structure, a frame of mind', *Harvard Business Review,* 68 (4) July/August: 138–145.

Bartlett, C.A. and Ghoshal, S. (1993) 'Beyond the M-form: toward a managerial theory of the firm', *Strategic Management Journal,* 14 (Winter special issue): 23–46.

Bartlett, C.A. and Ghoshal, S. (1995a) 'Changing the role of top management: beyond systems to people', *Harvard Business Review,* 73 (3) May/June: 132–142.

Bartlett, C.A. and Ghoshal, S. (1995b) *Transnational Management. Text, Cases, and Readings in Cross-Border Management.* London: Irwin.

Baruel, J. (1996) 'Spain in the context of European human resource management', in T. Clark (ed.), *European Human Resource Management.* Oxford: Blackwell. pp. 93–117.

Baum, J.A.C. (1996) 'Organizational ecology', in S. Clegg, C. Hardy and W. Nord (eds), *Handbook of Organization Studies.* London: Sage pp. 77–114.

BBC Group (1987) *BBC Annual Report.* Baden.

Beatty, R.W. and Schneier, C.E. (1997) 'New HR roles to impact organizational performance: from "partners" to "players"', *Human Resource Management,* 36 (1): 29–37.

Beer, M. (1997) 'The transformation of the human resource function: resolving the tension between a traditional administrative and a new strategic role', *Human Resource Management,* 36 (1): 49–56.

Bendix, R. (1956) *Work and Authority in Industry.* New York: Wiley.

Bennett, J.K. and O'Brien, M.J. (1994) 'The building blocks of the learning organization', *Training,* 31 (6) June: 41–49.

Bennis, P. (1959) 'Organizational developments and the fate of bureaucracy', *Industrial Management Review,* 7: 41–57.

Betts, M. (1995) 'Turn your company into a cybercorp. It's wired. It's virtual. It's agile', *Computerworld,* 29, 9 October: 41.

Biemans, W. (1992) *Managing Innovation within Networks*. London, Routledge.

Blackler, F. (1995) 'Knowledge, knowledge work and organizations: an overview and interpretation', *Organization Studies*, 16 (6) 1021–1046.

Blau, J. (1980) 'When weak ties are structured'. Unpublished paper, Department of Sociology, State University of New York at Albany.

Blau, P.M. (1956) *Bureaucracy in Modern Society*. New York: Random House.

Blau, P.M. (1970) 'A formal theory of differentiation in organizations', *American Sociological Review*, 35 (2) 201–218.

Blau, P.M. and Schoenherr, R.A. (1971) *The Structure of Organizations*. New York, Basic Books.

Boisot, M. (1995) *Information Space: A Framework for Learning in Organizations, Institutions and Culture*. London: Routledge.

Boorman, S.A. and White, H.C. (1976) 'Social structure from multiple networks. II. Role structures', *American Journal of Sociology*, 81: 1384–1446.

Borys, B. and Jemison, D.B. (1989) 'Hybrid arrangements as strategic alliances: theoretical issues and organizational combinations', *Academy of Management Review*, 14 (April): 234–249.

Boudès, T., Charue-Duboc, F. and Midler, C. (1998) 'Project management learning: a contingent approach', in R.A. Lundin and C. Midler (eds), *Projects as Arenas for Renewal and Learning Processes*. Boston: Kluwer Academic.

Bouwen, R. and Fry, R. (1991) 'Organizational innovation and learning', *International Studies of Management & Organization*, 21: 37–51.

Boxer, P. and Wensley, R. (1997) 'Design control to achieve strategic advantage', *Long Range Planning*.

Bransky, J., Chartoff, M. and Gavurnin, S.L. (1995) 'Finding the best path to the branch office', *Business Communications Review*, 25 (3) March: 35–38.

Brousseau, K.R., Driver, M. J., Eneroth, K. and Rikard, L. (1996) 'Career pandemonium: realigning organizations and individuals', *Academy of Management Executive*, 10 (4): 52–66.

Brown, S.L. and Eisenhardt, K.M. (1998) *Competing on the Edge. Strategy as Structured Chaos*. Boston, MA: Harvard Business School Press.

Brusco, S. (1982) 'The Emilian model: productive decentralization and social integration', *Cambridge Journal of Economics*, 6: 167–184.

Bryman, A. (1989) *Research Methods and Organization Studies*. London: Routledge.

Burns, T. and Stalker, G.M. (1961) *The Management of Innovation*. London: Tavistock.

Burt, R.S. (1978) 'Cohesion versus structural equivalence as a basis for network subgroups', *Sociological Methods and Research*, 7: 189–212.

Burt, R.S. (1987) 'Social contagion and innovation: cohesion versus structural equivalence', *American Journal of Sociology*, 92: 1287–1335.

Burt, R.S. (1992) *Structural Holes: The Social Structure of Competition*. Cambridge, MA: Harvard University Press.

Burt, R.S. (1997) 'The contingent value of social capital', *Administrative Science Quarterly*, 42: 339–365.

Burt, R.S. and Minor, M.J. & Associates (eds) (1983) *Applied Network Analysis: A Methodological Introduction*. Beverly Hills, CA: Sage.

Bush, John B. Jr and Frohman, Alan L. (1991) 'Communication in a "network" organization', *Organizational Dynamics*, Autumn: 23-36.

Cable, J. and Dirrheimer, M.J. (1983) 'Hierarchies and markets: an empirical test of the multidivisional hypothesis in West Germany', *International Journal of Industrial Organization*, 1: 43-62.

Cable, J. and Yasuki, H. (1985) 'Internal organization, business groups and corporate performance: an empirical test of the multi-divisional hypothesis in Japan', *International Journal of Industrial Organization*: 401–420.

Calori, R., Lubatkin, M., Very, P. and Veiga, J.F. (1997) 'Modelling the origins of nationally-bound administrative heritages: a historical institutional analysis of French and British firms', *Organization Science*, 8 (6): 681–96.

Camerer, C. and Vepsalainen, A. (1988) 'The economic efficiency of corporate culture', *Strategic Management Journal*, 9: 115–126.

Campion, M.A., Papper, E.M. and Medsker, G.J. (1996) 'Relations between work team characteristics and effectiveness: a replication and extension', *Personnel Psychology*, 49: 429–452.

Castells, M. (1996) *The Rise of the Network Society*. Oxford: Blackwells.

Catrina, W. (1991) *BBC Glanz–Krise–Fusion 1891–1991 von Brown Boveri zu ABB*, 2nd edn. Zürich: Orell Füssli.

Chakravarthy, B.S. and Doz, Y. (1992) 'Strategy process research: focusing on corporate self-renewal', *Strategic Management Journal*, 13: 5–14.

Chakravarthy, B.S. and Gargiulo, M. (1998) 'Maintaining leadership legitimacy in the transformation to new organizational forms', *Journal of Management Studies*, 35 (4): 435–456.

Chandler, A.D. (1962) *Strategy and Structure: Chapters in the History of the American Industrial Enterprise*. Cambridge, MA: MIT Press.

Chandler, A.D. (1980) *The Visible Hand: The Managerial Revolution in American Business*. Cambridge, MA: Harvard University Press.

Chang, S. J. (1995) 'International expansion strategy of Japanese firms: capability building through sequential entry', *Academy of Management Journal*, 38: 383–407.

Channon, D. (1973) *The Strategy and Structure of British Enterprise*. Cambridge, MA: Harvard University Press.

Child, J. (1972) 'Organizational structure, environment and performance – the role of strategic choice', *Sociology*, 6 (1): 1–22.

Ciucci, R. (1996) 'Kommunikation als Kernfähigkeit: Ein integrales Konzept der Hilti AG', *Thexis*, 3: 38–42.

Clark, K.B. and Fujimoto, T. (1991) *Product Development Performance*. Boston, MA: Harvard Business School Press.

Clark, T. (1997) 'Derek Pugh: his contribution to the advancement of organizational behaviour', in T. Clark (ed.), *Organizational Behaviour: Essays in Honour of Derek, S. Pugh*. Aldershot, Hants: Ashgate. pp. 1–7.

Clutterbuck, D. (1993) 'Clarify your purpose', *Managing Service Quality*, November: 5–6.

Cohen, W.M. and Levinthal, D.A. (1990) 'Absorptive capacity: a new perspective on learning and innovation', *Administrative Science Quarterly*, 35: 128–152.

Coleman, J.S. (1990) *Foundations of Social Theory*. Cambridge, MA: Harvard University Press.

Collins, H. (1993) 'The structure of knowledge', *Social Research*, 60: 95–116.

Contractor, F.J. and Lorange, P. (1988) *Cooperative Strategies in International Business*. Lexington, MA: Lexington Books.

Cook, K.S. (1977) 'Exchange and power in networks of interorganizational relations', *Sociological Quarterly*, 18: 62–82.

Cooper, D., Hinings, C. R., Greenwood, R. and Brown J. (1996) 'Sedimentation and transformation in organizational change: the case of Canadian law firms', *Organization Studies*, 17 (4): 623–637.

Costa, M.T. (1995) 'La empresa: características, estrategias y resultados', in J. L. García Delgado, R. Myro and J.A. Martínez (eds), *Lecciones de Economía Española*, 2nd edn. Madrid: Civitas, pp. 285–303.

Coulson-Thomas, C. and Coe, T. (1991) *The Flat Organization*. London: British Institute of Management.

Crane, D.B. and Bodie, Z. (1996) 'Form follows function: the transformation of banking', *Harvard Business Review*, 74 (2): 109–117.

Crouch, C. (1993) *Industrial Relations and European State Traditions*. Oxford: Clarendon Press.

Daft, R.L. and Lewin, A.Y. (1993) 'Where are the theories for the "New" organizational forms? An editorial essay', *Organization Science*, 4 (4) November: i–vi.

Damanpour, F. and Evan, W. (1984) 'Organizational innovation and performance: the problem of "organizational lag"', *Administrative Science Quarterly*, 29: 392–409.

D'Aveni, R.A. (1994) *Hypercompetition: Managing the Dynamic of Strategic Manoeuvring*. New York: Free Press.

Davenport, T.H., De Long, D.W and Beers, M.C. (1998) 'Successful knowledge management projects', *Sloan Management Review*, Winter: 43–57.

Davis, F.W. Jr (1993) 'Managing for flexibility and responsiveness', *Survey of Business*, 29 (1) Summer/Fall: 22–27.

Davis, J.H., Schoorman, F.D. and Donaldson, L. (1997) 'Toward a stewardship theory of management', *Academy of Management Review*, 22 (1): 20–47.

Davis, S.M. and Lawrence, P.R. (1977) *Matrix*. Reading, MA: Addison-Wesley.

Dean, J.W. and Sussman, G.I. (1989) 'Strategic responses to global competition: advanced technology, organization design, and human resource practices', in C.C. Snow (ed.), *Strategy, Organization, and Human Resource Management*. Greenwich, CT: JAI Press. pp. 297–331.

De Cock, C. (1998) 'Seems to fill my head with ideas: a few thoughts on postmodernism, TQM, and BPR', *Journal of Management Inquiry*, 7: 144–153.

DeFillippi, R.J. and Arthur, M.B. (1998) 'Paradox in project-based enterprise: the case of film making', *California Management Review*, 40: 125–139.

DeMent, J. (1996) 'Managers, leaders, and teams in a team-based environment', *Hospital Materiel Management Quarterly*, 18: 1–9.

Demsetz, H. (1991) 'The theory of the firm revisited', in O.E. Williamson and S. Winter (eds), *The Nature of the Firm*, New York: Oxford University Press. pp. 159–178.

Denison, D.R. (1997) 'Toward a process-based theory of organizational design: can organizations be designed around value chains and networks?' in *Advances in Strategic Management*, vol. 14. Greenwich, CT: JAI Press. pp. 1–44.

Denzin, N.K. (1978) *The Research Act*, 2nd edn. New York: McGraw-Hill.

DeSanctis, G. and Staudenmayer, N. (1998) 'Interdependence in virtual organizations'. Paper presented at the 14th EGOS Colloquium, Mastricht, The Netherlands, 9–11 July.

Djelic, M-L. (1998) *Exporting the American Model: The Postwar Transformation of European Business*. Oxford: Oxford University Press.

Dodgson, M. (1993) 'Organizational learning: a review of some literatures', *Organization Studies*, 14: 375–394.

Donaldson, L. (1996) *For Positivist Organization Theory*. London: Sage.

Donaldson, L. (1997) 'Derek Pugh: scientific revolutionary in organization studies', in T. Clark (ed.), *Organizational Behaviour: Essays in Honour of Derek, S. Pugh* . Aldershot, Hants: Ashgate. pp. 23–43.

Donovan, M. (1989a) 'Employees who manage themselves', *Journal for Quality & Participation*, 12 (1) March: 58–61.

Donovan, M. (1989b) 'Redesigning the workplace', *Journal for Quality & Participation*, December: 6–8.

Dore, R. (1983) *Taking Japan Seriously*. Stanford, CA: Stanford University Press.

Dow, S. (1995) 'Integrating hubs, switches and routers in virtual networks', *Computing Canada, Communications & Networking Supplement*, September: 33–34.

Drazin, R. and Van de Ven, A. H. (1985) 'Alternative forms of fit in contingency theory', *Administrative Science Quarterly*, 30 (4): 514–540.

Drucker, P.F. (1988) 'The coming of the new organization', *Harvard Business Review*, 66 (1) January/February 45–53.

Drucker, P.F. (1993) *Post-capitalist Society*. Oxford: Butterworth Heinemann.

Dyas, G.P. and Thanheiser, H.T. (1976) *The Emerging European Enterprise*. London: Macmillan.

Dyer, J.H. and Singh, H. (1998) 'The relational view: cooperative strategy and sources of interorganizational competitive advantage', *Academy of Management Review*, 23 (4): 660–679.

Easton, G. and Araujo, L. (1994) 'Market exchange, social structures and time', *European Journal of Marketing*, 28 (3): 72–84.

Eccles, R.J. (1981) 'The quasi firm in the construction industry', *Journal of Economic Behaviour and Organizations*, 2: 235–257.

Eisenhardt, K.M. (1989a) 'Making fast strategic decisions in high-velocity environments', *Academy of Management Journal*, 32: 543–576.

Eisenhardt, K.M. (1989b) 'Building theories from case study research', *Academy of Management Review*, 14 (4): 532–550.

Emery, F.E. and Trist, E.L. (1965) 'The causal texture of organizational environments', *Human Relations*, 18: 21–32.

Eriksson, S. (1995) *Global Shift in the Aircraft Industry*. Gothenburg: School of Economics and Commercial Law, University of Gothenburg.

Etzioni, A. (1961) *A Comparative Analysis of Complex Organizations*. New York: Free Press.

Evans, P. and Doz, Y.(1992) 'A paradigm for human resource and organizational development in complex multinational', in V. Pucik, N. M. Tichy and C. V. Bartlett (eds), *Globalizing Management*. New York, John Wiley.

Ezzamel, M. and Watson, R. (1993) 'Organizational form, ownership structure and corporate performance: a contextual empirical analysis of UK companies', *British Journal of Management*, 4 (3): 161–176.

Ezzamel, M., Lilley, S. and Willmott, H. (1994) 'The "new organization" and the "new managerial work"', *European Management Journal*, 12 (4): 454–461.

Ezzamel, M., Lilley, S. and Willmott, H. (1996) 'The view from the top: senior executives' perceptions of changing management practices in UK companies', *British Journal of Management*, 7 (2): 155–168.

Farley, J. and Kobrin, S. (1995) 'Organizing the global multinational firm', in E. H. Bowman and B.M. Kogut (eds), *Redesigning the Firm*. New York: Oxford University Press. pp. 197–217.

Fenton, E.M., Peck, S.I., Pettigrew, A.M. and Whittington, R. (1997) 'The new internal network organization: evidence from the UK.' Paper presented to the 17th Annual International Conference of the Strategic Management Society, Managing in an Interconnected World, Barcelona, 5–8 October.

Ferlie, E. and Pettigrew, A.M. (1996) 'Managing through networks: some issues and implications for the NHS', *British Journal of Management*, 7 (special issue) March: S81–S99.

Fligstein, N. (1990) *The Transformation of Corporate Control*. Cambridge, MA: Harvard University Press.

Friar, J. and Horwitch, M. (1985) 'The emergence of technology strategy: a new dimension of strategic management', *Technology in Society*, 72 (3): 143–178.

Friedrich, C.J. (1950) *Constitutional Government and Democracy*. Boston: Little, Brown.

Friedrich, C.J. (1952) 'Some observations on Weber's analysis of bureaucracy', in R. K. Merton et al. (eds), *Reader in Bureaucracy*. London: Collier-Macmillan.

Fulk, J. and DeSanctis, G. (1995) 'Electronic communication and changing organizational forms', *Organization Science*, 6: 337–349.

Galagan, P.A. (1992) 'Beyond hierarchy: the search for high performance', *Training & Development*, 46 (8), August: 20–25.

Galbraith, J. (1973) *Designing Complex Organizations*. Reading, MA: Addison-Wesley.

Galbraith, J.R. (1995) *Designing Organizations: An Executive Briefing on Strategy, Structure, and Process*. San Francisco: Jossey-Bass.

Galliers, R.D. and Baets, W.R.J. (eds) (1998) *Information Technology and Organizational Transformation*. Chichester: John Wiley.

Galunic, D.C. and Eisenhardt, K.M. (1994) 'Renewing the strategy–structure–performance paradigm', in L.L. Cummings and B.M. Staw (eds), *Research in Organizational Behaviour*, vol. 16. Greenwich, CT: JAI Press. pp. 215–255.

Galunic, D.C. and Rodan, S. (1998) 'Resource recombinations in the firm: knowledge structures and the potential for Schumpeterian innovation', *Strategic Management Journal*, 19 (12): 1193–1201.

García Delgado, J.L. (1995) 'Etapas y rasgos definidores de la industrialización española', in J.L. García Delgado, R. Myro and J.A. Martínez (eds), *Lecciones de Economía Española*, 2nd edn. Madrid: Civitas. pp. 21–47.

Gastil, J. (1994) 'A definition and illustration of democratic leadership', *Human Relations*, 47 (8): 953–975.

General Electric (1997) *Annual Report*.

Geroski, P. and Gregg, P. (1994) 'Corporate restructuring in the UK during the recession', *Business Strategy Review*, 5 (2) Summer: 1–19.

Ghoshal, S. and Bartlett, C. (1990) 'The multinational corporation as an interorganizational network', *Academy of Management Review*, 15 (4): 603–625.

Ghoshal, S. and Bartlett, C.A. (1995a) 'Changing the role of top management: beyond structure to process', *Harvard Business Review*, January/February: 86–96.

Ghoshal, S. and Bartlett, C.A. (1995b) 'Building the entrepreneurial corporation: new organizational processes, new managerial tasks', *European Management Journal*, 13 (2) June: 139–155.

Ghoshal, S. and Bartlett, C.A. (1997) *The Individualized Corporation*. San Francisco: Harper Business.

Ghoshal, S. and Bartlett, C.A. (1998) *The Individualized Corporation: A Fundamentally New Approach to Management*. London: Heinemann.

Ghoshal, S. and Moran, P. (1996) 'Bad for practice: a critique of transaction cost theory', *Academy of Management Review*, 21 (1): 13–47.

Ghoshal, S. and Nohria, N. (1993) 'Horses for courses: organizational forms for multinational corporations', *Sloan Management Review*, Winter: 23–35.

Glaser, B. and Strauss, A. (1967) *The Discovery of Grounded Theory: Strategies of Qualitative Research*. London: Weidenfeld & Nicolson.

Goldhar, J.D. and Lei, D. (1991) 'The shape of twenty-first century global manufacturing', *Journal of Business Strategy*, 12 (2) March/April: 37–41.

Gouldner, A.W. (1955) *Patterns of Industrial Bureaucracy*. London: Routledge & Kegan Paul.

Grandori, A. (1997) 'Governance structures, coordination mechanisms and cognitive models', *Journal of Management and Governance*, 1: 29–47.

Granovetter, M.S. (1973) 'The strength of weak ties', *American Journal of Sociology*, 78: 1360–1380.

Granovetter, M.S. (1982) 'The strength of weak ties: a network theory revisited', in P. Marsden and N. Lin (eds), *Social Structure and Network Analysis*. Beverly Hills, CA: Sage. pp. 105–130.

Granovetter, M.S. (1985) 'Economic action and social structure: the problem of embeddedness', *American Journal of Sociology*, 91: 481–510.

Granovetter, M.S. (1992) 'Problems of explanation in economic sociology', in N. Nohria and R.G. Eccles (eds), *Networks and Organizations: Structure, Form and Action*. Boston: Harvard Business School Press. pp. 25–56.

Grant, R.M. (1996a) 'Prospering in dynamically competitive environments: organizational capability as knowledge integration', *Organization Science*, 7 (4): 375–387.

Grant, R.M. (1996b) 'Toward a knowledge-based theory of the firm', *Strategic Management Journal*, 17 (Winter special issue): 109–122.

Gresov, C. and Drazin, R. (1997) 'Equifinality: functional equivalence in organizational design', *Academy of Management Review*, 22 (2): 403–428.

Grinyer, P.H., Yasai-Ardekani, M. and Al-Bazzaz, S. (1980) 'Strategy, structure, the environment and financial performance in 48 United Kingdom companies', *Academy of Management Journal*, 23 (2): 193–220.

Guia, J. and Camison, C. (1998) 'Co-ordination and control of sequential activities: a microlevel model of organization forms'. Paper presented to the 14th EGOS Colloquium, Subtheme 19: Relational perspectives on organizational forms, Maastricht, July.

Guillen, M.F. (1994) *Models of Management: Work, Authority and Organization in a Comparative Perspective*. Chicago: University of Chicago Press.

Gulati, R. (1995) 'Social structure and alliance formation patterns: a longitudinal analysis', *Administrative Science Quarterly*, 40: 619–652.

Gummer, B. (1995) 'Reinventing, restructuring, and the big band theory of organizational change', *Administration in Social Work*, 19 (3): 83–97.

Hagedoorn, J. (1991) 'Global strategies in innovation: networks in research and production', *International Journal of Technology Management*, 81–94.

Haige, J. and Aiken, M. (1967) 'Relationship of centralization to other structural properties', *Administrative Science Quarterly*, 12: 72–92.

Halal, W. (1993) 'The transition from hierarchy to . . . what?' in W. Halal, A. Geranmayeh and J. Pourdehnad (eds), *Internal Markets: Bringing the Power of Free Enterprise Inside Your Organization*. New York: Wiley.

Hall, L. and Torrington, D. (1998) *The Human Resource Function. The Dynamics of Change and Development*. London: Pitman Publishing.

Hambrick, D.C.(1983) 'An empirical typology of mature industrial product environments', *Academy of Management Journal*, 26: 213–230.

Hambrick, D.C. and Schecter, S. (1983) 'Turnaround strategies for mature industrial-product business units', *Academy of Management Journal*, 26: 231–248.

Hambrick, D.C., Davison, C. Snell, S., Scot, A. and Snow, C. (1998a) 'When groups consist of multiple nationalities', *Organization Studies*, 19 (2): 181–205.

Hambrick, D.C., Nadler, D.A. and Tushman, M.L.(eds) (1998b) *Navigating Change: How CEOs, Top Teams and Boards Steer Transformation*. Boston, MA: Harvard Business School Press.

Hamel, G. (1991) 'Competition for competence and inter-partner learning within international strategic alliances', *Strategic Management Journal*, 12: 83–103.

Hamel, G., Doz, Y.L. and Prahalad, C.K. (1989) 'Collaborate with your competitors – and win', *Harvard Business Review*, January/February: 133–139.

Hammer, M. and Champy, J. (1993) *Reengineering the Corporation*. New York: Harper Business.

Hampden-Turner, C. (1981) *Maps of the Mind. Charts and Concepts of the Mind and its Labyrinths*. New York: Collier.

Handy, C. (1990) *The Age of Unreason*. London: Arrow Books.

Handy, C. (1992) 'Balancing corporate power: a new federalist organization', *Harvard Business Review*, November–December. pp. 59–72.

Handy, C. (1996) 'Rethinking organizations', in T. Clark (ed.), *Advancement in Organizational Behaviour: Essays in Honour of Derek, S. Pugh*. Aldershot, Hants: Ashgate. pp. 187–195.

Hannan, M.T. and Freeman, J. (1977) 'The population ecology of organizations', *American Journal of Sociology*, 83: 929–964.

Hannan, M.T. and Freeman, J. (1989) *Organizational Ecology*, Cambridge, MA: Harvard University Press.

Hansen, M.T. (1999) 'The search-transfer problem: the role of weak ties in sharing knowledge across organizational subunits', *Administrative Science Quarterly*, 44: 82–111.

Hastings, C. (1996) *The New Organization. Growing the Culture of Organizational Networking*. London: McGraw-Hill.

Heckscher, C. (1994) 'Defining the post-bureaucratic type', in C. Heckscher and A. Donnellon (eds), *The Post-Bureaucratic Organization: New Perspectives on Organizational Change*. Thousand Oaks, CA: Sage. pp. 14–62.

Hedberg, B.L.T., Nystrom, P C. and Starbuck, W.H. (1976) 'Camping on seesaws: prescriptions for a self-designing organization', *Administrative Science Quarterly*, 21 (1): 41–65.

Hedlund, G. (1986) 'The hypermodern MNC: a heterarchy?' *Human Resource Management*, 25 (1): 9–35.

Hedlund, G. (1994) 'A model of knowledge management and the N-form corporation', *Strategic Management Journal*, 15 (Summer special issue): 73–90.

Hedlund, G. and Ridderstråle, J. (1997) 'Toward a theory of the self-renewing MNC', in B. Toyne and D. Nigh (eds), *International Business: An Emerging Vision*. Columbia, SC: University of South Carolina Press. pp. 329–354.

Heide, J.B. and John, G. (1992) 'Do norms matter in marketing relationships?' *Journal of Marketing*, 56 (April): 32–44.

Helgesen, S. (1995) 'Beyond teams', *Across the Board*, 32 (8): 43–48.

Hennart, J.F. (1993) *A Theory of Multinational Enterprise*. Ann Arbor: University of Michigan Press.

Hergert, M. and Morris, D. (1988) 'Trends in international collaborative agreeements', in F. Contractor and P. Lorange (eds), *Cooperative Strategies in International Business*. Lexington, MA: Lexington Books. pp. 99–109.

Hill, C.W.L. (1988a) 'Differentiation versus low cost or differentiation and low cost: a contingency framework', *Academy of Management Review*, 13: 401–412.

Hill, C.W.L. (1988b) 'Internal capital markets controls and financial performance in multidivisional firms', *Journal of Industrial Economics*, 37: 67–83.

Hill, C.W.L and Pickering, J. F. (1986) 'Divisionalisation, decentralisation and performance in large United Kingdom companies', *Journal of Management Studies*, 23: 26–50.

Hilti, M. (1995) *On his 80th Birthday*, Schaan: Hilti A.G.

Hinings, C.R., Thibault, L., Slack, T. and Kikulis, L.M. (1996) 'Values and organizational structure', *Human Relations*, 49 (7): 885–915.

Hirschhorn, L. (1991) *Managing in the New Team Environment*. Reading, MA: Addison-Wesley.

Horton, R.B. (1992) '"Surprise" governance', *Directors & Boards*, 16 (3) Spring: 9–11.

Hoskisson, R.E., Hill, C.W.L. and Kim, H. (1993) 'The multidivisional structure: organizational fossil or source of value?' *Journal of Management*, 19, (2): 269–298.

Huber, G.P. (1991) 'Organizational learning: the contributing processes and the literatures', *Organization Science*, 2: 88–115.

Hummel, R. (1990) 'Mit Beratungskompetenz zum Marktleader', *io Management Zeitschrift*, 59 (6): 8–15.

Ichijo, K. and Nonaka, I. (1998) 'Managing cross-divisional interconnections to create knowledge-based competence in a multidivisional firm', in M. A. Hitt, J.E. Ricart and R.D. Nixon (eds), *New Managerial Mindsets: Organizational Transformation and Strategy Implementation*. Chichester, UK: Wiley. pp. 151–166.

Ichniowski, C., Shaw, K. and Prenushi, G. (1997) 'The effects of human resource management practices on productivity: a study of steel finishing lines', *American Economic Review*, June, 291–314.

Ingram, P. and Baum, J. (1997) 'Opportunity and constraint: organizations' learning from the operating and competitive experience of industries', *Strategic Management Journal*, 18 (Summer special issue): 75–98.

Jaffe, D.T. and Scott, C.D. (1998) 'Reengineering in practice: where are the people? Where is the learning?' *Journal of Applied Behavioral Science.*, 34: 250–267.

Janssens, A. and Steyaert, C. (1999) 'The world in two and a third way out? The concept of duality in organization theory and practice', *Scandinavian Journal of Management*, 15: 121–139.

Jarillo, J.C. (1988) 'On strategic networks', *Strategic Management Journal*, 9: 31–41.

Jarvenpaa, S.L. and Ives, B. (1994) 'The global network organization of the future: information management opportunities and challenges', *Journal of Management Information Systems*, 10: 25–48.

Jensen, M.C. and Meckling, W.H. (1976) 'Theory of the firm: managerial behaviour, agency costs and ownership structure', *Journal of Financial Economics*, 3: 305–360.

Jessen, S.A. (1996) *The Nature of Project Leadership*. Oslo: Scandinavian University Press.

Jick, T.D. (1979) 'Mixing qualitative and quantitative methods: triangulation in action', *Administrative Science Quarterly*, December: 24.

Johansson, J. and Mattsson, L.-G. (1985) 'Market investments and marketing investments in industrial networks', *International Journal of Research in Marketing*, 3 (2): 185–195.

John, G. and Weitz, B. (1988) 'Forward integration and distribution: an empirical test of transaction cost analysis', *Journal of Law, Economics and Organization*, 2: 121–139.

Jones, C. (1991) 'Qualitative interviewing', in G. Allan, and C. Skinner (eds), *Handbook for Research Students in Social Sciences*. London: Falmer Press. pp. 203–214.

Jones, C., Hesterly, W.S. and Borgatti, S.P. (1997) 'A general theory of network governance: exchange conditions and social mechanisms', *Academy of Management Review*, 22 (4): 911–945.

Kagono, T., Nonaka, I., Sakakibara, K. and Okumura, A. (1985) *Strategic vs. Evolutionary Management: A US–Japan Comparison of Strategy and Organization*. Amsterdam: North-Holland Press.

Kanter, R.M. (1983) *The Change Masters*. New York: Simon & Schuster.

Kanter, R.M. and Eccles, R.G. (1992) 'Conclusion: making network research relevant to practice', in N. Nohria and R.G. Eccles (eds), *Networks and Organizations. Structure, Form, and Action*. Boston: Harvard Business School. pp. 521–527.

Kanter, R.M., Stein, B.A. and Jick, T.D. (1992) *The Challenge of Organizational Change. How Companies Experience It and Leaders Guide It*. New York: Free Press/Macmillan.

Keidel, R.W. (1990) 'Triangular design: a new organizational geometry', *Academy of Management Executive.*, 4: 21–37.

Ketchen, D.J., Thomas, J.B. and Snow, C. (1993) 'Organizational configuration and performance: a comparison of theoretical approaches', *Academy of Management Journal*, 36: 1278–1313.

Kets de Vries, M. (1994) 'Making a giant dance', *Across the Board*, 31 (9) October: 27–32.

Kim, W.C. and Mauborgne, R. (1997) 'Fair process: managing in the knowledge economy', *Harvard Business Review*, July–August: 65–75.

Knight, K.E. (1967) 'A descriptive model of the intra-firm innovation process', *Journal of Business*, 40: 478–496.

Knorr, R.O. (1990a) 'Managing resources for world-class performance', *Journal of Business Strategy*, 11 (1) January/February: 48–50.

Knorr, R.O. (1990b) 'Strategic restructuring for the 1990s', *Journal of Business Strategy*, 11 (3) May/June: 59–60.

Kogut, B. (1983) 'Foreign direct investment as a sequential process', in C. Kindleberger and D. Audretsch (eds), *The Multinational Corporation in the 1980s*. Cambridge, MA: MIT Press. pp. 38–56.

Kogut, B. (1992) 'National organizing principles of work and the erstwhile dominance of the American multinational corporation', *Industrial and Corporate Change*, 1 (2): 285–325.

Kogut, B. and Bowman, E.H. (1995) 'Modularity and permeability as principles of design', in E.H. Bowman and B. Kogut (eds), *Redesigning the Firm*. Oxford: Oxford University Press. pp. 243–260.

Kogut, B. and Zander, U. (1992) 'Knowledge of the firm, combinative capabilities and the replication of technology', *Organization Science*, 3: 383–397.

Köhler, C. and Woodard, J. (1997) 'Systems of work and socio-economic structures: a comparison of Germany, Spain, France and Japan', *European Journal of Industrial Relations*, 3 (1): 59–82.

Konstadt, P. (1990) 'Into the Breach', *CIO*, 11 (August) 71–73.

Krackhardt, D. (1990) 'Assessing the political landscape: structure, cognition and power in organizations', *Administrative Science Quarterly*, 35: 342–369.

Lado, A.A. and Wilson, M.C. (1994) 'Human resource systems and competitive advantage: a competency-based perspective', *Academy of Management Review*, 19 (4): 699–727.

Larson, E. and Gobeli, D. (1987) 'Matrix management: contradictions and insights', *California Management Review*, 29 (4) Summer: 126–138.

Lasserre, P. and Schütte, H. (1995) *Strategies for Asia Pacific*. London: Macmillan Press.

Lawler, E.E. (1992) *The Ultimate Advantage. Creating the High-involvement Organization*. San Francisco: Jossey-Bass.

Lawrence, P.R. and Lorsch, J.W. (1967a) 'Differentiation and integration in complex organizations', *Administrative Science Quarterly*, 12: 1–47.

Lawrence, P.R. and Lorsch, J.W. (1967b) *Organization and Environment: Managing Differentiation and Integration*. Boston, MA: Division of Research, Graduate School of Business, Harvard University.

Lee, J. (1993) 'The evolution of organizational adaptation in Korea', *Journal of Asian Business*, 9 (4) Fall: 72–89.

Leth, S.A. (1994) 'Critical success factors for reengineering business processes', *National Productivity Review*, 13 (4) Autumn: 557–568.

Levinthal, D.A. and March, J.G. (1993) 'The myopia of learning', *Strategic Management Journal*, 14 (Winter special issue): 95–112.

Levitt, B. and March, J.G. (1988) 'Organizational learning', *Annual Review of Sociology*, 14: 319–340.

Lewin, A.Y., Long, C. P. and Carroll, T. N. (1999) 'The co-evolution of new organization forms', *Organization Science*, 10 (5): 535–550.

Lewis, J.D. (1990) *Partnerships for Profit: Structuring and Managing Strategic Alliances*. New York: Free Press.

Liebeskind, J.P. (1996) 'Knowledge strategy, and the theory of the firm', *Strategic Management Journal*, 17 (Winter Special Issue) 93–107.

Lincoln, J.R. (1982) 'Intra-(and inter-) organizational networks', in *Research in the Sociology of Organizations*, vol. 1. Greenwich, CT: JAI Press. pp. 1–38.

Lindahl, G. (1999) 'Bereit für die Herausforderungen der Zukunft', *Die Volkswirtschaft – Magazin für Wirtschaftspolitik*, 3: 6–9.

Lindenberg, S. (1997) 'Solidarity and relational signalling: their workings and importance for contracting'. Paper presented to the 14th EGOS Colloquium, Subtheme 19: Relational Perspectives on Organizational Forms, Maastricht, July.

Little, B.L. and Madigan, R.M. (1997) 'The relationship between collective efficacy and performance in manufacturing work teams', *Small Group Research*, 28: 517–534.

Locke, R.L. (1996) *The Collapse of the American Management Mystique*. Oxford: Oxford University Press.

Loewenstein, G.F. and Elster, J. (eds) (1992) *Choice over Time*. New York: Russell Sage.

Lorange, P. and Roos, J. (1992) *Strategic Alliances: Formation, Implementation and Evolution*. Oxford: Blackwells.

Lorenzoni, G. and Ornati, O. (1988) 'Constellations of firms and new ventures', *Journal of Business Venturing*, 3: 41–57.

Lowendahl, B. (1997) *Strategic Management of Professional Service Firms*. Copenhagen: Handelshojskolens Forlag.

Lundin, R.A. and Midler, C. (1998) 'Evolution of projects as empirical trend and theoretical focus', in R.A. Lundin, and C. Midler (eds), *Projects as Arenas for Renewal and Learning Processes*. Boston: Kluwer Academic. pp. 1–10.

Lundin, R.A. and Sôderholm, A. (1998) 'Conceptualizing a projectified society: discussion of an eco-institutional approach to a theory on temporary organizations', in R.A. Lundin, and C. Midler (eds), *Projects as Arenas for Renewal and Learning Processes*. Boston: Kluwer Academic. pp. 24–24.

Maccoby, M. (1991) 'Move from hierarchy to heterarchy', *Research Technology Management*, 34: 46–49.

MacDuffie, J.P. (1995) 'Human resource boundless and manufacturing performance: organizational logic and flexible production systems in the world auto industry', *Industrial and Labour Relations Review*, 48: 197–221.

Malnight, T.W. (1995) 'Globalization of an ethnocentric firm: an evolutionary perspective', *Strategic Management Journal*, 16: 119–141.

Malone, T.W., Morton, M.S.S. and Halperin, R.R. (1996) 'Organizing for the 21st century', *Strategy and Leadership*, 24 (4): 6–10.

March, A. and Garvin, D.A. (1997) 'A Note on Knowledge Management', Harvard Business School Note 9–398–031.

March, J.G. (1991) 'Exploration and exploitation in organizational learning', *Organization Science*, 2: 71–87.

March, J.G. (1995) 'The future, disposable organizations, and the rigidities of imagination', *Organization*, 2 (3/4): 427–440.

March, J. G. (1999) *The Pursuit of Organizational Intelligence*. Oxford: Blackwell.

March, J.G. and Simon, H.A. (1958) *Organizations*. New York: John Wiley.

Mariotti, S. and Cainarca, G.C. (1986) 'The evolution of transaction governance in the textile-clothing industry', *Journal of Economic Behaviour and Organization*, 7: 351–374.

Mariti, P. and Smiley, R.H. (1983) 'Co-operative agreements and the organization of industry', *Journal of Industrial Economics*, 31 (4): 437–451.

Markides, C.C. and Williamson, P.J. (1996) 'Corporate diversification and organizational structure: a resource-based view', *Academy of Management Journal*, 39 (2): 340–368.

Martinez, J.I. and Jarillo, J.C. (1989) 'The evolution of research on coordination mechanisms in multi national corporations', *Journal of International Business Studies*, 20 (Fall): 489–514.

Martínez, M. (1998) 'Spain: regulating employment and social fragmentation', in A. Ferner and R. Hyman (eds), *Changing Industrial Relations in Europe*. Oxford: Blackwell. pp. 426–458.

McArthur, J. and Scott, B. (1968) *Industrial Planning in France*. Boston, MA: Harvard Business School.

McCollum, J. and Sherman, J. (1993) 'The matrix structure: bane or benefit to high tech organizations?' *Project Management Journal*, 24 (2) June: 23–26.

McHugh, P.P. (1997) 'Team-based work systems: lessons from the industrial relations literature', *Human Resource Planning*, 20: 44–47.

McKelvey, B. (1981) *Organizational Systematics*. Los Angeles: University of California Press.

McKelvey, B. (1997) 'Quasi-national Organization Science', *Organization Science*, 8 (4): 352–380.

McKenna, C.D. (1997) 'The American challenge: McKinsey & Company's role in the transfer of decentralisation to Europe', 1957–1975', *Academy of Management Best Paper Proceedings*, 226–231.

Meckstroth, D.J. (1994) 'Reengineering US manufacturing: implications of structural changes in the US economy', *Business Economics*, 29 (3): 43–49.

Melcher, A., Acar, W., DuMont, P. and Khouja, M. (1992) 'Standard-maintaining and continuous-improvement systems: experiences and comparisons', *Interfaces*, 20 (3) May/June: 24–40.

Melin, L., Ericson, T. and Müllern, T. (1999) 'Organizing is strategizing'. Paper presented to the INNFORM Symposium, US Academy of Management, Chicago, 9–11 August.

Merrill Lynch (1998) *Investor Relations Report on General Electric*. Merrill Lynch & Co. Research Department, 15 September.

Merton, R. K. (1940) 'Bureaucratic structure and personality', *Social Forces*, 23: 560–568.

Meyer, A.D., Goes, J.B. and Brooks, G.R. (1993a) 'Organizations reacting to hyperturbulance', in G. Huber and W. Glick (eds), *Organizational Change and Redesign*. New York: Oxford University Press. pp. 66–111.

Meyer, A.D., Tsui, A.S. and Hinings, C.R. (1993b) 'Introduction: configurational approaches to organizational analysis', *Academy of Management Journal*, 36: 1175–1195.

Meyerson, D., Weick, K.E. and Kramer, R.M. (1996) 'Swift trust and temporary groups', in R. M. Kramer and T. R. Tyler (eds), *Trust in Organizations: Frontiers of Theory and Research*. Thousand Oaks, CA: Sage. pp. 166–195.

Miles, M.B. and Huberman, A.M. (1994) *Qualitative Data Analysis. An Expanded Sourcebook*, 2nd edn. Thousand Oaks, CA: Sage.

Miles, R.E. and Creed, W.E.D. (1995) 'Organizational forms and managerial philosophies: a descriptive and analytical review', in B.M. Staw and L.L. Cummings (eds), *Research in Organizational Behavior*, vol. 17. Greenwich, CT: JAI Press. pp. 333–372.

Miles, R.E. and Snow, C.C. (1978) *Organizational Strategy, Structure and Process*. New York: McGraw-Hill.

Miles, R.E. and Snow, C.C. (1986) 'Network organizations: new concepts for new forms', *California Management Review*, 28: 62–73.

Miles, R.E. and Snow, C.C. (1992) 'Causes of failure in network organizations', *California Management Review*, 34: 53–62.

Miles, R.E. and Snow, C.C. (1993) 'Internal markets and network organizations' in W. E. Halal, A. Geranmayeh and J. Pardehnad (eds), *Internal Markets: Bringing the Power of Free Enterprise Inside Your Organization*, New York: John Wiley. pp. 67–86.

Miles, R.E. and Snow, C.C. (1994) *Fit, Failure, and the Hall of Fame*. New York: Free Press.

Miles, R.E. and Snow, C.C. (1995) 'The new network firm: a spherical structure built on a human investment philosophy', *Organizational Dynamics*, 23 (4): 4–15.

Miles, R.E., Snow, C.C., Mathews, J.A., Miles, G. and Coleman, Jr, H.J. (1997) 'Organizing in the knowledge age: anticipating the cellular form', *Academy of Management Executive.*, 11: 7–24.

Milgrom, P. and Roberts, J. (1990) 'The economics of modern manufacturing', *American Economic Review*, 80 (3): 511–528.

Milgrom, P. and Roberts, J. (1995) 'Complementarities and fit: strategy, structure and organizational change in manufacturing', *Journal of Accounting and Economics*, 19 (2/3): 179–208.

Miller, D. (1986) 'Configurations of strategy and structure: towards a synthesis', *Strategic Management Journal*, 7: 233–249.

Miller, D. (1987) 'The genesis of configuration', *Academy of Management Review*, 12 (4): 686–701.

Miller, D. (1996) 'Configurations revisited', *Strategic Management Journal*, 17: 505–512.

Miller, D. and Friesen, P.H. (1977) 'Strategy making in context: ten empirical archetypes', *Journal of Management Studies*, 14: 259–280.

Miller, D. and Friesen, P.H. (1978) 'Archetypes of strategy formulation', *Management Science*, 24: 921–933.

Miller, D. and Mintzberg, H. (1984) 'The case for configuration', in D. Miller and P. Friesen (eds), *Organizations: A Quantum View*. Englewood Cliffs, NJ: Prentice Hall. pp. 10–30.

Mingers, J. (1995) *Self-producing Systems: Implications and Applications of Autopoieses*. New York and London: Plenum Press.

Mintzberg, H. (1979) *The Structuring of Organizations*. Englewood Cliffs, NJ: Prentice Hall,

Mintzberg, H. (1983) *Power in and around Organizations*. Englewood Cliffs, NJ: Prentice Hall.

Mirvis, P.H. (1997) 'Human resource management: leaders, laggards, and followers', *Academy of Management Executive.*, 11: 43–56.

Mitsubishi Group (1998) *Annual Report*.

Moran, P. and Ghoshal, S. (1996) 'Value creation by firms', *Academy of Management Best Paper Proceedings*: 41–45.

Mowery, D.C. (ed.) (1988) *International Collaborative Ventures in US Manufacturing*. Cambridge, MA: Ballinger.

Nahapiet, J. and Ghoshal, S. (1998) 'Social capital, intellectual capital and the creation of value in firms', *Academy of Management Best Paper Proceedings*: 35–39.

Nelson, R. and Winter, S. (1982) *An Evolutionary Theory of Economic Change*. Cambridge, MA: Belknap.

Nienstedt, P.R. (1989) 'Effectively downsizing management structures', *Human Resource Management*, 12 (2): 155–165.

Nohria, N. (1992) 'Introduction: is a network perspective a useful way of studying organizations?' in N. Nohria and R.G. Eccles (eds), *Networks and Organizations: Structure, Form and Action*. Boston, MA: Harvard Business School Press. pp. 1–22.

Nohria, N. (1996) *From the M-form to the N-form: Taking Stock of Changes in the Large Industrial Corporation*. Harvard Business School, Working Paper 96–054.

Nohria, N. and Eccles, R.G. (1992) *Networks and Organizations*. Boston, MA: Harvard Business School Press.

Nohria, N. and Ghoshal, S. (1997) *The Differentiated Network: Organizing Multinational Organizations for Value Creation*. San Francisco: Jossey-Bass.

Nonaka, I. (1991) 'The knowledge creating company', *Harvard Business Review*, November/December: 96–104.

Nonaka, I. (1994) 'A dynamic theory of organizational knowledge creation', *Organization Science*, 5, 1: 14–37.

Nonaka, I. (1998) 'The concept of "Ba": building a foundation for knowledge creation', *California Management Review*, 40 (3): 40–53.

Nonaka, I. and Takeuchi, H. (1995) *The Knowledge-Creating Company: How Japanese Companies Create the Dynamics of Innovation*. Oxford: Oxford University Press.

Oertig, M. (1996) 'Wir leben Leadership', *Personalwirtschaft*, 1: 14–18.

Ohmae, K. (1989) 'The global logic of strategic alliances', *Harvard Business Review*, March/April: 143–154.

O'Leary, M. (1992) 'The CIO high performance 100: fancy footwork', *CIO*, 5 (16) August: 58–62.

Osborn, C.S. (1998) 'Systems for sustainable organizations: emergent strategies, interactive controls and semi-formal information', *Journal of Management Studies*, 35 (4): 481–509.

Ouchi, W. (1980) 'Markets, bureaucracies and clans', *Administrative Science Quarterly*, 25: 129–141.

Parkhe, A. (1991) 'Interfirm diversity, organizational learning, and longevity in global strategic alliances', *Journal of International Business Studies*, fourth quarter, 579–601.

Pennings, J.M. (1992) 'Structural contingency theory', *Research in Organizational Behaviour*, 14: 267–309.

Penrose, E. (1959) *The Theory of the Growth of the Firm*. New York: Wiley.

Pérez Díaz, V. and Rodríguez, J.C. (1995) 'Inertial choices: an overview of Spanish human resources, practices and policies', in R. Locke, T. Kochan and M. Piore (eds), *Employment Relations in a Changing World Economy*. Cambridge, MA: MIT Press. pp. 165–196.

Perlmutter, H.V. (1969) 'The tortuous evolution of the multinational corporation', *Columbia Journal of World Business*, January–February: 8–18.

Perrone, V. (1997) 'The coevolution of contexts and structures: the N-form', in T. Clark (ed.), *Organizational Behaviour: Essays in Honour of Derek S. Pugh*. Aldershot, Hants: Ashgate. pp. 145–163.

Perrow, C. (1967) 'A framework for the comparative analysis of organizations', *American Sociological Review*, 32: 194–208.

Perrow, C. (1970) *Organizational Analysis*. London: Tavistock.

Perrow, C. (1992) 'Small-firm networks', in N. Nohria and R.G. Eccles (eds), *Networks and Organizations*. Boston, MA: Harvard Business School Press. pp. 445–470.

Peters, T. (1992) 'Blow up the organization', *Adweek*, 33 (40) 5 October: 26–31.

Peters, T. and Waterman, R. (1982) *In Search of Excellence*. New York: Harper & Row.

Pettigrew, A.M. (1985a) *The Awakening Giant: Continuity and Change in ICI*. Oxford: Basil Blackwell.

Pettigrew, A.M. (1985b) 'Contextualist research: a natural way to link theory and practice', in E.E. Lawler, A.M. Mohrman, S.A. Mohrman, G.E. Ledford and T.G. Cummings (eds), *Doing Research That Is Useful for Theory and Practice*. San Francisco: Jossey-Bass. pp. 222–248.

Pettigrew, A M. (1990) 'Longitudinal field research on change: theory and practice', *Organization Science*, 1 (3): 267–292.

Pettigrew, A.M. (1992) 'The character and significance of strategy process research', *Strategic Management Journal*, 13 (Winter special issue): 5–16.

Pettigrew, A.M. (1997) 'What is processual analysis?', *Scandinavian Journal of Management*, 13 (4): 337–48.

Pettigrew, A.M. (1999a) 'Organizing to improve company performance', *Hot Topics–Warwick Business School*, 1(5): 1–4.

Pettigrew, A.M. (1999b) 'Complementarities in action: organizational change and performance in BP Amoco 1988–1998'. Paper presented to the INN-FORM Symposium, US Academy of Management, Chicago, 9–11 August.

Pettigrew, A.M. and Fenton, E.(1999) 'Complementary change in four professional service organizations'. Paper presented to the conference on Knowledge and Professional Service Organizations, University of Alberta, Edmonton, 23–25 September.

Pettigrew, A.M., Whipp, R. (1991) *Managing Change for Competitive Success*. Oxford, Blackwell.

Pettigrew, A., Ferlie, E. and McKee, L. (1992) *Shaping Strategic Change*. London: Sage.

Pettigrew, A.M., Whittington, R. and Conyon, M. (1995) 'The new internal network organization: process and performance'. Successful proposal to the ESRC. Centre for Corporate Strategy and Change, University of Warwick.

Pettigrew, A. M., Massini, S. and Numagami, T. (2000) 'Innovative forms of organizing in Europe and Japan'. *European Management Journal*. June.

Pfeffer, J. (1978) *Organizational Design*. Arlington Heights, IL: AHM Publishing.

Pfeffer, J. (1997) *New Directions for Organization Theory*. New York: Oxford University Press.

Pfeffer, J. (1998) *The Human Equation. Building Profits by Putting People First*. Boston, MA: Harvard Business School Press.

Pfeffer, J. and Salancik, G.R. (1978) *The External Control of Organizations: A Resource Dependence Perspective*. New York: Harper & Row.

Piore, M. J. (1979) 'Qualitative research techniques in economics', *Administrative Science Quarterly*, 24: 560–569.

Podolny, J.M. (1993) 'A status-based model of market competition', *American Journal of Sociology*, 98: 829–872.

Podolny, J.M. and Page, K.L. (1998) 'Network forms of organization', *Annual Review of Sociology*, 24: 57–76.

Porter, M.E. (1980) *Competitive Strategy*. New York: Free Press.

Porter, M.E. (1986) 'Competition in global industries: a conceptual framework', in M.E. Porter (ed.), *Competition in Global Industries*. Boston, MA: Harvard Business School Press. pp. 15–60.

Porter, M.E. and Fuller, M.B. (1986) 'Coalitions and global strategy' in M. Porter (ed.), *Competition in Global Industries*. Boston, MA: Harvard Business School Press. pp. 315–344.

Powell, W.W. (1990) 'Neither market not hierarchy: network forms of organization' in B. Staw (ed.), *Research in Organizational Behaviour*, Greenwich, CT: JAI Press: 12: pp. 295–336.

Powell, W.W. and Brantley, P. (1992) 'Competitive cooperation in biotechnology: learning through networks?' in N. Nohria and R.G. Eccles (eds), *Networks and Organizations: Structure, Form and Action*. Boston, MA: Harvard Business School Press. pp. 366–394.

Powell, W.W. and DiMaggio, P.J. (1991) *The New Institutionalism in Organizational Analysis*. Chicago: University of Chicago Press.

Prahalad, C.K. and Doz, Y.L. (1987) *The Multinational Mission: Balancing Local Demands and Global Vision*. New York: Free Press.

Prahalad, C.K. and Hamel, G. (1994) 'Strategy as a field of study: why search for a new paradigm?' *Strategic Management Journal*, 15: 5–16.

Presthus, R.V. (1958) 'Towards a theory of organizational behaviour', *Administrative Science Quarterly*, 3: 48–72.

Pugh, D.S. and Hickson, D.J. (1976) *Organizational Structure in its Context: The Aston Programme 1*. Farnborough, Hants: Saxon House; Lexington, MA: Lexington Books.

Pugh, D.S., Hickson, D.J. and Hinings, C.R. (1969) 'The context of organization structures', *Administrative Science Quarterly*, 14: 47–61.

Pugh, D.S., Hickson, D.J., Hinings, C.R., MacDonald, K., Turner, C. and Lupton, T. (1963) 'A conceptual scheme for organizational analysis', *Administrative Science Quarterly*, 8: 289–315.

Pugh, D.S., Hickson, D.J., Hinings, C.R. and Turner, C. (1968) 'Dimensions of organizational structure', *Administrative Science Quarterly*, 13: 65–105.

Putnam, R.D. (1993) *Making Democracy Work: Civic Traditions in Modern Italy*. Princeton, NJ: Princeton University Press.

Quinn, J.B., Anderson, P. and Finkelstein, S. (1996) 'New forms of organizing', in H. Mintzberg and J. B. Quinn (eds), *The Strategy Process*. Englewood Cliffs, NJ: Prentice Hall. pp. 350–362.

Rabobank (1988) Annual Report.

Ranson, S., Hinings, B. and Greenwood, R. (1980) 'The structuring of organizational structures, *Administrative Science Quarterly*, 25: 1–17.

Rapert, M.I. and Wren, B.M (1998) 'Reconsidering organizational structure: a dual perspective of frameworks and processes', *Journal of Managerial Issues*, 3 (10): 287–302.

Reason, P. and Hawkins, P. (1988) 'Storytelling as inquiry in reason', in *Human Inquiry in Action*. London: Sage. pp. 79–101.

Reich, R.B. (1991) *The Work of Nations*. London: Simon & Schuster.

Ripley, R.E. and Ripley, M.J. (1992) 'The innovative organization and behavioural technology for the 1990s', *SAM Advanced Management Journal*, 57 (4) Autumn: 30–36.

Roberts, P.W. and Greenwood, R. (1997) 'Integrating transaction cost and institutional theories: toward a constrained-efficiency framework for understanding organizational design adaptation', *Academy of Management Review*, 22 (2): 346–373.

Rockart, J.F. (1998) 'Towards survivability of communication-intensive new organization forms', *Journal of Management Studies*, 35 (4): 417–420.

Roost, A. and Meier, M. (1998) 'Mit Strom, Charme und neuen Chefs: Interview mit Göran Lindahl', *Bilanz*, September: 58–62.

Rosenzweig, P.M. and Nohria, N. (1994) 'Influences on human resource management practices in multinational corporations', *Journal of International Business Studies*, second quarter: 229–251.

Ross, S.C. (1993) 'Using free market principles to improve organizational effectiveness: guidelines for managers', *International Journal of Management*, 10 (1) March: 66–73.

Roth, K. and Nigh, D. (1992) 'The effectiveness of HQ-subsidiary relationships: the role of coordination, control and conflict', *Journal of Business Research*, 25: 277–301.

Rothschild, M. (1993) 'Coming soon: internal markets', *Forbes*, 7 June: 19–21.

Rugman, A. and Hodgetts, R. (1995) *International Business: A Strategic Management Approach*. New York: McGraw-Hill.

Ruigrok, W., Pettigrew, A.M., Peck, S. and Whittington, R. (1999) 'Corporate restructuring and new forms of organizing: evidence from Europe', *Management International Review*, 19, special issue (July).

Rumelt, R. (1974) *Strategy, Structure and Economic Performance*. Boston, MA: Harvard Business School Press.

Rumelt, R.P. and Stopford, J.M. (1996) 'Changing managerial logics', mimeo, London Business School, January.

Rummler, G.A. and Brache, A.P. (1991) 'Managing the white space on the organization chart', *Supervision*, 52 (5) May: 6–12.

Sabel, C., Herrigel, G., Kazis, R. and Deeg, R. (1987) 'How to keep mature industries innovative', *Technology Review*, 90 (3): 27–35.

Sanchez, R. and Mahoney, J.T. (1996) 'Modularity, flexibility and knowledge management in product and organization design', *Strategic Management Journal* (Winter special issue) 17: 63–76.

Schein, E.H. (1984), 'Coming to a new awareness of organizational culture', *Sloan Management Review*, 25 (Winter): 3–16.

Schumpeter, J.A. (1934) *The Theory of Economic Development: An Inquiry into Profits, Capital, Credit, Interest and the Business Cycle*. Cambridge, MA: Harvard University Press.

Scott, B. (1973) 'The new industrial estate: old myths and new realities', *Harvard Business Review*, March–April: 133–148.

Seidman, I. E. (1991) *Interview as Qualitative Research. A Guide for Researchers in Education and the Social Studies*. New York: Teacher College Press, Columbia University.

Selznick, P. (1949) *TVA and the Grass Roots*. Berkeley, CA: University of California Press.

Servan-Schreiber, J.J. (1967) *Le Défi Américain*. Paris: Denoël.

Sewell, G. (1998) 'The discipline of teams: the control of team-based industrial work through electronic and peer surveillance', *Administrative Science Quarterly*, 43: 397–428.

Shani, A.B. and Sena, J.A. (1994) 'Information technology and the integration of change: sociotechnical system approach', *Journal of Applied Behavioural Science*, 30 (2): June: 247–270.

Shani, A.B., Grant, R.M., Krishnan, R. and Thompson, E. (1992) 'Advanced manufacturing systems and organizational choice: sociotechnical system approach', *California Management Review*, 34 (4) Summer: 91–111.

Shaw, D.G. and Schneier, C.E. (1993) 'Making organization change happen: the keys to successful delayering', *Human Resource Planning*, 16 (1): 1–18.

Siemens (1997) *Annual Report*.

Siemens Internetpages (1998) http://www.siemens.de/en/investor_relations/Basic_ Information/index.html., 26.11.1998.

Siltkin, S.B. and Roth, N.L. (1993) 'Explaining the limited effectiveness of legalistic "remedies" for trust/distrust', *Organization Science*, 4: 367–392.

Silverman, D. (1985) *Qualitative Methodology and Sociology*. Aldershot, Hants: Gower.

Sinclair, A. (1992) 'The tyranny of a team ideology', *Organization Studies*, 13: 611–626.

Sisson, K. (1994) 'Personnel management: paradigms, practice and prospects', in K. Sisson (ed.), *Personnel Management*, 2nd edn. Oxford: Blackwell. pp. 3–50.

Skivington, J.E and Daft, R.L. (1991) 'A study of organizational "framework" and "process" modalities for the implementation of business-level strategic decisions', *Journal of Management Studies*, 28: 458.

Snow, C.C. and Ottensmeyer, E.J. (1990) 'Managing strategies and technologies', in M.W. Lawless and L.R. Gomez-Mejia (eds), *Strategic Management in High Technology Firms*. Greenwich, CT: JAI Press. pp. 181–193.

Snow, C.C. and Snell, S.A. (1993) 'Staffing as strategy', in N. Schmitt and W.C. Borman (eds), *Personnel Selection in Organizations*. San Francisco: Jossey-Bass. pp. 448–478.

Solenthaler, E. (1998) 'ABB bleibt ihrer Führungsstruktur treu: Interview mit Göran Lindahl', *Finanz und Wirtschaft*, 62 (15 August): 18–19.

Sommer, D., Stocher, H. and Weisser, L. (1994) *Ove Arup & Partners: Engineering the Built Environment*. Basel: Birkhauser.

Spender, J.C. (1989) *Industry Recipes: The Nature and Sources of Managerial Judgement*. Oxford: Basil Blackwell.

Spender, J.C. (1996) 'Making knowledge the basis of a dynamic theory of the firm', *Strategic Management Society* (Winter Special Issue) 17: 45–62.

Sryker, S. and Statham, A. (1985) 'Symbolic interaction and role theory', in G. Lindzey and E. Aronson, (eds), *Handbook of Social Psychology*. New York: Knopf.

Starbuck, W.H. (1981) 'A trip to view the elephants and the rattlesnakes in the garden of Aston', in A.H. Van de Ven and W.F. Joyce (eds), *Perspectives on Organization Design and Behaviour*. New York: Wiley. pp. 167–198.

Starbuck, W.H. (1993) 'Keeping a butterfly and an elephant in a house of cards: the elements of exceptional success', *Journal of Management Studies*, 30 (6): 885–921.

Steer, P. and Cable, J. (1978) 'Internal organization and profit: an empirical analysis of large UK companies', *Journal of Industrial Economics*, 30 (2): 173–211.

Steigmeier, A. (1991) *Brown Boveri and ASEA Brown Boveri: Highlights of a Century of Company History*. Zürich: ABB.

Stewart, T.A. (1992) 'The search for the organization of tomorrow', *Fortune*, 125 (10) 18 May: 92–98.

Stewart, T.A. (1997) *Intellectual Capital: The New Wealth of Organizations*. New York: Doubleday.

Stiles, P. (1999) 'Transformation at the leading edge', in L. Gratton, V. Hope-Hailey, P. Stiles, and C. Truss (eds), *Strategic Human Resource Management*. Oxford: Oxford University Press. pp. 153–169.

Stinchcombe, A.L. (1959) 'Social structure and organization', in J.G. March (ed.), *Handbook of Organizations*. Chicago: Rand McNally. pp. 142–193.

Storey, J. and Sisson, K. (1993) *Managing Human Resources and Industrial Relations*. Buckingham: Open University Press.

Taylor, S. (1992) 'Managing a learning environment', *Personnel Management*, 24 (10) October: 54–57.

Taylor, W. (1991) 'The logic of global business: an interview with ABB's Percy Barnevik', *Harvard Business Review*, March–April: 91–105.

Teece, D.J. (1981) 'Internal organization and economic performance: an empirical analysis of the profitability of principal firms', *Journal of Industrial Economics*, 30 (2): 173–211.

Teece, D.J. (1986) 'Profiting from technological innovation: implications for integration, collaboration, licensing and public policy', *Research Policy*, 15 (6): 285–305.

Teece, D. J. (1992) 'Competition, cooperation and innovation: organizational arrangements for regimes of rapid technological progress', *Journal of Economic Behaviour and Organization*, 18: 1–25.

Tersine, R., Harvey, M. and Buckley, M. (1997) 'Shifting organizational paradigms: transitional management', *European Management Journal*, 15 (1): 45–57.

Thanheiser, H. (1973) 'The strategy and structure of West German enterprise'. Unpublished PhD, Harvard Business School, Boston, MA.

Thompson, J.D. (1967) *Organizations in Action*. New York: McGraw-Hill.

Tolbert, P.S., Salancik, G.R., Krackhardt, D. and Andrews, S.B. (1995) 'Review essay – wanted: a good network theory of organization', *Administrative Science Quarterly*, 40 (2): 343.

Tompkins, J.A. (1993) 'Team-based continuous improvement: how to make the pace of change work for you and your company', *Material Handling Engineering*, 48 (11) November 71–72.

Truss, C., Gratton, L., Hope-Hailey, V., McGovern, P. and Stiles, P. (1997) 'Soft and hard models of human resource management: a reappraisal', *Journal of Management Studies*, 34 (1): 53–73.

Tsoukas, H. (1989) 'The validity of idiographic research explanations', *Academy of Management Review*, 14 (4): 551–561

Tsoukas, H. (1996) 'The firm as a distributed knowledge system: a constructionist approach', *Strategic Management Journal*, (Winter Special Issue) 17: 11–25.

Turner, J.R. (1999) *The Handbook of Project-Based Management*. London: McGraw-Hill.

Ulrich, D. (1997) *Human Resource Champions*. Boston, MA: Harvard Business School Press.

Ulrich, H. (1970) *Die Unternehmung als produktives soziales System: Grundlagen der allgemeinen Unternehmungslehre*. Bern: Haupt.

Uzzi, B. (1996) 'The sources and consequences of embeddedness for the economic performance of organizations: the network effect', *American Sociological Review*, 61: 674–698.

Uzzi, B. (1997) 'Social structure and competition in interfirm networks: the paradox of embeddedness', *Administrative Science Quarterly*, 42: 35–67.

Van de Ven, A. (1986) 'Central problems in the management of innovation', *Management Science*, 32 (5): 590–607.

Van de Ven, A.H., Delbecq, A.L. and Koenig, R. Jr. (1976) 'Determinants of coordination modes within organizations', *American Sociological Review*, 41 (2): 322–338.

Van de Ven, A.H., Angle, H.L. and Poole, M.S. (1989) *Research on the Management of Innovation: The Minnesota Studies*. New York: Ballinger/Harper & Row.

Van den Bosch, F.A. J. and Van Wijk, R.A. (1999) 'Transition processes towards the N-form corporation: implications for knowledge flows', in M.A. Hitt and R.D. Nixon (eds), *Resources and Gaining a Competitive Position*. New York: John Wiley. pp. 223–244.

Van den Bosch, F.A.J. and Van Wijk, R.A. (2000) 'Creation of managerial capabilities through managerial knowledge integration: a competence-based perspective', in R. Sanchez and A. Heene (eds), *Knowledge Management and Organizational Competence*. Chicester: John Wiley.

Van Wijk R.A. and Van den Bosch F.A.J. (1998a) 'Coordination mechanisms and property rights assignments from a knowledge perspective: the case of the N-form corporation'. Paper presented to the 14th EGOS Colloquium, Maastricht, 9–11 July.

Van Wijk, R.A. and Van den Bosch, F.A.J. (1998b) 'Knowledge characteristics of internal network-based forms of organizing', in S. Havlovic (ed.), *Academy of Management Best Paper Proceedings*: B1–7.

Vergós, J.C. (1998) *Una política económica para el agua*. Madrid: Círculo de Empresarios.

Volberda, H.W. (1996) 'Toward the flexible form: how to remain vital in hypercompetitive environments', *Organization Science*, 7 (4): 359–374.

Volberda, H.W. (1998) *Building the Flexible Firm: How to Remain Competitive*. Oxford: Oxford University Press.

Watson, T. (1995) 'Rhetoric, discourse and argument in organizational sense making: a reflexive tale', *Organizational Studies*, 16 (5): 805–821.

Weber, M. (1947) *The Theory of Social and Economic Organization*. Glencoe, IL: The Free Press.

Weick, K. (1979) *The Social Psychology of Organizing*. Reading, MA: Addison-Wesley.

Weimann, G. (1980) 'Conversation networks as communication networks'. Abstract of PhD dissertation, University of Haifa, Israel.

Wellman, B. (1980) 'A guide to network analysis'. Paper presented to the American Sociological Association, New York, August.

Werner, H. and Hügli, T. (1995) 'Michael Hilti über Kerngeschäfte, Marktbesitz und Mitarbeiter', *Index*, 5/6: 20–21.

Wernerfelt, B. (1984) 'A resource-based view of the firm', *Strategic Management Journal*, 5 (2): 171–180.

White, H.C., Boorman, S.A. and Breiger, R.L. (1976) 'Social structure from multiple networks', *American Journal of Sociology*, 81: 730–780.

White, R.E. and Poynter, T.A. (1990) 'Organizing for worldwide advantage', in C. Bartlett, Y. Doz and G. Hedlund (eds), *Managing the Global Firm*. New York: Routledge. pp. 95–113.

Whitley, R. (1994) 'Dominant forms of economic organization in market economies', *Organization Studies*, 15 (2): 153–182.

Whittington, R. and Mayer, M. (1997) 'Beyond or behind the M-form? The structures of European business' in D. O'Neal, H. Thomas and M. Ghertman (eds), *Strategy Structure and Style*. Chichester: John Wiley. pp. 241–258.

Whittington, R., Mayer, M. and Curto, F. (1999a) 'Chandlerism in post-war Europe: strategic and structural change in France, Germany and the United Kingdom, 1950–1993', *Industrial and Corporate Change*, 8 (3): 519–550.

Whittington, R., Pettigrew, A.M., Peck, S.I., Fenton, E.M. and Conyon, M. (1999b) 'Change and complementarities in the new competitive landscape: a European panel study 1992–1996', *Organization Science*, 10 (5): 583–600.

Whittington, R., Pettigrew, A.M., Melin, L., Ruigrok, W. and Van Wijk, R. (1999c) 'Organizing/strategizing'. Paper presented to the INNFORM Symposium, US Academy of Management, Chicago, 9–11 August.

Wijffels, H.F. (1996) 'The transformation of the Rabobank Organization', *Bedrifskunde*, 68 (1): 4–8.

Williamson, M. (1994) 'Uniting nations', *CIO*, 7 (16) 1 June: 55–63.

Williamson, O.E. (1975) *Markets and Hierarchies: Analysis and Antitrust Implications*. New York: Free Press.

Williamson, O.E. (1981) 'The economics of organization: the transaction cost approach', *American Journal of Sociology*, 87: 548–577.

Williamson, O.E. (1985) *The Economic Institutions of Capitalism: Firms, Markets, Relational Contracting*. New York: Free Press.

Williamson, O.E. (1991) 'Comparative economic organizations: the analysis of discrete structural alternatives', *Administrative Science Quarterly*, 36: 269–296.

Williamson, O.E. and Bhargava, N. (1972) 'Assessing and classifying the internal structure and control apparatus of the modern corporations', in R. Marris and A. Woods (eds), *The Corporate Economy*. London: Macmillan.

Winter, S. (1991) 'On Coase, competence and the corporation', in O. Williamson, and S. Winter (eds), *The Nature of the Firm*. New York: Oxford University Press. pp. 179–195.

Winter, S.G. and Szulanski, G. (1998) 'Replication as strategy'. Working paper, Reginald H. Jones Centre for Management Policy, Strategy and Organization, Wharton School, Philadelphia, PA.

Wirtschaftswoche (1998) Article on ABB, untitled, 13 August.

Woodward, J. (1965) *Industrial Organization, Theory and Practice*. London: Oxford University Press.

Woodward, J. (ed.) (1970) *Industrial Organization: Behaviour and Control*. Oxford: Oxford University Press.

Wright, P.M. and McHan, G.C. (1992) 'Alternative theoretical perspectives for strategic human resource management', *Journal of Management*, 18: 295–320.

Yin, R.K. (1984) *Case Study Research: Design and Methods.* Beverly Hills CA; London: Sage.

Yin, R.K. (1989) *Case Study Research: Design and Methods,* (revised edn). Newbury Park, CA; London: Sage.

Yin, R.K. (1994) *Case Study Research: Design and Methods,* 2nd edn. CA; London: Sage.

Zaltman, G., Duncan, R. and Holbeck, J. (1973) *Innovations and Organizations.* New York: John Wiley.

Zeffane, R. (1992) 'Organization structures: design in the nineties', *Leadership & Organization Development Journal,* 13 (6): 18–23.

Zeffane, R. (1995) 'The widening scope of inter-organizational networking: economic sectoral and social dimensions', *Leadership & Organization Development Journal,* 16 (4): 26–33.

Zoller, M. (1998) 'Customer focus – der gesamtunternehmerische Ansatz der ABB Schweiz'. Internal document, 4 April, Baden, ABB.

Zysman, J. (1994) 'How institutions create historically rooted trajectories of growth', *Industrial and Corporate Change,* 3 (1): 243–283.

Index